barbri®

Multistate Maximizer

Simulated MBE Workshop

To be used in conjunction with the Summer 2009 and Winter 2010 BAR/BRI Bar Review Courses

MSE

Table of Contents

PRE-TEST YOUR BAR EXAM
WITH THE BAR/BRI SIMULATED MBE

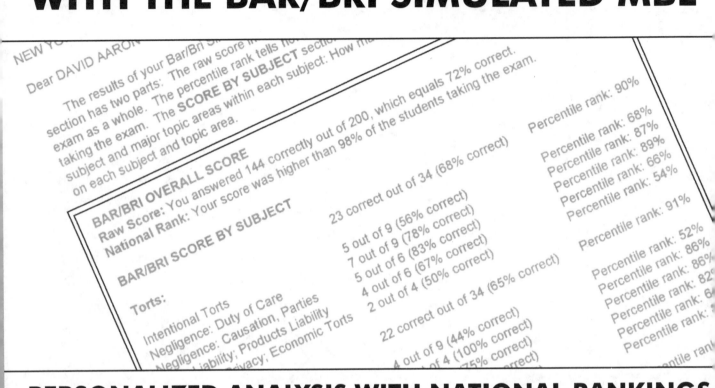

NEW YO...

Dear DAVID AARON

The results of your Bar/Bri S... section has two parts: The raw score i... exam as a whole. The percentile rank tells ho... taking the exam. The **SCORE BY SUBJECT** sectio... subject and major topic areas within each subject: How m... on each subject and topic area.

BAR/BRI OVERALL SCORE
Raw Score: You answered 144 correctly out of 200, which equals 72% correct.
National Rank: Your score was higher than 98% of the students taking the exam.

BAR/BRI SCORE BY SUBJECT

Torts: 23 correct out of 34 (68% correct)   Percentile rank: 90%
Intentional Torts   5 out of 9 (56% correct)   Percentile rank: 68%
Negligence: Duty of Care   7 out of 9 (78% correct)   Percentile rank: 87%
Negligence: Causation, Parties   5 out of 6 (83% correct)   Percentile rank: 89%
...iability; Products Liability   4 out of 6 (67% correct)   Percentile rank: 66%
...ivacy; Economic Torts   2 out of 4 (50% correct)   Percentile rank: 54%

                                                   22 correct out of 34 (65% correct)   Percentile rank: 91%
                                                   4 out of 9 (44% correct)   Percentile rank: 52%
                                                   ...of 4 (100% correct)   Percentile rank: 86%
                                                   ...5% correct)   Percentile rank: 86%
                                                                                                Percentile rank: 82...
                                                                                                Percentile rank: 6...
                                                                                                Percentile rank: ...

PERSONALIZED ANALYSIS WITH NATIONAL RANKINGS
THAT YOU CAN'T GET WITH ANY OTHER MBE COURSE

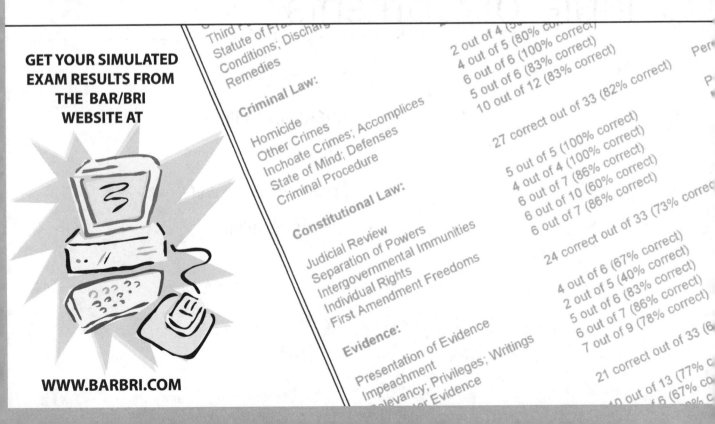

**GET YOUR SIMULATED
EXAM RESULTS FROM
THE BAR/BRI
WEBSITE AT**

Third ...
Statute of Fra...
Conditions; Discharg...
Remedies

Criminal Law:
Homicide
Other Crimes; Accomplices
Inchoate Crimes; Accomplices
State of Mind; Defenses
Criminal Procedure

Constitutional Law:
Judicial Review
Separation of Powers
Intergovernmental Immunities
Individual Rights
First Amendment Freedoms

Evidence:
Presentation of Evidence
Impeachment
...levancy; Privileges; Writings
...er Evidence

2 out of 4 (5... cor...)
4 out of 5 (80% correct)
6 out of 6 (100% correct)
5 out of 6 (83% correct)
10 out of 12 (83% correct)

27 correct out of 33 (82% correct)

5 out of 5 (100% correct)
4 out of 4 (100% correct)
6 out of 7 (86% correct)
6 out of 10 (60% correct)
6 out of 7 (86% correct)

24 correct out of 33 (73% correct)

4 out of 6 (67% correct)
2 out of 5 (40% correct)
5 out of 6 (83% correct)
6 out of 7 (86% correct)
7 out of 9 (78% correct)

21 correct out of 33 (6...
10 out of 13 (77% c...
...f 6 (67% co...

WWW.BARBRI.COM

Morning Exam

Simulated Multistate Bar Examination

A.M. EXAM

Time—3 hours

You will be given three hours to work on this test. Be sure that the question numbers on your answer sheet match the question numbers in your test book. You are not to begin work until the supervisor tells you to do so.

Your score will be based on the number of questions you answer correctly. It is therefore to your advantage to try to answer as many questions as you can. Give only one answer to each question; multiple answers will not be counted. If you wish to change an answer, erase your first mark completely and mark your new choice. Use your time effectively. Do not hurry, but work steadily and as quickly as you can without sacrificing your accuracy.

YOU ARE TO INDICATE YOUR ANSWERS TO ALL QUESTIONS ON THE SEPARATE ANSWER SHEET PROVIDED.

DIRECTIONS

Each of the questions or incomplete statements in this test is followed by four suggested answers or completions. You are to choose the **best** of the stated alternatives. Answer all questions according to the generally accepted view, except where otherwise noted.

For the purpose of this test, you are to assume that Articles 1 and 2 of the Uniform Commercial Code have been adopted. You are also to assume relevant application of Article 9 of the U.C.C. concerning fixtures.

The Federal Rules of Evidence are deemed to control.

The terms "Constitution," "constitutional," and "unconstitutional" refer to the federal Constitution unless indicated to the contrary.

You are also to assume that there is no applicable statute unless otherwise specified; however, survival actions and claims for wrongful death should be assumed to be available where applicable. You should assume that joint and several liability, with pure comparative negligence, is the relevant rule unless otherwise indicated.

DO NOT OPEN THE TEST UNTIL
YOU ARE INSTRUCTED TO DO SO.

Question 1

Federal narcotics officers suspected the defendant of growing marijuana in his greenhouse, which was adjacent to and connected to his house. The narcotics officers learned from an informant that the semi-opaque panes of glass on the greenhouse were being replaced during the night with a newer type of glass that let in more light without an increase in visibility. Without a warrant, the officers flew over the defendant's greenhouse in a helicopter that night. One of the officers focused on the greenhouse with a pair of "night vision" thermal imaging binoculars supplied by the Department of Defense and not available to the general public. He determined that marijuana was being grown. The officers then went to a magistrate, swore out a warrant, and arrested the defendant.

If the defendant moves to suppress any evidence gathered by virtue of the flyover, the motion most likely will be:

(A) Denied, because the police may conduct flyovers to gather evidence.

(B) Denied, because the defendant did not live in the greenhouse.

(C) Granted, because the "night-vision" binoculars were not available to the general public.

(D) Granted, because the greenhouse was within the curtilage.

Question 2

One of the provisions of federal anti-smoking legislation imposes restrictions on federal economic development grants, which were awarded to states to promote and assist small businesses in urban areas. The legislation mandates that grants will be reduced by 10% for any state that fails to require businesses engaged in the sale of cigarettes to take steps to avoid sales to minors, including checking drivers' licenses or photo ID cards. A tobacco-growing state that receives several million dollars under the federal grant program challenged the constitutionality of the provision in federal district court. The state established that the federal provision affects businesses that do not operate in interstate commerce.

Should the court uphold the federal provision?

(A) No, because the federal provision affects state regulation of businesses that do not operate in interstate commerce.

(B) No, because state distribution of economic development funds is an integral government function.

(C) Yes, because Congress may condition grants of money under its spending power.

(D) Yes, because the provision is substantially related to the important government interest of restricting minors' access to cigarettes.

Question 3

A large insurance company instituted a supplemental benefit plan for its own employees. Under the plan, any employee who had worked for the company for at least 25 years would be permitted to designate a charity to receive, on the employee's retirement, a donation in the employee's name of six months' worth of the employee's salary. The plan gave participating employees an unqualified right to change the beneficiary at any time before payment was made. An employee nearing retirement enrolled in the plan and named his favorite church as the beneficiary of the donation. The church received a letter from the company informing it that the employee had named it beneficiary of his plan and indicating the approximate amount that it would receive on the employee's retirement in 10 months. The letter did not inform the church of the employee's right to change beneficiaries before that time. Church elders, anticipating the gift, authorized restoration work to the church building, making plans to pay for the work with the funds from the employee's benefit program.

Six months later, the employee converted to a different religion and changed the beneficiary of his plan to his new church. When the employee retired, the company paid the benefit to his new church. His old church, which had paid for the restoration work on its completion, demanded payment of the benefit from the company. When payment was refused, the church sued the company to force payment.

The court should rule in favor of:

(A) The church, if the interests of justice require it.

(B) The church, because the employee did not have the power to change the beneficiary of his plan after the church's rights as third-party beneficiary had vested.

(C) The company, because the agreement between the employee and the company allowed the employee to change the beneficiary of the benefit plan.

(D) The company, because it had a duty to pay the employee's new church as the named beneficiary of his plan.

Question 4

A landowner sold a parcel of land to an investor for $100,000. The investor did not record the deed, and left the country for an extended trip. The landowner, seeing an opportunity to make a quick profit, partitioned the parcel of land and sold the front half to a friend in exchange for $50,000. The friend, who knew nothing about the investor's interest in the property, promptly recorded his interest. Two months later, the friend sold the front parcel to a buyer in exchange for $55,000. The buyer was aware of the investor's interest in the property but recorded his deed to the front parcel anyway. Meanwhile, the landowner executed a mortgage on the back half of the property to a bank in the amount of $40,000. The bank knew nothing of the landowner's transaction with the investor but neglected to record its mortgage interest. Six months later, the investor returned home and recorded her deed to the parcel of land.

A statute in the jurisdiction provides: "Any conveyance of an estate in land, other than a lease for less than one year, shall not be valid against any subsequent purchaser for value, without notice, unless the conveyance is recorded."

If the investor brings an action to quiet title in the parcel of land, a court will likely determine that her claim to the land is:

(A) Superior to the landowner's rights in the back half and the buyer's rights in the front half, and not subject to the bank's mortgage on the back half.

(B) Superior to the landowner's rights in the back half, inferior to the buyer's rights in the front half, and subject to the bank's mortgage on the back half.

(C) Superior to the landowner's rights in the back half, inferior to the buyer's rights in the front half, and not subject to the bank's mortgage on the back half.

(D) Superior to the landowner's rights in the back half and the buyer's rights in the front half, but subject to the bank's mortgage on the back half.

Question 5

A moving company specializing in local moves sent two employees on a typical job: a driver and a helper. The driver's responsibility was to drive the truck and load and unload the cargo. The helper's responsibility was to load and unload the cargo and generally assist the driver. While transporting furniture in a company truck, the driver failed to stop at a stop sign and collided with a car, causing the motorist to be seriously injured in the accident.

In a lawsuit brought by the motorist against the moving company on the theory of negligence by its employee, the motorist offered into evidence a written statement of the helper. The statement said that the driver was adjusting his portable radio and not observing the road when the accident occurred.

The helper's written statement is admissible if:

(A) The helper takes the witness stand and testifies that the driver was adjusting his radio and not observing the road.

(B) The helper is unavailable to testify.

(C) Evidence is introduced to establish that the helper is an employee of the moving company and his written statement is in the scope of his employment.

(D) The helper's statement was given under oath at a trial or other proceeding.

GO ON TO THE NEXT PAGE

Question 6

A police officer went to the defendant's house and placed him under arrest for operating an auto theft ring. As the defendant was being arrested, he told his wife, "You had better call our lawyer; I don't want to sign anything unless she's with me." The defendant was given *Miranda* warnings on the way to the police station. Meanwhile, the defendant's lawyer called the station and told the desk sergeant that she was on her way and to have the defendant call her as soon as he arrived. The sergeant assured her that the defendant would be held without questioning for several hours until the district attorney arrived. When the defendant arrived at the station, the arresting officer and another officer immediately put the defendant in an interrogation room and questioned him about a bank robbery that had taken place two days ago. They did not inform him of the call from his lawyer, but he agreed to talk as long as he did not have to put anything in writing or sign anything without her okay. He made incriminating statements about the robbery, and he was eventually indicted for that crime as well. At a preliminary hearing on the robbery charge, the defendant's lawyer moved to suppress the arresting officer's testimony about the defendant's statements.

The court should:

(A) Deny the motion, because the questioning was about a different crime from the one for which the defendant was in custody.

(B) Deny the motion, because the defendant's statements were made voluntarily after receiving *Miranda* warnings.

(C) Grant the motion, because the defendant was not informed that his lawyer was trying to see him, and his lawyer was misinformed that he would not be questioned right away.

(D) Grant the motion, because the defendant's refusal to write or sign anything indicates that he did not knowingly and intelligently waive his right to the assistance of counsel.

Question 7

A landowner who had owned and operated a small airport notified the electric company that he was discontinuing operations and that it should shut down the electrical current that had supplied his communications equipment. The equipment was surrounded by a fence with signs warning of high voltage. Because the electric company maintained a transformer next to the landowner's communications equipment that contained many valuable and reusable parts, it decided to leave the power on to prevent theft until it could schedule removal of the transformer. Three days later, a trespasser who knew that the airport had closed went onto the property looking for something to steal. He could find nothing of value except the transformer. He noticed the signs warning of the high voltage but believed that the power had since been turned off. He scaled the fence with the intent to dismantle the transformer. As soon as he touched the transformer, he was seriously injured by the electric current.

If the trespasser asserts a claim against the electric company to recover damages for his injuries, the trespasser will:

(A) Prevail, because the electric company was not the owner of the land on which the trespasser trespassed.

(B) Prevail, because the electric company used unreasonable force to protect its property.

(C) Not prevail, because the trespasser was a trespasser on the landowner's land.

(D) Not prevail, because the trespasser intended to steal the electric company's transformer.

GO ON TO THE NEXT PAGE

Question 8

To encourage minority business and foster pride in minority heritage, a state adopted legislation exempting magazines and other periodicals from the state's receipts tax if 20% of the magazine is devoted to articles concerning minorities (a commission was set up to sample magazines to determine on a yearly basis whether they should be exempt). A publisher produced a sports magazine in the state that occasionally contained articles about minority athletes, but the commission determined that the publisher's magazine was not eligible for the receipts tax exemption. After paying the tax assessed on her magazine, the publisher sued for a refund.

The court will most likely rule:

(A) Against the publisher, because taxpayers do not have standing to challenge tax exemptions.

(B) Against the publisher, because the state has a compelling interest in encouraging minority business.

(C) In favor of the publisher, because the tax violates the Equal Protection Clause.

(D) In favor of the publisher, because the tax violates the First Amendment freedoms of speech and press.

Question 9

A homeowner who regularly borrowed garden tools from his neighbor went to the neighbor's house to borrow the neighbor's leaf blower. The neighbor was not at home, but the leaf blower was in his unlocked garage with his other garden tools, and so the homeowner took it. Unbeknownst to the homeowner, the neighbor had drained the oil from the leaf blower's motor. The homeowner ran the leaf blower for an hour; the motor was totally destroyed because it had no oil.

The value of the leaf blower at the time that the homeowner took it was $300. An identical, new leaf blower costs $500. The cost of repairing the motor is $150. A new motor will cost $250.

If the neighbor sues the homeowner on a theory of conversion and is successful, he is entitled to:

(A) $300, but the homeowner will keep the leaf blower.

(B) $500, but the homeowner will keep the leaf blower.

(C) $150.

(D) $250.

Question 10

A state statute prohibited the state and any county, municipality, or other governmental unit within the boundaries of the state from hiring as a civil engineer any person who is not a citizen. A well-qualified engineer who is not a United States citizen read that the state's department of transportation needed a new drafting engineer. The foreign engineer applied for the position and had the required qualifications. However, the hiring official turned down the engineer's application, explaining that he could not hire her because of the state statute. The engineer filed suit in federal court, claiming that the statute violates her right to equal protection under the Fourteenth Amendment.

If the engineer prevails, it will most likely be because:

(A) The engineer proved that the statutory provision is not necessary to achieve a compelling government interest.

(B) The engineer proved that the statutory provision is not rationally related to a legitimate government interest.

(C) The state has failed to prove that the law is necessary to achieve a compelling government interest.

(D) The state has failed to prove that the law is substantially related to an important government interest.

Question 11

A patient had been taking a prescribed anti-seizure medicine, which had prevented him from having seizures while he had been taking it, but which had caused unpleasant side effects. His physician gradually weaned the patient off the medicine. One year later, the patient was driving when he suddenly suffered a seizure and lost control of his car, which crashed into the car in front of him. The driver of that car suffered serious injuries and sued the patient and the physician.

If the physician is not liable to the driver, it will be because:

(A) It was not reasonably foreseeable that removing the patient from medication could cause harm to third parties.

(B) The physician warned the patient about driving once he was off the medication.

(C) Given the side effects, it was medically reasonable to take the patient off of the medicine.

(D) The patient was judged not liable to the driver.

GO ON TO THE NEXT PAGE

Question 12

A motorist lapsed into unconsciousness while driving. Her car crossed the center line, which was marked with a double yellow line. A statute made it illegal for any person operating a motor vehicle on the highways of the state to cross a double yellow line. The motorist's car collided with another vehicle, and the driver of that vehicle was seriously injured. The driver sued the motorist for his injuries. At trial, the parties stipulated to the above facts. The motorist testified that she had not previously lapsed into unconsciousness while driving. At the close of the evidence, the driver moved for a directed verdict in his favor.

The court should:

(A) Grant the motion, because the motorist's vehicle crossed into the driver's lane and caused the driver's injuries.

(B) Grant the motion, because the driver has established negligence per se from the violation of an applicable statute that was intended to prevent the type of harm that occurred.

(C) Deny the motion, because the jury could find that the motorist had no reason to believe that she would lapse into unconsciousness.

(D) Deny the motion, because it was impossible for the motorist to comply with the statute.

Question 13

An owner purchased a parcel of property adjoining a five-foot-wide strip, which was a private right-of-way. Unsure where the exact boundaries of her property were located, the owner planted a garden on the five-foot right-of-way strip and enclosed it with a wire fence two weeks after taking up occupancy. The owner maintained the fence and garden for 20 years, at which time she removed the fence and smoothed out the ground where the garden had been located. Five years later, the owner entered into a written contract to sell the property to a buyer. The description in the contract included the five-foot strip. After research in the county recorder's office, the buyer discovered that the strip was a private right-of-way when the owner purchased the property. After properly notifying the owner of the problem prior to closing, the buyer refused to tender the purchase money to the owner when the closing day arrived. The owner sued the buyer for specific performance of the real estate sales contract. The jurisdiction's statutory adverse possession period is 15 years.

Who will prevail?

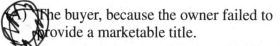

(A) The buyer, because the owner failed to provide a marketable title.

(B) The buyer, because the owner surrendered her adverse possession rights when she removed the fence, as her possession was no longer open, notorious, and continuous.

(C) The buyer, because one may not adversely possess a right-of-way.

(D) The owner, because she held the right-of-way for a longer time than the minimum required by the state adverse possession statute.

GO ON TO THE NEXT PAGE

Question 14

A jogger found a stray dog in the park. She took the dog home with her and placed an ad in the paper to try to find the dog's owner. Soon thereafter, the owner of the dog contacted the jogger. He came to the jogger's home and identified the dog as his. He offered to pay the jogger a $200 reward at the end of the week. The jogger thanked the dog owner but turned down the reward.

At the end of the week, however, the jogger changed her mind, so she called the dog owner and told him that she would like the reward after all. He refused to pay her, and she sues him for breach of contract.

What will the jogger recover?

(A) Nothing, because she rejected the dog owner's offer.

(B) Nothing, because there was no consideration to support a contract.

(C) $200, because the technical defense of the Statute of Frauds will be overcome by the dog owner's moral obligation to pay.

(D) $200, because the dog owner could not have revoked his offer until the end of the week, and he failed to do so before the jogger accepted.

Question 15

Two brothers who were certified public accountants were in business together practicing their chosen profession. The older brother was concerned about his younger brother's apparent inability to show up at his job by 9 a.m. each morning, sober and clear-eyed. One day, after the younger brother showed up late for work yet again, the older brother told him that if he would show up at the office sober and ready to work by 9 a.m. each morning for the next 10 months, he would pay him $15,000 at the end of that time. The younger brother accepted the offer, and complied with its terms from that day forward. Nine months later, the older brother died unexpectedly. One month after that, the younger brother filed a claim with his brother's estate for the $15,000.

Will the younger brother prevail in his claim?

(A) No, because he will be unable to prove the terms of the oral contract between him and his brother, because his brother is dead.

(B) No, because his brother's offer to pay was terminated on his death.

(C) Yes, because he has performed under a valid contract, and thus his brother's estate must now perform.

(D) Yes, because he changed his position for the worse in reliance on his brother's promise, and thus his brother's executor is estopped from denying that the contract existed.

GO ON TO THE NEXT PAGE

Question 16

A distributor of bottled spring water sent a letter to the manager of an upscale fitness center offering to meet the fitness center's requirements for bottled water for the next 12 months, at a price of $80 per case. The fitness center manager accepted the distributor's offer and they entered into a written contract formalizing the terms of their agreement. Two months later, the distributor wrote to the manager, informing him that because of increased costs, it would be necessary to increase the price of the bottled water to $120 per case. The manager balked at the price increase, reminding the distributor that they had a contract for $80 per case. The distributor replied, "No we don't, and in any case there's no way I can supply the bottled water to you now at $80 per case." The manager ordered bottled water from one of the distributor's competitors at a price of $95 per case, the best price he could get. The competitor's bottled water proved to be far less popular than the distributor's brand, and bottled water consumption at the fitness center declined, as did profits from their sale. The fitness center sued the distributor for damages.

If the fitness center is successful in its suit, the court should award it:

(A) Nominal damages.

(B) $15 times the number of cases of the competitor's bottled water purchased from the time of the seller's breach through the end of the contract period.

(C) The lost profits resulting from the reduced sales of the bottled water.

(D) $15 times the number of cases of the competitor's bottled water purchased from the time of the seller's breach through the end of the contract period plus the lost profits resulting from the reduced sales of the bottled water.

Question 17

The driver of a Zamboni machine at an ice rink began to clean the ice without making sure that all of the doors to the rink were closed, contrary to established procedures. A young child who had just completed a skating lesson went back onto the ice through an open door to retrieve a water bottle from the bench. A bystander saw what was happening and worried that the Zamboni driver would not see the child, and the machine's engine was too loud to yell to the driver or child. Intending to get the child off of the ice, the bystander darted through another door to the rink just in front of the approaching Zamboni machine, but she slipped and fell in front of it. She suffered serious injuries when she was struck by the machine.

The bystander sued the ice rink to recover damages for her injuries in a jurisdiction that has adopted a modified ("partial") form of comparative negligence. The trier of fact determined that the bystander was 45% at fault and the Zamboni driver was 55% at fault. The Zamboni driver was employed by a reputable rink maintenance company that contracted with the ice rink for its services.

The bystander will:

(A) Recover 45% of her damages from the ice rink because she was less at fault than the Zamboni driver.

(B) Recover 55% of her damages from the ice rink because she was less at fault than the Zamboni driver.

(C) Not recover damages from the ice rink because she assumed the risk of falling by going onto the ice.

(D) Not recover damages from the ice rink because the Zamboni driver was employed by a rink maintenance company rather than by the rink itself.

Question 18

A farmer died, devising his farm "to my wife for life, then to my son and my daughter in fee simple absolute." The wife occupied the farmhouse and operated the farm herself. After expenses of operation, the wife earned about $25,000 per year from the farm. Neither the son nor the daughter did anything to assist the wife with farm chores or expenses. The wife has consistently failed to pay the annual $2,000 county tax assessment and continues to refuse to pay it, despite threats from county tax collection authorities. With the taxes three years in arrears, the county has ordered a tax sale of the farm using proper procedures authorized by state law.

What are the rights and obligations of the parties?

(A) The wife is personally liable for the taxes, but a tax sale will cut off the rights of the son and the daughter.

(B) The son and the daughter are personally liable for the taxes if the wife does not pay them.

(C) The daughter will have to pay one-half of the taxes if the son pays one-half.

(D) The wife is personally liable for the taxes, and the tax sale will affect only her rights and not the rights of the son and the daughter.

Question 19

The defendant, a player for a professional ice hockey team, had a reputation for being a dirty, vicious player. During a game, a player for the opposing team skated toward the defendant at a high rate of speed; his hockey stick was raised in a threatening manner. The player did not intend to actually harm the defendant, but wanted to show him how it felt to be threatened by a large man traveling at a high rate of speed with a hockey stick. As the player approached the defendant, the defendant smashed his stick into the other player's face, causing a serious injury.

If the defendant is charged with the crime of battery and found not guilty, it will be because:

(A) He did not intend to injure the other player.

(B) Professional hockey players consent to being hit by hockey sticks during a game.

(C) He reasonably believed that he was under attack and his actions were reasonable.

(D) The other player was the original aggressor.

GO ON TO THE NEXT PAGE

Question 20

A certain city was the county seat and had a population of about 250,000. The city council consisted of 20 members, each of whom was elected at large. Although at one time the city had individual member districts, the city charter was revised in 1954 to provide for at-large election of all council members. The political life of the city had been dominated by members of the Alpha Party, and its full slate of candidates almost always won election. During the long period that the city had used the at-large election system, only one African-American had ever been elected to the city council, and only because of the support of the Alpha Party. When he ran for reelection, he did not receive the Alpha Party's support because he raised concerns of minority voters. He was soundly defeated, even though he received 95% of the African-American vote. Since then, no member of a minority group has served on the city council, nor has a member of a minority group been slated as a candidate by the Alpha Party. Among the population of the city are now 60,000 African-Americans, 20,000 Hispanics, 3,000 Asians, and 2,000 Native Americans.

If a minority coalition association brings suit to compel the city to provide for single member districts, it would be most likely to win its case with arguments based on which of the following provisions of the United States Constitution?

(A) Equal Protection Clause.

(B) Due Process Clause.

(C) The Fourteenth Amendment Privileges or Immunities Clause.

(D) Article I, Section 2, Clause 4.

Question 21

A philanthropist told his friend, who was a state governor, that he planned to build a museum. The governor thought that the museum would bolster the state's tourism industry and offered to arrange to have the state purchase land and grant it to the museum to enable the philanthropist to build a bigger museum with his money than originally planned. The philanthropist agreed and the museum was built.

The philanthropist undertook the hiring of the museum's senior staff. He was of German descent and was ashamed of Germany's actions during World War II. To assuage his own conscience, he refused to hire anyone whom he believed to be of German descent. A restoration expert applied for a job as chief curator of the museum, but the philanthropist refused to hire him because of his German background. The restoration expert discovered the philanthropist's rationale and brings suit against the museum, claiming that the hiring practice violates his constitutional rights.

The court will most likely find that the philanthropist's hiring policy is:

(A) Constitutional, because the museum is a private entity and so may constitutionally hire and fire as it desires.

(B) Constitutional, to the extent necessary to remedy past discrimination.

(C) Unconstitutional under the Equal Protection Clause, because the grant of the land is sufficient state involvement to render the museum's actions state action.

(D) Unconstitutional under the Equal Protection Clause, because the state will benefit from the museum and this creates a sufficient nexus to find state action.

GO ON TO THE NEXT PAGE

Question 22

A retailer of personal watercraft agreed to sell to a buyer a speedboat for $10,000. The written contract specified delivery within 30 days and a down payment of $2,000, but did not contain a liquidated damages clause. Two weeks after making the down payment, the buyer told the retailer that he could not afford to go through with the purchase, and asked for his down payment back. The retailer, which could get as many of that model of speedboat as it required from the manufacturer for a wholesale price of $7,000, put the boat back in its inventory. The retailer then sold it to someone else for $9,500. The buyer sues the retailer to get back his deposit; the retailer counterclaims for damages.

Excluding incidental costs, which of the following amounts represents the most likely recovery?

(A) The buyer will recover $2,000.

(B) The buyer will recover $1,500.

(C) The retailer will recover $3,000.

(D) The retailer will recover $1,000.

Question 23

A fleeing bank robber ran into a school and took the principal hostage at gunpoint. The police, who had received a detailed description of the clothing the robber was wearing, surrounded the school and demanded that the robber come out with his hands up. When it began to get dark, the robber ordered the principal to undress, and the robber switched clothing with the principal. He tied the principal's hands to his side and pushed the principal out the door first. Seeing that the first person out of the door did not emerge with hands up and that the person was wearing clothing the robber was described as wearing, a police sharpshooter shot and killed the principal. The robber was captured and put on trial for the murder of the principal.

The jury should find the robber:

(A) Guilty, because the police were justified in using deadly force under the circumstances.

(B) Guilty, because changing clothes with the principal was an act taken with extreme indifference to an unjustifiably high risk to human life.

(C) Not guilty, because it was not foreseeable under the circumstances that the police would use deadly force.

(D) Not guilty, because the robber was not responsible for the police shooting the principal.

GO ON TO THE NEXT PAGE

Question 24

A nephew asked his uncle, who like him was a farmer, to guarantee a loan to buy a new tractor. The local bank had already refused to extend credit to the nephew alone to buy the tractor. The uncle was inclined to refuse, but then decided that he could benefit from his own use of the tractor, so he told his nephew that he would guarantee the loan if he could use the new tractor without cost for 10 days during his harvest season. The nephew agreed to his uncle's proposal. The uncle went to the bank and told the loan officer that he was willing to guarantee the proposed loan to his nephew. This prompted the loan officer to agree to extend the requested credit to the nephew. Although the loan officer did not make the uncle sign any papers, the uncle provided consideration and the bank issued the nephew a loan commitment statement. That evening, the uncle had a change of heart. The next day, he telephoned the loan officer and told him to forget about his guaranteeing any loan to his nephew. Despite the uncle's phone call, the loan officer did not stop the check from being issued, and the nephew received the money to purchase the tractor. He drove the tractor over to the uncle's farm and delivered it for the uncle's 10-day use, as promised. The uncle told his nephew that he did not want to use the tractor and that he was not guaranteeing his loan. Within six months, it became clear that the nephew could not make good on the loan.

If the bank sues the uncle for the unpaid portion of the loan:

(A) The bank will win, because the suretyship agreement was supported by consideration between the bank and the uncle.

(B) The bank will win, because the uncle's main purpose in making the agreement with the bank was to benefit himself, not his nephew.

(C) The uncle will win, because the suretyship agreement was not in writing.

(D) The uncle will win, because he withdrew his promise before the nephew received the money or the tractor.

Question 25

A husband and a wife owned a parcel of land in joint tenancy. They conveyed a 10% interest in the land to their daughter. Six months later, they conveyed a 10% interest in the land to the daughter's husband, their son-in-law. The jurisdiction in which the land is located does not recognize tenancy by the entirety.

Which of the following best describes the ownership of the land after the conveyances?

(A) The husband and the wife have an 80% interest as joint tenants, the daughter has a 10% interest as a tenant in common, and the son-in-law has a 10% interest as a tenant in common.

(B) The husband and the wife have an 80% interest as tenants in common, the daughter has a 10% interest as a tenant in common, and the son-in-law has a 10% interest as a tenant in common.

(C) The husband and the wife have an 80% interest as tenants in common, and the daughter and the son-in-law have a 20% interest as joint tenants.

(D) The husband and the wife have an 80% interest as joint tenants, and the daughter and the son-in-law have a 20% interest as joint tenants.

Question 26

A homeowner borrowed $50,000 from a bank, secured by a mortgage on his home. Shortly thereafter, the homeowner sold his home to a buyer for $70,000 by a deed containing a recital signed by both parties that title passed "subject to" the bank's mortgage, "which obligation grantee expressly assumes." The buyer paid the homeowner $20,000, took possession of the house, and began making monthly payments of principal and interest to the bank. A few years later, a chemical manufacturing firm built a huge sulfur processing plant just down the road from the home, which caused the house to immediately decline in value to $35,000. Subsequently, the buyer stopped making the monthly payments to the bank. The bank exercised its contractual right of nonjudicial foreclosure and sold the house at a public auction for $34,000. The bank then brought suit against the homeowner and the buyer for $14,000, the difference between the proceeds of the foreclosure sale and the $48,000 principal remaining due on the original loan to the homeowner. The jurisdiction does not bar deficiency judgments.

The bank should be granted a judgment for $14,000 against:

(A) Both the homeowner and the buyer.

(B) Only the homeowner.

(C) Only the buyer.

(D) No one.

Question 27

A patient sought psychiatric treatment from a psychiatrist. During the treatment, which consisted of hour-long analysis sessions twice a week, the psychiatrist, unbeknownst to the patient, videotaped her. No sound recording was made of the sessions, but the psychiatrist was conducting a study on "body language" and planned to use the videotapes in those experiments. The patient learned that the psychiatrist had been videotaping their analysis sessions and

brought an action against him on a theory of invasion of privacy.

Which of the following arguments best supports the patient's claims in this action?

(A) The psychiatrist has placed the patient in a false light.

(B) The psychiatrist has publicly displayed private facts of the patient's life.

(C) The psychiatrist has misappropriated the patient's likeness.

(D) The psychiatrist has intruded upon the patient's physical seclusion.

Question 28

The owner of a restored 1957 Chevrolet told his neighbor that he was interested in selling his car but did not know what price to ask. The neighbor said that he would pay $12,000 for the car "if he could get the financing." The car owner hesitated, and the neighbor suggested that the car owner give him 10 days to obtain financing. The car owner agreed and promised, in writing, that he would sell the car to the neighbor if he came up with $12,000 within 10 days.

Which of the following best describes the agreement between the car owner and the neighbor?

(A) A promissory estoppel situation.

(B) A quasi-contract.

(C) An offer for a unilateral contract.

(D) An option contract.

Question 29

A quilter who had restored a rare Civil War-era quilt spoke with an old friend whose business was selling new and vintage quilts. When the friend learned of the quilter's latest restoration, she told her that for 15% of the gross, she could find her a buyer who would pay at least $5,000 for it. The quilter said nothing in reply. The next morning, the friend telephoned the quilter and told her that she had a prospective buyer who was willing to pay $5,200 for the quilt, sight unseen. The quilter asked for the buyer's phone number, which the friend gave to her, and then called the buyer and arranged a sale. The quilter refused to pay her friend the 15% commission, disclosing to her that another party had expressed interest in the quilt and she instead could have sold it to that party for at least $5,200. The friend sues the quilter for breach of contract, seeking her 15% sales commission.

What will be the probable outcome?

(A) The quilter will win, because 15% is unconscionably large as a finder's fee in such a transaction.

(B) The quilter will win, because there was no consideration for any promise to pay that might have been implied from her conduct.

(C) The quilter will win because she could have sold the quilt to another party who would pay at least $5,200 for it.

(D) The friend will win, because she obtained a buyer for the quilt and a purchase price over $5,000 was paid.

Question 30

In January, an owner executed and delivered a mortgage on her property to a bank to secure a $50,000 loan. Due to a clerical error, the mortgage was not recorded at that time. On February 15, the owner entered into a contract to sell the property to a buyer for $150,000. On February 16, the owner took out a $30,000 mortgage on the property with a finance company. The finance company promptly and properly recorded its mortgage. Knowing nothing about either of the mortgages, the buyer closed on the property on April 1, tendering $150,000 to the owner. The owner gave the buyer a warranty deed to the property. On April 3, the bank discovered its error and properly recorded its mortgage that same day. The buyer recorded his deed to the property on April 6.

A statute of the jurisdiction in which the property is located provides: "No conveyance or mortgage of real property shall be valid against a subsequent purchaser for value and without notice whose conveyance is first recorded." The bank brings an appropriate action to determine the status of its mortgage on the property.

The court should hold that:

(A) The buyer holds the property subject to both mortgages, and the bank's mortgage is subordinate to the finance company's mortgage.

(B) The buyer holds the property subject to both mortgages, and the bank's mortgage is superior to the finance company's mortgage.

(C) The buyer holds the property subject only to the finance company's mortgage.

(D) The buyer holds the property subject only to the bank's mortgage.

2

Question 31

After a widely publicized accident in which an elderly motorist drove onto the sidewalk and struck and killed several pedestrians, the state legislature revised its motor vehicle statutes. The new legislation required motorists over the age of 70 to undergo more frequent and more thorough testing to maintain their driver's licenses. A 75-year-old former race car driver who was required by the new legislation to be tested every year to maintain his driver's license brought suit in the federal district court in the state, alleging that the legislation results in unconstitutional age discrimination.

Which of the following statements best reflects the burden of persuasion that the court will apply in the driver's suit?

(A) The state must show that the law is substantially related to an important government purpose.

(B) The state must show that the law is rationally related to a legitimate government interest.

(C) The driver must show that the law is not rationally related to a legitimate government interest.

(D) The driver must show that the law is not substantially related to an important government purpose.

Question 32

The plaintiff sued a local restaurant, claiming that she injured her teeth, gums, and mouth when she bit into a hamburger that contained a large jagged piece of glass. The plaintiff called to the stand a waiter for the restaurant, who testified that, when he heard the plaintiff scream, he looked in her direction and saw her remove a piece of glass from her bleeding mouth. On cross-examination, the defense asked the waiter, "Isn't it a fact that three months ago you were fired by the restaurant for serving drinks to your friends and not charging for them?" The waiter responded, "Yes, but I wasn't trying to steal anything. I just forgot to charge them." The defense then asked, "Isn't it a fact that last month you threw a rock through the plate glass window at the restaurant?" The waiter replied, "That's not true; I was there but I didn't throw the rock." The defense then offered the testimony of a witness who was prepared to testify that she saw the waiter throw the rock through the restaurant's window.

Assuming that there have been no criminal charges filed as a result of the broken window, the witness's testimony is:

(A) Inadmissible, because specific acts of misconduct that did not result in a conviction cannot be used to impeach a witness, either on cross-examination or through extrinsic evidence.

(B) Inadmissible, because specific acts of misconduct that did not result in a conviction cannot be established through extrinsic evidence.

(C) Admissible as evidence of bias.

(D) Admissible to establish that the waiter lied under oath.

GO ON TO THE NEXT PAGE

Question 33

In a wrongful death action for the death of his wife in an automobile accident, the plaintiff alleged that the accident was caused by a mudflap assembly that fell off the truck of the defendant. The plaintiff wishes to introduce the testimony of a witness, another truck driver who was on the same highway at the time, who heard some-one tell the defendant over CB radio that he had noticed at the truck stop that the defendant's mudflap assembly on his truck was loose. The witness does not know the identity of the person who gave the warning.

If the defendant objects to admission of the testimony, the court should rule that it is:

(A) Admissible to prove that the defendant was notified that the mudflap assembly was loose.

(B) Admissible both to prove that the defendant was notified that the mudflap assembly was loose and as substantive evidence that it was loose.

(C) Inadmissible, because the witness cannot identify who made the statement.

(D) Inadmissible, because it is hearsay not within any recognized exception.

Question 34

A large Midwestern wheat producer and a large food distributor located on the Pacific coast entered into a contract calling for the wheat producer to sell and the food distributor to buy 10,000 bushels of winter wheat for $5 per bushel. The contract stated that the wheat producer would deliver the wheat "F.O.B. St. Louis Railroad depot." The wheat producer hired a trucking company to transport the wheat from its silos to the St. Louis Railroad depot, where the wheat would be loaded onto railroad hopper cars bound west. En route to St. Louis, the trucks carrying the wheat were stopped and the wheat was carried off by highway robbers. The wheat producer brings suit against the food distributor, which refused to pay for the wheat.

What will the wheat producer likely recover in damages?

(A) Nothing.

(B) The amount necessary to replace the stolen wheat.

(C) The full contract price.

(D) The profits it would have realized under the contract.

GO ON TO THE NEXT PAGE

Question 35

On April 25, a smoothie stand operator and a fruit processor entered into a written contract providing that the processor would deliver to the operator each month 20 barrels each of bananas, strawberries, blueberries, and raspberries at a price of $25 per barrel, with the first barrels to be delivered on May 1, and the same number of barrels to be delivered on the first of each month thereafter for the next 11 months, with payment made on the 15th of each month to a creditor of the fruit processor. The parties had actually agreed that the contract price per barrel of fruit would be $15, but the manager of the fruit processor had inadvertently written $25 in the contract, and neither party noticed before signing. The creditor first learned of the agreement between the parties on April 27. The next day, the operator and the processor agreed that the contract price for the barrels of fruit would be $20 per barrel instead of $25 per barrel. The first delivery was made one day late, on May 2. On May 15, the operator refused to pay any money to the creditor, and the creditor filed suit against the smoothie stand for the first month's payment of $2,000.

Which of the following would *not* provide a partial defense for the smoothie stand operator in the litigation?

(A) The parties had agreed on April 28 that the contract price per barrel of fruit would be $20 instead of $25.

(B) The parties had originally agreed that the contract price per barrel of fruit would be $15, but the manager of the fruit processor had inadvertently written $25 in the contract, and neither party noticed before signing.

(C) The fruit processor owed its creditor only $1,800.

(D) The fruit processor was late with its first delivery.

Question 36

A state statute prohibited the sale or possession of any food product containing more than one part per billion of a dangerous pesticide. An out-of-state driver taking her recreational vehicle through a corner of the state was stopped at a state inspection station. When the state trooper learned that the pantry of her RV was stocked with food, he asked to test a few samples of her baked goods. The samples contained about 600 parts per billion of the prohibited pesticide, and all of the other baked goods in her possession were tested and found to have the same level of pesticide. All of her baked goods, worth about $150, were confiscated and destroyed.

The state in which the driver lived has no laws governing the pesticide level of baked goods. A federal law designed to protect agricultural workers requires that any food product containing more than 500 parts per billion of the toxic pesticide must be labeled as such and be in special containers. The driver brings an action in federal court asserting that the state statute is invalid because it is preempted by the federal law.

How should the court rule as to this claim?

(A) For the state, because the purposes of the federal law are different from those of the challenged statute.

(B) For the state, because regulation of food quality is a power reserved to the states by the Tenth Amendment.

(C) For the driver, because the federal law does not expressly permit states to enact more stringent pesticide level controls.

(D) For the driver, because the federal law and the state statute regulate the same subject matter.

GO ON TO THE NEXT PAGE

Question 37

A developer owned several acres zoned for mixed use development. The developer prepared a subdivision of his various parcels, filed a subdivision map showing commercial lots, obtained all the necessary approvals, and began selling the lots. Each of the deeds conveying lots sold by the developer contained the following:

> It is hereby covenanted by the seller that the property conveyed shall be used for commercial or residential purposes only, that no industrial, warehouse, or other manufacturing structures shall be erected or maintained thereon, and that this covenant shall bind the buyer, his heirs and assigns, and their successors.

Two years later, after all but two of the lots had been developed as small businesses, the developer sold his remaining two lots to a real estate speculation firm. The deed to the firm did not contain any language restricting the use of the property. The firm then sold the property to a giant supermarket chain, which intended to construct a warehouse and distribution center thereon. A shopkeeper who had purchased a lot from the developer located next to the proposed warehouse brings suit against the supermarket chain seeking to enjoin construction of the warehouse. Her attorney argues that the lots sold by the developer to the firm and then to the supermarket chain are bound by the same restrictions on use that are contained in the deed by which the shopkeeper took her property.

The shopkeeper will likely:

(A) Win, because the developer established a common development scheme for his entire subdivision and the subdivision appeared to conform to the scheme.

(B) Lose, because the firm and the supermarket were not aware of the restrictions when they purchased the property.

(C) Lose, because the restrictions in the shopkeeper's deed bind only the purchaser of the land.

(D) Lose, because the deed by which the firm took the property from the developer did not contain any restrictions on use.

Question 38

The defendant became very intoxicated one night. As he was staggering home, he came upon a construction site in which several large pieces of heavy equipment were parked. Having had heavy equipment training in the military, the defendant decided it would be fun to rearrange all the machines so that the operators would be very surprised when they returned to work the next day. He started up the largest piece of heavy equipment and drove it toward the edge of the site, but because he was so intoxicated, he lost control of it, and it rumbled out into the street, weaved along for about a quarter mile, and then crashed into a house, flattening it. In this jurisdiction, it is a misdemeanor to tamper with heavy equipment on a construction site. The defendant is prosecuted on the tampering charge, as well as for reckless damage of the house.

Should he be convicted of the reckless damage charge?

(A) Yes, because he was tampering with heavy equipment on a construction site, in violation of law, when he damaged the house.

(B) Yes, because he was intoxicated while driving a huge piece of earthmoving equipment.

(C) No, because at most he could be found guilty of criminal negligence.

(D) No, because he must have been aware that his conduct would cause damage to the house in order to be found guilty of reckless damage.

Question 39

A computer programmer sent a computer virus anonymously via e-mail to a business. The programmer believed that the virus would just disable the business's e-mail program for a short time without causing any additional damage, although he was aware that it very infrequently caused widespread damage to the infected computer. However, because of a hidden bug in the business's e-mail program, the virus infected the computer's entire hard drive, eventually rendering it unusable. Not only did the business lose important data, it also had to replace the computer, at a cost of over $1,000. The jurisdiction in which this occurred has a modern criminal code patterned after the Model Penal Code. One of its statutes makes it a criminal offense to "knowingly cause over $200 in damage to another's property." May the programmer be found guilty of violating the statute?

(A) No, because the programmer did not know that the virus would cause damage to the computer's hard drive.

(B) No, because the programmer did not intend to cause the damage to the computer's hard drive.

(C) Yes, because the programmer knew that he was sending a virus to the business's e-mail program.

(D) Yes, because the programmer was aware that in a very small percentage of cases the virus could cause widespread damage to a computer system.

Question 40

During the defendant's prosecution for robbery, the prosecutor asks the court to take judicial notice of the fact that at that latitude, the sun is still up at 5:30 p.m. on June 21. The court so finds.

The effect of the court's action is that:

(A) The burden of persuasion is now on the defendant to prove otherwise as to the fact judicially noticed.

(B) The fact judicially noticed is established beyond a reasonable doubt.

(C) The prosecutor's burden of producing evidence on the fact judicially noticed is satisfied.

(D) The fact judicially noticed is conclusively established.

GO ON TO THE NEXT PAGE

Question 41

A homeowner offered to pay a roofer $500 to replace the bad shingles on his roof, provided the roofer could finish the job by October 1. The roofer told the homeowner he would get back to him after he had checked out prices at a local supply store. The next day, the roofer phoned the homeowner, who was not at home, and left a message on his answering machine that he could not do the work for less than $650. The roofer did not hear from the homeowner for several days. Because October 1 was still two weeks away, the roofer phoned the homeowner again and left another message on his answering machine stating that he would do the job for $500 and that he would do the work the next weekend unless that would be inconvenient for the homeowner. The homeowner replayed the second message just as he was leaving town on a business trip and did not contact the roofer. That weekend, unbeknownst to the homeowner, the roofer went to the homeowner's house and repaired the roof. When the homeowner returned home, the roofer presented him with a bill for $500, which represented the actual value of the work done. The homeowner refused to pay the bill.

If the roofer sues solely for breach of contract, who will likely prevail?

(A) The roofer, because he accepted the homeowner's offer before the latter materially changed his position in reliance on the first telephone message.

(B) The roofer, because the work he did was actually worth $500.

(C) The homeowner, because he was unaware that the roofer was doing the roof repair while he was out of town.

(D) The homeowner, because he did not accept the roofer's offer to do the roof repair for $500.

Question 42

A seller entered into an enforceable written agreement to sell her house to a buyer for $425,000. The agreement provided that closing would take place on September 18, and on that date the seller would provide marketable title, free and clear of all encumbrances. The agreement was silent as to risk of loss if the house was damaged prior to closing and as to any duty to carry insurance. On August 31, the seller cancelled her homeowners' insurance when she moved out of the house. Consequently, when the house was destroyed by wildfires on September 15, it was uninsured. The buyer refused to close on September 18 and the seller immediately brought an action against him for specific performance. The buyer countersued for the cancellation of the contract and return of his earnest money. Both parties stipulate that the value of the property without the house is $225,000.

In this jurisdiction, which has no applicable statute, the seller will most likely:

(A) Prevail, but the price will be abated to $225,000.

(B) Prevail for the full contract price.

(C) Not prevail, because the seller had a duty to carry insurance until the closing date.

(D) Not prevail, because the seller could not convey marketable title.

GO ON TO THE NEXT PAGE

Question 43

The plaintiff was driving her daughter to school when their car was struck broadside by a car driven by the defendant at an intersection controlled in all directions by stop signs. The plaintiff and her daughter were taken by ambulance to the hospital. In a personal injury action brought by the plaintiff and her daughter against the defendant, pretrial discovery revealed that both cars were in perfect mechanical condition just before the accident, and the defendant was on his way home from work at the time of the accident, but had stopped off at a bar before he reached the intersection at which he struck the plaintiff's car. There is no witness available to testify as to how much the defendant had to drink at the bar that day.

At trial, the plaintiff calls a co-worker of the defendant, who testifies over objection that the defendant has a reputation as a hard drinker who tolerates alcohol well but who always drinks a great deal at any one drinking occasion, as witnessed by the co-worker at numerous company events. Was it error for the trial court to admit his testimony?

(A) Yes, because in a civil matter, evidence of a party's character may not be introduced until he has put his character at issue.

(B) Yes, because the plaintiff may not attempt to prove that the defendant acted in a particular way on one occasion in conformity with his reputation as to that behavior.

(C) No, because the co-worker had personal knowledge of the defendant's drinking habits from having observed him while drinking.

(D) No, because there exists no unbiased eyewitness who can testify as to how much the defendant actually drank at the bar before he had the accident with the plaintiff.

Question 44

While driving home after an evening spent drinking at a local bar, the plaintiff passed out at the wheel. His car went through a red light at an intersection and was struck by a car driven by the defendant. The plaintiff, under the influence of alcohol, staggered from his car. The defendant, believing that the plaintiff had been injured in the accident, said "It's my fault. I was not paying attention. I'll take care of all your medical bills." Later that night, the plaintiff was treated for minor injuries at a nearby hospital.

The plaintiff sued the defendant for damages, alleging that the defendant was driving negligently at the time of the accident. The plaintiff offered the testimony of a witness who was prepared to testify that, after the accident, the defendant stated in a clear, calm voice, "I was not paying attention. I'll take care of all your medical bills."

Assuming the proper objection, should the witness's testimony concerning the defendant's statement be admitted?

(A) No, because the defendant's statement is a settlement offer.

(B) No, because the plaintiff was negligent per se.

(C) The defendant's statement "I was not paying attention" should be admitted, but the statement "I'll take care of all your medical bills" should not.

(D) Yes, as an admission by the defendant.

GO ON TO THE NEXT PAGE

Question 45

A logger was confronted by a protester who called him "a moronic treekiller." The logger warned the protester to leave and swung his axe as if to strike her, intending to frighten her away. Unfortunately, the manufacturer of the axe had neglected to insert a metal pin that secured the axe handle to the blade, and the blade had become loosened from previous chopping. Consequently, the blade flew off the handle and struck and injured the protester.

If the protester brings an action for battery against the logger, will she recover?

(A) No, because the logger did not intend to cause harm to the protester.

(B) No, because the defective axe was the cause in fact of the protester's injuries.

(C) Yes, because the logger intended to frighten the protester.

(D) Yes, because the protester provoked the logger.

Question 46

An owner of three acres of lakefront property subdivided it and sold two acres to a buyer, retaining the one acre actually fronting on the lake. The deed for the two acres expressly included an easement over the westernmost 30 feet of the one-acre parcel retained by the owner for access to the lake. The buyer recorded his deed in the county recorder's office, which maintained an alphabetical grantor-grantee index only. Fifteen years later, the owner died, leaving the one-acre parcel to his wife. She sold it to a developer that planned to build condominiums. A month later, the buyer died, and his two acres passed by will to his nephew. Three weeks after taking title to the property, the nephew visited the property and discovered that the developer had erected a chain link fence all along the boundary between the nephew's land and the acre of lakefront land. The nephew brings an action to enjoin the developer from obstructing his easement across the acre of lakefront property.

Which of the following best describes why the nephew should prevail in this litigation?

(A) Because the developer and the nephew can trace their predecessors in interest to a common grantor whose covenants run with the land, the developer is estopped from interfering with the nephew's use of the easement.

(B) The nephew's easement is a legal interest that the developer has record notice of, even though there is no tract index.

(C) Because there is no tract index, the developer was under an obligation to determine the riparian rights of any adjacent landowners before erecting the chain link fence.

(D) The nephew's easement is a legal interest that attaches not just to a legal estate but to the land itself and, running with the land, it binds successive owners of the servient estate whether or not they have notice of it.

Question 47

The food and beverage manager of an exclusive country club received a letter in the mail dated December 3 and signed by the sales director of a distiller, offering to meet the club's requirements for vodka for the next calendar year. The offer provided for delivery on the 15th of each month at $120 per case. The manager promptly wrote back, accepting the offer per the terms provided in the letter. At the same time, the manager placed a modest order for the distiller's vodka, which was duly delivered at the stated price on January 15. The manager placed orders of similar size throughout the rest of the year, and they were delivered at the stated price.

The agreement between the distiller and the club is best described as:

(A) A single bilateral contract.

(B) A series of unilateral contracts.

(C) A series of option contracts.

(D) Not an enforceable contract.

Question 48

A father wanted his adult daughter to stop smoking, and one day he told her that if she gave up smoking for the next 12 months, at the end of that time he would give her $10,000. She agreed to stop smoking, but later that day had doubts about whether her father would actually pay up if she complied. She contacted her stepmother, who told her to go ahead and quit smoking, and she would make good on the father's promise to pay her if he refused to do so. That very day, the daughter quit smoking and never smoked again. Eleven months after his conversation with his daughter, the father died.

One month later, the daughter sought payment of the $10,000 from her father's estate, which refused to pay. The daughter then asked her stepmother for the $10,000 but the stepmother also refused to pay. The daughter filed a claim against her stepmother for $10,000. She proves at trial that she has submitted a claim for $10,000 to the executor of her father's estate and has been refused payment.

What is the best argument for the court's rejecting this claim against her stepmother?

(A) The contract between the daughter and her stepmother was illusory.

(B) The daughter has not been damaged by any breach because the only effect—that she quit smoking—was salutary.

(C) The contract between the daughter and her stepmother was oral.

(D) No consideration flowed to the stepmother under the contract.

Question 49

The accused was driving his beat-up old car along a narrow road when he was passed by the victim in her new car. The victim's daughter was lying down in the back seat and could not be seen. The accused sped up, drew even with the victim, and repeatedly rammed his car into the side of the victim's car. After several collisions, the victim was forced off the road, rolling down a cliff for several yards. Due to the rolling, both the victim and her daughter were severely injured. The accused was charged with attempted murder of both of them. At his trial, he testifies that he was angry because of the cavalier way the victim passed him in her new car, and that his only intent in smashing into her car was to scratch and dent it so that she would not be so haughty in the future. Assuming that the jury believes this testimony, the accused may be convicted as to:

(A) The victim.

(B) The victim's daughter.

(C) Both the victim and her daughter.

(D) Neither the victim nor her daughter.

Question 50

At the trial of the plaintiff's breach of contract action against the defendant, the plaintiff called her accountant as a witness to testify about the difference in gross sales, gross income, and net profit caused by the defendant's failure to supply the promised quantity of ice cream to the plaintiff's ice cream shop. When the plaintiff's attorney asked the accountant to state the gross income figures for the year prior to formation of the contract between the plaintiff and the defendant, the accountant replied that he could not remember the exact amounts. The plaintiff's counsel then handed the accountant a copy of the federal tax return submitted by the plaintiff for that year, and asked him to read it. Counsel then asked, "Now that you have read the tax return, can you remember what the gross income of the plaintiff's ice cream shop was for the relevant period?" The defendant's counsel objects.

How should the court rule?

(A) Sustained, because the plaintiff's counsel is seeking to elicit testimony based on inadmissible hearsay.

(B) Sustained, because the accountant's testimony is not the best evidence.

(C) Overruled, because the accountant's hearsay testimony is admissible as a past recollection recorded.

(D) Overruled, because the accountant's testimony is admissible evidence relating to the plaintiff's damages.

Question 51

A landowner owns 15 acres of undeveloped property. He plans to build a stadium complex on the property to house a football team two years from now, but would like to open the 15 acres to public use for picnicking and similar activities until then.

Which of the following would best accomplish the landowner's goal?

(A) Dedicate the 15 acres for use as a public park.

(B) Lease the 15 acres to the city for two years.

(C) Grant the city an easement for public recreational uses for two years.

(D) Covenant that the city may use the 15 acres for recreation for two years.

Question 52

After leaving ceremonies at which the chief justice of a state supreme court had been named distinguished jurist of the year, an associate justice was interviewed by the press. The associate justice told a reporter that the chief justice "is a senile imbecile who lets his clerks write all his opinions. He hasn't had a lucid thought in decades, and he became a judge by being on the payroll of the mob." Enraged, the chief justice brought an action for defamation against the associate justice.

Which of the following, if established by the chief justice in his defamation action, would permit recovery against the associate justice?

(A) The associate justice negligently made the statements, which were false, and caused the chief justice actual injury.

(B) The associate justice made the statements knowing they were false.

(C) The associate justice made the statements because he hated the chief justice and wished to destroy his reputation in the legal community.

(D) The associate justice made the statements in order to ensure that the chief justice's political career was nipped in the bud.

2

GO ON TO THE NEXT PAGE

Question 53

After a long period of marital problems, a wife told her husband that she was going to file for a divorce. Because the wife had recently inherited a large sum of money, the husband was determined not to let her go through with the divorce. He contacted an ex-convict and offered him $10,000 if he would kill his wife. The ex-convict agreed and they picked a time when the wife would be in the house by herself. When the ex-convict broke into the house, however, the wife called the police and fled out the back door. The ex-convict shot and wounded the wife as she was running away, but he was apprehended by the police before he could do any further harm.

After the ex-convict implicated the husband, both were charged with attempted murder and conspiracy to commit murder, and the husband was also charged with solicitation of murder. As part of a plea bargain, the ex-convict agreed to testify against the husband and plead guilty to aggravated battery in exchange for the attempted murder and conspiracy to commit murder charges being dropped.

Which of the following best states the crimes for which the husband can be convicted?

(A) Solicitation, attempted murder, and conspiracy to commit murder.

(B) Attempted murder and conspiracy to commit murder.

(C) Solicitation and attempted murder.

(D) Attempted murder only.

Question 54

State statutory law requires that a person who is suspected of committing a crime must be informed of the nature of that crime before questioning may begin. The state supreme court has held that statements obtained in violation of a suspect's statutory interrogation rights may not be admitted into evidence. The defendant, who was arrested on suspicion of committing an arson, was told: "You have the right to remain silent, anything you say can and will be used against you in a court of law, you have the right to the presence of an attorney during questioning, and if you cannot afford an attorney, one will be appointed for you." The defendant immediately gave a statement implicating himself in the arson. He was charged and brought to trial in state court for arson.

At trial, should the statement be excluded from evidence?

(A) Yes, because the *Miranda* warnings were not proper.

(B) Yes, because the questioning violated state law.

(C) No, because proper *Miranda* warnings were given in compliance with federal constitutional requirements.

(D) No, because the requirement of informing the suspect of the nature of the charges against him is not a state constitutional requirement.

GO ON TO THE NEXT PAGE

Question 55

A buyer entered into a contract with a seller to buy a parcel of land for $40,000. Although the buyer was expecting to receive a large inheritance in a few weeks, he had very limited funds on hand and was able to personally finance only $10,000. To cover the remaining balance, the buyer obtained a loan from the seller for $30,000, giving the seller a promissory note in that amount secured by a mortgage on the land and orally promising to pay the seller in full when he received his inheritance money. A few weeks later, the seller negotiated the mortgage note to an investor for $25,000 without informing the buyer. The next day, the seller received a check from the buyer in the amount of $30,000. A few days later, the seller left the country with the $65,000 she had made on the sale of the land. The jurisdiction permits deficiency judgments.

If a foreclosure action is instituted by the investor, which of the following correctly states his rights against the buyer?

(A) The investor has no enforceable interest in the land and no rights against the buyer because the seller did not transfer the mortgage to him and the buyer paid the mortgage amount in full.

(B) The investor has an enforceable interest in the land to the extent of $25,000, but cannot recover against the buyer personally for any deficiency.

(C) The investor has an enforceable interest in the land to the extent of $30,000, but cannot recover against the buyer personally for any deficiency.

(D) The investor has an enforceable interest in the land to the extent of $30,000, and can recover against the buyer personally for any deficiency.

Question 56

A driver borrowed $75,000 from a bank to purchase a tract of land on which to operate his trucking company, securing the debt with a mortgage on the land. The bank promptly and properly recorded its mortgage. A few years later, the driver financed the installation of a truck wash on the land with a $50,000 loan from a finance company, secured by a mortgage on the land. The finance company promptly and properly recorded its mortgage. The driver subsequently defaulted on the bank's mortgage, leaving an outstanding balance on the bank's loan of $60,000. However, the driver continued to make payments to the finance company. The bank brought a foreclosure action, joining the finance company in the proceeding. The jurisdiction provides a statutory right of redemption for lienholders.

Does the finance company have any recourse prior to the foreclosure sale to protect its interest?

(A) Yes, the finance company may pay off the bank's mortgage to preserve its own interest on the land.

(B) Yes, it can exercise its statutory right of redemption.

(C) No, because the driver has not defaulted on the finance company's mortgage.

(D) No, because only the mortgagor holds the right to redeem the property.

Question 57

The plaintiff is suing the defendant for injuries he suffered when his car was struck by the defendant's truck, allegedly because the defendant had fallen asleep at the wheel after driving all night. At trial, the defendant's girlfriend testified that she had been with the defendant in the truck and had taken over the driving duties for several hours that night while the defendant napped. The plaintiff calls to the stand an acquaintance of the defendant's girlfriend, to testify that the girlfriend told him that she had been unable to get out of bed the weekend the accident occurred because of severe back pain.

The testimony of the acquaintance is:

(A) Admissible for impeachment purposes only.

(B) Admissible for impeachment purposes and as substantive evidence as a declaration of physical condition.

(C) Inadmissible, because this means of impeachment can be done only through cross-examination.

(D) Inadmissible, because the plaintiff has not first given the girlfriend an opportunity to explain or deny the statement.

Question 58

The defendant is charged with having been one of two men who robbed a tavern and its patrons at gunpoint at 5:30 p.m. on December 16.

The defendant calls a witness to testify that he was at the defendant's house at about 9:30 a.m. on December 16, and that as he was leaving, the defendant said to him, "I'm going to my mother-in-law's house this afternoon for a birthday party."

Is the witness's testimony admissible?

(A) No, it is hearsay not within any exception.

(B) No, it is irrelevant.

(C) Yes, it is not being offered to prove the truth of the matter stated, so it is not hearsay.

(D) Yes, it is hearsay within an exception, and thus admissible.

Question 59

A state legislature was concerned about the number of households headed by single teenage mothers and the deleterious effects of overpopulation. It enacted legislation requiring any person under the age of 25 to obtain a certificate of responsibility before having children. Under the statutes, any fetus whose parents do not both have a certificate of responsibility is required to be aborted, and any child born into the same circumstances is required to be placed up for adoption. Parents who violate the statute are subject to fine, imprisonment, or both.

A 22-year-old male resident of the state brings an action in federal court seeking to enjoin enforcement of the legislation on the ground that it violates his constitutional rights. In his complaint, he alleges that he plans to marry and father children before he is 25.

Which of the following provides the strongest justification for dismissing the action?

(A) It involves a nonjusticiable political question.

(B) It is not ripe for adjudication.

(C) There is no substantial federal question involved.

(D) The 22-year-old's future wife is not also a party to the action.

Question 60

A state's defamation statutes require as a prerequisite for the filing of a libel suit against a public newspaper that the plaintiff demand in writing that the defendant retract the allegedly defamatory material. In the plaintiff's defamation suit against the defendant, the publisher of a public newspaper, the plaintiff calls as a witness a former employee of the defendant who was the secretary to the editor during the period in which the events underlying the plaintiff's suit occurred. The witness will testify that two days after the allegedly defamatory story was run in the newspaper, she remembers receiving a letter to the editor of the newspaper delivered by the plaintiff. The plaintiff has already testified that he wrote a letter to the editor demanding a retraction, and that the letter was delivered by him the same day that the defamatory story was published.

Should the court admit the witness's testimony over the defendant's objection?

(A) No, because the witness is no longer employed by the defendant.

(B) No, because the letter itself is the best evidence.

(C) Yes, because the witness's testimony is evidence of a matter in issue.

(D) Yes, because the witness's testimony is an admission by a party-opponent.

Question 61

A debtor owed a creditor $1,200 on a promissory note that was due on August 1. After the debtor told the creditor that he might not be able to pay the note on its due date, the creditor agreed to extinguish the debt if the debtor, who was the manager of a discount electronics store, bought a new entertainment system that sold for $1,200 and had it delivered to the creditor's home by August 15. Because the debtor would have to pay only $600 for the system due to his manager's discount, he agreed and the parties signed a written contract on July 26.

Is the new agreement between the debtor and the creditor legally enforceable?

(A) No, because the debtor incurred no additional detriment that would serve as consideration for the new agreement.

(B) Yes, because it would have cost the creditor $1,200 to purchase the entertainment system himself.

(C) Yes, because the debtor incurred a different obligation than he originally had.

(D) Yes, because the new agreement between the debtor and the creditor is enforceable with or without consideration as long as it was made in good faith.

GO ON TO THE NEXT PAGE

Question 62

A buyer of a new car owed the car dealership where she purchased the vehicle $1,000 on a promissory note that was due on December 30. The buyer determined that she would be unable to pay the note on its due date, and she informed the owner of the dealership of that fact. The owner told her that she would not have to pay the debt if she bought him four tickets to a popular concert on January 15 that had been sold out for weeks, because she worked as publicist for the concert venue. She agreed to do so, and the parties memorialized their agreement in a signed writing on December 18. On January 2, the dealership filed suit against the car buyer for failure to pay the $1,000 promissory note, before the car buyer had secured the concert tickets for the owner.

May the car buyer have this action enjoined by introducing evidence of the December 18 agreement?

(A) Yes, because the December 18 agreement between the parties suspended the car buyer's obligation on the promissory note.

(B) Yes, because the December 18 agreement between the parties discharged the car buyer's obligation on the promissory note.

(C) No, because the car buyer has not yet bought the concert tickets in reliance on the owner's promise to extinguish the debt.

(D) No, because the car buyer's only remedy is to sue for damages for breach of the December 18 agreement.

Question 63

A petty thief and a felon decided to meet at the mall, armed with a gun or knife, to look for elderly women wearing expensive jewelry, intending to follow them home and rob them. The thief began to have second thoughts when he considered that the felon had already done time for armed robbery and assault with a deadly weapon, and that he had vowed that he

would never "do time" again because "somebody finked to the cops." The thief told the felon when they met at the mall that he had changed his mind and wanted no part of the action, and went home. That evening, the felon robbed and beat an elderly woman returning home from the mall. Because of her ill health and age, the woman had died as a result of the beating.

The thief is guilty of:

(A) No crime.

(B) Conspiracy.

(C) Murder.

(D) Murder and conspiracy.

Question 64

A shopper headed out of a store at the same time as a shoplifter, whose stolen items triggered the store's inventory control alarm. A security guard at the exit requested that the shopper stop so that his bags could be checked, but the shopper said he was in a hurry and did not want to wait. The guard then requested that the shopper immediately step to the side, and pulled out a pair of handcuffs as she reached for his arm. On seeing the handcuffs, the shopper agreed to step over to the side and wait.

If the shopper is not successful in an assault action against the store, it will be because:

(A) The shopper suffered no injury from the guard's actions.

(B) The guard did not intend to injure the shopper when she pulled out the handcuffs and reached for the shopper's arm.

(C) The guard acted reasonably in dealing with a suspected shoplifter.

(D) A reasonable person would have complied with the guard's initial request.

Question 65

A security officer employed by a mall was patrolling the mall parking lot which had suffered numerous thefts from cars when she heard a car alarm go off. She then saw a teenager stand up from behind the car. She immediately stopped the teenager and asked him what he was doing behind the car, and he said he was tying his shoe. Reasonably suspecting that he may have been trying to break into the car, she asked him to wait in the back seat of her car. The teenager complied, and waited in the back of the car while the security officer ate her lunch in the front seat and made a variety of personal calls. The teenager was humiliated because several of his friends and their parents, as well as some neighbors, saw him sitting in the security officer's car. Finally, after about an hour, the officer let the teenager go and advised him not to loiter in the parking lot anymore.

If the teenager brings a false imprisonment action against the mall, will he be able to recover for the humiliation that he felt on sitting in the security officer's car in view of his friends and neighbors?

(A) No, humiliation is not actionable.

(B) No, because the security officer reasonably suspected that he was trying to break into a car.

(C) Yes, if the jury determines that the security officer's conduct was extreme and outrageous.

(D) Yes, because he was falsely imprisoned.

Question 66

A landowner owned an undeveloped parcel of land, through which a creek ran. The creek also ran through his neighbor's downstream parcel. The neighbor drew off water from the creek to irrigate her crops and to water her livestock. The neighbor's use of her parcel and the creek water has been continuous and uninterrupted for 18 years. Two years ago, the landowner constructed a residence on his parcel and began to draw off the waters of the creek for his domestic use. The following summer, there was adequate water in the creek for all of the landowner's domestic purposes and for all of the neighbor's agricultural purposes. However, the flow of the creek is irregular and the water level dropped dramatically this summer. The amount of water in the creek is sufficient to meet either all of the neighbor's needs and none of the landowner's or all of the landowner's needs and one-half of the neighbor's. Both the landowner and the neighbor file suit, claiming they are entitled to sufficient water from the creek to meet all their respective needs. The jurisdiction in which the parcels are located has a statutory 10-year prescription and adverse possession period, and follows the riparian doctrine of reasonable use.

In the resulting trial of the case, who will prevail?

(A) The neighbor, because she has a prior reasonable use of the water.

(B) The neighbor, because she is entitled to the water by prescription.

(C) The landowner, because his use of the water does not totally deprive the neighbor of water for her needs.

(D) The landowner, because the neighbor's use of the water is not a natural use.

Question 67

A state statute prohibited, under criminal penalties, the sale or furnishing of any alcoholic beverage to a minor. A 16-year-old minor went to his neighborhood liquor store and asked a patron who was about to enter if the latter would purchase some beer for him. The patron agreed, took the minor's money, and returned with a six-pack of beer. At the moment that the beer changed hands, an official of the State Bureau of Alcohol Control leapt from behind a nearby car and announced that both the patron and the minor were under arrest. The patron ran to his car and escaped. The minor is now being prosecuted under the statute as having aided and abetted the patron in its violation.

Which of the following is his best argument in defense?

(A) He cannot be convicted as an aider and abettor unless the principal is first convicted.

(B) He cannot be convicted as an aider and abettor of violating a statute designed to protect the class of which he is a member—minors.

(C) He cannot be convicted of aiding and abetting any crime because he is a minor.

(D) He cannot be convicted alone of committing a crime that requires at least two parties to commit a violation.

Question 68

In a civil action tried to a jury, the defendant objected to the introduction by the plaintiff of certain evidence without the judge's first making a preliminary ruling on the admissibility of the evidence.

For which evidence is the defendant's objection not appropriate?

(A) Opinion testimony regarding the structural integrity of a building by an engineer called by the plaintiff, without a preliminary determination by the judge that the engineer is an expert.

(B) Hospital records pertaining to the plaintiff offered by the plaintiff, without a preliminary determination by the judge that they were made as a regular activity of the hospital staff.

(C) Contract negotiations between the plaintiff and a third party, without a preliminary determination by the judge that the third party was the defendant's agent.

(D) A paramedic's testimony that the plaintiff's wife, before she died, said that the defendant's car went through a red light before hitting her, without a preliminary determination by the judge that she made the statement under a sense of impending death.

GO ON TO THE NEXT PAGE

Question 69

A state statute has adopted the common law definition of larceny. Another statute provided as follows:

> It shall be an affirmative defense to a crime if the defendant establishes by clear and convincing evidence that, due to a mental disease or defect, he was unable to appreciate the criminality of his conduct or conform his conduct to the requirements of the law. *MPC*

A homeowner was leaving town for two weeks and he asked his neighbor to stop by the house each day and water the plants. While at the homeowner's home, the neighbor found the keys to the homeowner's new car. The neighbor took the car and drove it into town to show his friends. The neighbor told all of his friends that he had purchased the car. The homeowner returned home three days early, saw that the car was missing, and called the police. Later that day, the neighbor was arrested and charged with larceny.

At the neighbor's trial, the neighbor testified that he intended to return the car. Additionally, two psychiatrists testified that, due to a mental defect, the neighbor suffered from an extreme inferiority complex and delusions of grandeur. The doctors further testified that his mental condition caused him to take the car and to tell other people that he owned it. At the conclusion of the evidence, the court's instructions to the jury included the following:

1. If you find by a preponderance of the evidence that the defendant intended to return the car, you should find the defendant not guilty.

2. If you find by a preponderance of the evidence that, due to a mental disease or defect, the defendant was unable to appreciate the criminality of his conduct or conform his conduct to the requirements of the law, you should find the defendant not guilty.

The neighbor was found guilty and he appealed, claiming that the jury instructions violated his constitutional rights.

The appellate court should rule that:

(A) Both instructions were constitutional.

(B) Both instructions were unconstitutional.

(C) Instruction 1 was unconstitutional; Instruction 2 was constitutional.

(D) Instruction 1 was constitutional; Instruction 2 was unconstitutional.

Question 70

A state legislature enacted a program by which students in the public schools could request instruction as to specific religions and religious beliefs, and thus participate in public school programs in which leaders of the religions involved gave religious instruction and performed religious practices on school grounds. The program provided instruction on any religion requested by a student.

Which of the following would *not* be relevant in assessing the constitutionality of the state religious instruction program?

(A) The substantial effect of the legislation is to promote the religions studied.

(B) The primary purpose of the statute is to foster belief in the religions studied.

(C) The state does not have a compelling interest in instructing public school students about specific religions.

(D) The legislation requires that religious leaders and school officials interact constantly and frequently.

Question 71

A motorist purchased a new sport utility vehicle from his local dealer. Standard equipment on the vehicle included a set of top-of-the-line tires from a premium tire company. However, the motorist was able to save $400 on the purchase price by allowing the dealer to substitute a lower priced tire manufactured by a discount tire manufacturer. Unbeknownst to the motorist and the dealer, the tire manufacturer had negligently designed the tires, with the result that a tire would occasionally blow out when the car was traveling at a high rate of speed in hot weather. On an exceptionally hot day, the motorist was traveling 80 m.p.h. in a 55 m.p.h. zone. A tire exploded, resulting in damage to the vehicle and injury to the motorist.

If the motorist sues the dealer on a theory of strict liability, is he likely to prevail?

(A) Yes, because the tire was in a dangerously defective condition when the motorist purchased the car.

(B) Yes, because the dealer is responsible for the negligence of the tire manufacturer, because the dealer used its tires.

(C) No, because the motorist assumed the risk when he substituted the discount tires in exchange for $400.

(D) No, because the motorist was misusing the tire when he was traveling at 80 m.p.h.

Question 72

A farmer kept a pet bear at his farm. The bear was very old and had no teeth, no claws, and very little energy, but people liked to see the bear when they visited the farmer because no one else in the region had a pet bear. When the farmer first obtained the bear many years ago, he had a large steel cage constructed to house the animal. The cage had an electronic lock that only opened with a security code. Even though the bear was now old and harmless, it was always kept locked in the cage. One night during a severe storm while the farmer was out of town, a bolt of lightning hit the cage and the door opened. The bear left the cage and wandered off. The next morning, a 10-year-old girl was waiting on a rural road for her school bus. The bear emerged from a wooded area about 100 feet from where the girl was standing and headed towards her. She screamed and turned to run, tripping on the road and breaking her arm when she fell.

If the girl sues the farmer on a theory of strict liability for her bodily harm, will she prevail?

(A) No, because the bear was in fact a nondangerous animal.

(B) No, because the damage she suffered was not the type of damage that a bear would normally cause.

(C) Yes, because the bear is a wild animal.

(D) Yes, because pet bears were not commonly kept in the community.

GO ON TO THE NEXT PAGE

Question 73

Concerned about the rising death toll on the state's highways, a state legislature enacted a statute providing for a summary one-year suspension of the driver's license of any person convicted of three speeding violations within a 12-month period. The statute provided that an administrative hearing is immediately available upon request. However, that hearing is limited to a determination of whether the licensee is the same person who was convicted of the speeding violations.

A driver received three speeding citations in a three-week period and was convicted of all three charges. Her license was promptly suspended under the authority of the state statute. Without first seeking an administrative hearing, the driver files a suit in federal district court challenging the constitutionality of the statute.

The court should rule that the state law is:

(A) Constitutional, because driving an automobile on the state's highways is a privilege and not a right.

(B) Constitutional, because the state's interest in promptly removing unsafe drivers from its roads outweighs the driver's right to a prior hearing under these circumstances.

(C) Unconstitutional, because the law creates an irrebuttable presumption that all drivers falling within the ambit of the statute are unsafe.

(D) Unconstitutional, as a denial of due process without a prior hearing.

Question 74

In connection with its agricultural products price support program, the United States Department of Agriculture regularly sent marketing and price information via email to its numerous field offices in various states. Recently, sophisticated criminals began using electronic devices to intercept the transmitted information, which they then used to gain an unfair advantage over other traders in the nation's commodities markets. To alleviate the problem, Congress enacted legislation making it a criminally punishable offense to "intercept marketing and/or price information in any fashion or to transmit such intercepted information to any other person in any fashion." A citizen opposed to the federal agricultural price support program learned the identity of the individuals who are intercepting the Department of Agriculture transmissions and, in exchange for not revealing their identities, obtained copies of every transmission they intercepted. He published these in his weekly newsletter.

If the citizen is prosecuted for violation of the federal statute prohibiting transmission of intercepted marketing or price information, what is his strongest argument that the statute is unconstitutional as applied to him?

(A) The statute denies him the equal protection of the law as guaranteed by the Fourteenth Amendment.

(B) The statute violates his right not to be deprived of liberty without due process of law.

(C) The statute violates his First Amendment right to free speech.

(D) The statute is an undue burden upon interstate commerce.

GO ON TO THE NEXT PAGE

Question 75

A farmer was arrested after selling her surplus fruits and vegetables for several days at a vacant lot in the nearby town. A statute provides that it is a misdemeanor, punishable by a fine of up to $500 and/or imprisonment in county jail for up to one year, to sell any product without a business license, except for informal sales held on the property of the seller no more often than once every three months. At the farmer's trial, she requested but was refused appointed counsel.

Assuming that she would otherwise qualify as indigent, if she is convicted of violating the statute, what is the maximum penalty that may be imposed on her?

(A) Imprisonment for six months.

(B) A $500 fine.

(C) Imprisonment for six months and a $500 fine.

(D) No penalty, because her conviction is void as having been obtained in violation of her right to counsel under the Sixth Amendment.

Question 76

The plaintiff sued the defendant, a computer dealer engaged in buying and selling used computers, alleging that he was not given credit for a DVR drive that he had on the computer that he had sent back for resale. The defendant's bookkeeper testified that it was company practice when a boxed computer was returned to have one clerk open the box and identify the type of computer and its components and have another clerk record the information in the inventory ledger. The defendant seeks to enter into evidence the original ledger entry, which the bookkeeper authenticated, showing that a DVR drive was not checked off on the components list for the plaintiff's computer. The plaintiff objects to the admission of the ledger.

The ledger is:

(A) Admissible, because it is a record of a transaction for which the bookkeeper does not have any present recollection.

(B) Admissible, because it was regular company practice to record receipt of the components in the inventory ledger.

(C) Inadmissible as hearsay within hearsay, because even if a hearsay exception permits introducing the record itself rather than requiring testimony by the employee who made it, that employee was just recording hearsay because he had no personal knowledge of what he was recording.

(D) Inadmissible hearsay, because absence of the notation implies a statement that no DVR return was received, and the evidence is being offered as proof of that assertion.

Question 77

To combat fraud and misuse of driver's licenses, a state's department of motor vehicles enacted new regulations for the issuance of driver's licenses. One of the regulations, which were authorized by state law, required for the first time that driver's licenses display a photograph of the person whose name is on the license. The regulations did not provide for any exemptions from this requirement. Living entirely within the state was a religious sect whose followers devoutly believed that allowing oneself to be photographed was sinful. However, because much of the state was rural and sparsely populated, members of the sect needed to travel by automobile to obtain necessary services and to gather for worship. A member of the sect who was refused a driver's license because he would not allow himself to be photographed challenged the state regulation in federal court.

Is the court likely to uphold the application of the regulation to the religious group?

(A) Yes, because exempting the church's members from the regulation would not have a secular purpose and would constitute improper state advancement of, and entanglement with, religion.

(B) Yes, because enactment of the regulation was not motivated by a desire to interfere with religion.

(C) No, unless the state shows that the regulation is necessary to promote a compelling governmental interest.

(D) No, because the opposition to the regulation arises from a sincerely held religious belief.

Question 78

A buyer entered into a contract with a seller to purchase the seller's farm. The contract of sale referred to the farm as containing 250 acres. The agreed-on price was $1 million. Before the date on which escrow was to close, the buyer learned from a surveyor he had hired that the farm actually contained 248 acres. On the date the sale was to close, the buyer instructed the escrow agent to release all but $8,000 of the purchase money because he was not getting what he bargained for. The seller refused to proceed with the sale. The buyer brings an action for specific performance and also seeks a reduction of the agreed-upon contract price.

What will be the probable outcome of the litigation?

(A) The seller will win, because the buyer refused to tender the contract price when the seller tendered substantially what the contract called for her to perform.

(B) The seller will win, because both parties had seen the farm before the contract was formed.

(C) The buyer will win, because he is not receiving what he bargained for under the contract.

(D) The buyer will win, because the difference of two acres is material and the $8,000 reduction in price is not an excessive variance from the parties' agreement.

GO ON TO THE NEXT PAGE

Question 79

A strawberry farmer held his farm open to the public to pick strawberries for a fee. The farmer knew that many patrons would eat as many strawberries out in the field as they would bring home with them, so he advertised that no chemical pesticides or fertilizers were used on his strawberries. The owner of the land adjacent to the farm began operating a soap factory, a use allowed by the zoning code. Flakes of an unavoidable chemical byproduct of the soap-making process would drift over onto the farm whenever the wind was blowing in that direction and settle onto the strawberry plants. The flakes caused no harm to the plants themselves but detracted from the appearance of the strawberries as well as their taste if eaten right off the plant; consequently, the farmer's business declined. On several occasions, the farmer complained to the factory owner, but the owner did nothing, in part because a visit to the county recorder of deeds office had convinced him that he was the true owner of a large part of the strawberry farm, although in fact it was just a recording error.

Can the farmer recover damages for the harm caused to his business from the factory owner?

(A) Yes, because the discharge from the owner's factory entered the farmer's land.

(B) Yes, because the factory owner intended to conduct the activities that caused the particles to fall on the farmer's land.

(C) No, because the factory owner had no intent to cause harm to the farmer's property.

(D) No, because the factory owner's belief that he owned the property, although erroneous, was reasonable.

Question 80

At a popular barbecue restaurant, the barbecue was prepared in a large, outdoor pit in the back of the restaurant. Cooking meat outdoors in a commercial establishment violated a city health code regulation, designed to assure that the food was not exposed to flies and other insects. On windy days, smoke from the barbecue pit sometimes blew into a neighbor's backyard. Although most people would not be bothered by the smoke, the neighbor had extremely sensitive eyes. They watered and stung every time that he was exposed to any form of smoke. When the barbecue smoke drifted onto his property, the neighbor could not use his backyard.

If the neighbor sues the restaurant because he often cannot use his backyard, the neighbor will likely:

(A) Prevail, because the restaurant's action interfered with the neighbor's use and enjoyment of his yard.

(B) Prevail, because the restaurant was violating a health code regulation.

(C) Not prevail, because the smoke would not disturb a person of ordinary sensibilities in the community.

(D) Not prevail, because the health code regulation was not designed to protect against the type of harm suffered by the neighbor.

GO ON TO THE NEXT PAGE

Question 81

Late one night, a young couple in a car was struck by a speeding truck as the couple's car crossed an intersection with the light green in their favor, killing them immediately. Several weeks later, a burglar awaiting trial on burglary charges asked a jail officer to let him speak with a highway patrol officer. When the highway patrol officer came to the cell, the burglar told him that he was the driver of the truck that had struck the car, and had been speeding away from a burglary when the accident occurred.

The burglar was put on trial for felony murder, on the theory that he had not yet reached a place of temporary safety when the accident occurred. The prosecution seeks to introduce the statements made by the burglar to the highway patrol officer regarding the events of the night of the accident. The burglar's attorney objects.

Which of the following is the strongest argument for permitting the statements into evidence?

(A) The burglar had not been charged in connection with the auto accident at the time the statements were made to the highway patrol officer.

(B) The burglar made the statements spontaneously, without inducement or interrogation by the police.

(C) The highway patrol officer had no connection with the burglary investigation for which the burglar had been incarcerated.

(D) The burglar's statements were not the product of coercion by the police officers.

Question 82

At the beginning of the second day of the defendant's trial for arson, a bailiff approached the defendant and got him to admit that he had burned down the house in question. When the trial resumed, the defendant testified that he had nothing to do with the fire in question. In rebuttal, the prosecution seeks to put the bailiff on the stand to testify as to the defendant's statements, but the defendant's attorney objects.

Which of the following is the strongest argument to exclude the bailiff's testimony as to the defendant's statements?

(A) The bailiff did not give the defendant *Miranda* warnings.

(B) The bailiff did not tell the defendant's attorney that he was going to question him.

(C) The statements were made in the absence of the defendant's counsel.

(D) The statements were made to a law enforcement officer and therefore were not voluntary.

GO ON TO THE NEXT PAGE

Question 83

At the defendant's trial for armed robbery, the prosecutor offers indisputable evidence tending to show that the defendant committed two other armed robberies in the year preceding the present offense, and that he committed all three robberies to obtain money for his heroin habit. The defendant has no prior convictions and has chosen not to take the stand in his defense.

Should the court admit this evidence over the defendant's objection?

(A) No, because the defendant was not convicted of the other robberies.

(B) No, because the defendant has not testified at his trial.

(C) Yes, unless the court determines that the probative value of the evidence is substantially outweighed by its prejudicial effect.

(D) Yes, because the prosecution can establish by clear and convincing evidence that the defendant committed the robberies.

Question 84

A backpacker came upon another hiker who had been bitten by a rattlesnake. The backpacker carried the bitten hiker back to his vehicle and drove him toward the nearest hospital. On the way there, while exceeding the posted speed limit, the backpacker lost control of his vehicle and crashed into a tree by the side of the road. He was uninjured, but the snakebitten hiker's leg was broken. An ambulance soon arrived and took the hiker to the hospital. The emergency room physician committed malpractice that resulted in the loss of the hiker's leg. The hiker is now suing the backpacker.

Which of the following is the most likely reason why the backpacker will be held liable for the hiker's injuries?

(A) Having undertaken to rescue the hiker, the backpacker is strictly liable for injuries resulting from the rescue.

(B) The emergency room physician's malpractice is a foreseeable intervening cause that does not relieve the backpacker of liability.

(C) The backpacker did not conduct himself as a reasonably prudent person in carrying out the rescue of the hiker.

(D) The backpacker committed negligence per se when he exceeded the posted speed limit.

Question 85

Congress enacted a statute that provided for direct money grants to the various states to be distributed by them to police agencies within their jurisdictions for the purpose of purchasing gas-efficient patrol vehicles. One of the objectives of the statute was to help reduce the dependency of the United States on imported oil.

Which of the following would provide the best constitutional justification for the statute?

(A) The Commerce Clause.

(B) The power to tax and spend for the general welfare.

(C) The Necessary and Proper Clause.

(D) The power to conduct the foreign relations of the United States.

GO ON TO THE NEXT PAGE

Question 86

A passenger on a commuter train left his seat to go to the lavatory at the front of the car. While he was in the aisle, the car moved across intersecting tracks, causing the car to rock. He stumbled and bumped his knee against the lavatory door, aggravating a preexisting circulation problem in his leg that had been controlled by medication. As a result, he had to have several surgeries to correct the circulation problem.

The passenger brought suit to recover damages against the agency that operated the train system. At the jury trial, the following evidence was presented: The passenger testified as to how he was injured and introduced evidence of his medical expenses. His physician testified that the bump aggravated the circulation problem. The engineer of the train testified that the train had not been exceeding the speed limit for that stretch of track, and the agency introduced a report indicating that a subsequent inspection disclosed no problems with the track. The agency also presented uncontroverted evidence that a person in normal health would not have been injured by the bump. At the close of the evidence, the agency moved for a directed verdict.

The court should:

(A) Grant the motion, because there is no evidence that the agency or its employees operated the train negligently.

(B) Grant the motion, because the agency established that a person in normal health would not have been injured by the bump.

 (C) Deny the motion, because the jury could find that the agency, as a common carrier, breached its high duty of care to its passenger.

(D) Deny the motion, because the fact that the severity of the passenger's injuries was not foreseeable does not cut off the agency's liability.

Question 87

On August 5, the owner of a hot dog plant and the proprietor of a local ballpark concession stand entered into a written agreement providing, among other things, that if the local team wins the state championship, the plant owner will deliver to the proprietor 500 hot dogs on each of the following days: September 5, 7, and 9. The price was set at 25¢ per hot dog, with payment to be made on September 10 by the proprietor to a creditor of the plant owner. On August 15, the plant owner decided that he wanted to avoid his obligation to deliver the hot dogs. The creditor has not become aware of the agreement between the plant owner and the proprietor.

Which of the following is the most accurate statement?

(A) The plant owner cannot rescind the contract without the permission of both the proprietor and the creditor.

(B) The plant owner cannot rescind the contract without the permission of the proprietor.

(C) The plant owner can repudiate the agreement because the promise to perform by the proprietor is illusory.

(D) The plant owner can revoke the offer to sell hot dogs if the team does not win the state championship.

GO ON TO THE NEXT PAGE

Question 88

A large-scale bakery in the South entered into a written contract with a commercial apple orchard in the upper Midwest to purchase 200 bushels of apples at a cost of $8 per bushel. The contract provided that the apple orchard would deliver the apples "F.O.B. Louisville Railroad Depot," where the apples would be loaded onto a train headed south. The orchard assigned all of its rights under the contract to a large produce distributor which, in turn, hired a trucking company to deliver the apples to Louisville. En route to Louisville, the truck skidded off the road due to inclement weather and overturned, and the apples were destroyed. The bakery brought suit against the apple orchard for breach of contract.

What will be the probable outcome of the litigation?

(A) The bakery will lose.

(B) The bakery will recover the amount necessary to replace the destroyed apples, over the contract price.

(C) The bakery will recover the full contract price.

(D) The bakery will be able to compel specific performance of the contract.

Question 89

As permitted by state law, a large city in the state adopted an ordinance legalizing slot machines in shopping malls within the city. Several prominent city residents were upset by the new ordinance because gambling violates one of the main tenets of their religion. Seeking relief, the citizens contacted their representative in Congress and asked the representative to sponsor a bill making it illegal to place gambling machines in shopping malls throughout the country. The representative sponsored such a bill. Congress made a factual finding that the activity regulated has a substantial economic effect on interstate commerce and passes such a statute.

If the statute banning gambling machines in shopping malls is challenged on constitutional grounds by a proper plaintiff in federal court, would the court likely uphold the statute?

(A) No, because it was based on the citizens' religious tenets and so violates the First Amendment Establishment Clause.

(B) No, because the statute does not regulate the channels or instrumentalities of interstate commerce.

(C) Yes, because Congress has made a factual finding that the activity regulated has a substantial economic effect on interstate commerce.

(D) Yes, because there is a conceivable rational basis for concluding that the activity regulated, in aggregate, substantially affects interstate commerce.

Question 90

During a nationwide trucker's strike, striking drivers committed repeated acts of violence against independent truckers and railroad shipments that had replaced truck transportation. This prompted Congress to enact an emergency measure directing the President to dispatch United States Army troops to specified cities and rail and highway locations to preserve order and ensure the continued flow of commerce.

This enactment is probably:

(A) Unconstitutional, because it infringes on the President's authority to faithfully execute the laws of the United States.

(B) Unconstitutional, because it infringes on the President's authority as Commander in Chief of the armed forces.

(C) Constitutional, under Congress's power to regulate commerce.

(D) Constitutional, under Congress's power to raise and support the armed forces.

GO ON TO THE NEXT PAGE

Question 91

The defendant is on trial for shoplifting. As part of his defense, the defendant calls to the stand a restaurant cashier, who will testify that the defendant is a regular customer and has corrected an undercharge on her bill several times.

Is the testimony of the cashier admissible?

(A) Yes, because a defendant may offer evidence of her good character in a criminal case.

(B) Yes, because the evidence is relevant and its probative value outweighs the danger of unfair prejudice or confusion of the issues.

(C) No, because the cashier's testimony is hearsay.

(D) No, because the evidence is not a proper means for proving good character.

Question 92

A patient was scheduled to undergo nonemergency surgery for the removal of her appendix by her family doctor. The day of the surgery, the doctor was called out of town because of a family illness. Even though the surgery could be postponed, the doctor asked the surgeon on call, who was an expert in appendectomies, to take his place. The patient was not informed of the switch in doctors.

If the patient sues the surgeon on a battery theory, who will prevail?

(A) The patient, as long as she establishes damages at trial.

(B) The patient, regardless of whether she establishes damages at trial.

(C) The surgeon, because he was at least as qualified as the doctor.

(D) The surgeon, because the doctor requested that the surgeon take his place.

Question 93

A felon planned to break into the rental storage unit next to his that contained valuable electronic equipment. He went to a hardware store to purchase a crowbar. The proprietor sold him the crowbar even though he told her that he needed it to break into someone's storage unit. After the purchase, the felon went to the storage facility with his friend. The felon told the friend that he had lost the key to his storage unit and did not have time to contact the facility's manager, so they needed to break into the unit to get his equipment. Because the felon had a bad back, the friend pried open the door with the crowbar and carried the equipment out to the car. A silent alarm was triggered and the pair were apprehended shortly after leaving the facility.

Can the proprietor and the friend be convicted as accomplices to larceny?

(A) Yes as to the proprietor, because she knew that the felon was going to break into someone's storage unit with the crowbar.

(B) Yes as to the friend, because he carried out the theft of the items from the storage unit.

(C) Yes as to both the proprietor and the friend.

(D) No as to both the proprietor and the friend.

GO ON TO THE NEXT PAGE

Question 94

One provision of a federal law provided that state governments may enact legislation regulating any form of pinball machine or video game, including location and hours of operation. In response, a Western state enacted legislation providing, among other things, that any video game sold or operated within the state use a particular LCD screen designed to minimize eyestrain.

A corporation that designs and manufactures video games for sale throughout the United States and in Europe is based in the Midwest. Approximately 10% of its gross sales are made in the Western state that has regulated the LCD screens. The corporation's machines are not manufactured using the special eye-protecting LCD screens; to install such screens in all machines manufactured would cause the price of the machines to increase by 20%, and to use the screens in machines sold only in the Western state would increase the cost of those machines by 50%. The corporation files suit in federal court to enjoin enforcement of the state video game statute.

How should the court rule?

(A) For the state, because the challenged legislation is within the powers specifically reserved to the states by the Tenth Amendment.

(B) For the state, because Congress has acted within its power to authorize video game regulation by the states.

(C) For the corporation, because the challenged statute violates the Commerce Clause.

(D) For the corporation, because the challenged statute is overbroad and exceeds the permissible bounds of regulation as authorized by Congress.

Question 95

An off-duty mall security guard was at a bar with his girlfriend when he got into an argument with another patron. The argument escalated and the guard drew out the pistol he had been given at work and shot the patron in the chest, killing him. The survivors of the dead patron brought a wrongful death action against the security agency that hired the guard. At trial, they established that the guard had been required to fill out an application listing references and indicating whether he had any prior convictions for offenses involving violence or use of a weapon, which would disqualify him by law from a position as a security officer. The guard had listed as references some aunts and uncles who had not seen him in some time, and he stated that he had no prior convictions. In fact, the guard had several times been convicted of violent assaults using firearms, and records of these convictions were available in a public database. The agency, however, had not investigated the statements on his application.

The survivors will likely:

(A) Prevail, because a reasonable employer would have discovered the guard's prior convictions.

(B) Prevail, because the agency employed the guard and gave him the pistol he used to kill the patron.

(C) Not prevail, because the agency owed no duty to the patron which was violated.

(D) Not prevail, because the guard's actions occurred while he was acting outside the scope of his employment.

GO ON TO THE NEXT PAGE

Question 96

The plaintiff was injured when the bus in which she was riding braked too abruptly and threw her into a support stanchion, breaking her hip. She has brought an action against the bus company for damages from personal injuries on theories of respondeat superior and negligent hiring.

During the bus company's case in chief, its counsel calls the company's personnel director as a witness and asks him if the driver of the bus had been required to provide proof that he had had no convictions for crimes relating to vehicle use before being hired. The witness answers, "It's been several years since he was hired, but my best recollection is that we did not ask for such proof." Counsel then prepares to question the witness about his statement, made at a deposition taken 18 months before trial, that he had personally requested and received a statement from the driver before he was hired that he (the driver) had no such convictions.

May counsel for the bus company pursue this matter in this fashion?

(A) Yes, but the jury must be instructed that the evidence may be considered only for impeachment of the witness.

(B) Yes, the evidence may be admitted for both impeachment and substantive purposes.

(C) No, because it is hearsay not within any exception.

(D) No, counsel may not impeach its own witness.

Question 97

A landowner and his neighbor owned adjoining tracts of land. The boundary line between the two properties was never properly determined or clearly known. Twenty-five years ago, the landowner installed a gas-powered generator on land he thought he owned, but which was in fact owned by the neighbor. The generator was housed in a small shed and surrounded by a fence. Ten years later, the neighbor was found to be mentally incompetent. She died last year, and her executor filed suit to eject the landowner and quiet title. The statute of limitations in ejectment is 20 years.

With respect to the land on which the generator was installed:

(A) The landowner cannot claim title by adverse possession because the statute of limitations was tolled by the neighbor's incompetency.

(B) The landowner cannot claim title by adverse possession because his occupation was not under claim of right.

(C) The landowner has acquired title by adverse possession.

(D) The landowner has acquired a prescriptive easement.

Question 98

A lumberjack conveyed his forested land by deed "to my sister, her heirs, and assigns; but if my sister should die without producing issue, then to the American Cancer Society." At the time of the conveyance, the forest produced a net annual value of $25,000 in timber and had proven reserves of $250,000. Shortly after the conveyance, the American Cancer Society brings an action to enjoin the sister from harvesting any more timber.

The court should rule in favor of:

(A) The American Cancer Society, because it has a contingent remainder.

(B) The American Cancer Society, because it has an executory interest.

(C) The sister, because she has a defeasible fee simple.

(D) The sister, because timber was being harvested prior to the lumberjack's conveyance.

GO ON TO THE NEXT PAGE

Question 99

A company manufactured parachutes that it sold exclusively to the United States Army. To meet the standards required by the Army, each parachute was subjected to a 15-point inspection by the company before it could be approved for sale. When a parachute did not pass inspection, it was stored in another section of the company's plant. At a later time, a further inspection of the defective parachute would be made to determine whether the defects could be corrected or whether the parachute should be destroyed.

One night, the plant was burglarized through no fault of the company and a large number of parachutes, including the defective ones, were stolen. The defective parachutes eventually were sold on the black market to a member of a skydiving club who made purchases for the club. One week later, the member was using one of the parachutes when it failed to open, causing his death.

If the member's estate brings a wrongful death action against the company on a theory of strict liability in a jurisdiction retaining traditional contributory negligence rules, the company's best defense would be that:

(A) The company acted reasonably in storing the defective parachutes.

(B) The company did not sell or place into the stream of commerce the defective parachute.

(C) The member did not purchase the parachute from the company.

(D) The member was negligent when he purchased the parachute on the black market.

Question 100

A bank hired a security guard after a routine background check of the guard's references. The bank issued the guard a gun that he was allowed to take with him during his off-duty hours. However, bank policy required that all bullets be removed from the gun when the guard was off duty. Each security guard was required to sign a statement that he would abide by the unloaded gun policy. While the guard was driving home one evening, he got into a traffic altercation with another driver. The dispute escalated and the guard jumped out of his car, waving his gun. It was loaded and accidentally went off. The plaintiff suffered a gunshot wound.

The plaintiff brought an action against both the bank and the guard for his injuries. He alleged that the bank was negligent in entrusting the weapon to the guard, and that the guard was negligent in his handling of the weapon. The plaintiff offers the testimony of the guard's former co-worker, who worked with the guard for 10 years at another bank. The former co-worker is prepared to testify that, during the time that he worked with the guard, the guard had a reputation for being a hothead, keeping his weapon loaded during off-duty hours, and threatening people with his gun whenever he got into an argument.

Assuming proper objection, how should the court rule regarding the admissibility of the testimony?

(A) The former co-worker's testimony is character evidence, inadmissible in a civil case.

(B) The former co-worker's testimony is character evidence admissible against the bank if it can be established that the bank knew of the guard's reputation.

(C) The former co-worker's testimony is character evidence admissible against the bank whether or not the bank knew of the guard's reputation.

(D) The former co-worker's testimony is admissible to help establish that the guard may have acted negligently at the time of the accident.

STOP

A.M. ANSWER SHEET

1. _____	26. _____	51. _____	76. _____
2. _____	27. _____	52. _____	77. _____
3. _____	28. _____	53. _____	78. _____
4. _____	29. _____	54. _____	79. _____
5. _____	30. _____	55. _____	80. _____
6. _____	31. _____	56. _____	81. _____
7. _____	32. _____	57. _____	82. _____
8. _____	33. _____	58. _____	83. _____
9. _____	34. _____	59. _____	84. _____
10. _____	35. _____	60. _____	85. _____
11. _____	36. _____	61. _____	86. _____
12. _____	37. _____	62. _____	87. _____
13. _____	38. _____	63. _____	88. _____
14. _____	39. _____	64. _____	89. _____
15. _____	40. _____	65. _____	90. _____
16. _____	41. _____	66. _____	91. _____
17. _____	42. _____	67. _____	92. _____
18. _____	43. _____	68. _____	93. _____
19. _____	44. _____	69. _____	94. _____
20. _____	45. _____	70. _____	95. _____
21. _____	46. _____	71. _____	96. _____
22. _____	47. _____	72. _____	97. _____
23. _____	48. _____	73. _____	98. _____
24. _____	49. _____	74. _____	99. _____
25. _____	50. _____	75. _____	100. _____

Afternoon Exam

Simulated Multistate Bar Examination

P.M. EXAM

Time—3 hours

You will be given three hours to work on this test. Be sure that the question numbers on your answer sheet match the question numbers in your test book. You are not to begin work until the supervisor tells you to do so.

Your score will be based on the number of questions you answer correctly. It is therefore to your advantage to try to answer as many questions as you can. Give only one answer to each question; multiple answers will not be counted. If you wish to change an answer, erase your first mark completely and mark your new choice. Use your time effectively. Do not hurry, but work steadily and as quickly as you can without sacrificing your accuracy.

YOU ARE TO INDICATE YOUR ANSWERS TO ALL QUESTIONS ON THE SEPARATE ANSWER SHEET PROVIDED.

DIRECTIONS

Each of the questions or incomplete statements in this test is followed by four suggested answers or completions. You are to choose the *best* of the stated alternatives. Answer all questions according to the generally accepted view, except where otherwise noted.

For the purpose of this test, you are to assume that Articles 1 and 2 of the Uniform Commercial Code have been adopted. You are also to assume relevant application of Article 9 of the U.C.C. concerning fixtures.

The Federal Rules of Evidence are deemed to control.

The terms "Constitution," "constitutional," and "unconstitutional" refer to the federal Constitution unless indicated to the contrary.

You are also to assume that there is no applicable statute unless otherwise specified; however, survival actions and claims for wrongful death should be assumed to be available where applicable. You should assume that joint and several liability, with pure comparative negligence, is the relevant rule unless otherwise indicated.

DO NOT OPEN THE TEST UNTIL
YOU ARE INSTRUCTED TO DO SO.

Question 101

A petroleum company operated refineries in several states and was also engaged in the manufacture of a variety of petrochemical products. The company hired an industrial cleaning service to thoroughly clean one of its refineries. While one of the cleaning service's employees was engaged in routine cleaning activities at the refinery, one of the support legs on a crane suddenly gave way, causing part of the crane to fall onto a pipe carrying hot oil, cracking it open. The employee had his back to the pipe at the time and hot oil squirted over his back and legs, causing severe burns. The employee filed suit against the petroleum company for his injuries.

The parties stipulated for trial that the crane had been designed and constructed by a crane construction specialist and was serviced at regular intervals by a reputable crane maintenance company selected by the crane construction company. The employee testified at the trial that he was injured when the pipe cracked open and submitted his medical bills and other evidence of damages. The employee introduced no further evidence. At the conclusion of the employee's case, the petroleum company moved for a directed verdict in its favor.

Should the directed verdict be granted?

(A) Yes, because the employee has done nothing to connect the petroleum company to any negligent activity that might have caused the accident.

(B) Yes, because the petroleum company did not owe a duty to an employee of an independent contractor.

(C) No, because the petroleum company is strictly liable to the employee for his injuries.

(D) No, because a jury could reasonably conclude, based on the evidence presented by the employee, that the petroleum company was negligent.

Question 102

On July 26, a manufacturer of computer accessories received a purchase order form from a retailer who ordered 2,000 ergonomic mouse pads for delivery no later than September 1 for a total price of $10,000, as quoted in the manufacturer's current catalog. Two days later, the manufacturer faxed its own purchase order acceptance form to the retailer, who was a first-time customer. This form stated that it was an acceptance of the specified order, was signed by the manufacturer's shipping manager, and contained all of the terms of the retailer's form, but it also contained an additional printed clause stating that all disagreements under this sale are subject to arbitration by the American Arbitration Association.

Assuming no further communication between the parties, which of the following is an accurate statement of the legal relationship between the manufacturer and the retailer?

(A) There is an enforceable contract between the parties whose terms do not include the arbitration clause in the manufacturer's form.

(B) There is an enforceable contract between the parties whose terms include the arbitration clause in the manufacturer's form.

(C) There is no enforceable contract between the parties because the manufacturer's form constituted a rejection of the retailer's offer and a counteroffer by the manufacturer.

(D) There is no enforceable contract between the parties because the manufacturer's form added an additional term that materially altered the terms of the retailer's offer.

Question 103

The defendant was charged with embezzling $1 million from his employer, a bank, by transferring the funds to a secret offshore account in the bank's name. Only the defendant and the bank's vice president were authorized to draw funds from the account. The defendant testified that he had wired $1 million to the account but had done so at the direction of the bank's vice president. The defendant stated under oath that he had no intent to embezzle bank funds. The government's cross-examination of the defendant concentrated exclusively on his relationship and conversations with the vice president, who has committed suicide.

The defense now seeks to call a second witness, who is prepared to testify that he had worked with the defendant for 10 years and that the defendant had a reputation in both the business and general communities as being a very honest person.

The witness's testimony is:

(A) Admissible, because a defendant has a constitutional right to call witnesses in his own behalf.

(B) Admissible, to help show that the defendant did not embezzle funds.

(C) Inadmissible character evidence.

(D) Inadmissible, because you cannot bolster the credibility of your own witness unless the credibility of the witness has been attacked.

Question 104

A patient went to a dermatologist for treatment of a skin condition on his face that had resisted standard treatment. The dermatologist prescribed a new topical antibiotic cream that was recommended by her associate. She gave the patient instructions on how and when to apply the cream but did not discuss potential side effects. The patient purchased the cream at his local pharmacy and applied it as instructed. Shortly thereafter his skin turned a distinct shade of green and he felt a strong burning sensation when he tried to wash it off. The color took almost a week to fade away, during which time he avoided going out in public and took time off from work.

The cream was packaged with a lengthy printed insert that listed a number of possible side effects of varying degrees of probability. A "green pallor" and "irritation" were listed as uncommon side effects. The patient sued the dermatologist for prescribing the medicine and established the above facts. He also testified that he would not have taken the medicine had he been informed of all of the potential side effects.

If the patient does not prevail, it will be because:

(A) A reasonable person in the patient's position would have used the cream even when told of the potential side effects.

(B) The printed insert that came with the cream listed possible side effects similar to the reaction the patient experienced.

(C) The severity of the reaction the patient experienced was unforeseeable.

(D) The jurisdiction does not apply a "national" standard of care to specialists.

GO ON TO THE NEXT PAGE

Question 105

On January 1, a singer entered into a written contract with the owner of a nightclub to sing nightly at the nightclub for a period of two years at $54,000 per year, commencing February 1. On January 25, the singer phoned the nightclub owner and told him that he had not finished relocating from out of state and might not be ready to start singing until February 10. Furious, the nightclub owner located a substitute act for the month of February.

Can the nightclub owner bring an immediate suit against the singer?

(A) Yes, because the singer's telephone call was a repudiation.

(B) Yes, because he changed his position in reliance on the singer's telephone call.

(C) No, because the singer's telephone call did not constitute a repudiation.

(D) No, because a repudiation must be in writing to be given effect.

Question 106

At the defendant's trial for grand theft auto and other offenses, the prosecution offers to introduce the testimony of a police officer. The officer will testify that he showed a photographic lineup containing the defendant's picture to a witness who had seen the defendant fleeing from the stolen vehicle at the conclusion of a high-speed chase, and the witness selected the defendant's picture. The witness has left the state and refuses to return.

Should the court admit the evidence?

(A) Yes, because the witness is unavailable to testify.

(B) Yes, because it is a prior identification.

(C) No, because it is inadmissible hearsay.

(D) No, because the picture has not been properly authenticated.

Question 107

On April 1, an acclaimed tennis instructor entered into a written contract with a country club owner, calling for the instructor to conduct lessons and clinics at the club six days per week for a period of one year, beginning May 1. The instructor would be paid $48,000 for the year's work. After the instructor failed to appear at the club on May 1, the club owner read in the newspaper that the instructor had been hit by a car and was expected to be in the hospital for two months. The club owner hired a retired tennis pro to conduct lessons at his club for two months at a salary of $6,000 per month.

Can the club owner recover from the instructor the additional $2,000 per month salary that he must pay the tennis pro?

(A) Yes, because the instructor failed to give the club owner timely notice of his hospitalization.

(B) Yes, because of the general rule that the nonbreaching party may recover the expenses of mitigation from the breaching party.

(C) No, because the replacement instructor's salary was not reasonable.

(D) No, because in a personal services contract, performance is excused by illness of the party performing the personal service.

Question 108

A debtor owed a creditor $5,000, but the debt was barred by the applicable statute of limitations. The debtor agreed to assign to the creditor a $4,000 debt that was owed to him by a third party and was coming due in a week. The debtor called the third party to inform him of the assignment. When the debt became due, the third party refused to pay the creditor. The creditor brings an action to collect the debt against the third party.

Will the creditor likely prevail?

(A) Yes, because the creditor's agreement to accept a lesser amount than the original debt constituted consideration for the assignment.

(B) Yes, because an assignment need not be in writing to be enforceable.

(C) No, because the third party may raise the debtor's statute of limitations defense on the original debt.

(D) No, because a new promise to pay a legal obligation barred by law must be in writing.

Question 109

A homeowner decided to destroy his home by fire in order to collect the insurance. A neighbor's house was located a short distance from the homeowner's home. The homeowner knew that there was a strong wind blowing towards the neighbor's home; while he did not want to burn the neighbor's home, he nevertheless set fire to his own home. The fire department was unable to save the homeowner's house. They did manage to put out the fire moments before it spread to the neighbor's home, which suffered damage from smoke and soot. The jurisdiction's arson statute covers burning one's own dwelling as well as the dwelling of another, but is otherwise unchanged from the common law.

If the homeowner is charged with attempted arson of the neighbor's home, he will most likely be found:

(A) Not guilty, because he did not intend to burn the neighbor's house.

(B) Not guilty, because the fire was put out before any part of the neighbor's home was burned.

(C) Guilty, because he intended to burn his own home and took a substantial step toward burning the neighbor's house.

(D) Guilty, because he acted with malice and took a substantial step toward burning the neighbor's house.

GO ON TO THE NEXT PAGE

Question 110

Recently enacted legislation required farmers in certain counties of a western state to use drip irrigation systems instead of traditional methods in order to conserve water for agricultural and other uses. A farmer who refused to use the drip system was charged pursuant to the enforcement provisions of the legislation. A state court enjoined him from using other irrigation methods and fined him.

The farmer appealed to the state supreme court, renewing his trial court claims that the irrigation legislation violated a state constitutional provision prohibiting certain governmental intrusions into private commercial activities and that it was preempted by federal water management statutes. The state supreme court held that the state constitution prohibited the challenged legislation, and construed the relevant statutes as being within the parameters of the federal statutes, and thus preempted.

If the state petitions for certiorari to the United States Supreme Court, how should the Court rule on the petition?

(A) Grant the petition, to determine whether the state court's interpretation of the scope of the federal statutes was incorrect.

(B) Grant the petition, because, under principles of federalism, a state court cannot be the final arbiter of the validity of its own legislation when it is alleged to be in conflict with federal law.

(C) Deny the petition, because there is no substantial federal question that is dispositive of the case.

(D) Deny the petition, because a state government may not seek review of decisions of its own courts in the United States Supreme Court.

Question 111

An uncle validly executed a deed conveying his beach house to his nephew, and then validly recorded the deed. When the nephew, who was experiencing financial difficulties, learned of the recordation of the deed, he immediately told his uncle that he did not want the beach house and could not accept such an expensive gift anyway. Later, the nephew filed for bankruptcy and the trustee in bankruptcy asserted an ownership interest in the beach house on behalf of the debtor's estate. The bankruptcy court ruled that the property belonged to the uncle and not to the nephew, and thus was not part of the debtor's estate subject to distribution.

Which of the following is the strongest reason in support of the bankruptcy court's ruling?

(A) There was no presumption of delivery created by recordation of the deed because the nephew did not know of the recordation.

(B) The nephew's statements to the uncle were a constructive reconveyance of the property.

(C) There was never an effective acceptance of delivery of the deed by the nephew.

(D) The recordation of the deed was invalid because it was done without the nephew's permission.

Question 112

An aunt executed and delivered a valid warranty deed conveying her home to her niece as a gift. The niece did not record the deed. Two years later, the aunt was involved in an auto accident. She had allowed her auto insurance to lapse and the other driver's insurance company obtained a judgment against her for $100,000, which it recorded.

A statute in the jurisdiction provides: "Any judgment properly filed shall, for 10 years from filing, be a lien on the real property then owned or subsequently acquired by any person against whom the judgment is rendered."

When the aunt died five years later, her will left all of her property to the niece. The insurance company filed a claim in probate against the estate for $100,000. The niece, as executrix, seeks a determination from the probate court that the home is not part of the aunt's estate, having already been conveyed to the niece.

The court should rule that the home is:

(A) Part of the estate and must be utilized to satisfy the $100,000 claim.

(B) Part of the estate, but is not subject to the $100,000 claim.

(C) Not part of the estate and thus is not subject to the claim.

(D) Not part of the estate, but is nevertheless subject to a $100,000 lien in favor of the insurance company.

Question 113

At the trial of the plaintiff's personal injury action against the defendant, a pedestrian, who was near the accident scene but did not see what happened, testifies that an eyewitness to the accident shouted, "Good Lord! The green car just ran through a red light and hit the red car!" Previous evidence had established that the defendant drove a green car and the plaintiff a red one. The defendant offers to call to the stand the brother of the eyewitness, who will testify that he spoke with the eyewitness the day after the accident, and he said that the light was green when the green car drove through the intersection. The eyewitness had moved to a foreign country prior to trial.

Should this evidence be admitted over the plaintiff's objection?

(A) No, because the eyewitness is not available to explain or deny the contradiction.

(B) No, because it is hearsay not within any exception.

(C) Yes, for the purpose of impeachment and as substantive evidence.

(D) Yes, for the purpose of impeachment only.

GO ON TO THE NEXT PAGE

Question 114

A landlord entered into a 10-year lease of a building with an auctioneer, who planned to use the building itself for a storage area and the covered porch at the front of the building for auctions. A term in the auctioneer's lease stated, "Lessor agrees to maintain all structures on the property in good repair." Four years into the lease, the landlord sold the property to a buyer. The buyer did not agree to perform any obligations under the lease. As instructed, the auctioneer began paying rent to the buyer. In the fifth year of the lease, the porch roof began to leak. Citing the lease terms, the auctioneer asked the buyer to repair the roof. He continually refused to do so. The auctioneer finally repaired the roof herself at a cost of $2,000. The auctioneer then brought an appropriate lawsuit to recover the money.

Absent any other facts, the auctioneer is likely to recover:

(A) $2,000 from the landlord only, because the sale of the property did not sever his obligation to the auctioneer.

(B) $2,000 from the buyer only, because a covenant to repair runs with the land.

(C) $1,200 from the buyer and $800 from the landlord, because that represents their pro rata shares.

(D) $2,000 from either the buyer or the landlord, because they are both in privity with the auctioneer.

Question 115

A resort maintained an outside bar adjacent to its pool. When the bar was closed, it was secured by a metal gate that reached up towards the roof of the bar, but which left about a three-foot gap between the top of the gate and the roof. The resort had installed motion detectors inside the bar linked to an alarm system because of several previous thefts of liquor by persons climbing over the gate. Late one night, an intoxicated guest of the resort who wanted to keep partying after hours began to climb over the gate to get into the bar through the gap at the top, intending to take some bottles of wine. The brackets attaching the gate to the walls, which had been gradually deteriorating and pulling away from the walls for some time, suddenly gave way as he reached the top. The gate collapsed, causing him to fall back onto the concrete patio. He sustained a severe concussion and other serious injuries.

If the guest sues the resort for his injuries, is he likely to prevail?

(A) No, because the guest did not have invitee status when he was climbing over the gate.

(B) No, because the guest intended to steal alcohol belonging to the resort.

(C) Yes, because the resort operators were aware that persons had climbed over the gate in the past.

(D) Yes, because the brackets attaching the gate to the walls were in a weakened condition that could have been detected by a routine inspection.

GO ON TO THE NEXT PAGE

Question 116

A state prohibited the sale of heated grips for motorcycles within its borders to discourage motorcyclists from riding in dangerously cold conditions. The owner of a cycle shop that sells heated grips within the state that are purchased from an out-of-state manufacturer seeks an injunction in state court prohibiting the state from enforcing its statute. The owner claims that the statute unreasonably interferes with interstate commerce.

If the state court rules that the relevant statute is valid and denies injunctive relief, which of the following is the proper next step for the corporation to take to obtain review of the state court decision?

(A) Appeal to the state appellate courts.

(B) Petition for removal to the federal district court within the state.

(C) Appeal to the federal circuit court of appeals with jurisdiction over cases from the state.

(D) Petition for certiorari to the Supreme Court of the United States.

Question 117

The owner of a chain of natural food stores located within a particular state contracted with landowners and construction firms in a neighboring state in preparation for the opening of several new stores in the neighboring state. The chain's products are stored and sold in bulk within the stores. Consumers remove the amount of product they want from bins within the stores, place the product in plastic bags, and then present their bags at a checkout counter. Statutes in the neighboring state in which the chain owner would like to open his new stores prohibit the sale of food in bulk due to the health hazards associated with bulk storage and contamination from consumer access to food sold from bins. The state has prosecuted other grocers' violations of the statute in the past.

If the chain store owner seeks an injunction against state officials in the federal district court with jurisdiction over the matter and the state officials seek dismissal on the ground that the corporation lacked standing to sue, what would be the probable outcome?

(A) The suit would be dismissed, because the owner has suffered no injury.

(B) The suit would be dismissed, because the challenged state legislation has no effect on civil liberties.

(C) The federal court would hear the suit, because a federal question—interstate commerce—is involved.

(D) The federal court would hear the suit, because the owner has undertaken substantial steps to open outlets in the state.

GO ON TO THE NEXT PAGE

Question 118

A masked gunman held up a convenience store. Due to the poor quality of the surveillance recording, it was very difficult to identify the masked gunman. Nonetheless, the defendant was arrested and charged with the robbery. At the preliminary hearing, the magistrate, on seeing the poor quality of the tape, determined that there was not probable cause to prosecute the defendant. After that, the county prosecutor presented the case to a grand jury, but the grand jury refused to indict the defendant. After waiting a couple of months, the prosecutor presented the case to a different grand jury. The grand jury indicted the defendant and the case went to trial. At trial, the jury was unable to reach a verdict. After this trial, the county prosecutor again tried the case before a jury; in this instance, the jury acquitted the defendant of all charges. At a third trial, the county prosecutor was finally successful in having the defendant convicted. The defendant appeals on double jeopardy grounds.

On appeal, the court will find that:

(A) Jeopardy had attached after the magistrate determined that there was insufficient evidence to prosecute.

(B) Jeopardy had attached after the first grand jury refused to indict the defendant.

(C) Jeopardy had attached after the first trial had ended in a hung jury.

(D) Jeopardy had attached after the second trial had ended in an acquittal.

Question 119

A factory foreman was suspected of having murdered, for pay, the rival of a local union leader. After the police arrested the foreman at his home and he was taken to the police station, the officers who remained at the house asked the foreman's aunt, who was visiting him for the week, if she knew where any firearms could be found in the house. She went into the bedroom and returned with a pistol. Ballistics experts established that the pistol had been used to murder the victim, and the foreman's fingerprints were all over the pistol. At a subsequent grand jury proceeding, the district attorney introduced the pistol and the related ballistics and fingerprint evidence, and the grand jury indicted the foreman.

If the foreman seeks to quash the indictment, he will:

(A) Not prevail, because the evidence was offered before a grand jury, not a court.

(B) Not prevail, because the pistol was obtained by a private citizen, not the police.

(C) Prevail, because the police did not have probable cause to seize the pistol.

(D) Prevail, because the foreman's aunt was acting as an agent of the police when she obtained the pistol.

Question 120

The defendant is charged with arson for hire in the burning down of an old office building. The prosecution offers to introduce the testimony of a neighbor of the defendant, who will state that the day after the fire, she went to the defendant's apartment. The defendant had burnt a roast in her oven, and the apartment was full of smoke. The neighbor, coughing and choking, said, "What did you do, burn down that old office building again?" The defendant made no reply. Should this evidence be admitted over the defendant's objection?

(A) No, it is hearsay not within an exception.

(B) No, if the court determines that a reasonable person would not deny such a statement under the circumstances.

(C) Yes, it is an admission by silence.

(D) Yes, it is a declaration against penal interest.

GO ON TO THE NEXT PAGE

Question 121

The defendant, a competitive athlete, was charged with the murder of another athlete against whom she was scheduled to compete in two weeks. Autopsy results revealed that the victim was poisoned with a lethal mixture containing a variety of substances. During the prosecution's case in chief, evidence was introduced establishing that a bottle of a particular drug, which was among the substances listed in the autopsy report, was discovered in the defendant's medicine cabinet when she was arrested. On direct examination by her own attorney, the defendant states that when she was arrested and the bottle of the drug was found, she told the officers, "My doctor prescribed that for me to cope with the excruciating back pain from which I suffer." If the prosecution moves to strike this testimony, how should the court rule?

(A) For the defendant, because it is a prior consistent statement.

(B) For the defendant, because it tends to explain prosecution evidence.

(C) For the prosecution, because it is hearsay not within an exception.

(D) For the prosecution, because it is a self-serving statement.

Question 122

On November 1, a trapeze artist entered into a written contract with a circus manager to perform his act for the traveling circus for the upcoming season, commencing December 1. On November 30, the trapeze artist faxed the circus manager, stating that, due to circumstances beyond his control, he would not be able to start performing under their contract until December 10. The circus manager got the message the same day and was unfazed, because he had another performer who could take his place in the interim. However, when a tightrope walker approached the circus manager a couple of days later about a job, offering to work for significantly less money, the manager hired the newcomer to take the trapeze artist's place.

Can the circus manager cancel the contract with the trapeze artist?

(A) Yes, because the trapeze artist failed to begin performing on December 1, when performance was due.

(B) Yes, because having to go through with the contract when there was another trapeze artist willing to work for significantly less money would create a hardship for the circus.

(C) No, because the breach was minor.

(D) No, because the trapeze artist notified the circus manager of his delay in performance in a timely fashion.

Question 123

While walking down a city street, the plaintiff was seriously injured when a rotten limb fell off of a tree and hit him on the head. The tree was located on a vacant lot next to the defendant's house. The lot appeared to be a part of the defendant's property. The plaintiff sued the defendant to recover damages for his injuries, alleging that the defendant was negligent with respect to the care of the tree. The defendant's defense was that he did not own the lot or the tree, and that both the lot and the tree were the property of the city. At trial, the plaintiff calls a witness to testify that shortly after the plaintiff was taken to the hospital, he observed the defendant cutting down the rotten limbs on a number of trees on the vacant lot.

The witness's testimony is most likely:

(A) Admissible, to help prove that the defendant was negligent in not removing the rotten limbs sooner.

(B) Admissible, to help prove that the defendant owned the lot.

(C) Inadmissible, because subsequent repairs are encouraged for reasons of public safety.

(D) Inadmissible, because the evidence does not prove that the defendant owned the lot.

GO ON TO THE NEXT PAGE

Question 124

A daughter owed her father $1,250. The father's best friend was having financial difficulties and the father wanted to help him, so the father told his daughter to pay the $1,250 to his friend when the debt came due in three days. Immediately after directing his daughter to pay his friend, the father called his friend and told him he should expect to get $1,250 from his daughter in three days. When the debt came due, the daughter tendered the $1,250 to her father instead of to his friend, and the father accepted the money. The friend sues the daughter for $1,250.

Which of the following is the most likely result?

(A) The friend will recover, because the father effectively assigned his right to collect the $1,250 to his friend.

(B) The friend will not recover, because the father's acceptance of $1,250 from his daughter revoked his gift to his friend.

(C) The friend will not recover, because the daughter was never indebted to him and cannot be forced to pay him.

(D) The friend will not recover, because the daughter's tender of $1,250 to her father, and her father's acceptance of the money, constituted a novation.

Question 125

A homeowner wanted to have his driveway resurfaced. He called seven resurfacing companies and received one bid for $4,400 and six other bids ranging from $5,200 to $6,000. The homeowner entered into a contract with the low bidder to have the driveway resurfaced. Shortly before the low bidder was scheduled to begin work, he called the homeowner and told him that his secretary made a mistake in adding figures and he could not possibly do the work for less than $5,400.

Can the homeowner enforce the contract for $4,400?

(A) No, if the court finds that the homeowner had reason to know of the mistake.

(B) No, because the homeowner has not relied on the bid to her detriment.

(C) No, because the $1,000 error has a material effect on the agreed-on exchange.

(D) Yes, because the low bidder assumed the risk of bid computation errors.

Question 126

The defendant bought a new bow and arrow set at a local sporting goods store and went to a public park to try it out. Based on prior experience, the defendant knew that practicing his marksmanship at the park was a violation of park regulations and constituted a misdemeanor. Right at the moment that the defendant fired his first arrow, a park ranger yelled at him from a distance to "stop shooting, stupid." Perturbed that he was caught so early, the defendant decided to fire an arrow a couple of feet above the ranger's head. Unfortunately, the defendant's aim was slightly off, and the arrow struck the ranger right between the eyes, killing him instantly.

The defendant is charged with homicide for the park ranger's death. At trial, the jury was given instructions on common law murder and manslaughter.

If the jury believes the defendant's testimony that he did not intend to hit the park ranger with the arrow, the most serious charge for which the jury may find him guilty is:

(A) Murder.

(B) Voluntary manslaughter.

(C) Involuntary manslaughter based on criminal negligence.

(D) Misdemeanor manslaughter.

GO ON TO THE NEXT PAGE

Question 127

Based on a tip from a reliable informant that an attorney was illegally selling automatic weapons and ammunition from his storefront office, the police obtained a warrant to search for weapons at the office. When they arrived at the building, they saw a client exiting the attorney's office and placing what appeared to be a weapon inside his jacket. The police stopped the client on the street and an officer patted down his outer clothing but found no weapon. However, the officer felt a bag with several small tube-shaped objects in it, and she immediately placed him under arrest. The contents of the bag were later determined to be marijuana cigarettes.

At a preliminary hearing on the narcotics charge, the client sought to suppress introduction of the marijuana as evidence. The arresting officer testified at the suppression hearing that, based on her long experience as a narcotics officer, she concluded immediately that the bag contained marijuana cigarettes when she first touched it.

If the officer's testimony is believed, the motion to suppress the marijuana evidence should be:

(A) Denied, because the search was incident to a lawful arrest.

(B) Denied, because the police had a reasonable suspicion that the client might be armed and dangerous.

(C) Granted, because the scope of an officer's patdown during an investigatory detention is limited to a search for weapons.

(D) Granted, because the search warrant did not authorize the police to search the client despite the fact that he was just present at the place to be searched.

Question 128

During the investigation of a large gambling operation, the police obtained a warrant to search a bookie's home based on the affidavit of an informant. The informant was a rival bookie who had never acted as an informant before, and much of the substance of the rival's information came from third-party sources. During the search, the police seized a variety of gambling evidence, including betting slips and a check from the defendant. The bookie and the defendant were arrested for violating the state's gambling laws, and separate trials were ordered. At a preliminary hearing for the bookie, the court held that the search warrant for the bookie's home was not supported by probable cause and suppressed introduction of the evidence seized. The defendant moved to suppress introduction of the betting slips and the check on the same basis.

If the court agrees that the search warrant of the bookie's home was not supported by probable cause, the defendant's motion should be:

(A) Granted, because the rival bookie was not a reliable informant.

(B) Granted, because the evidence is the fruit of an unlawful search.

(C) Denied, because the client's legitimate expectation of privacy was not constitutionally violated.

(D) Denied, because the police acted reasonably in relying on the issuance of the warrant.

GO ON TO THE NEXT PAGE

Question 129

A tenant entered into a written five-year lease to rent an office from a landlord for $6,000 per year beginning October 1. The lease required that rent in the amount of $500 be paid on or before the first of each month. Two months before the five-year term was up, the tenant received a new lease identical to the one he had already signed, except that the lease term began on the upcoming October 1 and the stated amount of rent per month was $600. The tenant returned the lease to the landlord unsigned, with a letter stating that he did not intend to renew the lease and would be moving out on September 30. The tenant did not move out on September 30. On October 1, the landlord received a check for $500 from the tenant. The notation on the check indicated that it was for the October rent. The landlord deposited the check in her account. She then sent a letter to the tenant stating that he was $100 in arrears in his rent. The tenant did not move out of the office during October, and the landlord did nothing to remove him.

Most courts would hold that the tenant has:

(A) A month-to-month tenancy at a rent of $500.

(B) A month-to-month tenancy at a rent of $600.

(C) A year-to-year tenancy at $500 per month.

(D) A year-to-year tenancy at $600 per month.

Question 130

Federal legislation provided that the marketing and sale of oranges was subject to the control of a local marketing authority. The marketing authority determined what quantity of oranges could be sold by each grower, the price, and the location of sale. These decisions were made by a council of local growers whose members were selected by the federal Department of Agriculture. The applicable federal legislation provided, in part, that when any grower subject to a marketing order challenged the propriety of that order, the council of the marketing authority must submit the controversy to the United States district court with geographical jurisdiction for a recommendation as to whether the order should be confirmed, modified, or rescinded. After the hearing in district court, the council must revote on the challenged marketing order.

A citrus grower brings suit in United States district court, seeking on constitutional grounds to enjoin enforcement of the federal legislation providing for the marketing order that the council issued with regard to his orange crop.

If the court rules on the constitutional issue, the grower will probably:

(A) Lose, because the federal government may properly regulate items in interstate commerce.

(B) Lose, because the marketing order system is a necessary and proper means of effectuating the commerce power.

(C) Win, because the federal legislation permits the federal district court to give an advisory opinion.

(D) Win, because the federal legislation deprives the grower of his property without due process of law.

GO ON TO THE NEXT PAGE

Question 131

A merchant owned a skate rental business that she operated out of a specially equipped van. She would drive to various parks and public beaches within her home state and rent roller skates, related safety equipment and lightweight stereo/earphone sets to passersby on an hourly basis. She also sold skates and skating equipment. About 50% of the merchant's time is spent in a single city, and she earns about 70% of her gross rental and sale income at that city's beach areas. After receiving numerous complaints from beachgoers about the sidewalks congested with roller skaters, the city council passed an ordinance prohibiting roller skating on public property between the hours of 7 a.m. and 9 p.m.

If the merchant seeks to enjoin enforcement of the ordinance in federal district court on the basis that it is unconstitutional, that court will probably:

(A) Reach the merits of the merchant's challenge to the ordinance, because it interferes with his right to free association.

(B) Reach the merits of the merchant's challenge, because enforcement of the ordinance will harm her business and the rights of the public are linked to her rights.

(C) Decline to hear the case, because the ordinance does not prohibit the rental of skating equipment.

(D) Decline to hear the case, because skating is not prohibited on private property, nor on public property from 9 p.m. to 7 a.m.

Question 132

A landowner leased a store to a grocer for a term of five years at $10,000 per year, payable in monthly installments. The lease permitted assignments and subleases. After occupying the premises for two years and paying the rent, the grocer transferred the remaining three years of the term to a florist. The agreement between the parties did not have a specific provision regarding payment of rent, instead just referring to the original lease provisions. The florist occupied the premises for two years but paid rent only for the first year. With one year left on the original lease, the florist transferred her leasehold interest to a barber. The barber occupied the premises for one year but did not pay any rent. The landowner brought an appropriate action against the grocer, the florist, and the barber to recover the rent.

Against whom may the landowner recover?

(A) The grocer and the florist jointly and severally for $10,000, and the grocer individually for $10,000.

(B) The grocer and the florist jointly and severally for $10,000, and the grocer and the barber jointly and severally for $10,000.

(C) The grocer and the florist jointly and severally for $10,000, and the grocer, the florist, and the barber jointly and severally for $10,000.

(D) The grocer and the florist jointly and severally for $20,000.

Question 133

A 12-year-old boy took his radio-controlled model airplane to the park to show his friends the stunts he could do with it. The weather that day was rainy, and the instruction manual for the plane warned against flying it in the rain, but the boy was able to get the plane off of the ground. However, because of the rain, he had trouble controlling it with the transmitter. He tried to have the plane make a loop but it veered off course and crashed through the fabric roof of a convertible, which was parked nearby on the street.

If the car owner sues the boy for damages to his car and prevails, it will be because:

(A) A child of the boy's age, education, intelligence, and experience would not have flown the airplane that day.

(B) A reasonable person would not have flown the airplane that day.

(C) The airplane instruction manual warned against flying in the rain.

(D) The boy committed a trespass to chattel with his airplane.

Question 134

A kidnapper and his cohort hatched a scheme to kidnap the son of a wealthy man and hold him for ransom. After conducting a surveillance of the wealthy man's home, they decided that they would have to have inside help to disable the alarm at the home. They agreed that the kidnapper would contact the man's butler, who they learned was heavily in debt and frequented a local racetrack during his time off. The butler would be offered money to disconnect the alarm on the night of the planned kidnapping. Shortly before the kidnapper was to go to the track to make contact with the butler, the cohort had a change of heart about the scheme and contacted the butler. He warned the butler not to have anything to do with the kidnapper. The butler met with the kidnapper anyway and pretended to go along with his proposal, accepting the down payment that the kidnapper offered. After meeting with him, the butler contacted the authorities.

The kidnapper and cohort are charged with conspiracy in a jurisdiction that follows the common law rule for conspiracy. The most likely result will be:

(A) Both the kidnapper and cohort are guilty of conspiracy because the cohort agreed with the kidnapper to commit the offense.

(B) The cohort is not guilty of conspiracy because he withdrew from the conspiracy by contacting the butler.

(C) The cohort is not guilty of conspiracy because he withdrew from the conspiracy by contacting the butler, and the kidnapper is not guilty of conspiracy with the butler because one cannot be a conspirator by oneself.

(D) The kidnapper is guilty of conspiracy with the butler.

GO ON TO THE NEXT PAGE

Question 135

A brother and sister decided to hire a professional hit man to kill their parents in order to inherit the family fortune. Shortly after this discussion, however, the sister realized that she could not go through with the plan, and she told her brother that she would not be participating. She then called the hit man and told him that she would call the police if anything happened to her parents. The brother met with the hit man, who accepted a payment but intended to inform the parents of the brother's actions with the hope of collecting a reward. The hit man did so, and the parents had the brother arrested. The brother and sister are charged with attempted murder in a jurisdiction following the modern rules for attempt.

Which of the following statements is most accurate?

(A) The brother can be found guilty, because he paid the hit man.

(B) The brother and the sister can be found guilty, because they conspired to kill their parents.

(C) The brother cannot be found guilty, because the hit man only pretended to agree to the proposal.

(D) Neither the brother nor the sister can be found guilty, because they did not form the mental state necessary for attempt.

Question 136

A homeowner wanted to have his house repainted. He called a number of house painters and received bids ranging from $8,500 to $9,000. A local painter submitted a bid to do the work for $8,000, and the homeowner entered into a contract with him to have the house repainted. Shortly before the painter was scheduled to begin work, he discovered that he could not make a profit if he were paid less than $8,600. He called the homeowner with this information. The homeowner agreed to pay him the extra $600. After the painter finished the job, the homeowner handed him $8,000 in cash, saying that that was all he was going to pay him because he had no right to raise the price.

If the painter sues the homeowner for the additional $600, who will prevail?

(A) The homeowner, because the promise to pay the additional money was not in writing.

(B) The homeowner, because the painter was already under a preexisting duty to paint the house for $8,000.

(C) The painter, because he relied to his detriment on the homeowner's promise to pay the additional money.

(D) The painter, because the promise to pay the additional money was the settlement of a good faith dispute.

GO ON TO THE NEXT PAGE

Question 137

A balloonist sued the manufacturer of defla-tion panels for hot air balloons after one of the panels failed while his balloon was descending, causing the balloon to crash and the balloonist to suffer severe injuries. At trial, the balloonist calls as a witness a structural engineer, who testifies that, common to industry practice, her opinion is based on several reports done by an independent laboratory on the burst strength and material composition of the deflation panel closures. The balloonist's attorney then asks the engineer whether, in her opinion, the closures caused the deflation panel to give way. The manufacturer objects. Should the court admit this testimony?

(A) No, because the engineer did not perform the laboratory tests herself.

(B) No, because the laboratory reports are hearsay not within an exception.

(C) Yes, but the balloonist must offer into evidence the reports to which the engineer referred, so that the manufacturer may cross-examine as to them.

(D) Yes, because structural engineers reason-ably rely on such reports in the course of their profession.

Question 138

The plaintiff sued the defendant, the owner of an art gallery, alleging that the defendant charged him a price higher than what was originally quoted to him for the purchase of a rare sculp-ture. During the plaintiff's testimony, he stated that he purchased the sculpture from the gallery on a particular date and then realized two days later that his credit card was charged in an amount over that which he was originally quoted by the defendant. During its defense, the defendant presented the testimony of the art gallery's clerk, who testifies that she remembers the plaintiff coming into the gallery and pur-chasing the sculpture a week before the date testified to by him, because he signed the pur-chase order with such an unusual signature. If the plaintiff objects to this testimony, should the trial court admit it?

(A) No, because the content of the purchase order is hearsay not within any exception.

(B) No, because the date of purchase is a collateral matter.

(C) Yes, because the purchase order is a past recollection recorded.

(D) Yes, because the clerk's testimony is relevant evidence as to the date the sculp-ture was purchased.

Question 139

A landowner conveyed her 20-acre tract of land to a developer and his heirs, "provided that no multi-family dwellings may be built on the property for a period of 25 years. If such construction is undertaken, the grantor may terminate the conveyance and retake the land." Two years later the landowner died, leaving her nephew as the sole beneficiary under her will. Shortly thereafter, the nephew discovered that the developer was constructing multi-family dwellings on the land. He promptly brought an ejectment action against the developer. The jurisdiction in which the land is located has a statute providing that all future interests are freely devisable and alienable inter vivos. There are no other applicable statutes.

The court should rule that ownership of the land belongs to:

(A) The nephew, because the developer began constructing multi-family dwellings on the land.

(B) The nephew, because the developer began constructing multi-family dwellings on the land and the nephew brought an action for ejectment.

(C) The developer, because the Rule Against Perpetuities applies.

(D) The developer, because the restriction in the conveyance is an invalid restraint on alienation.

Question 140

At the defendant's trial for assault with a deadly weapon, the defendant's counsel calls a witness to the stand and asks him, "What is the defendant's reputation for honesty and veracity in your community?" The prosecutor objects before the witness can answer.

Should the court admit the testimony?

(A) Yes, because reputation evidence is admissible under these circumstances to establish a character trait.

(B) Yes, because the prosecution put the defendant's character at issue when they filed charges against him.

(C) No, because the evidence offered is irrelevant to any material issue in the case.

(D) No, because the evidence offered is inadmissible hearsay.

GO ON TO THE NEXT PAGE

Question 141

In litigation over whether an uncle conveyed a parcel of land to his nephew, the nephew wishes to offer into evidence a tape recording of his uncle made by a well-known oral historian at the nearby state university. The voice on the tape is discussing various conveyances of the parcel of land and other property owned by the uncle. The nephew wishes to have the historian testify that the voice on the tape is the uncle's.

If the court allows the historian to testify, it will be because:

(A) The historian is testifying regarding an admission by a party-opponent.

(B) The historian has heard the uncle speak before.

(C) The historian became familiar with the uncle's voice before the dispute over the property arose.

(D) The historian's experience as an oral historian qualifies him as an expert in voice recognition.

Question 142

On March 1, the purchasing agent for a suburban school district faxed a "quotation request form" to a supplier of school furniture requesting an offer for the sale of 20 student chairs. The form was on school district letterhead and signed by the purchasing agent. It specified that the offer must be held open for four months and that the price term must be no higher than $30 per chair. The supplier telephoned the purchasing agent and told him that he would sell the school district 20 chairs at $20 per chair. He also agreed to hold the offer open for four months. The purchasing agent thanked the supplier for the offer and indicated that he would get back to him within that time period. On May 1, before the purchasing agent had responded to the supplier's offer or taken any action in reliance on it, the supplier faxed a letter to the purchasing agent stating that demand for student chairs had been higher than expected and that the offer was terminated. On May 2, the purchasing agent called the supplier, told him that the school district was treating his offer as still being open, and accepted it on its terms.

Did the purchasing agent's call on May 2 create a legally enforceable contract with the supplier?

(A) Yes, because the contract is for the sale of goods valued at less than $500.

(B) Yes, because the school district accepted the offer within three months.

(C) No, because the supplier did not sign the form specifying the length of time that the offer would be held open.

(D) No, because a firm offer under the U.C.C. is not effective if its term is more than three months.

GO ON TO THE NEXT PAGE

Question 143

An undercover agent for a federal drug enforcement agency informed a state law enforcement agency that a large amount of cocaine was being mailed to a resident of that state. The cocaine would be mailed in a large box and wrapped distinctively. The agent further informed the agency that the resident was not the purchaser of the cocaine, but was only acting as an intermediary. The cocaine would be picked up within a few days by the buyer, who was from a neighboring state. The agency immediately placed the resident's house under surveillance. In a few days, a large box wrapped as the undercover agent described was delivered by the post office. The agency did not make an arrest, but kept the house under surveillance. Two days later, a man driving a car with plates from the neighboring state arrived at the house. He entered the house and came back out shortly thereafter carrying what appeared to be the same box. The suspect placed the box in the trunk of his car and drove off. Two blocks later, the car was stopped, the suspect arrested, and officers for the agency searched the entire vehicle, acting without a warrant. The box in the trunk was opened and cocaine was found. The suspect was charged with possession of cocaine. At a preliminary hearing, he moved to suppress the cocaine.

The motion should be:

(A) Denied, because the officers had probable cause to search the trunk.

(B) Denied, because the search was incident to a valid arrest.

(C) Granted, because the officers should have obtained a warrant before opening the package.

(D) Granted, because the officers had no way of knowing that it was the same package that was delivered to the home.

Question 144

A police officer witnessed a car turn the wrong way from a bar's parking lot onto a one-way street. The officer immediately turned on his siren and pursued the car for a couple of miles. During that pursuit, the car repeatedly weaved in and out of its lane of traffic. Eventually, the car pulled over, and the officer placed the driver under arrest. After handcuffing the driver and placing him in the back seat of his squad car, the officer looked under a blanket lying on the floor of the car's passenger compartment. Under the blanket, he found an open bottle of whiskey. Before his trial on charges of drunk driving and driving with an open container of alcohol in the car, the defendant moves to suppress from evidence the open bottle of whiskey.

The motion should be:

(A) Denied, because when the police stopped the car, they had probable cause to search the car.

(B) Denied, because the search was incident to a lawful arrest.

(C) Granted, because the officer did not have probable cause to look under the blanket.

(D) Granted, because, after arresting the driver and placing him in the squad car, the car should have been impounded and a warrant obtained before the search.

GO ON TO THE NEXT PAGE

Question 145

A seller entered into a written contract to sell her land to a buyer for $200,000. Before the closing date, the buyer received the title search report, which indicated that a rancher conveyed the land to a farmer by quitclaim deed 25 years ago and that a landowner conveyed the land to the seller by warranty deed 13 years ago. The buyer notified the seller that the records did not indicate how the land was conveyed to the landowner (the seller's immediate transferor), and that the buyer was concerned about this. The seller replied that she had no knowledge of the matter but would look into it. At the date and time appointed for closing, the seller informed the buyer that she could not locate the land-owner or obtain any information as to the conveyance of the land to him. On hearing this, the buyer refused to tender the purchase money, and told the seller that he was rescinding the contract. The seller sued the buyer for specific performance.

Which party is more likely to prevail?

(A) The seller, because land is unique and therefore a proper subject for a specific performance action.

(B) The seller, because she took title from the landowner by warranty deed.

(C) The buyer, because there is a gap in the title.

(D) The buyer, because the seller cannot supply marketable title.

Question 146

Based on recommendations of a state commission studying the effect of pornographic films on violent criminal activity, a state adopted legislation banning films intended for commercial distribution that appealed as a whole to the prurient interest in sex of the average person in the community, portrayed sex in a patently offensive way to citizens of the state, and which a reasonable person in the United States would find had no serious literary, artistic, political, or scientific value.

In ruling on a constitutional challenge to the legislation from a film distributor in the state who was convicted of distributing films in violation of the legislation, the federal court will likely find the legislation:

(A) Constitutional, because it uses a national "reasonable person" standard for determining the social value of the work.

(B) Constitutional, because it uses a statewide standard rather than a community standard for determining whether the material is patently offensive.

(C) Unconstitutional, because it uses a state-wide standard rather than a national standard for determining whether the material is patently offensive.

(D) Unconstitutional, unless the court finds that the legislation is necessary to advance the state's compelling interest in reducing violent criminal activity.

GO ON TO THE NEXT PAGE

Question 147

On March 1, a builder entered into a contract with a buyer to build a home on land the builder owned and then transfer it to the buyer for $350,000. The builder and the buyer agreed that construction would be completed on August 1, and that escrow would close on the transaction on August 15. The contract also contained a time-is-of-the-essence clause at the insistence of the buyer, whose lease on his current home was set to expire on September 1.

State law required that a home builder have an architect's certificate of completion before any residence could be conveyed to a purchaser. The builder employed his own architect to design and oversee construction of his custom homes. Construction of the buyer's house was not completed until August 5. On August 8, the builder discovered that his architect had left the country without preparing the certificate of completion for the home. The builder was not able to obtain the certificate until August 20. When the builder attempted to place the deed and certificate of completion into escrow, he learned that the buyer had canceled escrow on August 16 and refused to proceed with the purchase.

The builder sold the home nine months later for its then reasonable market value of $330,000. He brings an action for damages against the buyer, seeking $20,000, the difference between the contract price and the amount he ultimately received for sale of the house.

Will the builder recover?

(A) No, because the duty to certify completion of the home cannot be delegated to an architect unfamiliar with the construction.

(B) No, because he was late in delivering the deed and certificate of completion into escrow.

(C) Yes, because the short time the builder was late in delivering the deed was not a material breach of the contract.

(D) Yes, because the buyer suffered no damages as a result of the delay.

Question 148

The owner of an apparel store faxed an order to her regular supplier for 100 pairs of wool gloves at $10 a pair, the supplier's list price. The supplier checked his inventory and discovered that he had only 90 pairs of wool gloves, which he shipped to the store owner along with 10 pairs of wool blend gloves that also had a list price of $10 a pair. The supplier also enclosed a note to the store owner explaining that he did not have enough stock of wool gloves to fill her order, and that, in the hopes she could use them, he was sending wool blend gloves at the same list price to make up the balance of the shipment.

On receipt of the shipment and note, what are the store owner's options?

(A) The store owner may accept the shipment, in which case she must pay the supplier $1,000 less any damages sustained because of the nonconforming shipment, or she may reject the shipment, in which case she has no further remedy against the supplier.

(B) The store owner may accept the shipment, in which case she must pay the supplier $1,000, or she may reject the shipment, in which case she may recover against the supplier for breach of contract.

(C) The store owner may accept the shipment, in which case she must pay the supplier $1,000, or she may reject the shipment, in which case she has no further remedy against the supplier.

(D) The store owner may accept the conforming part of the shipment and reject the nonconforming part, in which case she must pay the supplier $900 less any damages sustained because of the nonconforming part of the shipment, or she may reject the entire shipment, in which case she may recover against the supplier for breach of contract.

GO ON TO THE NEXT PAGE

Question 149

A father conveyed his property to his son and daughter "as joint tenants with right of survivorship, but if they ever attempt to sell the property during their lifetimes, a right of first refusal based on the sale price is hereby granted to my sister." Unbeknownst to the son or the sister, the daughter quitclaimed her interest in the property to a purchaser. The following month, the daughter was killed in a snowmobile accident. The purchaser of the daughter's interest filed a suit for partition of the property. The son filed an appropriate counterclaim for quiet title, asserting that he was the owner of the entire parcel. The sister also filed a counterclaim, asserting that her right of first refusal was valid and that she was prepared to exercise her option to purchase the property for the contract price.

In a jurisdiction in which the Rule Against Perpetuities is unmodified by statute, how should the court rule?

(A) For the purchaser, because the right of first refusal is invalid as an unreasonable restraint on alienation.

(B) For the son, because he succeeded to the entire ownership when the daughter died.

(C) For the son, because the right of first refusal violates the Rule Against Perpetuities.

(D) For the sister, because she has a valid right of first refusal.

Question 150

An owner devised his property by will to a friend "so long as one or more dogs are kept on the property; if dogs are no longer kept on the property, then to the American Society for the Prevention of Cruelty to Animals (ASPCA)." The will also provided that the residuary estate would go to the owner's niece.

In a jurisdiction that has not modified the common law Rule Against Perpetuities, what are the respective interests in the property on the owner's death?

(A) The friend has a fee simple subject to a condition subsequent and the niece has a right of entry.

(B) The friend has a fee simple determinable and the niece has a possibility of reverter.

(C) The friend has a fee simple determinable and the ASPCA has a remainder.

(D) The friend has a fee simple determinable subject to an executory interest and the ASPCA has a shifting executory interest.

GO ON TO THE NEXT PAGE

Question 151

A state provided generous state-subsidized health benefits to all residents who did not have an employer-funded program that met specified minimum requirements. To alleviate the burden on the state's budget, the legislation provided that a person must have resided in the state for at least one year to be entitled to any health benefits provided by the state. A consultant moved to the state last month to take a consulting job. The position does not provide health benefits, so she sought coverage through the state program and was denied. She then filed suit in federal district court, challenging the denial of the state benefits to her.

If the court finds in favor of the consultant, it will most likely be because:

(A) The restriction does not have a rational relationship to a legitimate state interest as required by the Equal Protection Clause of the Fourteenth Amendment.

(B) The restriction deprives the consultant of certain privileges and immunities in violation of the Interstate Privileges and Immunities Clause of Article IV, Section 2.

(C) The restriction improperly burdens the fundamental right of interstate travel in violation of the Equal Protection Clause of the Fourteenth Amendment.

(D) The restriction deprives the consultant of a property interest without due process of law in violation of the Due Process Clause of the Fourteenth Amendment.

Question 152

The owner of a self-propelled mower started the engine in preparation to mow when the clutch of the mower suddenly engaged, and it jerked forward rapidly. The owner was unable to grab the handle in time before the mower was out of reach and heading for the street. As he caught up with the mower and attempted to restrain it in the street, a motorist driving down the street swerved to avoid the mower and struck a tree. The motorist was injured and her car damaged. The motorist brought an action against the owner of the mower and was awarded damages. The owner then sought indemnification from the manufacturer of the mower in a jurisdiction following traditional indemnity rules.

If the owner prevails, it will be because:

(A) The owner was found to have taken reasonable care in maintaining the mower.

(B) The mower clutch engaged because of some defect in manufacture.

(C) The clutch assembly was manufactured and assembled by the manufacturer.

(D) The jurisdiction apportions damages based on relative fault in contribution cases.

GO ON TO THE NEXT PAGE

Question 153

An American tourist was visiting another country when he was warned by United States health authorities to go immediately to a hospital because he had a serious and extremely contagious disease that required him to be quarantined. He decided to ignore the warning and instead traveled on an airline flight back to the United States. Despite the tourist's belief that he would not be discovered and his best efforts to keep a low profile, the news media were tipped off to what he had done and publicized it. When a passenger who had been sitting next to the tourist on the plane learned about it, she became extremely upset, fearing that she would contract the disease. The passenger brought a negligence action to recover for the distress she suffered.

If the passenger does not prevail, it will be because:

(A) The tourist's conduct was not extreme and outrageous.

(B) The passenger did not suffer physical injury from her distress.

(C) The passenger did not contract the disease from the tourist.

(D) The tourist could not have reasonably foreseen that the other passengers would find out about what he had done.

Question 154

To gain progress on critical treaty negotiations with another country, the President issued an official pardon to the leader of a radical group who was in a state prison after being convicted of a violent crime in the state. The President directed the governor of the state to free the leader but the governor refused. The Justice Department brought an action in federal district court seeking an order compelling his release.

The federal court most likely will rule:

(A) For the state, because a state official acting pursuant to his state's constitution need not obey inconsistent orders from a federal official.

(B) For the state, because the President's constitutional power to pardon prisoners extends only to those convicted of federal offenses.

(C) For the state, because the President's order and the pardon given the convicted leader violate his duty to see that the laws of the United States are faithfully executed.

(D) For the federal government, because the President's actions are authorized by his power to enter into treaties with other nations.

GO ON TO THE NEXT PAGE

Question 155

A state's pension program provided supplemental state pension benefits to surviving spouses and children of state employees. The program provided that when the spouse remarried, that spouse's benefits would be gradually terminated based on a statutory formula. Because of statistics showing past disparities between the household income levels of male surviving spouses and female surviving spouses, different formulas were used for the termination schedule depending on whether the surviving spouse was male or female.

A widower of a state employee was informed after he remarried that his pension benefits would be terminated in 90 days according to the applicable formula. Upon learning that a similarly situated widow would have continued to receive benefits for six months after remarrying, the widower decided to file suit in federal court, alleging that the state program is unconstitutional because it is discriminatory and it unfairly burdens his right to marry.

Which of the following best states the burden of persuasion in this case?

(A) The state must demonstrate that the program is narrowly tailored to achieve a compelling government interest.

(B) The state must demonstrate that the program is substantially related to an important government interest.

(C) The widower must demonstrate that the program is not substantially related to an important government interest.

(D) The widower must demonstrate that the program is not rationally related to a legitimate government interest.

Question 156

A plaintiff was injured when the steering mechanism of a snowmobile failed. He brought a negligence action against the snowmobile manufacturer. The steering mechanism was designed and manufactured by a component manufacturer; the snowmobile manufacturer merely assembled the snowmobile, branded it, and distributed it directly to retailers.

To prevail against the snowmobile manufacturer, the plaintiff will need to prove that:

(A) The steering mechanism was in a defective condition unreasonably dangerous to users.

(B) The steering mechanism was in a defective condition unreasonably dangerous to users, and the plaintiff was the purchaser of the snowmobile, a member of the purchaser's family, or a guest of the purchaser.

(C) The steering mechanism was in a defective condition unreasonably dangerous to users, and the defect could have been discovered and corrected if the component manufacturer had exercised reasonable care in its quality control process.

(D) The steering mechanism was in a defective condition unreasonably dangerous to users, and the snowmobile manufacturer failed to inspect the mechanism before assembly of the snowmobile.

GO ON TO THE NEXT PAGE

Question 157

A testing lab purchased a wind tunnel as a complete unit from a machinery company. The machinery company used an electronics company for the design and installation of the unit's electronic control systems, which regulated air speed and triggered the emergency shut-off devices.

A technician was installing a scale model of a prototype aircraft that was to be tested in the wind tunnel when the electronic control system of the tunnel malfunctioned, causing the huge fans that created the air flow to start up. The powerful air flow pinned the technician against the grating covering the intake ducts, asphyxiating him before he was discovered and the fans could be shut off.

In an action by the technician's survivors against the electronics company, proof that the machinery company failed to inspect the wind tunnel has which of the following legal effects?

(A) If the electronics company is held liable to the plaintiffs, it may bring an action for indemnity against the machinery company based on the failure to inspect.

(B) The failure of the machinery company to inspect the tunnel is a superseding cause that relieves the electronics company of liability to the plaintiffs.

(C) The failure of the machinery company to inspect the tunnel is attributable to the electronics company under the doctrine of respondeat superior.

(D) The failure of the machinery company to inspect the tunnel has no legal effect on the electronics company's liability.

Question 158

A lawsuit involving a contract dispute between a resident of State Alpha and a resident of State Beta was properly filed by the State Alpha party in a State Alpha district court. The court dismissed the action because the statute of limitations had run. On learning that State Beta had a longer limitations period that would not have run, the plaintiff promptly filed an identical action in the appropriate State Beta court. However, on the defendant's motion, the State Beta court dismissed the action on the sole ground that it was obligated to accept the judgment of the State Alpha court under the Full Faith and Credit Clause of the federal Constitution.

Assuming that both courts had jurisdiction over the parties and the subject matter, was State Beta required to give full faith and credit to the judgment of the State Alpha court?

(A) Yes, because the State Alpha court had entered a final judgment in an identical case.

(B) Yes, because the defendant should not be penalized for the plaintiff's forum shopping.

(C) No, because the Full Faith and Credit Clause applies to judgments rendered by a federal court, not a state court.

(D) No, because the State Alpha court did not make a ruling on the merits of the case.

GO ON TO THE NEXT PAGE

Question 159

Thirty years ago, an owner deeded his land containing a general store to a merchant "for so long as tobacco is not sold on the premises." The deed was promptly and properly recorded. A few years later, the owner died, leaving his son as his only heir but devising "all of my interests in any real property" to his friend by a duly probated will. The next year, the friend conveyed "all of my interest in the general store and its land" to a purchaser by means of a quitclaim deed supported by valid consideration. The purchaser promptly and properly recorded the deed. Two months ago, the merchant began selling tobacco at the general store.

In a jurisdiction in which the common law Rule Against Perpetuities is unmodified by statute, who currently has title to the land and general store?

(A) The son, because the friend received an executory interest that was void under the Rule Against Perpetuities.

(B) The friend, because the interest she holds in the land is not transferable inter vivos.

(C) The purchaser, because tobacco is being sold on the land.

(D) The merchant, because no party has taken action to terminate her interest in the land.

Question 160

In January of 2007, the defendant proposed to his girlfriend. During the engagement, the defendant confided in her about various drug deals in which he was participating. The woman swore that she would never reveal any of his confidences. On January 1, 2008, the couple married. The defendant continued to share with his wife information concerning his illegal drug activity. The wife's only rule was that he could not participate in any illegal drug transactions in their home. On one occasion in 2008, the wife came home unexpectedly and saw the defendant completing a drug transaction in the living room. The defendant was not aware that his wife had observed the event. In 2009, the defendant was charged with 57 counts of illegal drug sales that occurred between 2006 and 2009. The prosecutor wishes to call the defendant's wife as a witness for the state.

Assuming that the defendant's attorney makes appropriate objections, which of the following statements is correct regarding testimony by the defendant's wife?

(A) She can testify about the defendant's 2008 statements if she desires.

(B) She must testify to the defendant's 2007 statements.

(C) The defendant can keep her from testifying about his 2007 statements.

(D) She can testify to the drug sale that she observed in 2008 if she desires.

GO ON TO THE NEXT PAGE

Question 161

While investigating the most recent of a series of murders, a homicide detective was approached by an onlooker who seemed to have detailed knowledge of the murders. The detective recalled the onlooker at some of the other murder scenes, and immediately suspected that he knew something about the crimes. The detective asked the onlooker not to leave until the detective had the opportunity to ask him a few questions. After finishing with the evidence he was gathering, the detective started to question the onlooker at the crime scene without giving him *Miranda* warnings. The onlooker eventually revealed details of the crimes that were never made available to the public. As a result, the onlooker was arrested and charged with several murders. At a preliminary hearing, the onlooker testified that he believed that he could not leave until he had spoken with the detective. The defense counsel moves to suppress the statements made to the homicide detective.

What is the most likely result?

(A) The motion will not be granted because the onlooker was not in custody.

(B) The motion will not be granted because the onlooker initiated the contact with the homicide detective.

(C) The motion will be granted because the onlooker believed that he was not free to leave.

(D) The motion will be granted because the detective was required to give the onlooker *Miranda* warnings once the detective suspected him of having committed the crime.

Question 162

The plaintiff sued the defendant dry cleaner, claiming that it had permanently ruined her $10,000 mink coat by cleaning it with a solvent that left an extremely offensive odor that smelled like "skunk." Further attempts to have the odor removed by other cleaning services were unsuccessful. The odor was so bad that she could no longer wear the coat.

At the trial, the plaintiff testified to the above facts. She then identified a mink coat as her coat that the defendant had ruined. She testified that it still smelled the same as it did after the defendant had cleaned it. The plaintiff's counsel offered to introduce the coat for the purpose of having the jury smell it. Defense counsel objected.

How should the court rule?

(A) The coat is admissible based on the plaintiff's testimony.

(B) The coat is admissible, but the plaintiff must first present extrinsic evidence sufficient to support a finding that the coat is the coat that she had cleaned by the defendant.

(C) The coat is not admissible because the plaintiff's testimony has not been impeached.

(D) The coat is not admissible because its limited probative value in resolving the case would be substantially outweighed by the prejudice that would result from the jury smelling the coat.

GO ON TO THE NEXT PAGE

Question 163

The National Park Service recently created a new personnel level for field employees, which became the highest salaried position available to Park Service field employees. The position is restricted to employees over six feet in height. A female ranger who is five feet, three inches tall seeks your advice as to whether she can challenge the validity of the height restriction in federal court.

If you decide to file suit on her behalf, which of the following would be your strongest argument against the validity of the restriction?

(A) Because most women are less than six feet tall, the restriction is unconstitutional as a violation of the Equal Rights Amendment.

(B) Because most women are less than six feet tall, the restriction is an invalid discrimination on the basis of gender in violation of the Due Process Clause of the Fifth Amendment.

(C) Because most women are less than six feet tall, the restriction is an invalid gender-based discrimination in violation of the Equal Protection Clause of the Fourteenth Amendment.

(D) The restriction denies the ranger a property right without an opportunity for a hearing before a neutral decisionmaker, in violation of the Due Process Clause of the Fifth Amendment.

Question 164

After drinking heavily at his bachelor party at a beachfront resort, the groom was helped into a speedboat by a few of his friends and transported to a small island off the coast as a joke. They left him on the island, which had a small shelter but no communication facilities, without telling anyone else. As a result, the groom missed his wedding the next day. One of the participants was charged with kidnapping, which is defined in the jurisdiction as the unlawful movement or concealment of a person without his consent. In his defense, the participant claims that he was so intoxicated that he did not realize what he was doing, and that the groom had consented to being left on the island.

Which of the following would *not* be helpful to his defense?

(A) The groom was not legally intoxicated that evening.

(B) Kidnapping is a general intent crime in the jurisdiction.

(C) Kidnapping is a specific intent crime in the jurisdiction.

(D) The participant had overheard the groom say that he was not sure about going through with the wedding.

GO ON TO THE NEXT PAGE

Question 165

A motorist was driving his expensive sports car down a two-lane road at 90 m.p.h. in a heavy rainstorm. Just after cresting a hill, the motorist observed a large tree that had been hit by lightning and was blocking the highway. To avoid hitting the tree, the motorist drove off the road and onto a landowner's property. In so doing, the motorist destroyed the landowner's mailbox and flower bed.

If the landowner sues the motorist for damages to his mailbox and flower bed, he will:

(A) Prevail, because the jury will likely find that the motorist was not exercising due care.

(B) Prevail, regardless of whether the motorist was exercising due care.

(C) Not prevail, because the motorist was acting under necessity when he drove onto the landowner's property.

(D) Not prevail, because even though the motorist was exceeding the speed limit, the tree in the road was an act of God, and a superseding intervening cause.

Question 166

A state statute prohibits leaving a child under the age of five years unattended in an automobile. A mother parked her car at a supermarket parking lot. She left her four-year-old son in the car with his seatbelt fastened while she did her grocery shopping. While the mother was shopping, the son undid his seatbelt, left the car, and started riding on the grocery carts that customers had left in the parking lot. The son crashed one of the carts into another shopper's car, causing damage. The shopper brought a negligence action against the mother to recover for the damage caused by the son. At trial, the shopper presented evidence of the statute and the facts stated above. At the conclusion of the shopper's case, the mother moved for a directed verdict in her favor.

Should the court grant the mother's motion?

(A) No, because the shopper has established negligence per se based on the mother's violation of the statute.

(B) No, because the jury could find that it was foreseeable that the son would cause damage to cars in the parking lot if the mother left him unattended.

(C) Yes, because the shopper has not presented evidence that the statute was designed to prevent children from causing damage to the cars of other customers.

(D) Yes, because a parent is not vicariously liable for the negligence of her child.

GO ON TO THE NEXT PAGE

Question 167

A builder entered into a contract with a landowner to build a warehouse for $500,000 by August 1. The agreement provided for five progress payments of $100,000 each at various stages of completion. On June 20, after the builder had spent $350,000 on performance and received $300,000 in progress payments, the builder notified the landowner that he was quitting the project. The landowner hired another contractor to complete the warehouse by August 1 for $250,000, which was a reasonable price given the short deadline.

Which of the following statements regarding the parties' remedies is correct?

(A) The builder can recover $50,000, the difference between the amount he expended on performance and the amount he was paid, to prevent the landowner's unjust enrichment.

(B) Neither party can recover anything, because the $50,000 extra that the landowner had to pay to complete the building is offset by the $50,000 difference between the builder's expenditures and the payments the landowner made to him.

(C) The landowner can recover $50,000, the difference between the contract price and the total amount he paid for completing the building.

(D) The landowner can recover $100,000, the difference between the contract price and the total amount spent constructing the building.

Question 168

A homeowner owned a parcel of land on which she built a single-family residence. To pay for the construction, she obtained financing from a bank in exchange for a mortgage on the land. The bank promptly and properly recorded its mortgage. When the house was completed, except for the absence of an oven in the kitchen, the homeowner leased the house to a tenant for a three-year term. There was no provision in the lease agreement regarding kitchen appliances. The tenant bought a professional-grade oven from an appliance company and had it installed in the space provided around the built-in cabinets in the kitchen. To make the purchase, the tenant signed a security agreement with the appliance company granting it a security interest in the oven in exchange for financing. The appliance company did not file or record its security interest in the oven.

By the end of the lease term, the homeowner was in serious default on her mortgage payments to the bank and the tenant was in serious default on his loan payments to the appliance company. In preparing foreclosure proceedings against the homeowner, the bank learned that the tenant was planning to remove the oven and take it with him when he moved out within the next few weeks. The bank filed an action against the tenant claiming ownership of the oven, and joined the homeowner and the appliance company as parties.

Which party has a superior claim to the oven?

(A) The bank, because its mortgage interest attaches to all fixtures on the real estate and it has priority over the appliance company.

(B) The tenant, because removal of the oven will not cause substantial damage to the real estate.

(C) The homeowner, because the oven was annexed to the real estate after the mortgage was given.

(D) The appliance company, because it has a valid security interest in the oven even though it was not recorded.

Question 169

A parcel of property was devised to a husband and a wife "as joint tenants with right of survivorship" through the will of the husband's mother. After title had passed to them, the husband and the wife experienced marital difficulties and legally separated. Unbeknownst to the husband, the wife quitclaimed her interest in the property to a bona fide purchaser for value. Shortly thereafter, the husband and the wife reconciled. The next month, the wife was killed in an auto accident. The purchaser of the wife's interest filed a suit for partition of the property. The husband filed an appropriate counterclaim for quiet title, asserting that he was owner of the entire parcel by right of survivorship.

How should the court rule?

(A) For the purchaser, because he owns an undivided one-half interest in the property.

(B) For the purchaser, because the husband and the wife are presumed to have taken title from the mother as tenants in common under modern law.

(C) For the purchaser, because the husband and the wife were legally separated when he purchased his interest from the wife.

(D) For the husband, because he succeeded to the entire ownership when the wife died.

Question 170

To encourage the development of local integrated circuit manufacturing operations, a state enacted legislation requiring that at least 50% of the units sold by electronic products retailers within the state incorporate locally manufactured microprocessors. The owner of a chain of computer stores in the state sells electronic devices manufactured entirely in other states.

If the computer store owner attacks the state legislation on constitutional grounds, which of the following would provide the strongest support for his position?

(A) The Equal Protection Clause of the Fourteenth Amendment.

(B) The Due Process Clause of the Fourteenth Amendment.

(C) The Commerce Clause.

(D) The Privileges and Immunities Clause of Article IV.

Question 171

An interior decorator entered into a detailed contract with a rug dealer to purchase an Oriental rug for a law firm's reception area. On the date specified in the contract, the rug dealer brought the rug to the law firm, where the decorator was waiting. On inspecting the rug, the decorator was shocked to discover that it was made in a factory just outside of town, albeit by weavers knowledgeable in the art of Oriental rugmaking. He rejected the rug because it was not an "authentic" Oriental rug.

The rug dealer filed a claim in equity court compelling the decorator to accept the rug. The decorator claims that both parties to the contract understood that the term "Oriental rug" meant only a rug meeting certain criteria established in the rug trade, including, most importantly, that the rug be made in an Asian country by native artisans.

Will the court permit the decorator to introduce evidence of trade usage supporting that understanding of the term "Oriental rug"?

(A) Yes, because there was a latent ambiguity in the expression of the parties' agreement.

(B) Yes, because trade usage is admissible to explain or supplement the terms of a contract.

(C) No, because the writing was a complete integration.

(D) No, because there is no evidence that the writing was intended as anything other than a final expression.

GO ON TO THE NEXT PAGE

Question 172

A large farming concern in the Midwest contracted with a pet food manufacturer to deliver 100 tons of processed cornmeal no later than November 15. The purchase price and delivery terms were specified in the contract, which permitted partial shipments. On November 1, the farming concern delivered 50 tons of cornmeal to the pet food manufacturer with the notification that the balance would be shipped by November 15. The pet food manufacturer rejected the shipment because the written documentation accompanying the shipment did not establish that the cornmeal came from an approved source, as required by the contract. The farming concern responded to this rejection by conceding that the shipment did not conform to the contract and promising to deliver all 100 tons of cornmeal by November 15 with proper documentation.

Which of the following best expresses the pet food manufacturer's options?

(A) The pet food manufacturer may notify the farming concern that the entire contract is terminated and that it is going to obtain the 100 tons of cornmeal from another source.

(B) The pet food manufacturer may notify the farming concern that the contract is terminated as to the 50 tons of cornmeal that was shipped and did not conform to the contract, but must accept the additional 50 tons when it is shipped if it conforms to the contract.

(C) The pet food manufacturer must allow the farming concern a commercially reasonable time to ship cornmeal that conforms to the contract before it can terminate the contract.

(D) The pet food manufacturer must allow the farming concern until November 15 to ship cornmeal that conforms to the contract before it can terminate the contract.

Question 173

The defendant and several of his friends went to a celebration at a club. After consuming numerous alcoholic beverages over a period of two hours, the defendant attempted to drive home. Two blocks away, due to his intoxication, he drove his car across the center line and collided head-on with the victim's car, killing her instantly. However, the defendant was only charged with driving while intoxicated. After a bench trial, he was convicted and sentenced to two years of probation. The resulting public outcry and media attention cost the district attorney the next election. His successor immediately filed a charge of reckless homicide against the defendant for causing the victim's death while driving drunk.

The defendant was tried and convicted of the reckless homicide charge and sentenced to five years in prison. The defendant asserts on appeal that his trial and conviction on the reckless homicide charge violates the Fifth Amendment provision against double jeopardy.

Is he likely to prevail?

(A) No, because the driving while intoxicated charge and the reckless homicide charge each require proof of an additional element that the other crime does not require.

(B) No, because the fact that the charges arose out of the same transaction does not prevent the imposition of separate punishments as long as they are imposed in separate trials.

(C) Yes, because the reckless homicide charge will require proof of the same conduct that constituted the driving while intoxicated charge.

(D) Yes, because the sentence for the reckless homicide conviction was greater than, and not concurrent with, the driving while intoxicated sentence.

GO ON TO THE NEXT PAGE

Question 174

A state's Commercial Code provides, in part, that "the minimum price of cheese sold in this state shall be $2.50 per pound."

As to which of the following persons would the state statute be most likely constitutionally applied?

(A) A resident of the state selling cheese in that state to a manufacturer of snack foods whose plant is located in a neighboring state.

(B) A resident of Canada selling cheese made in Canada to the citizens of the state.

(C) A resident of the state selling cheese to the Commissary at the United States Air Force base in the state.

(D) A resident of the state selling cheese to the state Department of Education for its use in its school lunch program.

Question 175

A landowner devised her land by will "to my husband for life, then to my nieces and nephews for life, then to the children of my nieces and nephews in fee simple." When the landowner died, she had one niece, who had a son. The husband died one year later. The following year, a nephew was born. At that time, the niece and her son were also alive. The jurisdiction's Rule Against Perpetuities is unmodified by statute.

What are the respective interests of the parties in the land at this point in time?

(A) The niece has a life estate, and the niece's son has a remainder.

(B) The niece has a life estate, and the landowner's heirs have a reversion.

(C) The niece and the nephew have a life estate, and the niece's son has a remainder.

(D) The niece and the nephew have a life estate, and the landowner's heirs have a reversion.

Question 176

A buyer purchased a parcel of property from a seller for $100,000, financing the purchase with a loan from the seller secured by a mortgage on the property. The seller promptly and properly recorded his mortgage. Shortly thereafter, the buyer obtained a loan from a credit union for remodeling secured by a mortgage on the property. The credit union promptly and properly recorded its mortgage. One year later, the buyer obtained a home equity loan from a bank secured by a mortgage on the property. The bank promptly and properly recorded its mortgage. A few months later, the buyer stopped making payments on the debt owed to the credit union. With proper notice to all parties, the credit union brought an action to foreclose on its mortgage. At that time, the buyer owed $20,000 on the seller's mortgage, $25,000 on the credit union's mortgage, and $30,000 on the bank's mortgage. At the foreclosure sale, the property was sold for $45,000. The jurisdiction in which the property is located permits deficiency judgments.

After the $25,000 debt owed to the credit union is satisfied from the proceeds, which of the following statements is most correct?

(A) The seller's mortgage and the bank's mortgage are both reduced by $10,000 and remain on the property.

(B) The seller's mortgage is satisfied in full and extinguished, while the bank's mortgage remains on the property.

(C) The seller's mortgage remains on the property, while the bank's mortgage is reduced by $20,000 and extinguished, leaving the buyer personally liable to the bank for the deficiency of $10,000.

(D) The seller's mortgage is satisfied in full and extinguished, and the bank's mortgage is also extinguished, leaving the buyer personally liable to the bank for the deficiency of $30,000.

Question 177

A chemical company located in a small city stored the components of a deadly nerve gas in its underground vaults. The two chemical agents that combined to create the nerve gas were harmless when kept separate, and the canisters for the delivery system had been manufactured under detailed specifications to stay intact for decades without deterioration. The chemical company's vaults were adjacent to an old underground storage chamber of the city's cable car system. Unbeknownst to the chemical company or the city, children living nearby had gotten access to the city's underground chamber and played in there from time to time. After a period of time, several of the canisters in the delivery systems began to leak, permitting the mixture of the two harmless agents into the deadly nerve gas. The chemical reaction caused by the mixture released a great deal of heat, which melted through the walls of the storage vault where it adjoined the city's underground storage chamber. The children playing in the chamber at the time were able to scramble out through a ventilation shaft, but one child fell and cut his leg while escaping. Fortunately, the authorities were able to flood the chamber with a neutralizing agent that rendered the nerve gas inert, and no one was harmed by its effects. Through his parents, the injured child brings an action against the chemical company.

Will he prevail?

(A) Yes, because the chemical company was engaged in an abnormally dangerous activity.

(B) Yes, because the chemical company was negligent.

(C) No, because the child's injuries were not foreseeable.

(D) No, because the underground chamber in which the child was injured was owned by the city, not by the chemical company.

GO ON TO THE NEXT PAGE

Question 178

A consumer bit into a hamburger at a restaurant and cut her gum on a piece of bone in the meat. The bone was over an inch long. The consumer sued the meat processor in strict liability and negligence. At trial, she presented evidence that the processor supplied the ground beef that the restaurant used to make its hamburgers and that she was injured from the piece of bone in the meat. The meat processor presented evidence that restaurant employees prepared the hamburger patties by hand from the ground beef supplied by the processor, and asserted that one of the employees would have found the piece of bone had they made a reasonable inspection of the meat while preparing it. At the close of the evidence, the meat processor moved for a directed verdict on the consumer's negligence claim.

Based on the facts above, the court should:

(A) Grant the motion, because the consumer has failed to show negligent conduct by the meat processor.

(B) Grant the motion, because the restaurant employees' failure to inspect the meat and discover the bone cuts off the processor's negligence liability.

(C) Deny the motion, because the jury could find that the bone was in the ground beef as a result of negligence by the processor.

(D) Deny the motion, because the jury could find that the processor was more at fault than the restaurant.

Question 179

The defendant is on trial for first degree murder for the shooting of a rival gang member. His defense is that the gun accidentally discharged while he was cleaning it and that he is not in any gang. The prosecution seeks to offer the testimony of an experienced police officer in the gang crimes unit who interrogated the defendant. The officer is prepared to testify that he saw a distinctive tattoo on the defendant's leg and that he recognized the tattoo as one worn by members of a gang that was a rival of the victim's gang, and intends to have the tattoo displayed in court. The defendant's attorney objects to this testimony.

How should the court rule on the admissibility of the testimony?

(A) Inadmissible, because the officer does not have personal knowledge that the defendant is in the gang.

(B) Inadmissible, because the officer has not been qualified by the court as an expert on gangs.

(C) Admissible, as circumstantial evidence that the defendant was a member of the rival gang.

(D) Admissible, because the tattoo will be displayed in court.

GO ON TO THE NEXT PAGE

Question 180

The manager of a bank branch announced to bank employees at a meeting that the corporate security staff would be staging a mock bank robbery that evening just at closing time, so that the employees could learn the proper responses to such a stressful situation and view bank security measures. At closing time that evening, the main bank's security chief, dressed in grubby clothes, entered the bank with an assistant and pointed his empty handgun at a bank teller, shouting, "Put all your money in this bag now! Get moving or I'll blow your head off!" The teller, who had been too busy with a crossword puzzle to listen to the manager's announcement at the meeting, thought that a real robbery was in progress. He nervously attempted to stuff the contents of his cash drawer into the bag while the security chief was threatening him and waving the gun at him. Believing that the teller was playing along, the security chief then demanded the teller's wallet and wristwatch, threatening to shoot the watch off if he did not hurry up. After giving the security chief what he wanted and watching him exit, the teller collapsed into a chair and suffered a mild heart attack before the security chief could return with his "loot" to discuss the exercise with the bank employees.

Which of the following crimes has the security chief committed with regard to the teller?

(A) Robbery.

(B) Larceny.

(C) Assault.

(D) No crime.

Question 181

The plaintiff brought an action against a major national department store alleging that the electric blanket she bought from them overheated, causing a fire that destroyed her home and all that it contained. The defendant contends that its blanket could not have overheated unless it was left on after the plaintiff left for work on the day of the fire. The plaintiff offers in rebuttal the testimony of her husband, who will state that he has been married to the plaintiff for seven years, that he has slept in the same bed with her for most of that period, and that the first thing she does every morning upon awakening is to turn the control on the electric blanket to "off."

Should this testimony be admitted?

(A) Yes, because prior conduct may be used to show conformity with habit.

(B) Yes, because evidence of habit may be used to show that a person acted in conformity with the habit on a particular occasion.

(C) No, because habit may only be established by opinion or reputation evidence, not specific conduct.

(D) No, because there is no corroboration of the husband's testimony by a nonparty witness.

GO ON TO THE NEXT PAGE

Question 182

A miner executed his will, bequeathing his property on which a gold mine was located "to my wife for life, remainder to my nephew." When the miner died, the gold mine was producing a net annual value of $100,000 in gold and had proven reserves valued at $2 million. Shortly after the miner's death, the nephew brings an action to enjoin the wife from operating the mine.

The injunction should be:

(A) Granted, because the nephew has a vested remainder subject to partial divestment.

(B) Granted, because the nephew has a vested remainder.

(C) Denied, because the wife has a freehold estate.

(D) Denied, because of the open mines doctrine.

Question 183

A homeowner and her neighbor purchased adjoining parcels of property 20 years ago. During the summer months, the homeowner ran electrical wires from her home to a guest house across land she knew belonged to the neighbor. The neighbor orally consented to the wiring's crossing his land. Two years ago, the neighbor sold his property to a purchaser. The following summer, the homeowner tried to run the wires across the purchaser's land, but the purchaser objected. The statute of limitations in ejectment is 15 years.

With respect to the land over which the electrical wires were laid:

(A) The homeowner has acquired title by adverse possession.

(B) The homeowner has acquired a prescriptive easement.

(C) The homeowner cannot claim any right on title because her use of the land in question was not continuous.

(D) The homeowner cannot claim any right on title because the neighbor consented to her use of the land for the wires.

Question 184

After a recent rainy season, a number of the communities in a western state suffered flooding and mudslides. A study commissioned by the state legislature determined that the extensive removal of a certain plant from hillsides within the state contributed significantly to the flooding and mudslides. The plant had an extensive root system that helped hold hillside soil in place, and it was being rapidly removed because its roots had recently gained national favor as a powerful herbal remedy. As a result, the legislature passed a statute prohibiting the removal of more than 50% of such plants from any hillside within the state.

A landowner within the state challenged the statute on federal constitutional grounds, alleging that he had regularly harvested substantially more than 50% of the plants from his property and needed to do the same this year to meet the demand for the root.

Is he likely to prevail in his challenge?

(A) Yes, because the statute substantially impairs the economic value of the landowner's property.

(B) Yes, because the statute effects a taking of private property for public use without just compensation.

(C) No, because the statute is rationally related to the legitimate government interest of preventing flooding damage to property.

(D) No, because the statute promotes a legitimate public purpose and permits the continued use of the landowner's property.

GO ON TO THE NEXT PAGE

Question 185

A vendor entered into a written contract with a purchaser for the sale of a large tract of land. The contract set forth an accurate metes and bounds description of the land based on a professional survey. At closing, the purchaser discovered that the deed was incorrectly transcribed and did not agree with the description of the land in the contract. The deed described the property to be conveyed as follows:

> (i) from the southwest corner of [a specified starting point], proceed South 45 degrees East 200 feet to [a specified point]; (ii) from that point, proceed South 45 degrees West 100 feet to [a specified point]; (iii) from that point, proceed North 45 degrees West 200 feet to [a specified point]; and (iv) from that point, proceed South 45 degrees East 100 feet to the starting point.

The purchaser refused to proceed with the closing and brought an action to reform the deed to make it conform to the intention of the parties.

Which of the following corrections should be made for the deed to properly describe the land?

(A) Direction (i) should be changed to "South 45 degrees East 100 feet."

(B) Direction (iii) should be changed to "North 45 degrees West 100 feet."

(C) Direction (iii) should be changed to "North 45 degrees East 200 feet."

(D) Direction (iv) should be changed to "North 45 degrees East 100 feet."

Question 186

A gun collector ordered a rifle from a gun catalog. The rifle had a barrel 16 inches long and a pistol-type grip instead of the more usual rifle stock, so that the entire weapon was only 22 inches long. The collector was aware of a state penal statute that prohibited the possession of "any sawed-off shotgun or rifle." He was also aware that another statute defined sawed-off shotgun or rifle so as to include any such weapon whose barrel was less than 16 inches in length. He was unaware that the same statute also included in its definition of the prohibited weapons any shotgun or rifle whose overall length was less than 24 inches. When the rifle he had ordered arrived in the mail, he carefully measured it to confirm that its barrel was exactly 16 inches in length.

While driving to the target range one day, the collector was stopped for having a defective taillight, and the traffic officer saw the rifle he had ordered lying on the back seat of his car in plain view. The collector was arrested and subsequently prosecuted for possession of a sawed-off rifle.

What will be the probable outcome of the trial?

(A) He will be acquitted, because he honestly did not know that a weapon with an overall length of less than 24 inches was in violation of the statute.

(B) He will be acquitted, because he conducted a reasonable investigation to ensure that he was in compliance with the statute.

(C) He will be convicted, unless the trier of fact determines that his failure to realize that the overall length of the weapon was in violation of the statute was reasonable.

(D) He will be convicted, because his reasonable investigation does not vitiate violation of the statute arising from a mistake of law.

GO ON TO THE NEXT PAGE

Question 187

In a civil lawsuit arising from a car accident, the plaintiff's witness testified that she observed the defendant drive through a red light before striking the plaintiff's car. The defendant then presented evidence impeaching the plaintiff's witness. The plaintiff now wishes to call someone else to testify as to his witness's good reputation for truthfulness.

The court is most likely to permit this testimony if the impeachment was by evidence that:

(A) The plaintiff's witness was convicted of the felony of aggravated battery five years ago.

(B) The plaintiff's witness had a previous dispute with the defendant.

(C) The plaintiff's witness was not wearing her prescription eyeglasses at the time of the accident.

(D) The plaintiff's witness was his mother.

Question 188

A woman chastised her roommate when she saw that neither the roommate nor her boyfriend wore a helmet when they rode on the boyfriend's motorcycle. The roommate said that helmets were too restricting. The woman's brother had died in a motorcycle accident because he had not worn a helmet, so she decided to do something to make a lasting impression on her roommate. She called her roommate at work one day and left a message that her boyfriend was in a motorcycle accident and was in the hospital on life support. The roommate was very upset when she got the message and left immediately for the hospital. When she found out later that the message was not true, she became even more upset.

If the roommate brings an action against the woman to recover for her emotional distress, is she likely to prevail?

(A) Yes, because it was foreseeable that the roommate would suffer severe emotional distress.

(B) Yes, because the woman knew that there was a high likelihood that the roommate would suffer severe emotional distress.

(C) No, because it does not appear that the roommate suffered physical injury from her distress.

(D) No, because the roommate and her boyfriend were not related.

Question 189

The victim collapsed at her desk while drinking her morning coffee. Her secretary came rushing to her aid. Gasping for breath, the victim said, "I don't think I have much time left. I want you to remember when they come looking for suspects that I believe my assistant would kill for my job." The victim soon lost consciousness. She regained consciousness briefly after arriving at the hospital, but the doctors would not allow her to speak to anyone, including the police. She again lapsed into a coma, and she remains in this vegetative state. It was determined that she was poisoned. The assistant is arrested and charged with attempted murder.

At the assistant's trial, the prosecution wishes to call the victim's secretary to testify to the victim's statement to him at the office before the ambulance arrived.

The court should find the statement:

(A) Admissible, because it is a dying declaration.

(B) Admissible, because it is a declaration of the victim's state of mind.

(C) Inadmissible, because dying declarations are never admissible unless the declarant is dead.

(D) Inadmissible, because it is hearsay not within any exception.

GO ON TO THE NEXT PAGE

Question 190

A father took his six-year-old son to a shopping mall. While the father was looking at the mall directory, the son went over to a small electric trolley that traveled around a small oval track. Four children, whose parents had paid admission to the ride operator, were already seated in the four seats in the trolley, and the operator started the ride. The son climbed over the low fence surrounding the ride and ran to the rear of the trolley. He grabbed onto the upper edge of the trolley and stood on a narrow ledge at the bottom as the ride advanced. He lost his grip as the trolley was moving and fell backward onto the track, injuring his head.

The son brought an action, through his guardian ad litem, against the manufacturer of the trolley ride on a theory of strict liability. The jurisdiction follows traditional contributory negligence rules.

Which of the following would provide the best defense for the manufacturer in this litigation?

(A) There is not privity of contract between the son and the manufacturer.

(B) The son was contributorily negligent in riding on the rear of the trolley.

(C) The trolley was not being used by the son in a reasonably foreseeable manner.

(D) The father was negligent in his supervision of the son.

Question 191

A writer contracted with a literary agent to obtain a publisher for his book. The parties' written agreement provided that the agent would receive 20% of what the writer earned from the sales of his book. The agreement also provided that the publisher procured by the agent would pay the writer an advance against royalties of at least $10,000.

The agent found a willing publisher who entered into a written contract with the writer providing for the standard royalty amount minus the $10,000 that the publisher promised the writer as an advance. The writer insisted that a clause be added to the contract providing for liquidated damages of $50,000 if the publisher breached the contract. Although the writer was unsure what his actual damages would be, he thought he could make $50,000 in royalties. The writer and the publisher signed the contract, and the publisher paid the writer $10,000 per their agreement.

A few weeks later, the publisher notified the writer that, due to unexpected financial constraints, it was no longer possible for him to publish the book. The publisher requested that the writer return the $10,000 but the writer refused, so the publisher filed suit. The agent intervened in the suit, demanding the $10,000 from the writer as her 20% share of the expected royalties.

Regarding the $10,000, what are the parties contractually entitled to?

(A) The writer is entitled to keep the $10,000 because the liquidated damages clause is reasonable.

(B) The publisher is entitled to get the $10,000 returned to him because his contractual duties were discharged by impossibility.

(C) The agent is entitled to get the $10,000 because she performed her part of the contract by finding a publisher.

(D) The writer is entitled to keep $8,000 and the agent is entitled to get $2,000, because the liquidated damages clause was reasonable and the agent is entitled to 20% of whatever the writer gets from the deal.

GO ON TO THE NEXT PAGE

Question 192

A pedestrian brought a negligence action against a motorist who struck him with her car in a shopping mall parking lot. The trier of fact determined that the pedestrian suffered $100,000 in damages and that he was 25% at fault for crossing in front of the motorist's car. The shopping mall was determined to be 30% at fault for allowing bushes to obscure the view of drivers, and the motorist was found to be 45% at fault for striking the pedestrian.

The jurisdiction involved has adopted pure comparative negligence and uses a comparative contribution system.

How much can the pedestrian recover from the motorist?

(A) $45,000, because the jurisdiction uses a comparative contribution system.

(B) $75,000, because the pedestrian's fault was less than the fault of the motorist.

(C) $75,000, but the motorist can recover $30,000 contribution from the shopping mall.

(D) $75,000, and the motorist cannot recover contribution from the shopping mall because the motorist's fault was greater.

Question 193

The defendant boarded a bus in New York for a trip to Florida to deliver two bricks of cocaine to a drug dealer. En route, in Georgia, an officer for the state motor vehicle department stopped the bus in order to conduct a safety check of the bus. The officer was accompanied by a state trooper. While the motor vehicle officer was conducting the safety inspection, the trooper boarded the bus. The trooper announced that, for homeland security purposes and to combat drug smuggling, he would be asking for identification, for the passengers to identify their luggage, and for permission to search inside the luggage. The trooper stated that the passengers had the right to leave the bus or to decline to show what was inside their luggage. The trooper then walked to the back of the bus to avoid blocking the aisle. The trooper pulled down a bag that another passenger indicated belonged to the defendant. The trooper then asked the defendant if the bag was his and whether he could search the bag, and the defendant responded by nodding his head.

The trooper opened the bag, found the two bricks of cocaine, and immediately placed the defendant under arrest and advised him of his rights under *Miranda*. Approximately one hour later, the motor vehicle officer finished his inspection, issuing the driver a citation for failing to keep his log book up to date. The defendant was charged with possession of cocaine with intent to deliver. Before trial, the defendant moves for suppression of the cocaine.

The most likely outcome is that:

(A) The cocaine will be suppressed as a violation of the Fourth Amendment.

(B) The cocaine will be suppressed as a violation of the Fifth Amendment.

(C) The cocaine will be suppressed as violations of both the Fourth and Fifth Amendments.

(D) The cocaine will not be suppressed.

GO ON TO THE NEXT PAGE

Question 194

The legislature of a state was concerned that the numerous and strident television, radio, and newspaper advertisements by auto dealerships annoy and mislead the public. Therefore, it enacted comprehensive legislation regulating the timing and content of such ads, limiting their duration, frequency, and the types of claims and information made and given.

Which of the following statements is most accurate as to the constitutionality of the state's ad regulation?

(A) It is unconstitutional, because it infringes on the First and Fourteenth Amendment rights of auto dealers to free speech.

(B) It is constitutional if it does not prohibit the dissemination of truthful information about price and the availability of products, and is narrowly tailored to serve a substantial government interest.

(C) It is constitutional, because it is within the police power of the state and no federal constitutional rights are infringed.

(D) It is unconstitutional, because it infringes on the rights of the auto dealers to enter into contracts for advertising.

Question 195

A chef wanted to open his own restaurant and a contractor offered to build the place for $160,000. Their written contract provided that the chef would pay the contractor $60,000 in cash on commencement of construction, scheduled for April 15 after the spring thaw. On completion of the restaurant on September 30, the contractor would be paid the remaining $100,000. The region had a late spring, and on April 30 the contractor had not yet commenced construction of the restaurant.

The contractor has:

(A) Not breached the contract, and the chef need not make the initial $60,000 payment.

(B) Not breached the contract, but the chef must make the initial $60,000 payment.

(C) Breached the contract in a nonmaterial particular; thus, the chef need not make the initial $60,000 payment.

(D) Breached the contract in a material particular; thus, the chef may treat the contract as at an end and sue for damages.

Question 196

A consortium of actors decided to open a new theater and almost immediately raised $130,000 of the $250,000 needed to build it. The contractor whom the consortium hired to build the theater agrees to be paid $50,000 in cash on commencement of construction, another $80,000 when construction was completed, and the remaining $120,000 in monthly payments of $1,000 principal plus 12% annual interest on the outstanding balance, once the theater started earning a profit. Their agreement was reduced to a writing that the parties signed.

The first installment was paid, construction was completed on time, and the second installment was paid. The theater opened, but business was not good, and the theater did not make any profit. The consortium found a buyer who paid them $260,000 for the theater. The contractor sues the consortium for the remaining $120,000 owing on the contract.

Will the contractor recover?

(A) No, because the consortium never earned a profit from its operation of the theater.

(B) No, because the failure to earn profits from the operation of the theater was an unforeseeable intervening event.

(C) Yes, because the provision governing payment of the outstanding balance of the construction cost merely established the time frame in which payment was to be made.

(D) Yes, because all of the conditions precedent to the consortium's duty to pay had occurred.

Question 197

An industrial city in the Midwest had approximately 300,000 inhabitants, and about half of them were members of a recognized racial minority. The latest census figures indicated that 33,501 minority residents of the city could be classified as "poor" under federal poverty guidelines. In contrast, only 7,328 of the approximately 150,000 nonminority residents of the city could be classified as "poor." To combat a budget deficit, the city's 10-member city council, including no minority members and no poor members, decided to raise bus fares during rush hour periods from 80¢ to $1. Because poor people and members of minority groups placed greater reliance on the city's bus lines than did the bulk of the nonpoor and nonminority population (many of whom drove to work), the effect of the transit fare increase was hardest on the poor and minority communities. Several activist groups representing the poor, various minority organizations, and some community action coalitions vowed to fight the fare increase in federal court.

Which of the following statements most accurately describes the constitutional status of the fare increase?

(A) The fare increase is unconstitutional because the city council is composed solely of nonpoor and nonminority members who cannot adequately represent the interests of poor persons, who need low bus fares to survive.

(B) The fare increase is unconstitutional, because the city cannot show that the resulting disparate impact of the fare increase is necessary for a compelling state interest.

(C) The fare increase is constitutional, because there is no evidence that the city council acted irrationally or was motivated by an intent to discriminate on the basis of race.

(D) The fare increase is constitutional, because a political question is involved and fares and fees may be increased if the city council deems such increases appropriate to cure deficits.

GO ON TO THE NEXT PAGE

Question 198

On completion of a major expansion project, a city's public library board adopted a usage policy for the new meeting room that was added to the facility. To alleviate the scheduling burden on the staff if the meeting room were open to all groups, the policy provided that the meeting room was to be used only for "library purposes" by the library staff, the library board, or groups affiliated with the library, such as the library's teen advisory group or volunteer "Friends of the Library" group. A local organization that promoted the political interests of an ethnic minority in and around the city requested use of the meeting room for an informational meeting that would be open to the public. Although no other event was scheduled for the meeting room at the time requested, the library director declined the organization's request, citing the meeting room policy adopted by the library board. The organization filed suit in federal district court, challenging the library's policy and seeking access to the meeting room. How is the court likely to rule?

(A) The library's policy is valid, because limiting the meeting room's use to library purposes is reasonably related to a legitimate government purpose.

(B) The library's policy is valid, because limiting the meeting room's use to library purposes is narrowly tailored to serve a significant government interest.

(C) The library's policy is not valid, because limiting the meeting room's use to library purposes is restricting speech based on its content.

(D) The library's policy is not valid unless there are alternative facilities in the area available for groups to hold meetings.

Question 199

A thief looking for targets in a hotel lobby one evening spotted the victim wearing what appeared to be expensive jewelry as she checked into the hotel. After finding out the victim's room number, the thief broke into a supply room and put on a bellhop's uniform. She then grabbed some flowers from a vase in the hall and knocked on the door to the victim's room, announcing the delivery of a bouquet of flowers. After the victim let her in, the thief scanned the room for the jewelry while putting the flowers in a vase. When she did not see the jewelry, she pulled out a knife and forced the victim to reveal the whereabouts of the jewelry, which turned out to be the hotel's safe. The thief made the victim call the front desk and ask that someone bring the jewelry to the room. The thief then locked the victim in the bathroom, changed out of the bellhop's uniform, and accepted the jewelry when it was brought to the room. She was apprehended a few days later trying to sell the jewelry.

Under these facts, what are the most serious crimes the thief can be convicted of?

(A) Burglary and larceny.

(B) Burglary and robbery.

(C) Larceny only.

(D) Robbery only.

Question 200

As a result of an automobile accident at an intersection, the plaintiff sued the defendant, claiming that the defendant's car was traveling at a high rate of speed and went through a red light just before the crash. A witness for the plaintiff testified that he observed the accident and that the plaintiff's car was traveling at a low speed with a green light at the time of the accident.

Which of the following will the court find inadmissible to admit to impeach the credibility of the witness?

(A) A certified copy of a certificate of conviction for felony assault and battery seven years ago.

(B) The testimony of the witness's friend that, last month, while having a drink at a bar, the witness told her that the plaintiff's light was red.

(C) A record of an arrest one week ago for embezzlement.

(D) On cross-examination of the witness, the question "Isn't it a fact that you lied to your employer last year concerning your meal expenses on a business trip?"

P.M. ANSWER SHEET

101. _____

102. _____

103. _____

104. _____

105. _____

106. _____

107. _____

108. _____

109. _____

110. _____

111. _____

112. _____

113. _____

114. _____

115. _____

116. _____

117. _____

118. _____

119. _____

120. _____

121. _____

122. _____

123. _____

124. _____

125. _____

126. _____

127. _____

128. _____

129. _____

130. _____

131. _____

132. _____

133. _____

134. _____

135. _____

136. _____

137. _____

138. _____

139. _____

140. _____

141. _____

142. _____

143. _____

144. _____

145. _____

146. _____

147. _____

148. _____

149. _____

150. _____

151. _____

152. _____

153. _____

154. _____

155. _____

156. _____

157. _____

158. _____

159. _____

160. _____

161. _____

162. _____

163. _____

164. _____

165. _____

166. _____

167. _____

168. _____

169. _____

170. _____

171. _____

172. _____

173. _____

174. _____

175. _____

176. _____

177. _____

178. _____

179. _____

180. _____

181. _____

182. _____

183. _____

184. _____

185. _____

186. _____

187. _____

188. _____

189. _____

190. _____

191. _____

192. _____

193. _____

194. _____

195. _____

196. _____

197. _____

198. _____

199. _____

200. _____

Explanatory Answers

ANSWER KEY AND SUBJECT MATTER KEY

	Answer	Subject Matter
1.	C	Criminal Law/Procedure—search and seizure
2.	C	Constitutional Law—spending power
3.	A	Contracts—promissory estoppel/third-party beneficiary
4.	B	Real Property—recording acts/priorities
5.	C	Evidence—vicarious admissions
6.	B	Criminal Law/Procedure—Fifth Amendment
7.	B	Torts—defense of property
8.	D	Constitutional Law—First Amendment
9.	A	Torts—conversion
10.	C	Constitutional Law—equal protection
11.	A	Torts—negligence
12.	C	Torts—negligence/violation of statute
13.	A	Real Property—marketable title/adverse possession
14.	B	Contracts—consideration
15.	C	Contracts—consideration
16.	D	Contracts/Sales—damages
17.	B	Torts—comparative negligence
18.	A	Real Property—life estate/doctrine of waste
19.	C	Criminal Law—self-defense
20.	A	Constitutional Law—voting rights/equal protection
21.	A	Constitutional Law—equal protection
22.	D	Contracts/Sales—lost profits damages
23.	B	Criminal Law—homicide
24.	B	Contracts—Statute of Frauds
25.	A	Real Property—joint tenancy
26.	A	Real Property—mortgages
27.	D	Torts—invasion of privacy
28.	C	Contracts—unilateral contract
29.	D	Contracts—offer and acceptance
30.	A	Real Property—priority of security interests
31.	C	Constitutional Law—equal protection
32.	C	Evidence—impeachment
33.	A	Evidence—hearsay rule
34.	A	Contracts/Sales—risk of loss
35.	C	Contracts—third-party beneficiary
36.	A	Constitutional Law—preemption
37.	A	Real Property—equitable servitude/common development scheme
38.	B	Criminal Law—requisite mental state
39.	A	Criminal Law—requisite mental state
40.	C	Evidence—judicial notice
41.	D	Contracts—offer and acceptance
42.	B	Real Property—land sale contract
43.	B	Evidence—character evidence
44.	C	Evidence—settlement offers
45.	C	Torts—battery
46.	B	Real Property—easements
47.	A	Contracts—requirements contract

borbri

48.	C	Contracts—Statute of Frauds
49.	D	Criminal Law—attempt/requisite intent
50.	D	Evidence—recollection refreshed
51.	C	Real Property—easement
52.	B	Torts—defamation of public figure
53.	B	Criminal Law—conspiracy/solicitation
54.	B	Criminal Law/Procedure—Fifth Amendment
55.	D	Real Property—transfer of security interests
56.	A	Real Property—priority of security interests/redemption
57.	A	Evidence—impeachment
58.	D	Evidence—hearsay
59.	B	Constitutional Law—ripeness
60.	C	Evidence—materiality of evidence
61.	C	Contracts—consideration
62.	A	Contracts—accord and satisfaction
63.	B	Criminal Law—conspiracy
64.	C	Torts—assault
65.	D	Torts—false imprisonment
66.	D	Real Property—riparian rights
67.	B	Criminal Law—accomplice liability
68.	C	Evidence—judge/jury responsibility
69.	C	Criminal Law/Procedure—burden of proof
70.	C	Constitutional Law—First Amendment Establishment Clause
71.	A	Torts—products liability based on strict liability
72.	C	Torts—strict liability for animals
73.	B	Constitutional Law—procedural due process
74.	C	Constitutional Law—First Amendment
75.	B	Criminal Law/Procedure—Sixth Amendment
76.	B	Evidence—hearsay
77.	B	Constitutional Law—First Amendment Free Exercise Clause
78.	D	Real Property—specific performance of land sale contract
79.	B	Torts—trespass to land
80.	C	Torts—nuisance
81.	B	Criminal Law/Procedure—Fifth Amendment
82.	C	Criminal Law/Procedure—Sixth Amendment
83.	C	Evidence—probativeness vs. prejudicial effect
84.	C	Torts—rescuer's liability
85.	B	Constitutional Law—taxing and spending power
86.	A	Torts—duty of care
87.	B	Contracts—rescission
88.	B	Contracts—assignment/damages
89.	D	Constitutional Law—federal commerce power
90.	B	Constitutional Law—executive power
91.	D	Evidence—character evidence
92.	B	Torts—battery
93.	D	Criminal Law—accomplice liability
94.	B	Constitutional Law—Commerce Clause
95.	A	Torts—respondeat superior
96.	B	Evidence—impeachment
97.	C	Real Property—adverse possession
98.	C	Real Property—future interests

99.	B	Torts—products liability based on strict liability
100.	C	Evidence—character evidence
101.	A	Torts—breach of duty
102.	A	Contracts/Sales—offer and acceptance
103.	B	Evidence—character evidence
104.	A	Torts—physician's standard of care
105.	C	Contracts—anticipatory repudiation
106.	C	Evidence—hearsay
107.	D	Contracts—impossibility of performance
108.	B	Contracts—assignment/consideration
109.	A	Criminal Law—attempt
110.	C	Constitutional Law—case or controversy requirement
111.	C	Real Property—recording of deed
112.	C	Real Property—recording acts
113.	D	Evidence—impeachment
114.	D	Real Property—assignment of leasehold
115.	A	Torts—negligence/landowner's duties
116.	A	Constitutional Law—judicial review
117.	D	Constitutional Law—standing
118.	D	Criminal Law/Procedure—double jeopardy
119.	A	Criminal Law/Procedure—grand jury/exclusionary rule
120.	B	Evidence—admission by silence
121.	C	Evidence—hearsay
122.	C	Contracts—material vs. minor breach
123.	B	Evidence—subsequent remedial measures
124.	B	Contracts—assignment and delegation
125.	A	Contracts—mistake
126.	A	Criminal Law—murder/requisite intent
127.	B	Criminal Law/Procedure—search and seizure
128.	C	Criminal Law/Procedure—search and seizure
129.	D	Real Property—termination of tenancy
130.	C	Constitutional Law—advisory opinions
131.	B	Constitutional Law—standing
132.	B	Real Property—assignment of lease
133.	A	Torts—child's standard of care
134.	A	Criminal Law—conspiracy
135.	A	Criminal Law—attempt
136.	B	Contracts—modification
137.	D	Evidence—expert testimony
138.	B	Evidence—impeachment
139.	B	Real Property—future interests
140.	C	Evidence—character evidence
141.	B	Evidence—authentication/opinion testimony
142.	C	Contracts/Sales—merchant's firm offer
143.	A	Criminal Law/Procedure—search and seizure
144.	B	Criminal Law/Procedure—search and seizure
145.	D	Real Property—marketable title
146.	A	Constitutional Law—First Amendment/obscenity
147.	B	Contracts—"time of the essence"
148.	C	Contracts/Sales—shipment of nonconforming goods
149.	D	Real Property—right of first refusal

150.	B	Real Property—fee simple determinable/Rule Against Perpetuities
151.	C	Constitutional Law—fundamental rights
152.	B	Torts—indemnity
153.	B	Torts—negligent infliction of emotional distress
154.	B	Constitutional Law—executive power
155.	B	Constitutional Law—equal protection
156.	C	Torts—products liability based on negligence
157.	D	Torts—causation/duty to inspect
158.	D	Constitutional Law—Full Faith and Credit
159.	C	Real Property—fee simple determinable
160.	D	Evidence—spousal privilege
161.	A	Criminal Law/Procedure—Fifth Amendment
162.	A	Evidence—relevancy/real evidence
163.	B	Constitutional Law—substantive due process
164.	B	Criminal Law—mens rea/kidnapping
165.	B	Torts—trespass to land/necessity
166.	B	Torts—parent duty of care
167.	C	Contracts—remedies
168.	D	Real Property—fixtures
169.	A	Real Property—joint tenancy
170.	C	Constitutional Law—Commerce Clause
171.	B	Contracts—parol evidence rule
172.	D	Contracts/Sales—seller's right to cure
173.	A	Criminal Law/Procedure—double jeopardy
174.	D	Constitutional Law—Commerce Clause
175.	B	Real Property—class gifts/Rule Against Perpetuities
176.	C	Real Property—foreclosure of mortgages
177.	A	Torts—strict liability
178.	C	Torts—strict products liability
179.	C	Evidence—lay opinion testimony
180.	D	Criminal Law—requisite mental state
181.	B	Evidence—habit evidence
182.	D	Real Property—doctrine of waste
183.	D	Real Property—prescriptive easement
184.	D	Constitutional Law—"Takings" Clause
185.	D	Real Property—description of deeds
186.	D	Criminal Law—mistake of law
187.	A	Evidence—impeachment
188.	B	Torts—intentional infliction of emotional distress
189.	D	Evidence—hearsay
190.	C	Torts—strict products liability
191.	A	Contracts—liquidated damages
192.	C	Torts—comparative contribution
193.	D	Criminal Law/Procedure—Fourth and Fifth Amendments
194.	B	Constitutional Law—First Amendment
195.	A	Contracts—condition precedent
196.	C	Contracts—promise vs. condition
197.	C	Constitutional Law—equal protection
198.	A	Constitutional Law—First Amendment
199.	B	Criminal Law—burglary/robbery
200.	C	Evidence—impeachment

Answer to Question 1

(C) The use of thermal imaging binoculars to observe the marijuana where it could not be observed by simply using the naked eye likely renders the search invalid. To be able to assert a Fourth Amendment right, a person must have a reasonable expectation of privacy with respect to the place searched or the item seized. There is no such expectation of privacy in objects or places held out to the public or that may be viewed from a public vantage point. Thus, the police may fly over an area to observe it with the naked eye, and even a low flyover by a helicopter to view inside a partially covered building is permissible. This is true even if the area is within the curtilage. However, the police may not use technologically enhanced methods that are not available to the public to search areas (at least as to areas within the curtilage). In the instant case, the police have flown over the defendant's greenhouse at night and used a means of enhancing their vision that is not available to the general public. This enabled them to see what could not have been observed with the naked eye, which likely constitutes an impermissible search. [*See* Kyllo v. United States (2001)] (A) is incorrect because it is too broad of a statement. The police generally may look into any area, even an area within the home or curtilage by means of a flyover, so long as they do so from a place the public has access to; ***however, the police may not use technological enhancements that are not available to the public***. In the instant case, the use of thermal imaging makes the police conduct unconstitutional. (B) is incorrect, as it does not properly define the concept of "open fields." Under the "open fields" doctrine, areas outside the "curtilage" (dwelling house ***and outbuildings***) are subject to police search, as these areas are held out to the public and are unprotected by the Fourth Amendment. (B) ignores the fact that an outbuilding may be deemed part of the curtilage. (In determining whether the building is part of the curtilage, the court will consider the proximity of the building to the dwelling, whether the area is enclosed in the same area as the dwelling, and the steps taken by the resident to protect the building from the view of passersby.) (D) is incorrect because it does not address the fact that police may use the naked eye to make observations from a public place even within the curtilage. For example, in the instant case, there would be no Fourth Amendment issue if the officer were able to make unaided observations from the helicopter. It is the fact that he needed technological assistance from sources unavailable to the public that make this search improper. Thus, the fact that the greenhouse may have been within the curtilage, alone, does not make this search improper.

Answer to Question 2

(C) The court should uphold the federal provision because it is within Congress's power to spend for the general welfare. Article I, Section 8, provides that Congress may spend to "provide for the common defense and the general welfare." This spending may be for any public purpose—not merely the accomplishment of other enumerated powers. Under this power, Congress may "regulate states by imposing explicit conditions on the grant of money to state or local governments." Such conditions will not violate the Tenth Amendment merely because Congress lacked the power to directly regulate the activity that is the subject of the spending program. [South Dakota v. Dole (1987)] Here, Congress has attempted to address a national problem—minors embarking on a potentially addictive habit that has been shown to damage health—by restricting access to the product causing the problem. Even if Congress's enumerated powers would not permit it to directly require businesses to take the steps specified by the legislation, it may use its spending power to encourage states to impose these steps. (A) is incorrect. The fact that the businesses involved could not be regulated directly under Congress's power over interstate commerce is irrelevant. As long as Congress is not inducing the states to do something that would not be within their constitutional power (which is not the case here), Congress can indirectly "regulate" activities that it could not regulate directly by imposing conditions on the grant of money to

states. (B) is incorrect because, as discussed above, making a grant of money to a state conditional on the state's taking governmental action does not violate the Tenth Amendment. (D) is incorrect because that is not the standard that the Court would use to test conditions on grants of federal funds. As long as the restrictions have some relevance to the federal interest involved, they will be upheld. Here, conditioning grants that the state will provide for businesses is relevant to the goal of getting businesses to restrict minors' access to cigarettes.

Answer to Question 3

(A) The church will be able to recover against the insurance company on a promissory estoppel theory because the interests of justice require it. Under the majority view, consideration is not necessary to make an agreement at least partially enforceable where the facts indicate that the promisor should be estopped from not performing. Under the Second Restatement, a promise is enforceable to the extent necessary to prevent injustice if the promisor should reasonably expect the promise to induce action or forbearance and such action or forbearance is in fact induced. Here, the insurance company sent a letter to the church informing it that the employee had named the church beneficiary under his employee benefits program. The company did not warn the church that the employee had the right to change his beneficiary and should have reasonably expected that the church would rely on the promise in some way; it is not necessary in charitable contribution cases that the promisor know of a specific expenditure that the recipient made or is going to make. Hence, to prevent injustice, as choice (A) states, the church can recover against the company. (B) is incorrect because the employee's contractual right to change his beneficiary was not affected by any reliance on the part of the church. In the usual case, an intended third-party beneficiary can prevent the contracting parties from rescinding or modifying the contract once his rights have vested. Vesting occurs when the beneficiary: (i) manifests assent to the promise in a manner invited or requested by the parties; (ii) brings suit to enforce the promise; or (iii) materially changes position in justifiable reliance on the promise. However, the parties may by agreement determine the issue of whether or when a third-party beneficiary's rights vest. This is commonly done in life insurance policies and employee benefit plans, such as the one in this case, by reserving to the policyholder or the employee the power to change the beneficiary at any time. The facts indicate that the employee retained an unrestricted right to change his beneficiary and that he exercised that right. The fact that the company contacted the church and the church detrimentally relied on the company's letter did not deprive the employee of the power to change the beneficiary of his benefit plan. The church's recovery will be on the basis of promissory estoppel against the company rather than as a third-party beneficiary of the agreement between the company and the employee. (C) is incorrect. As discussed above, the fact that the employee had the power to change the beneficiary of the benefit plan prevented the church's third-party beneficiary rights from vesting. However, it did not affect the liability the company incurred to the church under a promissory estoppel theory. (D) is incorrect for the same reason as (C): the company did have a duty to pay the new church because the employee had the power to change beneficiaries under the plan; however, the company also caused the first church to detrimentally rely on the statement in the letter that it was the beneficiary.

Answer to Question 4

(B) The investor has title to the back half subject to the bank's mortgage, and the investor has no rights in the front half. The recording statute in the question is a pure notice statute, which allows subsequent purchasers for value and without notice of a prior conveyance to prevail over the prior transferee, regardless of whether the subsequent purchaser records. In addition, the "shelter rule" allows a person who takes from a bona fide purchaser to prevail against any interest that the transferor-bona fide purchaser would have prevailed against, even if the transferee had actual knowledge of the prior unrecorded interest. Thus, the buyer would prevail over the investor even though the buyer was aware of the investor's interest in the parcel, because the buyer obtained title from the friend, a bona fide purchaser. Thus, the investor's rights in the front half of the parcel are extinguished. With regard to the back half, the investor has superior title to it over the landowner, but takes subject to the mortgage on it by the bank because mortgagees for value are treated as "purchasers" under recording statutes and because the bank had no notice of the investor's interest. (A) and (C) are wrong because the investor takes subject to the bank's mortgage, as discussed above. The fact that the bank did not record and the investor subsequently did record, while it would allow the investor to take free of the bank's mortgage under a *race-notice* statute, does not have this effect under the statute here, which is a *notice* statute. (A) and (D) are wrong because, as discussed above, the buyer prevails over the investor under the shelter rule despite his knowledge of the investor's interest in the property.

Answer to Question 5

(C) The helper's written statement is admissible if it qualifies as a vicarious admission. Federal Rule 801(c) defines hearsay as a statement, other than the statement made by the witness while testifying, offered into evidence to prove the truth of the matter asserted. The helper's written statement meets that definition. Therefore, it will be excluded by the hearsay rule unless the statement is removed from the definition of hearsay by 801(d) or is covered by one of the exceptions to the hearsay rule found in Rules 803 and 804. Federal Rule 801(d) provides that admissions by a party are not hearsay and, therefore, an admission will not be excluded by the hearsay rule. An admission is a statement by a party to the action offered by the opponent of the party. Admissions also include statements by a party's employees if made during and in the scope of the employment relationship. Thus, if it can be established that the helper is an employee of the moving company and that his statement was made in the scope of employment, the helper's statement will be admissible as an admission under 801(d). (A) is wrong because if the helper testifies, his written statement would be a prior consistent statement, which is generally only admissible to rebut a charge that the witness is lying or exaggerating because of some motive, and nothing of that nature is suggested by the facts. (B) is wrong. Even if the helper is unavailable to testify, his written statement meets the definition of hearsay under 801(c) and is neither removed from the definition by 801(d) nor qualifies as an exception (without the additional facts stated in choice (C) establishing it as a vicarious admission). (D) is too broad a statement. If the helper testifies in the current trial and contradicts his written statement, the prior inconsistent statement under oath would be removed from the definition of hearsay by 801(d). Alternatively, if the helper had testified in a previous trial and the motorist (or a predecessor in interest) had an opportunity to cross-examine the helper, his previous testimony would qualify under the former testimony exception to the hearsay rule. Neither situation is suggested by the facts presented.

Answer to Question 6

(B) The defendant's motion should be denied because his interrogation did not violate his Fifth Amendment right to counsel. At any time prior to or during interrogation, a suspect may invoke a *Miranda* (Fifth Amendment) right to counsel. However, the request must be unambiguous and specific. If the defendant agrees to answer questions orally, but requests the presence of counsel before making any written statements, the defendant's oral statements are admissible. The defendant's agreement to talk constitutes a voluntary and knowing waiver of the right to counsel, even if it could be argued that it indicates a misunderstanding of the evidentiary effect of oral statements. [Connecticut v. Barrett (1987)] Thus, (B) is correct and (D) is incorrect. (A) is incorrect because it is irrelevant to the defendant's Fifth Amendment right to counsel that the officers questioned him about a different crime. If the accused invokes his right to counsel under *Miranda*, all questioning must cease, even about a totally unrelated crime, because the Fifth Amendment right to counsel under *Miranda*, unlike the Sixth Amendment right to counsel, is not offense specific. Here, the statements are admissible because the defendant did not effectively invoke his right to counsel. (C) is incorrect because as long as *Miranda* warnings have been given and adversary judicial proceedings have not commenced, voluntary statements are admissible even if the police lie to the defendant's lawyer about their intent to question him and fail to inform the defendant that his lawyer is attempting to see him. [Moran v. Burbane (1986)]

Answer to Question 7

(B) The trespasser will prevail against the electric company because it did not have the right to use deadly force to protect its property. As a general rule, one may use reasonable force to prevent the commission of a tort against one's property. However, force that is likely to cause death or serious bodily harm is not permitted when the invasion is threatening property alone. Furthermore, one may not use indirect deadly force when such force could not lawfully be directly used. Because the trespasser was threatening only the property interest of the electric company, the use of deadly force would not be privileged against him. By leaving the power on to prevent theft, the electric company was using indirect deadly force to defend its property where such force could not lawfully be directly used. Hence, it will be liable to the trespasser for his injuries. (A) is incorrect because the electric company's status with respect to the land is irrelevant for the type of claim that the trespasser is asserting. In negligence actions, the limited duty to trespassers that a landowner has is not shared by persons with an easement or license to use the land; they owe a duty of reasonable care even to trespassers. Here, however, the theory of the trespasser's claim is not negligence but more likely battery, because the electric company intended to leave the power on to protect its property and will be deemed to have intended the consequences of that conduct. Even if the electric company had been the landowner, it would not have been privileged to leave the power on solely to protect its property from theft. (C) is incorrect because, as discussed above, the trespasser's status as a trespasser does not provide the electric company with a privilege to use deadly force against him. (D) is incorrect because the fact that the trespasser was attempting to steal the electric company's property would not, standing alone, give the electric company the right to use deadly force, either directly or indirectly, to protect the property.

Answer to Question 8

(D) The court should rule in favor of the publisher because the tax exemption regulates speech based on its content in violation of the First Amendment. The freedom of the press is guaranteed by the First Amendment. As with other areas within the First Amendment, the freedom does not prohibit all government regulation of the press, but it does place limits on regulation. The press and broadcasting companies can be subject to general business regulations and taxes, but generally may not be singled out for a special tax. Moreover, a tax impacting on the press or a subpart of the press cannot be based on the content of the publication absent a compelling justification. Although the state tax here appears to be a general receipts tax, the exemption is based on content, which means that the tax also is based on content (*i.e.,* a publication is subject to the tax unless it contains . . .). As discussed below, a compelling interest is not presented here, so the exemption is invalid and the tax should fail. (A) is incorrect because the publisher would certainly have standing to litigate her tax bill. To have standing, a plaintiff must show that she has suffered an injury in fact, caused by the government, that can be remedied by a court decision in her favor. If the tax here is unconstitutional, the publisher has suffered an injury because she was required by the government to pay the tax, and a decision in her favor will remedy her injury. Therefore, the publisher has standing. The doctrine that taxpayers do not have standing applies to cases where the taxpayer is litigating the way her tax money is spent rather than whether she owes a particular tax. (B) and (C) are incorrect because the facts are insufficient to establish whether the state has a compelling interest here; therefore, it cannot be determined whether the Equal Protection Clause has been violated. The Equal Protection Clause prohibits government discrimination absent a compelling interest, and laws that favor a minority are subject to the same strict scrutiny standard as laws that discriminate against a minority. However, the Supreme Court has found that remedying past discrimination against a minority—either by the government or by the public—is a compelling interest. Therefore, a government program favoring a minority will be upheld if it is narrowly drawn to remedy past discrimination. Here, we are not given any facts about past discrimination and so cannot decide whether the Equal Protection Clause has been violated. Therefore, neither (B) nor (C) is as good an answer as (D).

Answer to Question 9

(A) The neighbor is entitled to $300, but the homeowner will keep the leaf blower. If the plaintiff is successful in a conversion action, the measure of damages is the fair market value of the chattel converted. This value is generally computed as of the time and place of the conversion. The defendant is given title upon satisfaction of the judgment so that, in effect, there is a forced sale of the chattel. (Note that even if the defendant wishes to return the item, the plaintiff is not obligated to take it back once it has been converted.) Here, the value of the leaf blower at the time the homeowner took it was $300, so that is what the neighbor is entitled to. (B) is wrong because damages are measured not by the cost of replacing the converted chattel but by its fair market value at the time and place of conversion. (C) is wrong because damages based on the cost of repair of the motor are more appropriate as a measure of actual damages for a trespass to chattels action. For interferences with a chattel that are so serious as to constitute a conversion, the damages remedy is different. (D) is similarly wrong because it does not state the appropriate measure of damages for conversion.

Answer to Question 10

(C) If the engineer prevails, it will be because the state has failed to show that the law is necessary to achieve a compelling state interest, as required by the Equal Protection Clause of the Fourteenth Amendment. Under that clause, a governmental action involving classification of persons will be subject to strict scrutiny if a suspect classification is involved. The law will be struck down unless the government proves that it is necessary to achieve a compelling interest. State and local laws that classify persons based on alienage are subject to strict scrutiny unless the law is discriminating against alien participation in the functioning of the state government. In that case, the law will be upheld as long as it is rationally related to a legitimate government interest. Thus, a state can validly refuse to hire aliens as teachers or police officers because these positions have a direct effect on the functioning of government. On the other hand, a state law requiring citizenship for all civil service positions was held to be invalid. Similarly, a state law requiring a notary public to be a citizen was struck down under the strict scrutiny standard because a notary's responsibilities are essentially clerical. The engineer could argue that the civil engineer position involves engineering skills rather than the functioning of government. If she prevails it will most likely be because the court agreed with her position and the state failed to meet its difficult burden under the strict scrutiny test of proving that the ban was necessary to achieve a compelling government interest. (A) is incorrect because when the strict scrutiny standard is applied, the burden of proof is on the government rather than on the challenger. (B) is incorrect. It is very unlikely that a court

would decide that a civil engineer position has a direct effect on the functioning of government. If it were to decide this, it would require only that the law have a rational relationship to a legitimate government interest, and it would be very unlikely that the engineer could prove that the ban does *not* have a rational basis. Thus, (B) does not state the most likely basis for the engineer to prevail. (D) is incorrect because it states the standard for analyzing government actions based on quasi-suspect classifications such as gender and legitimacy. State law classifications based on alienage are subject to a different standard.

Answer to Question 11

(A) The physician would not be liable to the driver if it was not reasonably foreseeable that the patient's seizures might recur after the patient was removed from the medication and create an unreasonable risk of harm to third parties. A prima facie case for negligence consists of: (i) a duty on the part of the defendant to conform to the standard of care of a reasonable person for the protection of the plaintiff against an unreasonable risk of injury; (ii) breach of that duty; (iii) the breach was the actual and proximate cause of the plaintiff's injury; and (iv) damage to the plaintiff's person or property. If the recurrence of the patient's seizures following removal from the medication was not reasonably foreseeable, then the physician breached no duty to anyone by taking the patient off the medication. (B) is not as good a choice as (A) because a warning against driving may not have been sufficient to satisfy the duty of care. If there was a risk of seizures that the physician was aware of, it would likely be not reasonable to take the patient off the medication with just a warning against driving, given the likelihood that at some point he would resume driving. (C) is incorrect because the fact that the decision to suspend the medication may have been a reasonable medical decision as it applied to the patient (*i.e.,* the seizures had stopped, and the medication produced unpleasant side effects) does not resolve the physician's liability. The issue in the question relates to how the decision affected a third party. If the decision created an unreasonable risk of injury to persons such as the driver, and such risk was reasonably foreseeable, then the physician will not be insulated from liability for the resulting injury by the medical reasonableness of the decision for the patient. Thus, (C) is not as good a choice as (A). (D) is incorrect because the physician's liability is not dependent on the patient's liability. The patient might not be liable because he had no reason to anticipate that a seizure would occur, but that does not establish that the physician exercised reasonable care.

Answer to Question 12

(C) The court should deny the motion, because the jury could find that the motorist had no reason to believe that she would lapse into unconsciousness. If the motorist had no reason to believe that she might lapse into unconsciousness, her operation of the car breached no duty and she would be found not to be liable; the fact that she violated the statute would not necessarily make her liable, as discussed below. (A) is incorrect because it addresses the causation issue only, and does not address whether the motorist breached her duty. (B) is incorrect even though the statute sets a specific standard of care to be followed. The statute here makes it illegal to cross the double yellow line and was intended to prevent collisions with oncoming traffic. Thus, the driver is in the class intended to be protected by the statute, and the harm he suffered is of the type that the statute was designed to prevent. Consequently, the duty imposed by the statute will replace the more general common law duty of due care. In most states, violation of such a statute establishes a conclusive presumption of duty and breach of duty. However, violation of a statute may be excused where compliance would be beyond the defendant's control. Although the motorist's car did cross a double yellow line, it did so after she lost consciousness (a circumstance that may not have been reasonably foreseeable). Consequently, because compliance with the statute may have been beyond her control, the court should deny the motion for a directed verdict. (D) is incorrect because even though it was impossible to comply with the statute once the motorist lapsed into unconsciousness, her breach of duty may have occurred when she drove the car, if she had reason to believe that she might lapse into unconsciousness, and the jury needs to make that determination. If the jury determines that she did not breach her duty, it will be because it determined that she had no reason to believe that she would lapse into unconsciousness while driving.

Answer to Question 13

(A) Absent a judgment in an action to quiet title or other tangible proof that title to the five-foot strip has actually been acquired, most jurisdictions would not consider the owner's title marketable. All contracts for the sale of land contain, unless the contract expressly provides otherwise, an implied warranty by the seller that she will deliver to the buyer a marketable title at the date of closing. Marketability refers to freedom from the possibility of litigation concerning the title; title is marketable if a reasonably prudent buyer, ready and able to purchase, will accept it in the exercise of ordinary prudence. At times, sellers will rely on adverse possession to show that defects in title have been cleared. However, courts generally will not permit such reliance when proof of adverse possession rests only on oral evidence that will not be available to the buyer in the future. Here, title to the property described in the contract is unmarketable because the five-foot strip was a private right-of-way and not part of the owner's record title. The owner's adverse possession of the strip will not be sufficient by itself to establish marketable title; there is no longer any physical evidence of the owner's possession. Thus, at the least the owner must offer the buyer additional proof that the buyer can use to defend any lawsuit challenging title. (B) is wrong because the owner removed the fence after she had acquired title by adverse possession. While that makes it more difficult for her to establish marketable title in selling the property, it does not affect the ownership rights she gained by adverse possession. (C) is a misstatement of law. Although government property, including public rights-of-way, is generally exempt from the operation of statutes of limitations, the facts of this question specifically state that this is a private right-of-way. (D) is wrong because, as discussed above, the fact that the owner has title to the strip does not mean that she has marketable title.

Answer to Question 14

(B) The jogger will recover nothing because her finding the lost dog occurred prior to the dog owner's promise to pay the $200. An enforceable contract must be supported by consideration. Consideration consists of: (i) a bargained-for exchange between the parties; and (ii) an element of legal value to that which is bargained for. The majority rule is that legal value is present if the promisee has incurred a detriment (*i.e.,* has done something she is under no legal obligation to do or has refrained from doing something that she has a legal right to do). For the presence of "bargained-for exchange," the promise must induce the detriment, and the detriment must induce the promise. If something has already been given or performed before the promise is made, it will not satisfy the "bargain" requirement, because it was not given in exchange for the promise when made. Here, the jogger was under no legal obligation to return the dog to its owner. Thus, in doing so, she incurred a detriment. However, the jogger was not induced to so act by the dog owner's promise to pay $200. Because the jogger's actions regarding the dog were performed before the dog owner's promise, those actions were not given in exchange for the promise when made. Thus, the "bargain" element is absent. (A) is incorrect because for a communication to constitute an offer, the acceptance of which results in a contract, it must express a promise to enter into a contract on the basis of terms that are certain and definite. Here, the dog owner simply offered to pay $200 in gratitude for an act already performed by the jogger. This was not an expression of a commitment to enter into a contract. Thus, there was no "offer" that was capable of either acceptance or rejection. In addition, as detailed above, consideration was not present. Even if the jogger had not declined the dog owner's promise, she could not have enforced its performance. (C) is incorrect for two reasons: First, the technical defense bar, to which it apparently refers, is inapplicable to these facts. If a past obligation (*e.g.,* a promise to pay money) would be enforceable but for the existence of a technical defense (*e.g.,* statute of limitations, discharge in bankruptcy), a new promise is enforceable if it is written or has been partially performed. Here, the dog owner owed no past obligation to the jogger. Second, the Statute of Frauds is inapplicable here. The Statute of Frauds provides that certain agreements must be evidenced by a writing signed by the party sought to be charged. These agreements are: (i) a promise by an executor or administrator to pay the estate's debts out of his own funds; (ii) a promise to answer for the debt of another; (iii) a promise made in consideration of marriage; (iv) a promise creating an interest in land; (v) a promise that cannot be performed within one year; and (vi) a promise for the sale of goods for $500 or more. None of these types of promises is at issue here. Therefore, the Statute of Frauds does not come into play. (D) is also incorrect for two reasons: First, as explained previously, consideration is not present on these facts. Consequently, the jogger cannot enforce the promise to pay $200, regardless of any right of the dog owner to revoke his offer. Second, it is not true that the dog owner could not have revoked the offer until the end of the week. An offer not supported by consideration or detrimental reliance can be revoked at will by the offeror if revocation is communicated to the offeree prior to acceptance. Here, the jogger gave no consideration, nor did she detrimentally rely, so the dog owner could have revoked his offer at any time.

Answer to Question 15

(C)   The younger brother will prevail because he has performed under a valid contract. He entered into and performed a valid unilateral contract with his brother, who offered to give him $15,000 if he showed up at the office sober and ready to work by 9 o'clock each morning for the next 10 months. He accepted by fully performing; his giving up the right to do something that he had a legal right to do constitutes valid consideration. Because the younger brother fully performed his duties under the contract, the older brother's estate is bound to perform his duties and must now pay him. Therefore, (C) is correct. (A) is incorrect. An oral contract is valid and enforceable unless it falls within the Statute of Frauds; this contract does not. To prove the contract, the younger brother could have a witness from the workplace testify as to the oral contract; that testimony would be sufficient to prove the terms of the contract. (B) is incorrect because an offer will not be terminated by the death of the offeror if the offeror's power to revoke is limited by law, such as in the case of a valid unilateral contract. Here, the younger brother has begun performance, making the offer irrevocable during the time he was given to complete performance. (D) is incorrect because it contemplates promissory estoppel, which is a remedy that makes a promise enforceable when there is insufficient consideration to enforce the contract. It is not necessary to rely on promissory estoppel here because there is an enforceable contract, as discussed above.

Answer to Question 16

(D)   The fitness center is entitled to recover the difference between the price of the substitute bottled water and the contract price, as well as damages for lost profits resulting from reduced sales of bottled water, *i.e.,* consequential damages of which the distributor had reason to know. The measure of damages for breach of a contract for the sale of goods is found in the Uniform Commercial Code ("U.C.C."). Where the seller fails to deliver or repudiates, the buyer may measure his damages by the difference between the contract price and the amount he actually has to pay for replacement goods ("cover"). If the buyer chooses to fix damages in this manner, he must

make a reasonable contract for substitute goods in good faith and without unreasonable delay. [U.C.C. §2-712] In addition to such damages, the buyer is entitled to incidental and consequential damages (less expenses saved as a result of the seller's breach). Incidental damages include expenses reasonably incurred in inspection, receipt, transportation, care, and custody of goods rightfully rejected. Consequential damages include any loss resulting from the general or particular requirements and needs of which the seller had reason to know at the time of contracting, and which could not be prevented by purchasing substitute goods or otherwise. Where one party's words or actions make it clear that he is unwilling or unable to perform (*i.e.,* there has been an anticipatory repudiation), the aggrieved party may resort to any remedy for breach. [U.C.C. §2-610] The distributor's comments to the fitness center manager indicate unequivocally that the distributor will not sell any more bottled water to the fitness center at $80 per case, as provided for in the contract. Thus, the fitness center can treat this as a repudiation by the distributor, and may resort to its remedies for breach. Upon learning of the repudiation, the manager promptly and in good faith entered into a contract with a competitor for substitute bottled water. The competitor's bottled water cost $15 more per case than the distributor's bottled water would have cost under the contract. Thus, because the fitness center chose to cover, it can recover $15 (the difference between the contract price per case and the amount per case paid for replacement goods) times the number of cases composing that portion of its yearly requirements that the distributor failed to deliver (*i.e.,* the number of cases purchased from the competitor for the remainder of the contract period). The distributor knew at the time of contracting that the fitness center sold bottled water to its members. The distributor had reason to know that a breach on its part would result in the fitness center's losing profits from reduced sales of bottled water to its members, due to its being compelled to serve a bottled water brand with less appeal than the distributor's. Therefore, the fitness center can recover these lost profits as consequential damages. (B) is incorrect because it does not allow for recovery of the lost profits which, as explained above, are recoverable as consequential damages. (C) is incorrect because it does not allow for recovery of the cost of cover. Nominal damages may be awarded where a breach is shown but no actual loss is proven. Here, the fitness center has incurred lost profits as well as increased costs for the procurement of substitute bottled water. Consequently, (A), which would restrict recovery to nominal damages, is incorrect.

Answer to Question 17

(B) The bystander will recover 55% of her damages because she was less at fault than the Zamboni driver. Most comparative negligence jurisdictions have adopted a modified or partial form, whereby the plaintiff is permitted to recover damages only if her negligence is at or below a threshold level (49% or 50%). A plaintiff entitled to recover will have her damages reduced by the amount of her negligence. Hence, the bystander can recover 55% of her damages (100% minus 45%). (A) is incorrect because the amount of her fault (45%) is subtracted from her total damage recovery, resulting in a 55% recovery. (C) is incorrect. Most comparative negligence jurisdictions have abolished the separate defense of implied assumption of risk and would analyze the plaintiff's conduct here under comparative negligence principles. Because the trier of fact has determined that the bystander was only 45% at fault, she may recover in this jurisdiction regardless of whether she "assumed the risk" when she went onto the ice. (D) is incorrect because the fact that the Zamboni driver was not an employee of the ice rink will not negate the ice rink's liability. While the general rule is that a principal will not be liable for the tortious acts of its agent if the latter is an independent contractor, a broad exception applies for duties that are nondelegable on public policy grounds, such as the duty of a business to keep its premises safe for customers. Hence, the ice rink will be liable for the danger created by the Zamboni driver even though he is not an employee of the rink.

Answer to Question 18

(A) The wife, as the life tenant, is obligated to pay all ordinary taxes on the land to the extent of income or profits from the land. Thus, because the income from the farm has exceeded the taxes due, the wife is personally liable for the taxes. A tax sale, however, will cut off the rights of the remaindermen, the son and the daughter; so they definitely have an interest in paying the taxes. (B) misstates the law. The remaindermen are not liable in any way for these taxes. (C) is incorrect because the daughter cannot be forced to pay one-half of the actual tax bill. Note, however, that if to protect the property the son pays the full amount of the taxes owing (rather than just one-half), he can as a co-tenant seek a contribution from the daughter for her one-half share. (D) is incorrect because a tax sale cuts off the rights of remaindermen.

Answer to Question 19

(C) If the defendant is found not guilty, it will be because he acted reasonably in self-defense. Under principles of self-defense, a person who is without fault may use such force as reasonably appears necessary to protect himself from the imminent use of unlawful force upon himself. If the defendant is found not guilty, it will be because the jury determined that he was acting reasonably in self-defense. (A) is inaccurate. Common law battery can be established by showing that the defendant recklessly caused injury to the person of another. Therefore, this defendant could have been found guilty even if he did not intend to injure the other hockey player. (B) is wrong. Although there may be consent to the contact incident to the game, hockey players do not consent to the type of action engaged in by the defendant. (D) is wrong because it is too broad. Even though the other hockey player was the original aggressor, the defendant would be limited to the amount of force reasonably necessary to defend himself. He would be guilty of battery if the jury found that he acted unreasonably and with excessive force against the other player's aggression. Thus, (C) is a more accurate statement.

Answer to Question 20

(A) Because the city at-large election system appears to have been established and maintained for the purpose of suppressing the voting power of minority-race voters, the system violates the Equal Protection Clause. The Fourteenth Amendment Equal Protection Clause has been interpreted by the Supreme Court as prohibiting state dilution of the right to vote by malapportionment of electoral districts. In effect, this constitutes a ban on fewer representatives per voter in some districts than in others. This "one person-one vote" principle has also been applied to elections for local government bodies. Generally, an at-large system of election presents no one person-one vote problem, because such a system contains no electoral districts. However, where such a system has been established or maintained for the purpose of suppressing minority-race voting power, it has been found unconstitutional. Here, the Alpha Party, which dominates the city's political life, has only slated one member of a minority race as a candidate for the city council. When the Alpha Party did not support his reelection, he was defeated, even though his receipt of 95% of the African-American vote indicated that he enjoyed considerable support among the African-American community. The Alpha Party's withdrawal of support from that candidate because he raised issues of concern to minority voters and subsequent failure to slate any other minority candidates suggests a pattern of discrimination against minorities and unresponsiveness to their needs, thus supporting an inference of purposeful discrimination against minorities to suppress their voting power. Therefore, the city voting system could most likely be invalidated by relying on the Equal Protection Clause. (B) is incorrect. The Due Process Clause prohibits arbitrary governmental action, and comes into play where a law limits the liberty of all persons to engage in some activity. However, where a law limits the liberty of some persons but not others, there is an equal protection problem. The city voting system does not limit the voting powers of all persons; rather, it limits the voting power of minority races. Consequently, this question is more appropriately resolved as an equal protection matter rather than one of due process. (C) is incorrect. The Fourteenth Amendment Privileges or Immunities Clause has been interpreted as protecting only against state infringement of rights peculiar to *national* citizenship, *e.g.,* the right to vote in national elections. At issue here is the right to vote in a *local* election, which is not protected by that clause. (D) is incorrect. Article I, Section 2, Clause 4 of the Constitution directs the governor of a state to issue writs of election to fill vacancies in the United States House of Representatives. Because this question does not involve a vacancy in the House of Representatives, (D) is totally inapplicable.

Answer to Question 21

(A) The court should find that the museum is a private entity and that it may constitutionally hire and fire as it pleases because its actions do not constitute state action. The Equal Protection Clause prohibits states from discriminating against persons on the basis of race, alienage, or national origin unless the discrimination is necessary to achieve a compelling state interest. The museum's policy here of not hiring persons of German descent clearly violates the Clause's prohibitions. However, there is no constitutional violation here because there is no state action. The Equal Protection Clause prohibits only *government* infringement. This does not mean that only direct government action is proscribed. Private action may constitute state action where the private actor is performing an exclusive state function or the government is significantly involved in the private actor's activities. The running of the museum here, however, is not an exclusive government function (*e.g.,* running elections), and the state's grant of the land for the museum does not constitute significant state involvement in the museum's affairs (see below). Thus, there is no state action here and no constitutional violation. (Note that the museum's actions probably violate several civil rights statutes that apply to private citizens.) (B) is incorrect because it reaches the proper result on a faulty rationale. If the museum's acts were state action, the excuse of remedying past discrimination would not validate the discrimination. Remedying past discrimination has never been used as a basis for explicit discrimination against a suspect class, but rather has only been used to justify action favoring a group in limited circumstances. As noted above, discrimination against a suspect class will be upheld only if it is necessary to achieve a compelling interest, and only one case of explicit discrimination against a suspect class has been upheld—incarcerating United States citizens of Japanese ancestry during World War II. It is doubtful that the explicit discrimination would be upheld. (C) is incorrect because the grant of land simply does not constitute significant state involvement, which requires that the state affirmatively facilitate, encourage, or authorize the acts of discrimination. Merely granting land to an entity that then decides to adopt a discriminatory policy does not constitute the necessary affirmative action. (D) is incorrect for the reasons stated under (C)—there is no significant state involvement in the discrimination since the state is deriving no benefit from the discrimination and has not authorized or encouraged it. [*Compare* Burton v. Wilmington Parking Authority (1961)—state action found where city/landlord charged tenant high rent to operate a "whites only" restaurant in the city garage building]

Answer to Question 22

(D) The retailer will recover $1,000, which is the difference between its lost profits and the buyer's down payment. When the buyer repudiates or refuses to accept goods, the usual measure of the seller's damages is the difference between the contract price and the market price or the difference between the contract price and the resale price of the particular goods. However, neither of

those measures of damages gives adequate compensation for the buyer's breach where the seller can obtain or manufacture as many goods as it can sell (*i.e.*, a lost volume seller), because, but for the buyer's breach, the seller would have made two sales instead of one. In this type of case, lost profit is measured by the contract price less the cost to the dealer. Here, the retailer could have made two sales of that model of watercraft because it could get as many as it needed from the manufacturer. Hence, it lost a profit of $3,000 as a result of the buyer's breach. This amount is offset against the amount of the down payment that the buyer made, resulting in a net recovery of $1,000 by the retailer. (A) is incorrect because the retailer did suffer damages as a result of the buyer's breach. (B) is incorrect because it represents the difference between the contract price and the resale price for the goods, which does not adequately compensate the retailer for its damages from the buyer's breach. (C) is incorrect because $3,000 constitutes the retailer's lost profits from the buyer's breach, but it must be offset against the down payment that the retailer received from the buyer.

Answer to Question 23

(B) In forcing the principal to dress in the robber's clothing and to leave the school first, the robber exhibited extreme indifference to an unjustifiably high risk to human life; *i.e.*, the robber acted with malice aforethought. Murder is the unlawful killing of a human being with malice aforethought. Malice aforethought exists if the defendant has any of the following states of mind: (i) intent to kill; (ii) intent to inflict great bodily injury; (iii) awareness of an unjustifiably high risk to human life; or (iv) intent to commit a felony. When the robber forced the principal to dress in the robber's clothing and leave the school first, the robber knew that there was a high risk that the police would mistake the principal for the robber and shoot the principal, who could not raise his hands in the air. By compelling the principal to proceed into a situation that presented an unjustifiably high risk to the principal's life, the robber manifested extreme indifference to that risk. Thus, the robber acted with a state of mind that was sufficient to constitute malice aforethought. This state of mind, in conjunction with the robber's act of placing the principal in this position, makes the robber guilty of the murder of the principal. (C) is incorrect because, not only was it foreseeable that the police would use deadly force against what they perceived to be an armed and dangerous felon, but it was highly probable that they would do so. (D) is incorrect because, by consciously creating the appearance that the principal was actually the robber, an armed and dangerous felon, and compelling the principal to proceed out the door without his hands up, the robber is deemed to be responsible for the shooting of the principal. It may be true that, as (A) states, the police were justified in using deadly force under the circumstances. The police may use deadly force to apprehend an armed felon who poses a threat of serious bodily harm, and it appeared to the police that the principal was such a person. However, (A) is incorrect because it implies that the robber would not be guilty if the police were not justified in using deadly force. The robber's indifference to an unjustifiably high risk to human life does not depend on whether the police response was legally justified. In effect, (A) would make the robber's mental state dependent on his knowledge of the law regarding police use of deadly force. Even if the police response was not legally justified, there was still an unjustifiably high risk that the police would shoot under these circumstances. (B) addresses this risk, while (A) does not.

Answer to Question 24

(B) The uncle's main purpose in making the agreement was to benefit himself rather than his nephew, so the agreement is outside of the Statute of Frauds and is enforceable even though it was oral. Under the Statute of Frauds, certain agreements must be evidenced by a writing that contains: (i) the identity of the party sought to be charged; (ii) identification of the contract's subject matter;

(iii) terms and conditions of the agreement; (iv) recital of consideration; and (v) signature of the party to be charged, or of his agent. One type of agreement that is covered by the Statute of Frauds is a promise to answer for the debt or default of another where the promise is collateral rather than primary. However, where the main purpose or leading object of the promisor is to secure an advantage or pecuniary benefit for himself, the contract is not within the Statute of Frauds, even if the effect is still to pay the debt of another. The uncle guaranteed the loan to his nephew, which means that the uncle agreed to repay the loan only if his nephew refused to do so. Therefore, the uncle made a collateral promise to answer for the debt or default of the nephew regarding the loan from the bank. However, because the main purpose of the uncle's making the agreement was to benefit himself rather than his nephew (by, *e.g.*, being allowed to use the tractor without cost), the agreement is outside the scope of the Statute of Frauds and would be enforceable against the uncle even in the absence of a writing. (C) is incorrect because, although the lack of a writing would ordinarily render the agreement unenforceable, the additional statement of the uncle's purpose contained in (B) would result in the agreement's not falling within the Statute of Frauds. (A) is incorrect because separate consideration need not flow between the bank and the uncle to support the suretyship agreement. The bank's agreeing to engage in the loan transaction is sufficient to support the uncle's promise even if the uncle received no benefit from it. (D) is incorrect because the uncle did not withdraw his promise until after his offer of guarantee had been accepted by the bank (through the loan officer). An offeror may terminate an offer by communicating revocation to the offeree prior to acceptance. Here, the loan officer communicated directly to the uncle an absolute and unequivocal acceptance of the uncle's offer of guarantee. Thus, the uncle's attempted withdrawal of his promise came too late to constitute an effective revocation. While it could be argued that the uncle's repudiation required the loan officer to mitigate damages by stopping the check from being issued, damages must be reasonably certain of being incurred for the requirement of mitigation to apply. Here, any damages are only speculative at this point because the nephew has the primary duty to pay off the new loan and the uncle may not be required to do anything. The duty to mitigate damages does not require that the creditor forgo, for the guarantor's sake, a potentially income-producing transaction merely to avoid a *possibility* of breach by the principal.

Answer to Question 25

(A) The conveyances of 20% of the land to the daughter and the son-in-law sever the joint tenancy only as to that 20%, leaving the husband and the wife with an 80% interest as joint tenants. The daughter and the son-in-law, by virtue of the separate conveyances to them, each have a 10% interest as tenants in common. Creation of a joint tenancy requires four unities: (i) time (interests must vest at the same time); (ii) title (interests must be acquired by the same instrument); (iii) interest (interests must be of the same type and duration); and (iv) possession (interests must give identical rights to enjoyment). Under modern law, a joint tenancy results only when an intention to create a right of survivorship is clearly expressed. When two or more persons take property by a single conveyance, a tenancy in common is presumed rather than a joint tenancy. An inter vivos conveyance by all joint tenants of a portion of the property held in joint tenancy severs the joint tenancy as to the portion that is conveyed. However, the joint tenancy is preserved as to the unconveyed portion of the property. The transferee takes as a tenant in common, because she does not share the unities of time or title with the joint tenants (*i.e.*, her interest vested at a different time and was acquired by a different instrument). Here, the husband and the wife owned the land as joint tenants. When they conveyed 10% of the land to the daughter, the joint tenancy was severed as to that 10%. At that point, the husband and the wife held an interest in 90% of the land as joint tenants because, as between themselves, the four unities were preserved as to that 90%. The daughter did not share the unities of time or title with the husband and the wife. Thus, the

daughter took a 10% interest as a tenant in common rather than as a joint tenant. When the husband and the wife conveyed another 10% of the land to the son-in-law, the joint tenancy was further severed as to that 10%, leaving the husband and the wife with an 80% interest as joint tenants. The son-in-law, who did not share the unities of time or title with the husband and the wife, took his 10% interest as a tenant in common. (B) is incorrect because it indicates that the joint tenancy of the husband and the wife has been converted into a tenancy in common as to their 80% interest. As explained above, the husband and the wife retain a joint tenancy as to this 80%. (C) and (D) are incorrect in stating that the daughter and the son-in-law have a 20% interest as joint tenants. The daughter and the son-in-law took their interests in the land at different times. These interests were not conveyed to them together. Thus, the daughter and the son-in-law each hold a separate 10% interest rather than a single combined 20% interest. Even if the husband and the wife had conveyed a 20% interest to the daughter and the son-in-law together (so that the four unities would exist as between them), a tenancy in common (rather than a joint tenancy) would be presumed under modern law absent a clear expression of intent to the contrary.

Answer to Question 26

(A) Both the homeowner and the buyer are personally liable for the deficiency. If a sale of foreclosed property does not bring enough to satisfy the mortgage debt, the mortgagee/lender can bring a personal action against the mortgagor/debtor for the deficiency (as long as the jurisdiction does not bar deficiency judgments). When the mortgagor sells the mortgaged property and gives a deed, the grantee takes subject to the mortgage, which remains on the land. If the grantee does not sign an agreement to assume the mortgage, he does not become personally liable on the loan, and the original mortgagor remains primarily and personally liable. If the grantee does sign an assumption agreement, however, the lender is considered a third-party beneficiary of the agreement, and hence may sue either the original mortgagor or the assuming grantee on the mortgage note. Here, the buyer signed the recital providing for the assumption, so she will be personally liable on the loan; (B) is therefore incorrect. (C) is incorrect because the homeowner, the original mortgagor, did not extinguish his own personal liability on the loan by obtaining the assumption agreement from the buyer. He remains secondarily liable as a surety. Thus, the bank may sue the homeowner on the original mortgage agreement. (Note that while the bank may obtain a judgment against both of them, its maximum recovery will be the $14,000 deficiency.) (D) is incorrect because the facts indicate that the jurisdiction does not bar deficiency judgments.

Answer to Question 27

(D) The patient's best argument would be that the psychiatrist has intruded into her physical seclusion. One of the four branches of the tort of invasion of privacy is intrusion upon a person's seclusion, which can be proved by showing an act of intrusion upon the seclusion of the plaintiff that would be objectionable to a reasonable person, where the thing intruded upon is private. A person's body language while revealing inner secrets to a psychiatrist is probably sufficiently private to be the subject of such an action. The fact that the patient permitted the psychiatrist to observe her does not preclude her activity from being "private"; she did not consent to a permanent record being made of it. Therefore, (D) is correct. (A) is incorrect because "false light" requires revelation of facts that attribute to the plaintiff views she does not hold or action she did not take. Here, the psychiatrist would not be revealing anything untrue about the patient. She actually made whatever gestures the tape recorded. (B) is incorrect because public disclosure of private facts requires some publication or publicity concerning the private facts. Nothing in the facts indicates that the psychiatrist has shown the tapes to anyone yet, so they were not publicly displayed. If the psychiatrist had shown the tapes publicly, the prima facie tort would be present.

(C) is incorrect because misappropriation of a person's likeness requires use of the likeness for commercial advantage, and the psychiatrist has not yet published the videotapes or gained any commercial advantage from them.

Answer to Question 28

(C) An offer for a unilateral contract best describes the agreement between the car owner and the neighbor. An offer for a unilateral contract is a promise to perform in exchange for a requested performance. Here, all that the car owner promised was to sell the car to the neighbor if he performed by tendering $12,000. The contract would be unilateral because the car owner was requiring acceptance by completion of performance rather than by a return promise. Thus, (C) is correct. (A) is incorrect because grounds for promissory estoppel are not present. Promissory estoppel will arise where a promisee detrimentally relies on a promise that the promisor should foresee will cause such reliance. Here, the neighbor did nothing to detrimentally rely on the car owner's promise; in fact, there is no indication that he took any action whatsoever. (B) is incorrect because quasi-contract is a remedy to disgorge unjust enrichment and is not a description of an actual agreement. Quasi-contract is a legal fiction imposed to force one who has been unjustly enriched to return the unjust benefit to the person it should belong to where that person had a reasonable expectation of being compensated. Here, the car owner was not unjustly enriched. (D) is incorrect because the neighbor did not receive an option. An option is a promise to keep an offer open for an agreed-upon time in exchange for consideration; it is itself a contract and must meet the requirements of contracts to be enforceable. Here, there was no consideration given for his promise to keep the offer open, so the car owner had the right to revoke the offer at any time until the neighbor began performance. Thus, there was no option contract here. (Note that if the neighbor had begun performance, the offer would become irrevocable and, under the Second Restatement, an option contract would be implied, but here there is no indication that the neighbor did anything; hence, no option contract was created.)

Answer to Question 29

(D) The friend will recover the 15% commission because she obtained a buyer for at least $5,000. Whether the friend can recover depends on whether there is a contract between her and the quilter. The friend's statement that she could find a buyer for 15% of the price of at least $5,000 was sufficiently definite to be an offer. While the quilter did not accept the offer immediately, when the friend informed her that she had found a buyer, the quilter asked for the buyer's telephone number. This was a sufficient acceptance even though the quilter did not explicitly state that she was accepting, because acceptances are tested by an objective standard, and a reasonable person would presume that the quilter's statement was an acceptance—given that the quilter knew that the information was being supplied under the terms of the friend's offer. Thus, (D) is correct. (A) is incorrect because there is nothing in the facts that indicates that a 15% commission is unconscionable. Unconscionability is tested at the time a contract is formed. A contract will be found to be unconscionable where the court finds that the terms are extremely one-sided. Such contracts are often found where the parties are of unequal bargaining positions. Here, the parties appear to be in equal bargaining positions; indeed, the quilter did not need her friend's services at all. Thus, the contract was not unconscionable. (B) is incorrect because the quilter did receive consideration. Consideration is something of legal value given in exchange for a promise or performance. Here, the friend was under no obligation to tell the quilter the identity of the prospective purchaser, and her doing so was of legal value; thus, there was consideration for the quilter's promise to pay. (C) is incorrect because it is irrelevant. The friend discharged the only condition precedent to the quilter's duty to pay under the terms of the contract—providing a buyer for at least $5,000. It does not matter that the quilter could have found a buyer on her own.

Answer to Question 30

(A) The buyer holds the property subject to both mortgages, and the bank's mortgage is subordinate to the finance company's mortgage. The jurisdiction's recording act is a race-notice statute. Under this statute, a bona fide purchaser is protected only if he records before the prior transferee or mortgagee records. Here, the buyer had record notice of the finance company's mortgage, so he was not a bona fide purchaser protected by the recording statute as to that mortgage. As to the bank's mortgage, the buyer was a bona fide purchaser because he had no notice of that mortgage executed by the owner, but he did not record until after that mortgage was recorded. Hence, the buyer holds the property subject to both mortgages. The bank's mortgage is subordinate to the finance company's mortgage because mortgagees for value are treated as "purchasers" under the recording statutes, and the finance company executed its mortgage without notice of the bank's prior mortgage and recorded it before the bank recorded its mortgage. Thus, the finance company's mortgage has priority over the bank's mortgage, and (B) is incorrect. (C) is incorrect because the property is subject to the bank's mortgage also. Unlike in a notice jurisdiction, in a race-notice jurisdiction the fact that the buyer was a subsequent bona fide purchaser without notice of the bank's mortgage is irrelevant because the bank recorded before the buyer did. (D) is incorrect because the property is subject to the finance company's mortgage also. At the time of the conveyance of the property to the buyer on April 1, the buyer had record notice of the finance company's mortgage because it was recorded in February, so the buyer takes subject to it.

Answer to Question 31

(C) To prevail, the driver will be required to show that the law is not rationally related to a legitimate government interest. Because age is not a suspect or quasi-suspect class, government action based on age will be upheld if there is a conceivable rational basis for the classification. Under the rational basis standard, laws are presumed valid, so the challenger has the burden of proof. Here, the different treatment of drivers over the age of 70 will be upheld unless the driver satisfies the difficult burden of showing that the legislation is not rationally related to a legitimate government interest. (A) is incorrect because it states the likely burden of proof when quasi-suspect classifications are involved, such as gender and legitimacy. Age is not a quasi-suspect class. (B) is incorrect because, as stated above, the burden of proof is on the challenger for classifications tested under the rational basis standard. (D) is incorrect because it uses the test for quasi-suspect classifications, which does not include classifications based on age.

Answer to Question 32

(C) The witness's testimony is admissible to show bias. A witness can be impeached, either on cross-examination or by extrinsic evidence, with evidence that suggests a bias on the part of the witness, because it tends to show that the witness has a motive to lie. Evidence that the witness disliked the party he is testifying against would qualify as evidence of bias. The witness could testify that she saw the waiter throw the rock through the restaurant's window, because such evidence would help establish the waiter's bias against the restaurant. (A) is incorrect for two reasons: Federal Rule 608 provides that evidence of prior bad acts, if offered to impeach, may not be proved through other extrinsic evidence, but may be inquired into during cross-examination. Furthermore, if the prior bad act also helps establish bias, the courts have held that extrinsic evidence will be admissible. (B) is incorrect as well for this latter reason. (D) is too broad a statement. In a broad sense, the evidence is offered to impeach the credibility of the waiter and to suggest to the jury that he may be lying under oath. However, the reason it is relevant and does not constitute impeachment on a collateral matter is because it is offered to show bias, making (C) the better answer.

Answer to Question 33

(A) The court should rule that the witness's testimony is admissible nonhearsay for the limited purpose of showing that the defendant knew that the mudflap assembly was loose. Hearsay is a statement, other than one made by the declarant while testifying at trial, offered in evidence to prove the truth of the matter asserted. When the out-of-court statement is introduced for any other purpose, the statement is not hearsay. Thus, in a negligence case when knowledge of a danger is an issue, the third person's statement of warning is admissible for the limited purpose of showing knowledge or notice on the part of the listener. Here, the statement of the third person over the CB radio can be testified to by the witness to show that the defendant was notified of the loose mudflap assembly. (B) is incorrect because the testimony would not be admissible as substantive evidence that the assembly was loose. In that case, the statement would be inadmissible hearsay because it was made by an out-of-court declarant and offered to prove the truth of what the declarant stated. (C) is incorrect because it is not necessary that the out-of-court declarant be identified. Since the statement is being offered only to show that the defendant had notice of the loose mudflap assembly, it does not matter that the witness does not know who made the statement; he can still testify to what he heard spoken to the defendant. (D) is incorrect because, as stated above, the statement is admissible nonhearsay for the limited purpose of proving that the defendant had notice that the mudflap assembly was loose.

Answer to Question 34

(A) The wheat producer will lose and recover nothing, because the wheat producer had the risk of loss at the time the wheat was stolen. Because crops such as wheat are goods, this contract will be governed by the Uniform Commercial Code (U.C.C.). The U.C.C. modifies the common law rule that destruction of the subject matter without fault of either party discharges both parties of their obligations under the contract. Under the U.C.C., the risk of loss falls on the buyer or seller according to the terms of their contract. Here, the contract called for the wheat producer to deliver the wheat "F.O.B." (free on board) St. Louis. When a contract has an F.O.B. delivery term, the seller is obligated to get the goods to the destination indicated and make a reasonable contract for freight if the destination indicated is not the buyer's place of business. The seller has the risk of loss until the goods make it to the F.O.B. destination, and thereafter the buyer has the risk. Here, the theft occurred before the seller got the goods to the F.O.B. destination (St. Louis), so the risk of loss was on the seller (the wheat producer), who is in breach for nondelivery. Thus, the wheat producer will lose and recover nothing, (B) would be incorrect even if the wheat producer did not have the risk of loss. A seller's remedy if the goods are lost or destroyed when the risk of loss is on the buyer would be the contract price. If the seller were given the value of the stolen goods, he might recover more or less than the contract price (depending on the price agreed upon by the parties), whereas the aim of the U.C.C. is to put a nonbreaching party in as good a position as he would have been in had there not been a breach. (C) would be correct if the wheat producer did not have the risk of loss—as indicated above, the nonbreaching seller's remedy for stolen goods is the contract price. (D) would be incorrect even if the wheat producer did not have the risk of loss, because merely awarding a nonbreaching seller the profits on a contract where the goods are lost or destroyed rather than the full contract price will cause him a loss, because he had to pay for the manufacture or purchase of the goods and would not be recovering those costs.

Answer to Question 35

(C) Any defense that the fruit processor might have with respect to the money it owed to the creditor would not provide the operator with a defense in the litigation. If the promisor has made an

absolute promise to pay the third-party beneficiary (and not simply a promise to pay whatever the promisee owed him), the promisor cannot assert the promisee's defenses. Hence, the fact that the processor owed only $1,800, even if it could be asserted as a defense against the creditor, cannot be asserted as a defense by the operator. (A) is incorrect because the promisee and promisor in a third-party beneficiary contract are free to modify their contract until the third party's rights have vested. While the creditor learned of the agreement before the processor and the operator modified it, he did not (i) manifest assent, (ii) bring suit, or (iii) materially rely on the agreement before it was modified; thus, his rights did not vest. Assuming the processor has performed and the operator's duty to perform is now absolute, the operator would be liable to the creditor for only $1,600 under the contract as modified. Therefore, (A) is a partial defense. (B) is also a partial defense. When a third-party beneficiary sues the promisor on the contract, the promisor may raise any defense he would have had against the promisee. Under the doctrine of reformation, either of the parties to the contract may ask a court in equity to modify the terms of the contract where the writing, through mistake or misrepresentation, does not incorporate the terms orally agreed upon. Here, the parties' mistake in memorializing the contract permits the operator to have the contract reformed to show the parties' original agreement. This provides a partial defense that the operator can use against the creditor; the operator is liable at most for $1,200 rather than $2,000. (D) is incorrect for a similar reason. The processor's failure to perform according to the terms of the contract may be asserted as a defense by the operator. The operator's liability to the creditor would be offset by whatever lost sales the operator incurred as a result of the fruit processor's late delivery.

Answer to Question 36

(A)   The court should rule for the state because the purpose of the federal law is different from the purpose of the state law. The question here is whether the state law is preempted by the federal law. Preemption will be found where it was the intent of the federal government to occupy the entire field with its regulation or where the state law is found to interfere with the federal scheme of regulation. Because the federal law here is aimed only at occupational safety, no conclusion can be drawn that the federal government intended to occupy the entire field of regulation of pesticides, and the state law does not interfere with the federal law. Hence, the state law is not preempted, and (A) is correct and (D) is incorrect. (B) is incorrect because the Tenth Amendment reserves to the states only those powers not granted to the federal government by the Constitution, and the federal government has the power to regulate pesticides under the Commerce Clause, which gives Congress plenary power to regulate any activity that, either in itself or in combination with other activities, has a substantial economic effect on, or effect on movement in, interstate commerce. The production and distribution of food products containing pesticides would be such an activity. (C) is incorrect because there need be no specific authorization for a state to regulate, as long as federal preemption does not apply. While congressional power over interstate commerce is plenary, it is not exclusive—states may regulate local aspects of interstate commerce under certain conditions.

Answer to Question 37

(A)   The shopkeeper will win because the developer established a common development scheme for the entire subdivision and the subdivision appeared to conform to the scheme. An injunction against breaching a covenant may be obtained by enforcing the covenant as an equitable servitude. An equitable servitude can be created by a writing complying with the Statute of Frauds concerning a promise that touches and concerns the land and indicates that the servitude exists, as long as notice is given to the future owners of the burdened land. Here, there was a promise

that touched and concerned the land and indicated that a servitude existed (the deed restrictions), but the promise was not contained in the supermarket's deed. Nevertheless, the court will imply the covenant here. A court will imply a covenant—known as a reciprocal negative servitude— where evidence shows that the developer had a scheme for development when sales began and the grantee in question had notice of the plan. The covenant protects the parties who purchased in reliance on the scheme. Evidence of the scheme can be obtained from the general pattern of other restrictions, and notice can be from actual notice, record notice, or inquiry notice. Here, the supermarket had inquiry notice of the restriction regarding industrial use because of the uniform residential and commercial character of the other lots in the development. Thus, the covenant will be implied and (A) is correct. (B) is incorrect because actual awareness of the restriction on the part of the firm and the supermarket is not essential; they have inquiry notice (which is a type of constructive notice). On the other hand, mere notice of the restriction would not be enough if the other elements for an implied negative servitude (common scheme when sales began) are not present. (C) and (D) are incorrect because an implied negative servitude would bind subsequent purchasers whether or not the restriction appeared in their deeds, and despite the fact that the restrictive language in the shopkeeper's deed purported to bind only the buyer and her successors. Based on the developer's representations, the shopkeeper was entitled to rely on the fact that similar restrictions would be imposed on all other purchasers of the lots.

Answer to Question 38

(B) The defendant should be convicted because he was intoxicated when he damaged the property. The defendant is being charged with reckless damage to property. A person acts recklessly when he consciously disregards a substantial or unjustifiable risk that a prohibited result will follow and this disregard constitutes a gross deviation from the standard of reasonable care. Driving earthmoving equipment while intoxicated would be considered to be reckless because of the great potential for destruction arising from the huge size and power of the equipment. Therefore, (B) is correct. (A) is incorrect because merely driving the equipment in violation of statute would not necessarily be reckless. For instance, here, the statute likely was enacted to prevent untrained persons from driving dangerous equipment, but the defendant was trained to operate the heavy equipment in question; thus, if not for the fact that he was drunk, his action would not necessarily have been reckless. Violating the statute may be evidence of negligence, but negligence is insufficient to establish recklessness. (C) is incorrect for the same reason that (B) is correct—driving the equipment while intoxicated constitutes reckless conduct. Although voluntary intoxication is a defense to a crime that requires purpose or knowledge, it is no defense to crimes involving recklessness. Even though the defendant's condition may in fact have precluded him from being consciously aware of the risk, his initial act of becoming voluntarily intoxicated was sufficiently reckless to justify holding him liable for his conduct while intoxicated. (D) is incorrect because it states the mental state for knowing conduct—if the defendant is aware that his conduct will necessarily or very likely cause a certain result, he acts knowingly with respect to that result. Recklessness is a lesser standard of fault.

Answer to Question 39

(A) The computer programmer cannot be found guilty of violating the statute because he did not know that his act would cause the damage to the business's computer that it did. Under the Model Penal Code fault standards adopted by modern criminal codes, a person acts "knowingly" with respect to the nature of his conduct when he is aware that his conduct is of that nature or that certain circumstances exist. He acts knowingly with respect to the result of his conduct when he knows that his conduct will necessarily or very likely cause such a result. When a statute establishes a culpable state of mind without indicating to which material elements of the offense

it is to apply, the statute will be interpreted as requiring that state of mind for every material element of the offense. In this case, the statute requires that the defendant "knowingly cause over $200 in damage to another's property." The requirement that the damage caused be over $200 is a material element of the offense because it defines the harmful result that will trigger criminal liability under the statute. Thus, the programmer must have known that his act of sending the computer virus would necessarily or very likely cause over $200 in damage to the business's computer to be liable under the statute in this case. (B) is incorrect because intent is not required by the statute for the programmer to be liable. Under modern criminal codes, intent is equated with purpose, which is defined as having a conscious objective to engage in certain conduct or cause a certain result. Here, the programmer could be guilty under the statute even if he did not have the objective of causing that damage to the business's computer, as long as he knew that it was at least very likely to occur. (C) is incorrect because the fact that the programmer knew that he was sending a virus is not enough to establish guilt. As discussed above, the statute also requires that he know that his conduct will or is very likely to cause over $200 in damage to the business's computer. (D) is incorrect because, even if the programmer knew that there was a small chance that this damage *might* occur, he has not acted with the required degree of culpability under the statute. The programmer must have known, at a minimum, that his conduct was very likely to cause the damage to the business's computer. Being aware that such damage could occur in a very small percentage of cases may establish that the programmer acted recklessly, but it does not establish that he acted knowingly.

Answer to Question 40

(C) Judicial notice operates as a substitute for proof as to facts that are matters of common knowledge in the community or are capable of certain verification through easily accessible, well-established sources. When a court takes judicial notice of a fact under the federal rules in a criminal case, the jury may, but is not required to, accept the fact noticed; thus, its effect is only to relieve the prosecutor of her burden of producing evidence on that fact. (A) is incorrect because taking judicial notice does not affect the burden of persuasion, which is the burden of one litigant to overcome the case of the opposing litigant. (B) is incorrect because judicial notice of a fact does not establish proof of the fact beyond a reasonable doubt; as discussed above, the jury is not required to accept the fact noticed. (D) is incorrect because it is the rule for civil cases; in criminal cases, the jury is instructed that it may, but is not required to, accept as conclusive any fact judicially noticed.

Answer to Question 41

(D) The homeowner will likely prevail on the contract claim because he did not enter into a contract with the roofer. To form a contract, there must be a valid offer and acceptance. The homeowner made an offer, but the roofer rejected the offer the next day with his first phone call. Once an offer is rejected, the offeree's power of acceptance is destroyed. Thus, the roofer's second call was not an acceptance, but rather an offer. The homeowner did nothing to accept the roofer's offer, and this is not the type of case where silence will be deemed to be an acceptance (*e.g.,* where the parties have so agreed or where that has been their course of dealing). Thus, there was no acceptance and no contract. Therefore, (D) is correct and (A) is incorrect. (B) is incorrect because it suggests a restitutionary remedy in a quasi-contract action (which allows a party to recover the value of his services under some circumstances even if a contract cannot be established), and the question specifically states that the roofer's action is limited to a breach of contract claim. (C) is incorrect because whether the homeowner was bound depends on whether there was a valid offer and acceptance, not on whether he was aware of the performance. If the homeowner had accepted and did not know of the performance until he returned, there would still be an enforceable contract.

Answer to Question 42

(B) The seller will most likely prevail for the full contract price. Although jurisdictions differ as to which party has the risk of loss, the majority rule is that where property subject to an enforceable contract for sale is destroyed without the fault of either party before the date set for closing, the risk of loss is on the buyer. Thus, the buyer must pay the contract price despite a loss due to fire, unless the contract provides otherwise. Here, the house was destroyed by fire after the seller and buyer entered into their contract for the sale of the house, but before the closing date. The contract was silent regarding the risk of loss. Thus, under the majority rule, the risk of loss is on the buyer. As a result, the seller is entitled to receive specific performance of the contract, meaning that the buyer must pay the full contract price. (A) is incorrect because it allows the buyer to tender less than the full contract price. With the buyer bearing the risk of loss, he must pay the $425,000 contract price despite the decrease in the property's value due to the fire. (C) and (D) are incorrect because they conclude that the seller is not entitled to specific performance. As explained above, the seller is entitled to specific performance because the risk of loss is on the buyer. (C) is also incorrect because, absent a provision to the contrary, neither the seller nor the buyer has a duty to carry insurance on the property. However, both the seller and the buyer have insurable interests once the contract is signed (*i.e.,* either or both *could* obtain insurance). (D) is also incorrect because "marketable" title does not refer to whether the seller would be able to sell a destroyed house. It refers to a deed free of any possible dispute as to who is the owner of the property.

Answer to Question 43

(B) It was error to admit the reputation evidence from the co-worker because, in civil trials, character evidence is inadmissible to prove that the litigant acted in conformity with that character. An exception exists when the litigant's character is directly in issue (*e.g.,* in a defamation action), but that is not the case here. (A) is incorrect because it is not the rule in civil trials; it is, however, the rule for criminal trials—evidence of character is admissible only if the party puts his character in issue. (C) is incorrect because character evidence generally is inadmissible in civil cases whether or not the witness had personal knowledge of specific conduct of the litigant. Moreover, when character evidence is admissible, it is permissible to testify to the litigant's reputation in the community; knowledge of specific acts is not required. (D) is incorrect because there is no exception to the rule against reputation evidence in civil cases that would allow character evidence that can be verified by an unbiased witness. It would, however, be proper to call the unbiased witness to testify as to how much the defendant drank the night of the accident.

Answer to Question 44

(C) The witness can testify to one of the defendant's statements but not the other. An admission is a statement made by a party offered by the opponent of that party that is relevant to an issue in the case. If an out-of-court statement qualifies as an admission, it will not be excluded by the hearsay rule. However, it will be excluded if there is a specific rule excluding the admission. Federal Rule 408 provides that settlement offers and factual statements made during settlement negotiations are inadmissible if offered to prove liability, invalidity of the claim, or to establish the amount of damage. Rule 408 only applies, however, when there is a dispute between the parties. A statement made at the scene of an accident would rarely qualify. Federal Rule 409 excludes evidence

of the payment or offer to pay medical expenses if offered to help establish liability for an injury. Rule 409, however, does not exclude factual statements made in conjunction with the payment or offer. Such factual statements would be admissible as an admission by a party. Hence, the defendant's statement would not qualify as a settlement offer. His statement "I'll take care of your medical bills" would be excluded under Rule 409. His statement "I was not paying attention" would not be excluded by Rule 409 and would be admissible as an admission. (A) is wrong because the defendant's statement is not a settlement offer. (B) is tempting but wrong. Regardless of whether the plaintiff was negligent per se, the defendant's statement would probably be admissible on the issue of comparative fault or the issue of damages. (D) is too broad a statement. As discussed above, the defendant's statement "I'll take care of your medical bills" would be excluded.

Answer to Question 45

(C) The protester will recover because the logger intended to frighten her. To make out a prima facie case for battery, a plaintiff must show an act by the defendant that will bring about a harmful or offensive contact to the plaintiff, intent on the part of the defendant to do the act, and causation. Here, there was definitely a harmful contact, but the logger did not have the intent to cause the contact. Nevertheless, he will be liable for battery because he did have the intent to assault the protester (*i.e.,* he intended to cause the protester apprehension of immediate harmful or offensive contact). Under the doctrine of transferred intent, his intent to commit the assault will be transferred to the battery action to complete the prima facie case. Thus, (C) is correct, and (A) is incorrect. (B) is incorrect because although the defective axe may have been a cause in fact (*i.e.,* the "but for" cause) of the protester's injury, it did not break the causal connection between the defendant's act and the plaintiff's injury. As established above, the logger's act was also a cause in fact of the protester's injury and a substantial factor in bringing it about. Hence, he will be held liable for the unintended consequences of his act. (D) is incorrect because provocation is not a defense to battery. If the protester's remarks had caused the logger to reasonably believe that he was in danger, he would have had the defense of self-defense, but the protester's words were not sufficient to make such a claim.

Answer to Question 46

(B) The nephew should prevail because his interest is a legal interest in the property and could have been discovered by the developer in the grantor-grantee index. The owner granted the buyer an easement by express grant. The easement was properly recorded with the buyer's deed, and because it contained no limitation, it is perpetual. The easement here is appurtenant (*i.e.,* one benefiting the holder of the easement), because it benefits the buyer's land (the dominant tenement) and burdens the owner's land (the servient tenement). Where there is an easement appurtenant, it passes with a transfer of the dominant tenement, even though it is an interest in the servient tenement. Thus, the buyer's easement passed to his nephew. Because the easement is perpetual, it is binding on all of the owner's subsequent transferees regardless of whether the conveyance refers to the easement, as long as the transferees have notice of it. Many courts will find record or constructive notice here because the nephew's property is adjacent to the developer's property, is deeded from a common grantor (the owner), and includes the easement in the original deed from the owner. Thus, (B) is correct because it best describes the legal effect of the easement for the nephew to prevail. (A) is incorrect because the parties did not create a covenant to allow access to the lake (*i.e.,* a promise that is something less than an interest in land); rather, the owner expressly granted the buyer an easement, which is an actual interest in the land that is a legal incident of the property owned by the developer. Thus, the nephew need not resort to an estoppel argument to obtain the injunction. (C) is incorrect because it is untrue. Purchasers of land are subject to easements in their chains of title regardless of the type of recording index, because they are deemed to have constructive notice of any easement that was recorded. There is no independent duty to discover riparian rights when there is no tract index. The nephew can enforce the easement here only because it was in the chain of title of the developer's property. (D) is incorrect because it is too broad. An easement must comply with all formal requisites of a deed, and deeds are valid only as to those who have notice of them (actual, constructive, or inquiry). Hence, the easement must be recorded in the chain of title; if the easement is not properly recorded, it might not be binding on all successive owners.

Answer to Question 47

(A) The agreement between the distiller and the club is a single bilateral contract because it is an exchange of mutual promises, supported by valuable consideration. The existence of a contract requires mutual assent, *i.e.,* an offer and an acceptance. An offer creates a power of acceptance in the offeree and a corresponding liability on the part of the offeror. To be an offer, a communication must create a reasonable expectation in the offeree that the offeror is willing to enter into a contract on the basis of the offered terms. Such a reasonable expectation depends on whether there was: (i) an expression of a promise or undertaking to enter into a contract; (ii) certainty and definiteness in the essential terms; and (iii) communication to the offeree. If an offeror promises contractual liability in exchange for a counterpromise by the offeree to do a stipulated act, the exchange of promises creates a bilateral contract. On the other hand, if an offer makes acceptance possible only by performing a stipulated act, a unilateral contract is contemplated. Any objective manifestation of the offeree's counterpromise, whether by words or acts, is usually sufficient for acceptance and the formation of a bilateral contract, *i.e.,* where the offeree knowingly takes steps that a reasonable person would consider an acceptance. The December 3 letter from the sales director (on behalf of the distiller) expressed an undertaking to supply all of the club's vodka requirements for the next calendar year. This letter contained the essential terms of the transaction: (i) identity of the offeree and subject matter; (ii) price; (iii) time of delivery; and (iv) quantity (an agreement to buy all of one's requirements is capable of being made certain by reference to objective, extrinsic facts). The definiteness and certainty of these terms made reasonable an expectation on the part of the club that the distiller had expressed an intention to contract, and also rendered the agreement capable of enforcement. Consequently, the communication of these terms to the club constituted an offer. This offer could be accepted by the club's counterpromise to purchase all of its vodka requirements for the next calendar year from the distiller. Thus, a bilateral contract was contemplated. The manager's letter objectively manifested the club's counterpromise to satisfy its vodka requirements for the next calendar year through purchases from the distiller, on the terms stated in the distiller's letter. This was an acceptance. Consideration is present because: (i) the distiller is doing something that it is under no legal obligation to do (supplying the club with its vodka requirements for the year); and (ii) the club is refraining from doing something that it has a legal right to do (purchasing its vodka for the next year from a source other than the distiller). Consequently, there is an enforceable bilateral contract and (D) is incorrect. (B) is incorrect for two reasons: First, the agreement between the distiller and the club calls for the purchase and sale of a quantity of vodka sufficient to meet the needs of the club for the next calendar year. Thus, there is one contract, for the duration of one year. The fact that deliveries of varying size are made once a month does not convert this into a *series* of contracts. Second, the distiller's offer did not make acceptance possible only by performing a stipulated act; *i.e.,* the club could (and did) accept by making a counterpromise. Therefore, this was not a unilateral contract. Similarly, (C) is incorrect for two reasons: First, as explained in the analysis of (B), this is a single contract, not a series of contracts. Second, an option is a contract in which the offeree gives consideration for a promise by the offeror not to revoke an outstanding offer. The facts do not indicate the existence of such a contract.

Answer to Question 48

(C) The stepmother's best defense is that the contract was oral. Generally, contracts need not be in writing to be enforceable; however, under the Statute of Frauds, certain contracts must be evidenced by a writing signed by the party to be charged to be enforceable. One such contract is to pay the debt of another, such as the stepmother's promise here to pay the father's debt if he does not pay. Therefore, (C) is correct. (A) is incorrect because the promise was not illusory. A promise is illusory when there is not consideration on both sides of the contract. Here, the daughter will receive $10,000 if she performs, and the stepmother will receive the daughter's detriment of not doing something that she has a right to do, which is valid consideration (the benefit to the promisor need not have economic value). The daughter's performance is valid consideration even though she has already promised her father to refrain from smoking (*i.e.,* it is not a preexisting duty), because she was not bound by her promise to her father. The offer was for a unilateral contract (*i.e.,* one seeking performance rather than a promise to perform), and so could be accepted only by performance. The daughter had not yet performed when her stepmother made her own promise to her, so she had not yet accepted her father's contract and was not bound by her promise to refrain from smoking. Therefore, she was not under a preexisting duty, and the stepmother's promise served as additional consideration for her performance. Note also that a surety such as the stepmother will be bound by her promise to pay another's debt as long as she makes her promise before the creditor (the daughter) performs or promises to perform; the surety need not receive any separate consideration. (B) is incorrect because the daughter's giving up what she had a legal right to do—even if harmful—is sufficient consideration to support a contract, so the stepmother could be bound to pay even though the contract was beneficial to the daughter. (D) is incorrect because the daughter's quitting smoking was the consideration that the stepmother received. Moreover, as explained above, a surety need not receive consideration separate from the consideration of the person whose debt she is back-stopping.

Answer to Question 49

(D) The accused may not be convicted of attempted murder because he lacked the necessary intent. A criminal attempt consists of (i) conduct that brings the defendant in close proximity to the completed offense, and (ii) intent to commit the completed crime. In other words, the defendant must have the intent to perform an act and obtain a result that would constitute the crime charged if achieved. Regardless of the intent required for the completed offense, an attempt always requires a specific intent. Thus, attempted murder requires the specific intent to kill another person, even though the mens rea for murder itself does not require a specific intent—had the victim or her daughter died, the accused could be convicted of murder because malice aforethought can be established here by awareness of an unjustifiably high risk to human life (*i.e.,* "abandoned and malignant heart"). However, the accused did not have the intent to kill either victim, so he lacked the intent necessary for attempt. (D) is therefore correct, and (A), (B), and (C) are incorrect. In answering questions such as this, remember to be objective and answer the question asked. Although the accused is surely guilty of some crimes (*e.g.,* assault and battery), he is not guilty of the crime charged.

Answer to Question 50

(D) The objection should be overruled because the accountant's testimony is admissible. As the plaintiff's accountant, he has personal knowledge of the relevant financial information, and so may testify. Although the accountant indicated that he could not remember the plaintiff's income, the rules of evidence allow a witness's recollection to be refreshed by just about anything. The witness may not read from the writing while he testifies; it is used solely to jog his memory. While the opposing counsel is allowed to examine the item being used to refresh the witness's testimony and may cross-examine the witness about it, he may not object to it. Therefore, (D) is correct. (A) is incorrect because the item used to refresh a witness's memory is not admitted into evidence, so it is not offered for the truth of the matter it asserts. Therefore, it cannot violate the hearsay rule. (B) is incorrect because the best evidence rule requires only that when the contents of a writing are sought to be proved, the writing itself should be entered into evidence, if it is available. Here, the contents of the tax return are not being entered into evidence; rather, the accountant is merely using the tax return to refresh his memory. Therefore, the best evidence rule does not apply. (C) is incorrect because the tax return is not being offered as a past recollection recorded. If a witness cannot remember a fact while testifying, counsel may attempt to refresh his memory, as counsel has done here. If, unlike the facts here, the witness still cannot remember, the thing used to refresh the witness's recollection can be read into evidence if a proper foundation is laid for its admissibility. In such a case, the "thing" must be a writing made by the witness at a time when the facts were known to him, and this is known as a past recollection recorded. The device was not needed here since the accountant was able to recall the facts requested after he saw the tax return.

Answer to Question 51

(C) The best way for the landowner to accomplish his goals is to grant the city an easement for recreational use for two years. An easement would allow the city to use the land only for the purposes provided for in the easement, and the landowner could limit the purposes to recreational uses. Thus, (C) is the best answer. (A) would not be a good choice because if the landowner dedicated the land to public use, he would be giving title to the land to the government, so he would not be able to reclaim the land and build his stadium in the future. (B) would not be a good choice because a lease would give the city more control over the land than an easement, and would be more complicated to create. A lease grants the lessee the exclusive right to possess the premises, and broad rights to use them in any manner, unless specifically restricted. Thus, if the landowner leases the land to the city, he would not have access to the land, and if he wanted it used only for recreational purposes, he would have to specifically restrict any undesired uses. Any restriction not included in the lease will be unenforceable. An easement, on the other hand, grants only a limited interest in the land—to use it for only those purposes stated in the ease-ment; thus, it would be better than a lease. (D) is not a good choice because covenants usually are made in conjunction with a lease, deed, or other instrument; they promise some act or forbear-ance with respect to property and are generally not used to grant rights for access to property.

Answer to Question 52

(B) The chief justice could recover if the associate justice made the statements knowing that they were false. To make out a case for defamation, a plaintiff must show that the defendant published a defamatory statement of or concerning the plaintiff that damaged his reputation. If the plaintiff is a public figure (or public official) or a matter of public concern is involved, the plaintiff must also prove falsity and fault on the defendant's part. The type of fault required when a public figure or public official is involved is "actual malice," defined as knowledge that the statement was false or reckless disregard as to its truth or falsity. Here, the chief justice is a public official. Thus, he would be able to recover if the associate justice made the statement knowing that it was false, since all of the required elements would be present: (i) the statement was defamatory of the chief justice and communicated to a third person; (ii) damage to reputation is presumed because it was slander per se (it adversely reflected on his abilities in his profession); and (iii) if the

associate justice knew that the statement was false, there is fault and falsity. Thus, (B) is correct. (A) is incorrect because negligence and actual injury would not be sufficient to establish the prima facie case. Since the judge is a public official, malice must be proved, and malice can be shown only if the defendant made the statement knowing that it was false or in reckless disregard as to its truth; negligence is not enough. Once malice is established, actual injury is not required. (C) is incorrect because, even if the associate justice hated the chief justice and wanted to harm him, he would not be liable for defamation if the statements were true, since a public official such as the chief justice must prove that the statement was false. ("Malice" in the constitutional sense is different from malice in the sense of ill will.) Thus, it would not be enough merely to show that the associate justice had bad motives. (D) is essentially the same answer as (C) and is incorrect for similar reasons.

Answer to Question 53

(B) The husband can be convicted of attempted murder and conspiracy to commit murder. The husband is liable for attempted murder under principles of accomplice liability because he solicited the ex-convict to commit murder with the intent that his wife be murdered. Where the person solicited proceeds far enough to be liable for attempt, the solicitor will be a party to that attempt. Here, the ex-convict's conduct satisfies the act requirement for attempted murder; therefore, the husband is liable as an accomplice to attempted murder. The husband is also liable for conspiracy to commit murder because, acting with the intent to kill his wife, he entered into an agreement with the ex-convict to kill her. Under the majority rule, conspirators can be convicted of both criminal conspiracy and the crime they committed pursuant to the conspiracy; *i.e.,* there is no merger. (A) and (C) are incorrect because, unlike conspiracy, solicitation merges into the principal offense. Thus, the husband cannot be convicted of both solicitation and attempted murder, as those choices state. (D) is incorrect because, as discussed above, conspiracy does not merge into the completed crime. Also, the fact that the charge of conspiracy was dropped against the ex-convict does not preclude a conviction of conspiracy against the husband. Although an *acquittal* of the other party to a conspiracy precludes conviction of the remaining defendant, this rule does not apply when the other party is charged with a lesser offense or is no longer being prosecuted.

Answer to Question 54

(B) The statement should be excluded from evidence. In *Miranda v. Arizona,* the Fifth Amendment privilege against compelled self-incrimination became the basis for ruling on the admissibility of a confession. *Miranda* warnings and a valid waiver are *minimum* prerequisites to the admissibility of any statement made by the accused in a custodial interrogation. Nonetheless, states are free to provide greater protection to a defendant. Here, the state statute provides for greater rights, in that it requires the interrogator to inform the defendant about the nature of the crimes he wishes to discuss with the accused, and the state supreme court has held that statements obtained in violation of a defendant's statutory interrogation rights must be excluded. Thus, under state law, the statement should be excluded, making (B) the correct answer and (C) incorrect. (D) is incorrect; a state statute is sufficient to provide the right to an accused under the state supreme court ruling. (A) is substantively incorrect. The rights warning in this question would have complied with *Miranda.*

Answer to Question 55

(D) The investor has an enforceable mortgage for $30,000, and can enforce the promissory note against the buyer for any deficiency. All parties to a mortgage can transfer their interests. When a note is properly transferred, a mortgage will automatically follow it as a general rule; no special written assignment is necessary. If the note is negotiable, it is considered to embody the obligation, and payment will count only if made to the holder of the note. Any payment made by the mortgagor to the original mortgagee after a transfer of the note has taken place will not be binding on the holder, even if the mortgagor had no notice of the transfer. Here, the promissory note given to the seller by the buyer was properly negotiated to the investor, and the mortgage on the land automatically follows it; (A) is therefore incorrect. (B) and (C) are incorrect because the jurisdiction specifically allows for a deficiency judgment against the mortgagor. As holder of the note, the investor can recover against the buyer personally if the proceeds of the foreclosure action are insufficient to satisfy the mortgage debt. (B) is also incorrect because the investor is the holder of the note; even though he did not pay its face value, he can enforce it for that amount. Thus, as (D) states, the investor's mortgage interest is $30,000, and he can enforce the note against the buyer for that amount less the proceeds of the foreclosure sale.

Answer to Question 56

(A) The finance company may pay off the bank's mortgage to preserve its own mortgage interest on the land. Because foreclosure will destroy all interests that are junior to the mortgage being foreclosed, the junior mortgagee has the right to pay it off (*i.e.,* redeem it) to avoid being wiped out by its foreclosure. Hence, the finance company may pay off the outstanding balance of the bank's mortgage and be subrogated to the bank's rights against the mortgagor. (B) is incorrect because the junior lienholder's right is not dependent on the statutory right of redemption. A statutory right of redemption, available in about half the states, gives the mortgagor and sometimes junior lienholders a statutory right to redeem for some fixed period *after* the foreclosure sale has occurred; the amount to be paid is generally the foreclosure sale price, rather than the amount of the original debt. Here, regardless of the statute, the finance company has the right to pay off the bank's mortgage *before* the foreclosure sale to protect its interest. (C) is incorrect because a junior mortgage does not need to be in default for that lienholder to have a right to pay off the senior lien in default. Because the finance company's mortgage will be terminated regardless of whether it is in default, the finance company may pay off the bank's mortgage. (D) is incorrect. While the mortgagor holds an equitable right to redeem the land prior to foreclosure, a junior lienholder also has an equitable right to pay off the senior lien prior to foreclosure and become subrogated to the rights of the senior lienholder.

Answer to Question 57

(A) The testimony of the acquaintance is admissible, but only for impeachment purposes. For the purpose of impeaching the credibility of a witness, a party may show that the witness has, on another occasion, made statements that are inconsistent with some material part of her present testimony. Here, the acquaintance is prepared to testify that the girlfriend stated that she had been unable to get out of bed because of severe back pain at the time that she testified that she was with the defendant and had taken over the driving, a fact that would be material to the allegations in the lawsuit. Thus, the testimony is properly admissible for purposes of impeachment. (C) is incorrect because, under the Federal Rules, an inconsistent statement may be proved by either cross-examination or extrinsic evidence. (D) is incorrect because, while extrinsic evidence is admissible only if the witness is, at some point, given an opportunity to explain or deny the allegedly inconsistent statement, the opportunity need not come before the introduction of the statement under the Federal Rules; the testimony may be admitted now and the girlfriend subsequently be given an opportunity to explain or deny it. (B) is incorrect because the testimony is hearsay that is not admissible for substantive purposes because it does not fall under the exception for declarations of physical condition. Under the Federal Rules, declarations of present bodily condition are admissible as an exception to the hearsay rule when made to anyone, not just a physician, whereas declarations of past physical condition are admissible as a hearsay exception only if made to medical personnel to assist in diagnosing or treating the condition. Here, the girlfriend's statement to the acquaintance pertained to her past physical condition, and there is no indication that the acquaintance is her doctor. Hence, the girlfriend's statement does not fall within these or any other exceptions to the hearsay rule, and is admissible for impeachment purposes only.

Answer to Question 58

(D) The evidence is admissible because it is a declaration of the defendant's present state of mind, offered as circumstantial evidence that he carried out his intent to go to his mother-in-law's house. Hearsay is a statement, other than one made by the declarant while testifying at the trial or hearing, offered in evidence to prove the truth of the matter asserted. One exception to the hearsay rule is for statements of present state of mind. Declarations of an existing state of mind are admissible not only when the declarant's state of mind is directly in issue and material to the controversy, but also when the declarant's state of mind is not directly in issue, but the declarations of intent are offered to show subsequent acts of the declarant; *i.e.,* a declaration of intent to do something in the future is offered as circumstantial evidence tending to show that the intent was carried out. The defendant's statement that he was going to his mother-in-law's house is a statement made by the declarant out of court. This statement is offered to prove the truth of the matter asserted therein: that on the day of the alleged armed robbery, the defendant intended to go to his mother-in-law's house. This is being offered as circumstantial evidence that he did go to his mother-in-law's house. Thus, the statement is hearsay. However, the statement does come within the present state of mind exception. Although the defendant's state of mind is not directly in issue, his statement is a declaration of intent to do something offered to show that such intent was in fact carried out. Therefore, the statement is admissible under the present state of mind exception to the hearsay rule. [*See* Mutual Life Insurance Co. v. Hillmon (1892)] (A) incorrectly states that the evidence is not within any hearsay exception. As stated above, the evidence is within the present state of mind exception. (C) is incorrect because the evidence is being offered to prove the truth of the matter stated, that the defendant intended to go to his mother-in-law's house on December 16, because his intent provides circumstantial evidence that he did in fact do so. Thus, the statement is hearsay. (B) is incorrect because the evidence tends to make the defendant's absence at the time and place of the alleged crime more probable than it would be without the evidence. This fact is of consequence to the determination of the defendant's guilt of the crime charged. Thus, the evidence is relevant.

Answer to Question 59

(B) The strongest basis for dismissal is that the action is not ripe for adjudication. The Constitution gives the federal courts power to hear cases and controversies, and the Supreme Court has interpreted this to mean that the federal courts should hear a case only when there is some real harm or immediate threat of harm involved. There is no immediate threat of harm under the facts here because the man's action is only in the planning stage—he is not yet married and has not yet fathered a child. Thus, his case is not ripe and (B) is correct. (A) is not a good defense because the question presented is not a political question; it involves the man's constitutional rights. Political questions involve issues committed by the Constitution to other branches of the government and issues inherently incapable of judgment and enforcement by the courts. (C) is incorrect because the statute imposes on a woman's right to decide whether to have an abortion as well as on the right of a married couple to procreate, which are within the right of privacy protected by

the Fourteenth Amendment. Therefore, a substantial federal question is involved. (D) is incorrect because the man does not need his future wife to join in the litigation; the statute infringes on his own rights. Assuming the truth of his allegations, he has a personal stake in the outcome of the action because he wants to have children before he is 25 and the law may deter him from doing so. At this point, however, his claim is not yet ripe for adjudication.

Answer to Question 60

(C) The witness's testimony is admissible because it is evidence of a matter in issue. Generally, evidence is admissible if it is relevant. The Federal Rules define relevant evidence as any evidence tending to make the existence of any fact of consequence to the determination of the action (materiality) more or less probable than it would be without the evidence (probativeness). Whether the newspaper received the request for the retraction governs whether the statutory prerequisite for the defamation action here was met, so the testimony is material. The testimony is also probative because, if the newspaper received a letter from the plaintiff on the day in question, it is likely that it was the request for retraction; thus, the testimony makes it more likely that the fact sought to be proved (that the plaintiff requested a retraction) was true. Furthermore, the witness is competent to testify about receipt of the letter because people are competent to testify to facts within their personal knowledge, and whether the witness remembered receiving a letter from the plaintiff on the day in question is certainly within her personal knowledge. Thus, (C) is correct. (A) is incorrect because the witness's competency to testify as to whether she received a letter on a particular day is unaffected by her employment status. Her employment status may be relevant to other evidentiary issues (such as whether she may be treated as a hostile witness and whether her statement can be deemed to be an admission), but it is irrelevant here. (B) is incorrect because the best evidence rule is not relevant here. That rule provides that when the contents of a writing are sought to be proved at trial, the writing itself should be introduced if it is available. Here, the witness is not testifying as to the contents of the writing, but only to the fact that the newspaper received a letter from the plaintiff on the day in question. (The plaintiff is relying on his own testimony to create an inference that the letter was a request for retraction.) (D) is incorrect because the witness is not seeking to testify to an admission, which is a prior statement made or act done by a party. She is merely testifying to an event that she recalled: the receipt of a letter from the plaintiff. Hence, the testimony does not even raise a hearsay issue.

Answer to Question 61

(C) The new agreement between the two parties is enforceable as an accord. An accord is an agreement in which one party to an existing contract agrees to accept, in lieu of the performance that he is supposed to receive from the other party, some other, different performance. Generally, an accord must be supported by consideration, but the consideration may be of a lesser value than the originally bargained-for consideration in the prior contract, as long as it is of a different type or the claim is to be paid to a third party. Here, the debtor's obligation to provide the creditor with a new entertainment system was a sufficient new consideration to form a valid accord. (A) is incorrect because the preexisting legal duty rule does not apply when the party's duty is varied in some way, as the debtor's duty was here. (B) is incorrect because it is immaterial whether the benefit to the creditor in the accord agreement has the same value as the original debt here; courts will find sufficient consideration as long as the consideration is in any way new or different. Here, regardless of how much the entertainment system would have cost the creditor, the variance in the debtor's duty (*i.e.,* payment is in the form of an entertainment system rather than cash) is sufficient to support the accord agreement. (D) is incorrect because the original agreement was not a sale of goods contract under the U.C.C., which provides that an agreement modifying a

contract subject to Article 2 needs no consideration to be binding, as long as the parties were acting in good faith. Here, however, the original obligation was to pay a debt on a promissory note, so this provision does not apply.

Answer to Question 62

(A) The car buyer may enjoin the dealership's action because the dealership currently does not have the right to enforce the promissory note. A valid accord, taken alone, does not discharge the prior contract. It merely suspends the right to enforce it in accordance with the terms of the accord contract. The performance of the accord agreement, which is called satisfaction, discharges not only the accord agreement but the original contract as well. Where the accord agreement is breached by the creditor by suing on the original contract, as is the case here, the debtor may seek to have the action enjoined by raising the accord agreement as an equitable defense. (B) is incorrect because the accord agreement does not discharge the original obligation, it only suspends it. Hence, if the car buyer were to breach the accord agreement, the dealership could sue on either the original promissory note obligation or the accord agreement. (C) is incorrect because the car buyer does not need to establish promissory estoppel or detrimental reliance to enforce the accord agreement. Even if the car buyer has not yet relied to her detriment on the dealership's promise, she can enforce the accord agreement, which suspends her obligation on the original debt. (D) is incorrect because, while the car buyer may wait until she is damaged by the dealership's lawsuit and then sue for breach of the accord agreement, she is not limited to that remedy. As discussed above, she may enjoin the dealership's action by raising the accord agreement as an equitable defense.

Answer to Question 63

(B) The thief's withdrawal from the conspiracy absolves him of liability for the subsequent murder committed by the felon, but does not provide a defense to the crime of conspiracy. Conspiracy consists of: (i) an agreement between two or more persons; (ii) an intent to enter into an agreement; and (iii) an intent to achieve the objective of the agreement. In addition, most states require an overt act in furtherance of the conspiracy (although an act of mere preparation will suffice). Each conspirator is liable for the crimes of all other conspirators if such crimes were committed in furtherance of the objectives of the conspiracy and they were a natural and probable consequence of the conspiracy, *i.e.,* foreseeable. However, if a conspirator has made a legally effective withdrawal from the conspiracy at the time of commission of such a crime, he will not be liable for that crime. Withdrawal requires an affirmative act that notifies all members of the conspiracy and is done in time for them to have the opportunity to abandon their plans. Withdrawal, however, will not be a defense to the conspiracy charge itself. The thief and the felon agreed to rob elderly women whom they followed home from the shopping center. They intended to enter into this agreement and to achieve its objective (to rob the women). Coming to the shopping center at the agreed-on time, armed with a gun or a knife, constitutes a sufficient act in furtherance of the conspiracy. Consequently, the thief has satisfied all of the elements of conspiracy. Given that he cannot use withdrawal from the conspiracy as a defense to that charge, he will be convicted of conspiracy. (A) is therefore incorrect. Ordinarily, the thief would also be guilty of the woman's murder. The killing resulted from a beating administered during the course of the robbery; thus, it was committed in furtherance of the conspiracy's objective. Also, it was foreseeable that death might result where all of the intended victims were elderly women. However, the thief had withdrawn from the conspiracy prior to the time the killing was committed. He made an effective withdrawal when he explicitly told the felon that he no longer wanted any part of the plan at a time when there was still an opportunity to abandon the plan. Thus, criminal liability for the killing will not attach to the thief, and (C) and (D) are therefore incorrect.

Answer to Question 64

(C) If the shopper brings an action for assault against the store and does not prevail, it will be because the security guard acted reasonably under the shopkeeper's privilege. To make out a prima facie case for assault, the plaintiff must prove that the defendant's actions caused the plaintiff to be in reasonable apprehension of an immediate harmful or offensive contact, and that the defendant intended to cause this reaction. The shopper here can establish a prima facie case because the guard's pulling out the handcuffs and reaching for the shopper's arm created a reasonable apprehension of an immediate offensive contact, and the guard intended to create this apprehension so that the shopper would willingly step to the side to allow his bags to be checked. However, the store could raise the defense of recapture of chattels if the guard reasonably believed that the shopper was a shoplifter. This defense, which allows the property owner (or his agent) to use reasonable force or the threat of force to recapture his chattels from a tortfeasor who has stolen them, has a specialized application in the shopkeepers' privilege to reasonably detain individuals whom they reasonably believe to be in possession of shoplifted goods. Although the privilege usually applies as a defense to a false imprisonment action, it is equally applicable as a defense to other intentional torts. Hence, if the security guard's belief that the shopper was a shoplifter was reasonable, the defense would be available and the store would not be liable for the assault. (A) is incorrect because assault is actionable without alleging a specific injury or damages. (B) is incorrect because the only intent required for assault is the intent to place someone in apprehension of a harmful or offensive contact, and the guard had the requisite intent here. The plaintiff does not have to show that the defendant intended to harm him. (D) would be the best answer if (C) were not available, because it suggests that the guard was justified in acting because the shopper acted unreasonably. However, (C) is a better answer because it directly addresses the reasonableness of the guard's actions.

Answer to Question 65

(D) The teenager will be able to recover for his humiliation because he was falsely imprisoned. All of the elements of a prima facie case for false imprisonment are present in these facts: an act or omission by defendant that confined or restrained plaintiff to a bounded area, intent by the defendant to do so, and causation. Here, the confinement was brought about by the invalid use of legal authority by the security officer. The mall cannot avail itself of the shopkeepers' privilege for detaining a suspected shoplifter because the detention must be for only a reasonable period of time for the purpose of making an investigation, and here the hour-long detention clearly was unreasonable given the officer's failure to even make an investigation during the detention. On proof of the prima facie case, the plaintiff can recover all foreseeable damages that arise from the tort. Humiliation is a foreseeable consequence of a false arrest, so the teenager will be able to recover. (A) is incorrect. While humiliation is not an actionable tort in and of itself, humiliation is a recognized element of damages from the commission of an intentional tort. (B) is incorrect because it relies on the shopkeepers' privilege to detain, and the privilege was not available here even though the security officer reasonably suspected that the teenager was breaking into a car. The manner and length of detention must also be reasonable for the privilege to apply, and here the detention was for an unreasonable length of time under the circumstances. (C) is incorrect because the officer's action need not amount to extreme and outrageous conduct to make the mall liable for false imprisonment; it is sufficient that the officer intentionally detained the teenager without a right to do so.

Answer to Question 66

(D) The landowner will prevail because the neighbor's use of the water is not a natural use under the

riparian doctrine. In jurisdictions following the riparian doctrine for allocation of water in watercourses, the reasonable use theory permits each riparian owner (*i.e.*, owner of land bordering the watercourse) a reasonable use of the water, and a downstream owner cannot enjoin the reasonable use by an upstream riparian owner unless it substantially interferes with the downstream owner's comparable use. Under this doctrine, uses are categorized as natural or artificial. Natural uses (*e.g.*, household consumption, gardening, limited grazing) prevail over artificial uses (*e.g.*, irrigation, manufacturing); riparian owners can take all the water they need for natural uses, but cannot take water for artificial uses unless there is enough water for the domestic needs of all other riparian owners. Here, the neighbor's use of the creek for irrigation is an artificial use, so the landowner's use of the water for domestic purposes takes priority over the neighbor's use, even though the landowner's use may substantially interfere with the neighbor's use. (A) is incorrect because the fact that the neighbor's use was prior to the landowner's is determinative in a state following the prior appropriation doctrine, but not in a riparian doctrine state. (B) is incorrect because water rights cannot be acquired by prescription. (C) is incorrect because the fact that the landowner's use allows partial satisfaction of the neighbor's needs is not controlling. Because the landowner's use is a natural use and the neighbor's is an artificial use, the landowner would prevail even if his use totally deprived the neighbor of her water needs.

Answer to Question 67

(B) One who aids, counsels, commands, or encourages another in the commission of a crime and who is present when the crime is committed is generally guilty of the substantive crime by virtue of his aiding and abetting the principal (under the common law, a principal in the second degree). Because the statute makes furnishing alcohol to a minor illegal and a minor requested the patron to furnish him with alcohol, which the patron did, the minor could be found guilty as an aider and abettor of the substantive crime under the general rule. However, there are exceptions to the general rule, including an exception for members of the class sought to be protected by the statute that has been violated. Because the statute speaks in terms of selling or furnishing to a minor, without creating any punishment for the minor to whom the alcohol is furnished, it probably was intended for the protection of minors, and a legislative exemption for those same minors can be presumed that overrides principles of aiding and abetting. (A) is incorrect because in most jurisdictions an aider and abettor can be convicted even if the principal cannot be convicted, and this was true even under the common law as to principals in the second degree (aiders and abettors), such as the minor. (C) is an incorrect statement of law; there is no aiding and abetting exception for minors in general, and minors over age 14 can generally be found guilty of committing a crime. (Minors under age 14 may have the benefit of a presumption that they lack the necessary mental state.) (D) is an incorrect statement of law, and closely akin to (A); the patron violated the law and the minor can be convicted of the substantive crime as an aider and abettor even though the patron is never apprehended or convicted, unless some superseding principle intervenes, as in (B).

Answer to Question 68

(C) The defendant's objection to the contract negotiations is not appropriate because whether an agency relationship existed is determined by the jury. The Federal Rules of Evidence distinguish preliminary facts to be decided by the jury, which determine whether the offered evidence is relevant to the issues in the case, from preliminary facts to be decided by the judge, which determines whether the offered evidence is competent to be admitted at all. Whether an agency relationship existed between the defendant and a third party is a question of fact to be decided by the jury; if the jury decides that the third party was not the defendant's agent, it will disregard as irrelevant the evidence of contract negotiations undertaken by the third party. While the judge must find that the proponent of the contract negotiations has introduced enough evidence to allow the jury to find that an agency relationship existed, the ultimate determination of agency rests with the jury. (A) is incorrect because the judge must determine the qualifications of a witness called as an expert before permitting the witness to offer an opinion or conclusion on a matter appropriate for expert testimony. If the judge decides that the engineer does not qualify as an expert, he will not be permitted to testify on the structural integrity of the building. (B) and (D) are incorrect because all preliminary fact questions involving the standards of trustworthiness of exceptions to the hearsay rule must be determined by the court. Thus, the court must decide whether a purported business record was made in the regular course of business, and whether a statement offered as a dying declaration was made under a sense of impending death.

Answer to Question 69

(C) The appellate court should rule that only Instruction 2 was constitutional. Due process of law requires a state to prove each element of the crime charged beyond a reasonable doubt. However, as to affirmative defenses to the criminal charge, the Supreme Court has held that the state can place the burden of proof on the defendant without violating the defendant's constitutional rights. [Leland v. Oregon (1952)] Common law larceny is the taking and carrying away of property in the possession of another with the intent to permanently deprive the other of the property. Since the intent to permanently deprive is an element of the crime, the state cannot require the defendant to prove that he intended to return the car, which would negate the required intent for larceny. The state must prove beyond a reasonable doubt that he intended to permanently deprive. Hence, Instruction 1 is unconstitutional, making (A) and (D) wrong. Instruction 2 is constitutional. As to the defense of mental illness, the Supreme Court has held that the state can require (as federal courts do) that the defendant prove the defense by clear and convincing evidence. The state also can place the burden on the defendant to prove the defense of mental illness by a preponderance of the evidence, which is a lesser burden of proof. The fact that the instruction placed a lighter burden on the defendant than the statute specified would not make the instruction a violation of the defendant's constitutional rights. Thus, choices (B) and (D) are wrong.

Answer to Question 70

(C) The statement in (C) would not be relevant in assessing the program's constitutionality. The facts in (A), (B), and (D) would make the program unconstitutional under the Establishment Clause of the First Amendment. A state law may not respect the establishment of a religion. Unless a law prefers one religious sect over another, which is not the case here, it is unconstitutional if it fails to pass any of the three following tests: (i) it has a secular purpose; (ii) its primary effect neither advances nor inhibits religion; and (iii) it does not produce excessive government entanglement with religion. [Lemon v. Kurtzman (1971)] Here, (A) is relevant to test (ii); (B) is relevant to test (i); and (D) is relevant to test (iii). The statement in (C) is irrelevant; the fact that no compelling interest exists would not make the program unconstitutional if it satisfied the three-part *Lemon* test. Whether a compelling state interest exists would be relevant only if the state program had discriminated among religious sects.

Answer to Question 71

(A) The motorist will prevail because the dealer sold defective tires to him. In a strict liability action based on a defective product, a commercial supplier of a product who sells the product in a defective condition unreasonably dangerous to consumers will be held strictly liable for the damage caused by the defective product. The dealer was a commercial supplier of the product; the tires were in a dangerous condition when the dealer put the tires on the car and sold the car to the motorist. Thus, the motorist will likely prevail. (B) is wrong because the dealer would be liable on a strict liability theory regardless of whether the manufacturer was negligent, and also because the dealer's liability arises when it sells the car to the consumer, not when it "uses" the tires. (C) is wrong because there is nothing in the facts to suggest that the motorist knew of the risk that the tires were defective; the discount price is not sufficient. (D) is wrong. Misuse of a product is a defense to a strict liability claim only if the misuse was not foreseeable by the defendant. It would certainly be foreseeable that a new car owner might occasionally drive 80 m.p.h.

Answer to Question 72

(C) The girl will prevail because the bear is classified as a wild animal. An owner of a wild (*i.e.*, nondomestic) animal will be strictly liable for the damage caused by the animal. A bear, even a very tame one, will be classified as a wild animal. Therefore (C) is correct and (A) is wrong. (B) is wrong because the injury the girl suffered was within the "normal dangerous propensity" of the animal. Strict liability for wild animals includes liability for the harm that results when a person is attempting to flee from what is perceived to be a dangerous animal. (D) is wrong. The fact that the activity was uncommon in the locale would have some relevance if the lawsuit were based on a theory of strict liability for an ultrahazardous activity. It has nothing to do with strict liability for damage caused by animals.

Answer to Question 73

(B) The state law is valid because the prior judicial determinations that the driver violated the speeding laws satisfy the procedural due process requirements of the Fourteenth Amendment. Under the Due Process Clause of the Fourteenth Amendment, the state must provide some fair process or procedure before it may deprive a person of "life, liberty, or property." Fair procedure at a minimum requires an opportunity to present objections to the proposed action to a fair, neutral decisionmaker. Whether a prior evidentiary hearing is required and the extent of procedural requirements is determined by *weighing* (i) the importance of the individual interest involved, (ii) the value of specific procedural safeguards to that interest, and (iii) the governmental interest in fiscal and administrative efficiency. [Mathews v. Eldridge (1976)] Because the government has taken control of who may drive automobiles on public roads, which is a sufficiently important area of human activity that persons have a liberty interest in it, the government must provide fair procedure to those who are specifically barred from engaging in the activity. In applying the *Mathews v. Eldridge* balancing test, the Court has held that the state generally must afford a prior hearing before a driver's license is suspended or terminated. However, where the suspension is based on prior judicial determinations that traffic laws were violated, the driver has already had prior evidentiary hearings before unbiased decisionmakers on the significant factual issues involved. The governmental interest in keeping unsafe drivers off public roads and in not relitigating issues already fairly decided outweighs the driver's interest in keeping her driver's license. The procedural safeguards in the judicial proceedings in which she was convicted were sufficiently broad so that no additional prior hearing is necessary. Thus, the court should rule that the state law satisfies procedural due process requirements. (A) is incorrect because the liberty and property interests that a person cannot be deprived of without procedural due process do not turn on whether the interest involved is a "right" rather than a "privilege." That distinction has been rejected by the Supreme Court. (C) is incorrect because the presumption created by the law is rationally related to a legitimate state goal. If the government "presumes facts" against a person so that she cannot demonstrate that she is qualified for some important benefit or right, the

"irrebutable presumption" may be unconstitutional. If the presumption involves a fundamental right or a suspect or quasi-suspect classification, it will likely be held invalid under a strict scrutiny or intermediate scrutiny analysis. If some other right or class is involved, it will likely be upheld under the rational basis standard. Here, no suspect or quasi-suspect class is involved, and driving is not a fundamental right. Thus, the action will be upheld because suspending licenses of drivers convicted of speeding is rationally related to the legislature's goal of reducing the death toll on the state's highways. (D) is incorrect because, as discussed above, the prior judicial proceedings in which she was convicted provide sufficient due process; no additional prior hearing is necessary before her license is suspended.

Answer to Question 74

(C) The citizen's strongest argument is his right to freedom of speech. The First Amendment forbids Congress from abridging the freedom of speech or of the press. While there are numerous exceptions and qualifications to this right (and the citizen might not ultimately succeed), this is his strongest argument, because the statute purports to punish him for publishing information even though he is motivated only by political reasons (he disagrees with the price support program). (A) is incorrect because the Equal Protection Clause of the Fourteenth Amendment applies to state governments and the law here is federal. Additionally, equal protection only prevents states from treating classes of people differently, and here no classification is made. (B) is incorrect because nothing in the statute indicates that punishment will be imposed without a hearing, so the citizen will not be deprived of liberty without due process of law (*i.e.,* procedural due process). Nor does the statute violate substantive due process, because it does not affect any of the citizen's fundamental rights. (D) is incorrect because Congress has plenary power over interstate commerce and may adopt laws controlling interstate commerce—even ones burdening interstate commerce—as long as the laws do not otherwise violate the Constitution.

Answer to Question 75

(B) The farmer may be fined under the statute but not imprisoned. The right to counsel under the Sixth Amendment gives the defendant the right to be represented by privately retained counsel or to have counsel appointed for her by the state if she is indigent. However, the right to counsel applies to misdemeanor trials only when a sentence of imprisonment is ***actually*** imposed (including a suspended sentence). Thus, even though the misdemeanor statute permits a potential jail term, its alternative penalty of a fine may constitutionally be imposed on the defendant despite the refusal to provide her with counsel. (A) and (C) are incorrect because the right to counsel would apply to any misdemeanor trial in which imprisonment is actually imposed. The failure to provide the farmer with counsel would preclude the imprisonment sentence. (D) is incorrect because, as discussed above, the misdemeanor's alternative penalty of a fine may be imposed without violating the constitutional right to counsel at trial.

Answer to Question 76

(B) The ledger is admissible under the business records exception to the hearsay rule. Any writing or record of any act or transaction is admissible as proof of that act or transaction if the record was made in the regular course of a business and if it was customary to make the type of record involved (*i.e.,* the entrant was under a business duty to make the entry). Here, testimony has established that it was the defendant's customary practice to have one clerk identify the type of computer and its components and have another clerk record the information. Thus, the authenticated record showing that no DVR drive was indicated for the plaintiff's computer is admissible

as a business record. (A) is incorrect because the ledger entry is not being used as evidence of a past recollection by a testifying witness. That exception to the hearsay rule allows a writing to be read into evidence when a witness has insufficient recollection of the event to enable him to testify accurately, even after consulting the writing to refresh his recollection. Here, the entry is being offered into evidence standing alone as a business record, rather than as the recollection of a witness on the stand. (C) is incorrect because most business record statutes do not require that the person making the entries have personal knowledge of the event. As long as the one with personal knowledge and the one making the record are both employees of the business with a duty to report and record the information accurately, the business records exception applies to both hearsay statements—the statement by the first clerk and the record made by the second clerk. (D) is incorrect. While the absence of the notation is being offered as an implied statement that no DVR drive was returned, such a statement falls within the business records exception. Modern business records statutes, including Federal Rule of Evidence 803(7), permit a record to be used to prove the nonoccurrence of a matter if it was the regular practice of the business to record all such matters.

Answer to Question 77

(B) The law will be upheld because it is a neutral law that is applicable to all drivers in the state. The Free Exercise Clause does not require exemptions from government regulations for a person whose religious beliefs prevent him from conforming his behavior to the requirements of the law. Unless the law was motivated by a desire to interfere with religion, it can be applied to regulate the conduct of one whose religious beliefs conflict with the law. Here, the sect member must allow his photograph to be taken if he wants to obtain a driver's license; the state is entitled to enforce this regulation because it is a neutral law of general applicability. (A) is incorrect because it may be possible for a state to make accommodations for groups objecting to a particular state regulation without violating the Establishment Clause, even though it is not *required* to do so under the Free Exercise Clause. The state here could permit an exemption from the photograph requirement for persons who present legitimate reasons for it; such an accommodation would not be an impermissible advancement of religion. (C) is incorrect because the "compelling interest" test is not currently used to judge the validity of neutral laws that happen to interfere with a person's religious practices. (D) is incorrect because the sincerity of the sect member's beliefs does not provide a basis for avoiding application of the law to them.

Answer to Question 78

(D) This answer states the traditional rule where the amount of land in a land sale contract is less than as agreed. When a buyer has a remedy of specific performance in a land sale contract, a court of equity will order a seller to convey the title if the buyer tenders the purchase price. If the seller cannot provide marketable title under the terms of the contract, but the buyer wishes to proceed with the transaction, the buyer can usually get specific performance with an abatement of the purchase price in an amount reflecting the title defect. A defect as to the quantity of land conveyed is usually corrected by a pro rata abatement of the price. (D) states the factors that a court of equity will look for when deciding whether to grant specific performance with abatement. (A) is incorrect because the parties' contract did not merely refer to the farm as a named parcel of land; it recited that it contained 250 acres. Based on this recital, a court could readily conclude that the difference of two acres is a material change in the terms of the contract and that the seller's tender of 248 acres was not substantial performance. (B) is incorrect because viewing the property did not put the buyer on notice as to the discrepancy; the buyer is not required to visually calculate the amount of acreage a parcel of land contains. (C) is not as good an answer as (D) even though it is probably a true statement. Not only must the defect as to quantity be material, so that the buyer is not receiving what he bargained for, but the abatement amount must be appropriate and not an excessive variance from the parties' agreement.

Answer to Question 79

(B) The farmer can recover damages for trespass to land because the factory owner intended to conduct the activities that caused the trespass. To establish a prima facie case for trespass to land, plaintiff must prove: (i) an act of physical invasion of plaintiff's real property by defendant; (ii) intent on defendant's part to bring about the physical invasion; and (iii) causation. Here, flakes of the chemical byproduct of the factory owner's soap factory physically invaded the farmer's property when the wind blew. The factory owner intended to bring about the trespass because, after the farmer had complained, the factory owner *knew with substantial certainty* that the flakes would continue to fall on the farm whenever the wind was right. Finally, the factory owner's operation of the soap factory was the cause of the flakes settling on the farmer's strawberries, completing the prima facie case of trespass to land. (A) is incorrect because the fact that the factory owner's discharge entered the farmer's land is not enough to establish liability. The factory owner is not engaged in an abnormally dangerous activity, for which strict liability would apply. If the discharge had been a single accidental occurrence, the factory owner would not have had the intent for trespass to land. (C) is incorrect because an intent to harm or to cause injury is not necessary for liability; only an intent to enter on the land is required. (D) is incorrect because mistake as to the lawfulness of the entry is no defense, even if reasonable. Because the factory owner knew that the particles would enter the land when the factory continued to operate, he had the "intent" to bring about the physical invasion of property owned by the farmer.

Answer to Question 80

(C) The neighbor will not prevail because the smoke would not disturb a person of ordinary sensibilities. The neighbor's lawsuit is based on nuisance. For a private nuisance action to lie, the interference with the plaintiff's use or enjoyment of his land must be substantial. This means that it must be offensive, inconvenient, or annoying to an *average person* in the community. It will not be characterized as substantial if it is merely the result of plaintiff's hypersensitivity. Here, because the neighbor is unable to use his yard when the smoke blows into it only because of his extremely sensitive eyes, the interference will not be characterized as substantial. Hence, the neighbor will not prevail given the condition stated in (C). (A) is incorrect because it is not sufficient that the restaurant's conduct interfered with the neighbor's use and enjoyment of his yard; the interference must be both substantial and unreasonable for the neighbor to prevail. (B) is incorrect because the restaurant's violation of a health code regulation does not establish that an actionable nuisance is present. While violation of a zoning ordinance or regulation may be a factor in balancing whether the severity of the injury outweighs the utility of the defendant's conduct and is therefore unreasonable, it is not determinative. (D) is incorrect for the opposite reason. The fact that the health code regulation was not designed to protect against the harm suffered by the neighbor does not establish that the restaurant's activity was not a nuisance; it could constitute a nuisance even if it complied with the regulation.

Answer to Question 81

(B) The best argument is that the burglar made the statements spontaneously. Prior to a suspect's being charged with a crime, the Fifth Amendment privilege against compelled self-incrimination is the usual basis for ruling on the admissibility of a confession. [Miranda v. Arizona (1966)]

Under *Miranda*, statements made during custodial interrogations are inadmissible unless the defendant is first warned of his right to remain silent and his right to an attorney. Thus, *Miranda* applies only when the defendant is in custody and only when the defendant's statements are the result of interrogation. Although almost *any* words or actions on the part of the police that they should know are reasonably likely to elicit an incriminating response qualify as interrogation, *Miranda* does not apply to spontaneous statements not made in response to interrogation. Here, the police did nothing to solicit the statement from the burglar; it was spontaneous. Thus, (B) is correct. (A) is incorrect because the defendant need not yet be charged for *Miranda* rights to apply as long as he is in custody (*i.e.,* not free to leave). Being in jail on another charge (as the burglar was) satisfies the custody requirement. (C) is incorrect because the fact that the officer who took the burglar's admission had nothing to do with the investigation of the burglary does not alter the rules of *Miranda*—questioning that is totally unrelated to the matter for which the accused is in custody may still violate the accused's *Miranda* rights. (D) is incorrect. Due process requires that a confession be voluntary (*i.e.,* not the product of police coercion). The *Miranda* rule, however, goes beyond voluntariness. It makes inadmissible all statements obtained without *Miranda* warnings or without a valid waiver of *Miranda* rights, not just statements actually coerced by the police.

Answer to Question 82

(C)   The strongest argument to exclude is that the statements were made in the absence of the defendant's counsel. This question illustrates the operation of the Sixth Amendment right to counsel approach, which you should use to evaluate the admissibility of any statements made *after* the defendant has been charged with the relevant crime. The Sixth Amendment provides defendants with a right to counsel at any post-indictment interrogation. Since the defendant was on trial for arson, any interrogation relating to those charges must take place, if at all, in the presence of the defendant's counsel unless the defendant has knowingly and intelligently waived the right. Nothing indicates that the arsonist knowingly waived his right to counsel, so (C) is correct. (A) is incorrect because the failure to give *Miranda* warnings, which may violate the Fifth Amendment privilege against self-incrimination, does not prevent use of otherwise voluntary statements for impeachment purposes, as in this case. In contrast, evidence obtained from a direct violation of the Sixth Amendment right to counsel (the bailiff's questioning of the defendant in the absence of his counsel) has not been held to be admissible, even for only impeachment purposes. [*See* Michigan v. Harvey (1990)] (B) is not the best answer because the Sixth Amendment right to counsel is the right of the defendant rather than the attorney; the defendant could have waived his right without the knowledge or consent of his attorney. The failure to inform the defendant's attorney does not, by itself, establish that his right to counsel was violated. [*See* Moran v. Burbine (1986)] (D) is not the strongest argument because the bailiff's status as a law enforcement officer does not, by itself, make the statements involuntary or otherwise inadmissible; the critical issue in this question is whether the bailiff obtained the statements in violation of the defendant's right to counsel.

Answer to Question 83

(C)   This choice states the critical factor for admitting evidence of other crimes or misconduct to show motive, while the other choices raise issues that are relevant only when other crimes evidence is being offered for impeachment purposes. *It is essential that you keep the impeachment rules distinct from the rules for admitting other crimes evidence when the evidence is independently relevant—the bar examiners will often mix these issues in the answer choices for this type of question.*

One of the most important areas where recurring relevance questions have developed into established rules is the use of character evidence. The well-settled rule is that extrinsic evidence of other crimes is not admissible to show a criminal disposition or conduct in conformity with the other crimes. On the other hand, Federal Rule 404(b) permits this evidence to be introduced for other purposes, such as to show motive, opportunity, intent, or identity, whenever these issues are relevant in the case. Because of the potential for unfair prejudice of this type of evidence, the balancing test of Federal Rule 403 (paraphrased in choice (C)) is particularly important. Even though evidence of the other robberies is relevant to show motive, the court may find that its probative value is substantially outweighed by the danger of unfair prejudice, especially because the other crimes are of the same type as the crime charged. (A) is incorrect because a conviction is not required for other crimes evidence used for this purpose. Only when extrinsic evidence of another crime is being used to impeach a testifying defendant is an actual conviction required. (B) is incorrect because whether the defendant has testified is relevant only when the other crimes evidence is being used for impeachment, since a defendant only puts his credibility at issue if he takes the witness stand; it is irrelevant when the other crimes evidence is used to show motive. (D) is incorrect. For independently relevant uncharged misconduct by the defendant to be admissible, there need only be sufficient evidence to support a jury finding that the defendant committed the prior act; clear and convincing evidence is not required.

Answer to Question 84

(C) If the backpacker undertakes to rescue the hiker, he must be reasonably prudent in doing so. The general rule in tort law is that no legal duty is imposed on any person to affirmatively act for the benefit of others. However, one who gratuitously acts for the benefit of another is then under a duty to act reasonably. If he acts negligently, he will be liable for damage caused thereby. (A) is an incorrect statement of the law—a rescuer is not strictly liable for a victim's injuries, but rather is liable only for negligent acts. (B) is an accurate statement of the law but does not take into account that the backpacker must be negligent to be liable at all. (D) is incorrect because it is not necessarily true. A violation of a statute will not be negligence per se where compliance would cause greater risk of harm than violation, such as in an emergency. If it was necessary to speed to get the hiker to the hospital for treatment of the snakebite, it may have been excusable to exceed the posted speed limit. If the backpacker was not otherwise negligent, this would not establish negligence at all.

Answer to Question 85

(B) The statute is authorized by Congress's spending power. Article I, Section 8 gives Congress the power to spend "to provide for the common defense and general welfare." This power allows Congress to spend for any public purpose as long as it does not infringe on other specific constitutional restrictions (such as the Bill of Rights). The statute here is clearly for a public purpose and is not otherwise unconstitutional; it is therefore within Congress's spending power. (A) is not as good a choice as (B). The statute arguably does involve the commerce power, because Congress has plenary power to regulate interstate commerce, including any kind of commerce or transportation within a state that has a substantial economic effect on interstate commerce. However, that power is generally invoked for federal legislation that directly regulates the state activity. Here, no government action is involved except for the grant of money, which more closely implicates the spending power. (C) is incorrect because the Necessary and Proper Clause is not by itself a basis of power; it merely gives Congress power to execute specifically granted powers. The grant of money falls within a specific enumerated power of Congress; the Necessary and Proper Clause is not the primary source of authority here. (D) is incorrect because the power to conduct foreign relations is vested in the President. Congress shares some of this power in

such cases as approval of treaties, but the President's power to act for the United States in day-to-day foreign relations is paramount.

Answer to Question 86

(A) The court should grant the agency's motion because the passenger has not established a prima facie case of negligence against the agency. To establish a prima facie case for negligence, a plaintiff must show: (i) a duty of care, (ii) breach of that duty, (iii) actual and proximate cause, and (iv) damages. As a common carrier, the agency may have owed the passenger a high duty of care, and therefore would be liable for slight negligence. However, the passenger has offered no evidence to establish that the agency breached its duty, and res ipsa loquitur is not applicable to these facts because the rocking motion of a train is not the type of event that would occur only as a result of negligence. Because the passenger failed to establish a breach of duty, the court should grant the agency a directed verdict. (B) is incorrect because the agency's introduction of that evidence does not conclusively establish its exercise of due care. While evidence that a person in normal health would not have been injured by the bump may support the agency's other evidence that it exercised due care, it is not necessary because the passenger has failed to offer evidence that the agency breached its duty. On the other hand, if the agency had breached its duty of care to its passengers, the fact that a person in normal health would not have been injured by the bump on the knee would not be a defense to liability. Where a defendant's negligence causes an aggravation of plaintiff's existing physical illness, defendant is liable for the damages caused by the aggravation. (C) is incorrect because, as discussed above, the passenger has failed to present evidence that the agency breached even a high duty of care that it owed to its passengers. (D) is incorrect even though it is a true statement of law, as discussed above. The reason the agency prevails is because the passenger has failed to establish a prima facie case.

Answer to Question 87

(B) The proprietor must agree to a rescission of the agreement. A party to a contract may not unilaterally rescind it if the contract is valid (*i.e.,* in the absence of mistake, misrepresentation, etc.). However, both parties to a contract may agree to rescind and discharge their contractual duties as long as the duties are still executory on both sides. Here, neither party has performed under the contract, so the contract will be mutually rescinded if the proprietor gives his assent to the plant owner. (A) is incorrect because the creditor's rights as a third-party beneficiary of the contract have not yet vested; thus, his consent to the rescission is not needed. An intended beneficiary such as the creditor can enforce a contract only after his rights have vested, which will occur when he (i) manifests assent to the promise in a manner invited or requested by the parties, (ii) brings suit to enforce the promise, or (iii) materially changes his position in justifiable reliance on the promise. Here, the creditor has not even become aware of the agreement between the plant owner and the proprietor, so his rights cannot have vested. (C) is incorrect because conditional promises are not illusory. They are enforceable, no matter how remote the contingency, unless the "condition" is entirely within the promisor's control. Here, the fact that both parties' performance is conditioned on the team's winning the state championship does not make the contract illusory because neither party (presumably) can control the occurrence or nonoccurrence of the condition. (D) is incorrect because an offer can only be revoked before it has been accepted, and here the offer has already been accepted and a contract formed. Whether the team wins the state championship is merely a condition precedent to the parties' duty of performance.

Answer to Question 88

(B) If the bakery brings an action against the apple orchard, the bakery will be able to recover the

costs of replacing the destroyed apples, because the apple orchard remained liable on the as-signed contract and it had the risk of loss. Although most contractual duties may be assigned—unless they are personal—and the obligee must accept performance from the delegate, the delegating party (delegator) remains liable on his obligation. Thus, an assignment of a contract that includes a delegation of duties does not relieve the assignor from its duty to perform. Here, the bakery did not receive the performance that was due (the apples), so it could sue the apple orchard to recover for the breach. When a nonbreaching buyer does not receive the contracted goods, it has several options: it can cancel the contract and recover any incidental damages, or it can purchase replace-ment goods and sue for the cost of replacement—"cover." Damages under the latter option are measured by the difference between the contract price and the amount the buyer actually has to pay for the replacement goods. Thus, (B) is correct and (A) is incorrect. Note that (A) would have been correct if U.C.C. section 2-613 were applicable, because it provides for avoidance of the contract when goods are lost without fault of either party before risk of loss passes to the buyer. However, that section applies only when particular goods are identified to the contract *when the contract was made*; here, there is no designation of specific bushels of apples until shipment. (C) is not a proper measure of damages unless the bakery had already paid for the apples and wished to cancel (and the facts do not indicate this to be the case), because the con-tract price may not be enough to purchase replacement goods if the price of apples has risen, and would be too much if the price has dropped. (D) is incorrect because specific performance is usually not available for goods unless the circumstances call for it—for example, if replacement goods could not be obtained or the goods are unique. Here, the goods are not unique and there is no indication that replacement apples are not available.

Answer to Question 89

(D) The court would likely uphold the statute against a constitutional challenge because there is a conceivable rational basis for concluding that gambling, in aggregate, substantially affects inter-state commerce. Under the Commerce Clause, Congress may regulate: (i) the channels of inter-state commerce; (ii) the instrumentalities of interstate commerce, as well as persons and things in interstate commerce; or (iii) activities that have a substantial effect on interstate commerce. When Congress attempts to regulate intrastate activities under the third of the preceding prongs, the Court will uphold the regulation if it involves economic or commercial activity as long as there is a conceivable basis for concluding that the activity in aggregate substantially affects interstate commerce. Here, it is conceivable that gambling machines in shopping malls, in aggregate, could substantially affect interstate commerce. Therefore, the statute would be upheld. (A) is incorrect because the citizens' motivation for requesting the law would not taint it. A regulation not involv-ing a sect preference will be upheld under the Establishment Clause if (i) it has a secular purpose, (ii) its primary effect neither advances nor inhibits religion, and (iii) it does not produce exces-sive government entanglements. Banning gambling machines from shopping malls does not involve any sect preference, it has a secular purpose (*e.g.,* preventing the ills associated with gambling), its primary effect neither advances nor inhibits religion, and it does not produce any religious entanglements. (B) is incorrect because, under the Commerce Clause, Congress also has the power to regulate activities that have a substantial effect on interstate commerce. (C) is incorrect because it states the test applicable to situations where Congress seeks to regulate noneconomic or noncommercial intrastate activity under the Commerce Clause (*e.g.,* possession of a gun in a school zone); gambling in shopping malls would likely be found to be an economic or commercial activity.

Answer to Question 90

(B) Although the President has no power to declare war, Article II, Section 2 makes the President

commander in chief of the military, which affords the President extensive power to deploy military forces against any enemy, foreign or domestic. Congress lacks such power. Therefore, (B) is correct; this statute directly infringes upon the President's authority as commander in chief to make such orders as he deems proper with respect to the armed forces, and thus violates the doctrine of separation of powers. (A) is incorrect because the duty to execute the laws of the United States is an obligation, not a grant of authority. (C) is incorrect because even if the measure has some effect upon interstate commerce, it is still a violation of the separation of powers doctrine. Congress's power under the Commerce Clause does not supersede other powers that the Constitution has specifically bestowed on another branch of government. (D) is incorrect because the enactment does not appropriate money to support the armed forces, but seeks to control their activities.

Answer to Question 91

(D)   The cashier's testimony is not admissible to prove good character. Generally, a criminal defendant can introduce evidence of her good character to show that she did not commit the crime charged. This is accomplished through the reputation or opinion testimony of a witness. The testimony must relate to the trait involved in the case and the witness cannot testify to specific acts of conduct. Here, the defendant is entitled to call the restaurant cashier to the stand to testify to her good character, but she can do so only by giving her personal opinion or by testifying to the defendant's reputation concerning honesty (the trait involved in a shoplifting case). The cashier's testimony in this case is impermissible because she is attempting to testify to the defendant's history of correcting undercharges on her bill, which are specific acts of conduct. Thus, her testimony is inadmissible. (A) is incorrect because, as stated, a defendant can introduce evidence of good character but not by testimony of specific acts of conduct. (B) is incorrect because, while the evidence may be relevant and nonprejudicial, the fact remains that it is still an impermissible form of character evidence, and therefore inadmissible. (C) is incorrect because the testimony is not hearsay. Hearsay is an out-of-court statement offered to prove the truth of the matter asserted. Here, the cashier is not testifying as to any statement that was made, nor is the evidence being offered to prove the truth of the matter asserted (*i.e.*, that the defendant actually corrected the undercharges). Thus, (C) is incorrect.

Answer to Question 92

(B)   The patient can establish a prima facie case for battery regardless of whether she establishes damages at trial. The prima facie case for battery requires an act by defendant that will bring about a harmful or offensive contact to the plaintiff, intent on the part of defendant to do the act, and causation. Here, the surgeon's performing the operation would be offensive contact because it was unconsented to: The patient had selected her doctor to perform the operation and did not consent to the surgeon's participating in the procedure. (A) is incorrect because damages is not an element of the prima facie case for battery. Even if the patient cannot establish damages, she can obtain a judgment in her favor and at least nominal damages. (C) is incorrect because the fact that the surgeon is considered an expert in this type of operation is irrelevant; the patient did not consent to his involvement. (D) is incorrect because the doctor had no authority to approve the substitution of the surgeon. Since no emergency existed, there was no justification for not obtaining the patient's consent to the substitution.

Answer to Question 93

(D)   Neither the proprietor nor the friend would be convicted as accomplices to larceny. An accomplice is one who, with the intent that the crime be committed, aids, counsels, or encourages the

principal before or during the commission of the crime. Here, the friend is not liable as an accomplice because nothing in the facts suggests that he disbelieved the felon's claim that it was his own storage unit. Hence, he had no intent to commit larceny, which requires an intent to permanently deprive another of his interest in the property. Therefore, (B) and (C) are incorrect. To be convicted as an accomplice under the prevailing rule, a person must have acted with the intent to aid or encourage the principal in the commission of the crime charged. Absent a statute, most courts would hold that mere knowledge that a crime may result from the aid provided is insufficient for accomplice liability, at least where the aid involves the sale of ordinary goods at ordinary prices. Here, the proprietor's sale of the crowbar in the ordinary course of business would not make her liable as an accomplice under the prevailing rule even if she believed that the purchaser was going to use it to break into someone's storage unit. Hence, (A) and (C) are incorrect.

Answer to Question 94

(B) The state will prevail because Congress has consented to the state regulation of interstate commerce. A state may regulate local aspects of commerce (*i.e.,* ***intrastate*** commerce), but state regulation that discriminates against or substantially burdens ***interstate*** commerce may be held invalid under the Supremacy Clause, because of Congress's plenary power to regulate interstate commerce under the Commerce Clause. Here, the state statute, standing alone, might have been held invalid because its substantial burden on interstate commerce could have been found to outweigh any legitimate local interest in reducing eyestrain. However, the federal statute changes the equation. Because Congress's power over interstate commerce is plenary, Congress may allow a state to adopt legislation that would otherwise be invalid as an unconstitutional burden on interstate commerce; this is what Congress did here. By allowing the state regulation, it is actually exercising the federal commerce power—it simply allows for nonuniform (state-by-state) rules. Therefore, (B) is correct and (C) is incorrect. (A) is incorrect because the Tenth Amendment merely reserves to the states the powers not delegated to the federal government, and the power to regulate interstate commerce—the power in question here—was not reserved to the states because it was granted to Congress by the Constitution. (D) is incorrect because the statute, as far as described in the problem, appears to be exactly what Congress authorized. There is no information indicating that the statute is overbroad or exceeds the authorization, which apparently allows a broad range of regulation beyond just location and hours of operation.

Answer to Question 95

(A) The agency is likely to be liable because it should have known of the guard's prior convictions. Under the doctrine of respondeat superior, an employer is not vicariously liable for the acts of an employee outside the scope of his employment. However, the employer may be liable for its own negligent selection if it has some reason to be on notice that the actions that resulted in harm were likely to occur. Thus, because the plaintiffs can show that a reasonable employer could have learned of the guard's violent crimes from public records, the agency likely did not act with reasonable care by not even investigating the guard's statements on his application (and hiring someone as an armed guard who was barred by law from that type of job). (B) is incorrect because merely giving the guard the pistol does not breach the agency's duty—the agency must have had some reason to know of the guard's dangerous propensities. (C) is incorrect because a duty can arise in circumstances such as those stated in (A). (D) is incorrect because the rule it states is only for an employer's vicarious liability, and negligent selection of an employee is not vicarious liability; it is independent negligence on the part of the employer.

Answer to Question 96

(B) The witness's prior inconsistent statement is admissible both for impeachment and as substantive

evidence. One of the most common means of impeaching the credibility of a witness is by showing that the witness has, on another occasion, made statements that are inconsistent with some material part of his present testimony. While the witness is still on the stand, he may be questioned as to the prior statement and given an opportunity to explain or deny it. [*See* Fed. R. Evid. 613(b)] Furthermore, the prior statement may be considered by the jury as substantive proof of the facts stated if the statement was given under oath at a prior trial or a deposition. [Fed. R. Evid. 801(d)(1)] Here, the witness's prior statement is inconsistent with his in-court statement and was made at a deposition; hence, it is admissible as substantive evidence as well as for impeachment. (A) is incorrect because the Federal Rules admit prior inconsistent statements not only for impeachment purposes but also as substantive evidence when made under oath at a prior trial or a deposition. Although it would ordinarily be hearsay when used as substantive evidence (because it is being offered for the truth of the matter asserted), the Federal Rules specifically categorize such statements as nonhearsay. [Fed. R. Evid. 801(d)(1)(A)] (C) is incorrect because, as stated above, a prior inconsistent statement is nonhearsay and therefore admissible. (D) is incorrect because Federal Rule 607 provides that the credibility of a witness may be attacked (such as through a prior inconsistent statement) by any party, including the party that called him.

Answer to Question 97

(C) The landowner has acquired title to the land on which the generator was installed by adverse possession. One may obtain title to land by taking and maintaining possession of it for the statutory period provided by the jurisdiction. The possession must be actual and exclusive, open and notorious (sufficient to put the true owner or the community on notice of the fact of possession), hostile (without the true owner's permission), and continuous (used in a way that the actual owner would use it). Here, the landowner's installation and maintenance of the generator for more than the 20 years provided by the statute of limitations for ejectment satisfies the requirements for him to acquire title by adverse possession. (A) is incorrect because the statute of limitations is not tolled by an *intervening* disability. The neighbor's mental incompetence would have benefited her against the landowner only if she was suffering from it at the *inception* of the adverse possession. (B) is incorrect because claim of right is not an essential element of adverse possession under the majority view. It does not matter whether the possessor believes he is on his own land, knows he is trespassing on someone else's land, or has no idea who owns the land. (D) is incorrect because a prescriptive easement, like easements generally, is a nonexclusive right to use the land rather than an exclusive right to possess and enjoy the land. The typical easement gives its holder the right of access across a tract of land (*e.g.,* a utility line or road) without precluding the owner of the land from also using it; here, the landowner's installation and enclosure of the generator amounted to a permanent and exclusive possession of the land on which the generator rested.

Answer to Question 98

(C) The sister owns a fee simple, albeit subject to a divesting condition subsequent (her dying without having had children). Thus, the sister is entitled to harvest the timber on the land, and the American Cancer Society cannot prevent her from doing so. A defeasible fee is a fee simple estate that is of potentially infinite duration, but which may terminate on the happening of a specified event. One such estate is a fee simple subject to an executory interest. This estate is subject to a divesting condition subsequent that, if the condition occurs, will vest title in a third person rather than in the grantor. Here, according to the language of the lumberjack's deed, the sister has a fee simple in the land. However, this fee simple is subject to a divesting condition subsequent, in that title will vest in the American Cancer Society if the sister dies without having produced issue. The Society is a transferee whose future interest is not capable of taking on the natural termination of a preceding life estate; *i.e.*, it divests the interest of another. Thus, the interest of the Society is classified as an executory interest, meaning that the sister has a fee simple subject to an executory interest. Although title will vest in the Society if the sister dies without having produced children, this may never happen. Thus, the sister's estate is of potentially infinite duration. As a result, the Society (in whom title may never vest) cannot prevent the sister from harvesting the timber on the land. (A) incorrectly classifies the Society's interest. A remainder is a future interest created in a transferee that is capable of becoming a present interest upon the natural termination of the preceding estates created in the same disposition. Remainders follow life estates. Here, the sister has a fee simple, rather than a life estate. Thus, the Society's future interest will not take on the natural termination of the preceding estate, but will divest the interest of the sister (if she dies without having produced issue). Consequently, the Society's interest is an executory interest rather than a remainder. (B) is incorrect because, although the Society has an executory interest, this does not confer on it the right to prevent the holder of the fee simple from harvesting the timber on the land. While a remainderman may assert certain rights against a life tenant, the holder of an executory interest cannot assert these rights against the holder of a fee simple. Thus, (D) is also incorrect. Generally, a life tenant may not consume or exploit natural resources on the land (*e.g.*, timber) unless the land was used in exploitation of such natural resources prior to the grant. Here, the sister is not a life tenant. As the holder of a fee, the sister could have harvested the timber on the land even if it were not being harvested when she took her interest.

Answer to Question 99

(B) The company's best defense is that it did not breach a duty to the member because it did not place the parachutes in the stream of commerce. To establish liability in a strict liability action based on a defective product, the plaintiff must prove that the defendant is a commercial supplier of the product in question and that the product is expected to be supplied to the consumer without substantial change in the condition in which it is supplied. To establish breach of duty, the plaintiff need not prove that the defendant was at fault in supplying a defective product, just that it supplied the defective product, either by selling it or producing it and placing it into the stream of commerce. Here, the company produced the defective parachutes but did not place them into the stream of commerce and did not intend to do so. Thus, it did not breach a duty to the member with regard to the defective parachutes. (A) is incorrect because it is not a defense in a strict liability action that the defendant acted reasonably (*i.e.,* without fault). The element of negligence need not be proved in a strict liability case. (C) is incorrect because the fact that the member was not in privity of contract with the company is not a defense. A strict liability action may be maintained against a commercial supplier not only by the buyer but also by the buyer's family, friends, and employees, and by foreseeable bystanders. (D) is incorrect because ordinary contributory negligence is not a defense in a strict liability action where the plaintiff failed to discover the defect or guard against its existence. While voluntarily and unreasonably encountering a *known* risk is a defense, there is no indication that the member knew that the parachutes might be defective just because they were sold on the black market.

Answer to Question 100

(C) The former co-worker's testimony is admissible character evidence. Under Federal Rule 404, in a civil case, evidence of the character of a person generally is inadmissible if offered to prove that the person may have acted in conformity with his character on a particular occasion. If, however,

the character evidence is offered for some other purpose, such as where a person's character itself is one of the issues in the case, Rule 404 will not exclude the evidence. The testimony is evidence of the guard's character but, if offered against the bank, it would be offered to show that the bank may have been negligent when it entrusted the gun to the guard. Thus, the evidence would not be excluded by Rule 404. In addition, the evidence would be relevant even if the bank did not know of the guard's reputation, because the jury could find that a reasonable investigation by the bank would have uncovered the information and the bank should have known of the guard's reputation. (A) is too broad a statement. In a civil case, character evidence is not admissible to help prove that a person acted in conformity with their character, but it may be admissible for the purpose it is offered here. (B) is too narrow a statement. The evidence clearly would be admissible if the bank knew of the guard's reputation. Thus, (B) is technically a correct statement. However, since the theory of the case against the bank is "negligent entrustment," the evidence could be admitted even if the bank did not know of the guard's reputation but should have known. Thus, (C) is a more complete statement than (B). (D) is wrong. Under Rule 404, the evidence is not admissible to help establish that the guard may have acted negligently.

Answer to Question 101

(A) The court should grant the petroleum company's motion for a directed verdict in its favor because the employee has not established a prima facie case against the petroleum company. The question does not indicate the theory of liability for the employee's lawsuit; however, because strict liability is not applicable against the petroleum company for operation of the refinery (as discussed below) and because there is no evidence to establish that the petroleum company is vicariously liable for another party's negligence here, the employee's only feasible theory of liability is that the petroleum company itself was negligent. While the employee has established the negligence elements of duty, causation, and damages, he has not established the element of breach of duty. While breach of duty is ordinarily a question for the trier of fact, plaintiff's failure to offer *any evidence* on that element of the prima facie case will permit a directed verdict for defendant. Under certain circumstances, the fact that a particular injury occurred may itself establish or tend to establish a breach of duty owed, permitting the trier of fact to infer defendant's liability. This is the doctrine of res ipsa loquitur. However, for the doctrine to apply, plaintiff must show that: (i) the accident causing his injury is the type that would not normally occur unless someone was negligent; (ii) the negligence was attributable to defendant; and (iii) the injury was not attributable to plaintiff. For the second requirement, plaintiff must establish that this type of accident ordinarily happens because of the negligence of someone in defendant's position. This can often be done by showing that the instrumentality causing the injury was in the exclusive control of the defendant. Here, however, the crane that caused the injury was designed and constructed by a company other than the petroleum company and was serviced and maintained by still another company not selected by the petroluem company. Even assuming that the collapse of the crane was the type of accident that does not normally occur unless someone was negligent, there is no evidence that the petroleum company was the source of that negligence. The accident could well be attributable to negligence on the part of the manufacturer or the company hired by the manufacturer to service the crane, or simply to a defect in the materials used to construct the crane, and there is no basis for the petroluem company's being vicariously liable for the actions of either company, since the exceptions that impose vicarious liability for the conduct of an independent contractor do not apply. Since no other evidence of breach of duty was established, the petroleum company's motion for a directed verdict should be granted. (B) is incorrect because the petroleum company owed a duty to the employee, since the employee was an invitee on the petroleum company's property. An invitee is one who enters onto the premises in response to an express or implied invitation of the landowner or occupier, including those who

enter for a purpose connected with the business interests of the landowner. Here, even though the employee was an employee of an independent contractor, he was on the premises for the benefit of the petroleum company's refinery operations and at its invitation. Thus, he is an invitee to whom the petroleum company owed a duty of reasonable care. (C) is incorrect because the refinery operation is not an abnormally dangerous activity. For strict liability to apply to an activity, the activity (i) must create a foreseeable risk of serious harm even when reasonable care is exercised by all actors, and (ii) must not be a matter of common usage in the community. Because an oil refinery can be operated in many locations without the risk of serious harm as long as due care is exercised, a court probably would not find it to be an abnormally dangerous activity; hence, the petroleum company would not be strictly liable to the employee. (D) is incorrect because, as discussed above, the employee has presented no evidence of the petroleum company's negligence and has therefore failed to establish his prima facie case.

Answer to Question 102

(A) The manufacturer and the retailer have a contract without the arbitration clause. In contracts for the sale of goods, a definite expression of acceptance operates as an acceptance even if it states additional terms. Between merchants, additional terms proposed by the offeree in an acceptance automatically become part of the contract unless: (i) they *materially* alter the original terms of the offer (*e.g.,* they change a party's risk or the remedies available); (ii) the offer expressly limits acceptance to the terms of the offer; or (iii) the offeror objects to the additional terms within a reasonable time. Most courts consider a clause requiring that disagreements be subject to arbitration to be a material alteration because such a clause affects the remedies that the parties can pursue. Hence, the acceptance is effective to create a contract but the arbitration clause would not become part of the contract. (B) is therefore incorrect. (C) is incorrect because it reflects the common law "mirror image" rule, which the U.C.C. has rejected in sale of goods cases. (D) is incorrect because under the U.C.C. rule, the inclusion of a material additional term does not prevent formation of a contract; instead, a contract is formed without the inclusion of that additional term.

Answer to Question 103

(B) The witness's testimony is admissible. Under Federal Rule 404(a), a criminal defendant is allowed to present relevant character evidence to help establish that he may not have committed the crime charged. Thus, evidence that the defendant had a reputation for being an honest person would be admissible to show that he might not have embezzled funds because embezzlement is a crime of dishonesty. (A) is too broad a statement. While, as a general matter, a defendant does have a constitutional right to call witnesses, the testimony of the witnesses must comport with the rules of evidence (unless the rule itself is declared unconstitutional), including the requirement that character evidence must be relevant to the crime charged. (C) is wrong because, as discussed above, Federal Rule 404 specifically allows such evidence. (D) is wrong. It is true that a party may not present evidence to bolster the credibility of his own witness until the witness has been impeached. However, if the evidence of good character is offered for any other legitimate purpose, the fact that it also helps bolster the credibility of the witness will never result in the exclusion of the evidence. Here the evidence is admissible to show that the defendant may not have embezzled funds; hence, the rule excluding evidence offered to bolster credibility would not apply.

Answer to Question 104

(A) If the patient does not prevail, it will be because a reasonable person in the patient's position

would have used the cream even after being told of the potential side effects. As part of the physician's duty of care, a doctor proposing a course of treatment has a duty to provide the patient with enough information about its risks to enable the patient to make an informed consent to the treatment. If an undisclosed risk was serious enough that a reasonable person in the patient's position would have withheld consent to the treatment, the doctor has breached her duty. Here, whether the dermatologist breached her duty to the patient by not warning him of possible side effects would be determined ultimately by the trier of fact. If the trier of fact finds against the patient, it will likely be because a reasonable person in the patient's position would have consented to using the cream even after being informed of the potential side effects. (B) is incorrect because the listing of side effects on a printed insert does not necessarily satisfy the dermatologist's duty to provide enough information for the patient to make an informed consent. If the information was buried in a lengthy insert that a reasonable person was not likely to read through, the dermatologist may have had a duty to verbally disclose side effects, and she will have breached that duty if a reasonable person in the patient's position would have withheld consent to the treatment if given the information. (C) is incorrect because the dermatologist could be liable regardless of the severity of the reaction the patient experienced. If she should have warned about the particular side effects the patient experienced even though they are ordinarily less severe, the fact that the patient suffered an unforeseeably severe reaction to the medicine does not relieve her from liability. (D) is incorrect. Even if the jurisdiction requires only that the dermatologist exercise the knowledge and skill of a physician in good standing in similar communities, rather than apply a national standard typically used for specialists, that does not establish whether the duty was breached here. The duty issue here is whether she provided the patient with enough information to allow him to make an informed consent, for which the factor in (A) is determinative.

Answer to Question 105

(C) Because the singer's statement did not amount to an anticipatory repudiation of the contract, the nightclub owner may not bring an immediate suit for breach of contract. Anticipatory repudiation requires that the promisor unequivocally indicate that he cannot or will not perform when the time comes, or act in a manner rendering him unable to perform. When this happens, the nonrepudiating party may treat the anticipatory repudiation as a total breach and sue immediately. Here, the singer merely expressed doubt that he would be able to perform. An expression of doubt does not constitute an anticipatory repudiation. (A) is therefore wrong. (B) is wrong because the nightclub owner did not have to change his position in reliance on the singer's telephone call because it was not a repudiation. However, the call did indicate a prospective inability to perform on the singer's part, which would allow the nightclub owner to demand adequate assurances of performance from the singer. Only after the singer's noncompliance with such a demand could the nightclub owner safely change his position (*e.g.*, by hiring a substitute performer), because the failure to give assurances may be treated as a total repudiation. (D) states incorrect law. A repudiation also may be oral or by conduct, as long as it is unequivocal.

Answer to Question 106

(C) The court should not admit the evidence because it is hearsay not within any exception. The officer is attempting to testify to the statement of a witness (an out-of-court declarant) that the defendant was the person she saw fleeing from a stolen vehicle. The testimony is being offered to prove the truth of the matter asserted—that the witness saw the defendant flee from a stolen vehicle. This constitutes inadmissible hearsay because it does not fit within any exception to the hearsay rule and should not be admitted. (A) is incorrect because the declarant's unavailability to testify is relevant to the admission of hearsay only when the statement is: (i) the former testimony of the declarant, (ii) a statement against interest, (iii) a dying declaration, (iv) a statement

of personal or family history, or (v) a statement offered against a party procuring the declarant's availability. The statement made by the witness that she saw the defendant fleeing from a stolen vehicle does not fall within any of these categories; thus, the statement is not admissible merely because she is unavailable. (B) is incorrect because a statement of prior identification of a person made after perceiving him is hearsay unless the witness is subject to cross-examination. Here, the witness who made the prior identification is not testifying. Thus, the statement of identification remains hearsay. (D) is incorrect because the picture of the defendant is not even being offered into evidence.

Answer to Question 107

(D) The club owner will not recover the additional salary. A duty to perform under a personal services contract will be discharged where it has become impossible to perform, *e.g.*, because of physical incapacity. (If the impossibility is only temporary, the duty is only suspended and "springs back" into existence when performance once more becomes possible.) Here, the instructor's physical incapacity discharged his duty to perform during the two months he would be in the hospital, and he will not be liable for the additional costs that the club owner incurred in hiring a replacement. (A) is incorrect because notice is not required before duties are discharged on the basis of impossibility. (B) is incorrect because physical incapacity that makes it impossible to perform is not a breach of contract. Rather, it discharges the incapacitated person's duty to perform (as discussed above). Because there was no breach here, the general rule about paying mitigation expenses does not apply. (C) is incorrect because, although mitigation costs must be reasonable, this is not a case where mitigation of damages applies because there has been no breach of contract (as discussed above).

Answer to Question 108

(B) The creditor will prevail because the debtor has made an effective assignment of his right to collect the debt from the third party. The general rule is that a writing is not required to have an effective assignment. Here, the oral assignment to the creditor of the debtor's right to the $4,000 was effective and enforceable by the creditor. (A) is incorrect for two reasons: The creditor's agreement to accept $4,000 did not constitute consideration because he no longer had a right to enforce the original debt. Furthermore, consideration is not required for an assignment; a gratuitous assignment is effective. The absence of a writing or consideration may allow the assignor (the debtor) to revoke an assignment, but will not prevent the assignee from enforcing it against the obligor. (C) is incorrect. While the obligor may raise contract defenses on the obligation he owes to the assignor (the debtor), he may not raise defenses that the assignor might have had against the assignee (the creditor) on a different obligation as a means of avoiding his own obligation. Here, there are no apparent defenses to the third party's liability to the debtor for the $4,000 debt, and the third party is not entitled to assert the debtor's statute of limitations defense to the debt that the debtor owed to the creditor. (D) is incorrect for a similar reason. The general rule is that a new promise to pay a legal obligation barred by law must be in writing to be enforceable; hence, if the debtor had made an oral promise to the creditor to pay him $4,000, the creditor may have had difficulty enforcing it against the debtor. However, the third party has a separate obligation to the debtor that is not barred by any defense; the debtor's gratuitous assignment to the creditor of his right to the $4,000 does not allow the third party to raise a defense that the debtor may have had against the creditor.

Answer to Question 109

(A) The homeowner will be found not guilty because he did not have the requisite mental state. To

convict a person for an attempted crime, the prosecution must establish that the defendant had an actual specific intent to cause the harm prohibited by the statute and committed an act beyond mere preparation in furtherance of that intent. Those elements—specific intent and act—are required regardless of the mental state required by the target offense. A person who took a substantial step towards commission of the crime but was only reckless with respect to the target offense could not be found guilty of attempt. The homeowner did not intend to burn the neighbor's home. Therefore, he cannot be guilty of attempted arson of the neighbor's home. (B) is wrong. The fact that the fire was put out before it burned any of the neighbor's home would not preclude a conviction of attempted arson if the elements of attempted arson were otherwise established. (C) is wrong. To be guilty of attempted arson of the neighbor's home, the homeowner must have intended to burn the neighbor's home. The doctrine of transferred intent does not apply to attempt. (D) is wrong. A specific intent to burn the home is required for attempted arson. While malice satisfies the state of mind requirement for the completed crime of arson, it will not suffice for attempt.

Answer to Question 110

(C)   The state's challenge to the decision of the state supreme court presents no substantial federal question and will be denied. The Supreme Court's appellate jurisdiction under 28 U.S.C. section 1257 extends to reviewing the decision of the highest court of a state where the validity of state legislation is called into question on the ground that it is unconstitutional or contrary to federal statutes. However, the Supreme Court will hear a case from a state court only if the state court judgment turned on federal grounds. The Court will refuse jurisdiction if it finds adequate and independent nonfederal grounds to support the state decision, because a different interpretation of the federal statutes would have no effect on the judgment rendered by the state court, so that the Supreme Court, in effect, would be rendering an advisory opinion. Here, even if the state court was incorrect in holding that federal statutes preempted the state legislation, it also held that the state constitution prohibited the state legislation. Hence, a different interpretation of the federal preemption issue would have no effect on the outcome of the case. (A) is incorrect because, as discussed above, the nonfederal grounds are fully dispositive of the case. Even if the federal grounds were wrongly decided, it would not affect the outcome of the case. (B) is incorrect because the state court has interpreted its legislation so that it also conflicts with its state constitution. Thus, its determination of whether its legislation conflicts with federal law has no effect. (D) is incorrect because the Supreme Court has complete discretion under its appellate jurisdiction to review cases from the highest state court where a state statute allegedly violates state law; it is irrelevant that the state is challenging its state court decision.

Answer to Question 111

(C)   The nephew's express rejection of the deed was sufficient to rebut any presumption of acceptance. As a general rule, delivery of the deed is the final operative act to complete a conveyance of title to the grantee, because courts will infer the grantee's acceptance if the conveyance is beneficial to him. However, all courts will consider evidence that is contrary to the presumption or inference. Hence, the nephew's express rejection of the gift is sufficient to establish that no conveyance of the property took place. (A) is an incorrect statement of law. If the grantor intends the recording of the deed to be the final act in vesting title in the grantee, then such recording creates a presumption of delivery even where the grantee did not know of the recordation. (B) is wrong because there is no such thing as a constructive reconveyance. Had the nephew accepted the gift (completing the conveyance) and later changed his mind, the nephew would have had to execute a new deed to convey the property back to the uncle. (D) is wrong because knowledge or permission of the grantee has no effect on the validity of the recordation; rather, it determines whether there has been an effective acceptance.

Answer to Question 112

(C) The home is not subject to the judgment lien even though the niece never recorded the deed. Under the recording acts, a subsequent mortgagee or bona fide purchaser for value generally prevails over the grantee of a prior unrecorded conveyance. However, most recording statutes do not protect subsequent judgment creditors on the theory that the creditor is not offering consideration at the time its lien is created, and the language of the recording statute generally extends protection to "purchasers," defined as those obtaining an interest in exchange for consideration. Also, courts generally interpret a judgment lien statute like the one in the question to apply to "any land" *actually owned* by the judgment debtor rather than any land for which the judgment debtor has record title. Hence, (C) is correct and (A) is incorrect; the home was validly conveyed to the niece and is not subject to the claim of the lien creditor. (B) is incorrect because if the home were part of the estate, it would be subject to any claim against the testator. (D) is incorrect because the insurance company's lien only applies against the judgment debtor or her estate. Even though the niece is sole beneficiary and executrix, she has no responsibility to pay charges against the estate out of what she already owns.

Answer to Question 113

(D) The evidence is admissible for impeachment purposes as an inconsistent statement of a hearsay declarant. Because the credibility of a hearsay declarant is as much at issue as the credibility of an in-court witness, Federal Rule 806 allows statements of a hearsay declarant to be impeached to the same extent as those of an in-court witness. Thus, a statement of the declarant made at any time that is inconsistent with his hearsay statement may be offered into evidence for impeachment purposes. Here, the eyewitness's hearsay statement (which probably qualified as an excited utterance) was testified to by the pedestrian. The eyewitness's subsequent statement to his brother is inconsistent with his hearsay statement and is therefore admissible to discredit that statement. (A) is wrong because the general requirement that an impeached witness be given an opportunity to explain or deny an apparently inconsistent statement does not apply to hearsay declarants. Because hearsay statements are often admissible at trial after the declarant has died or is otherwise unavailable, Rule 806 provides that the declarant need not be given an opportunity to explain or deny statements that are inconsistent with the declarant's hearsay statement. (B) is wrong because the statement is admissible for purposes of impeachment; hence, it does not fall within the definition of hearsay. (C) is wrong because the statement would be hearsay not within any exception if it were offered as substantive evidence as well as for impeachment. Under Federal Rule 801(d)(1), prior inconsistent statements are not admissible as substantive evidence unless made under oath at a prior trial or deposition.

Answer to Question 114

(D) The auctioneer may recover the cost of repair from either the landlord or the buyer. A landlord's promise in a lease to maintain the property does not terminate because the property is sold. Although no longer in privity of estate, the original landlord and tenant remain in privity of contract, and the original landlord remains liable on the covenant unless there is a novation. A novation substitutes a new party for an original party to the contract. It requires the assent of all parties, and completely releases the original party. Because neither the auctioneer nor the buyer has agreed to a novation, the landlord remains liable for the covenant because he and the auctioneer remain in privity of contract even after the sale. Thus, the promise to repair can be enforced

against the landlord. When leased property is sold, the purchaser may be liable for his predecessor's promises if the promise runs with the land. A covenant in a lease runs with the land if the parties to the lease so intend and the covenant touches and concerns the land. Generally, promises to do a physical act, such as maintain or repair the property, are considered to run with the land. Thus, the buyer is liable because he is in privity of estate with the auctioneer and the covenant to repair runs with the land. Consequently, both the landlord and the buyer are potentially liable to the auctioneer for the repairs. While it is true that the sale/assignment to the buyer did not sever the landlord's obligation to the auctioneer, as explained above, the landlord is not the only person who is liable to the auctioneer. Because both the landlord and the buyer are potentially liable for the repairs, (A) is incorrect. (B) is incorrect because although it is true that a covenant to repair touches and concerns the land and runs with it on assignment, the landlord as well as the buyer can be held liable. (C) is incorrect because the auctioneer may recover the *full amount* from either the landlord or the buyer.

Answer to Question 115

(A) The guest is not likely to prevail because he did not have invitee status when he was climbing over the gate. The duty owed by an owner or occupier of land to those on the land depends in most jurisdictions on whether the person on the land is characterized as a trespasser, licensee, or invitee. A trespasser is one who comes onto the land without permission or privilege. A licensee is one who enters on the land with the landowner's permission, express or implied, for his own purpose or business rather than the landowner's benefit. An invitee is one who enters onto the premises in response to an express or implied invitation of the landowner. However, a person loses his status as an invitee if he exceeds the scope of the invitation—*e.g.,* if he goes into a portion of the premises where his invitation cannot reasonably be said to extend. Here, the guest was an invitee while on the grounds of the resort, but he lost invitee status when he began climbing over the gate to get into the closed bar. He became a trespasser because he clearly did not have express or implied permission to climb into the bar, and a landowner owes no duty to an undiscovered trespasser. On the other hand, a landowner owes a discovered or anticipated trespasser the duty to warn of artificial conditions known to the landowner that involve a risk of death or serious bodily harm and that the trespasser is unlikely to discover. Here, while the guest can argue that he was an anticipated trespasser because others had climbed over the gate in the past, there is no evidence that the resort knew of the dangerous condition of the brackets, so the resort has breached no duty to the guest under these facts. (B) is incorrect because the intent to steal is not the reason why the guest will lose. The guest is still a trespasser on that part of the resort's property regardless of his intent in climbing over the gate; he would not prevail even if he were only trying to borrow a corkscrew. (C) is incorrect because, as discussed above, the resort's awareness of previous thefts from the bar may make the guest an anticipated trespasser rather than an undiscovered trespasser, but it does not make the resort liable to the guest under these circumstances. (D) is incorrect because the failure to inspect or discover the dangerous condition does not make the resort liable here. The guest could argue that the resort operators should have known of the dangerous condition of the gate, but that would not establish liability here. The landowner must *know* of a highly dangerous artificial condition to be liable to trespassers, and nothing indicates that any resort employee knew that the gate would collapse.

Answer to Question 116

(A) The proper next step for the corporation is to appeal to the state appellate courts. A plaintiff bringing an action in a state trial court is required to exhaust its state appellate remedies before seeking review in federal courts, even where federal issues are involved. (B) is incorrect because only a defendant may petition for removal under 28 U.S.C. section 1441 when the action could have been brought in the federal district court. The plaintiff, having initially selected the state court to file its suit, must pursue its state appellate remedies before seeking review in the federal courts. (C) is incorrect because a federal court of appeals never hears appeals from a state trial court. (D) is incorrect because a party may file a petition of certiorari only from a decision of the *highest* court of the state where a state statute allegedly violates the United States Constitution. [28 U.S.C. §1257]

Answer to Question 117

(D) The owner has standing to sue because it can demonstrate a concrete stake in the outcome of the controversy and an impairment of its rights by the state statute. Courts will not consider a constitutional challenge to government action unless the person challenging the action has "standing" to raise the constitutional issue. Under the Supreme Court test, the person must have "such a personal stake in the outcome of the controversy as to ensure the concrete adverseness which sharpens the presentation of issues." Here, the store owner has taken substantial steps to open outlets in the state by contracting with landowners and construction firms in that state, but cannot begin to operate these outlets without violating the state statutes; obtaining the injunction against enforcement will eliminate the problem. The court will therefore hear the suit. (A) is incorrect even though the store owner has not yet been prosecuted for violating the statute. A person challenging the constitutionality of a statute does not need to violate it and await prosecution as the sole means of seeking relief. Where there exists a clear threat of prosecution if the person fails to comply with the statute (such as previous prosecutions of others), injury in fact is established. (B) is incorrect because threatened economic injury as well as threatened injury to civil liberties will create standing. (C) is incorrect even though a federal question is involved. If the court accepts the state official's claim that the store owner lacked standing to sue, it would dismiss the suit regardless of the issues involved.

Answer to Question 118

(D) The court will find that jeopardy had attached after the second trial ended in an acquittal. The Fifth Amendment right to be free of double jeopardy for the same offense has been incorporated into the Fourteenth Amendment. The general rule is that once jeopardy attaches, the defendant may not be retried for the same offense. In jury trials, jeopardy attaches when the jury is empanelled and sworn, but the state may retry a defendant even if jeopardy has attached when the first trial ends in a hung jury. Hence, (C) is incorrect. (A) is incorrect. Because the jury had not been empanelled and sworn when the magistrate had found insufficient grounds to prosecute, no jeopardy had attached yet. Likewise, the jury deciding the case would not have been empanelled or sworn when the case was presented to a grand jury. Thus, jeopardy had not attached when the case was presented to the grand jury. As a result, (B) is incorrect. (D) is correct because the jury would had to have been empanelled and sworn (and thus jeopardy had attached), and no exception exists for a case ending in an acquittal.

Answer to Question 119

(A) The factory foreman will not succeed in quashing the indictment even though it may be based on illegally obtained evidence. A grand jury may consider any evidence available to it in determining whether probable cause exists to return an indictment against the defendant. Because the exclusionary rule does not apply, a grand jury may base its indictment on evidence that would not be admissible at trial. Thus, even if the pistol was the product of an illegal search and seizure, and the grand jury based its indictment on this evidence, the foreman will not prevail in his

attempt to quash the indictment. (B) is incorrect because it is irrelevant. If the foreman's aunt could be characterized as an "agent" of the police because she was acting at their request, the search may have been illegal, but the evidence would still be admissible at the grand jury proceeding. (C) is incorrect because, as discussed above, the grand jury may consider evidence obtained without probable cause. (D) is incorrect regardless of whether the foreman's aunt could be characterized as an agent of the police. As discussed above, even if the search is treated as a police search, the evidence can be considered by the grand jury.

Answer to Question 120

(B) The defendant's silence cannot constitute an implied admission if the defendant reasonably did not respond to the neighbor's statement. An admission is a statement or act done that amounts to a prior acknowledgment by one of the parties of one of the relevant facts. An admission can be express or it can be inferred from conduct, including silence in response to another person's statement. However, for silence to constitute an adoptive admission of the other person's statement, the circumstances must establish that the party would naturally have responded to it were it untrue. Here, the prosecution is offering the neighbor's testimony to show that the defendant impliedly admitted the neighbor's charge by not replying to it. However, if the court determines that the defendant would not reasonably deny the statement under these circumstances (because it apparently was made in jest), it will not qualify as an implied admission and the court will not admit the evidence. (A) is not correct. To the extent that the evidence is being offered to prove the matter asserted, it would be admissible as an admission, which is not hearsay under the Federal Rules. The court's refusal to accept the evidence as an implied admission would be because it is not probative evidence on the matter asserted (it does not tend to establish anything as to the defendant). (C) is incorrect because, as explained above, an admission by silence requires a statement or charge to which one would naturally respond were it untrue. (D) is incorrect because declarations against interest apply only to a person unavailable as a witness. A statement by a defendant qualifies as an admission by a party regardless of whether it is against his interest.

Answer to Question 121

(C) This question illustrates that a hearsay problem can arise even when the out-of-court declarant and the in-court witness are the same person. The defendant is attempting to testify as to a statement made by her out of court, and this statement is being offered to prove the truth of the matter asserted. Thus, the statement is hearsay. Because it is not within any exception to the hearsay rule, it must be excluded. Hearsay is a statement, other than one made by the declarant while testifying at the trial or hearing, offered in evidence to prove the truth of the matter asserted. [Fed. R. Evid. 801(c)] The defendant's out-of-court statement is being offered to prove the truth of the matter asserted therein, *i.e.*, that she used the drug for her back pain. The defendant is free to make that assertion as part of her in-court testimony, but cannot use her out-of-court statement for that purpose. Thus, the statement is hearsay. (A) would be correct if the prosecution had made a charge that the defendant is lying or exaggerating about her explanation for the drug. A prior statement by a testifying witness is not hearsay if it is consistent with the declarant's in-court testimony and is offered to rebut a charge that the witness is lying or exaggerating because of some motive. Here, the prosecution has not charged that the defendant has fabricated her explanation for the drug. Thus, the defendant's out-of-court statement is not admissible as a prior consistent statement. It is true that, as (B) states, the defendant's testimony tends to explain prosecution evidence. However, this does not provide a ground for the admission of hearsay. Thus, (B) is incorrect. (D) is incorrect because the fact that a statement is self-serving is not grounds for its exclusion. All of a criminal defendant's evidence can be considered self-serving in the sense that it furthers her claim of innocence.

Answer to Question 122

(C) While the trapeze artist clearly breached the contract, because he was under an absolute duty to perform and failed to do so, the circus manager would only be entitled to cancel the contract if the breach is material (*i.e.*, if the nonbreaching party did not receive the substantial benefit of his bargain). Where the breach is only minor, the nonbreaching party is not entitled to cancel the contract (although he will have an action for any damages suffered). Six factors that courts look at to determine materiality of breach are: (i) amount of benefit the nonbreaching party will receive ("substantial benefit" test); (ii) adequacy of damages remedy; (iii) extent of performance already completed by the breaching party; (iv) hardship to the breaching party; (v) whether the breaching party's behavior was negligent or willful; and (vi) likelihood of the breaching party completing performance. Here, although the trapeze artist has not yet begun performance, his delay was for only nine days and the contract was for the entire season; also, the circus has an adequate remedy for damages for the nine-day period. The trapeze artist's conduct does not appear to be negligent or willful, and there is nothing in the facts to indicate that he will not perform the remainder of his contract. Moreover, the circus has a full roster of performers and another performer already in the circus's employ could take the trapeze artist's place until he was ready to commence performance, so his absence for nine days would not work a hardship on the circus. Thus, the breach would be minor and the manager could not cancel the contract. (A) is incorrect because it only establishes that a breach occurred, and does not address the issue of whether the breach was material or minor. (The circus manager would only be entitled to cancel the contract if the breach was material.) (B) is incorrect because, while hardship is one of the factors to consider in determining whether a breach is material, and it might be viewed as a hardship to pay the contracted rate for 10 months (less nine days) when the tightrope walker will work for less, this is not the type of hardship that is contemplated by this test. Rather, the hardship that would result from the trapeze artist's absence during the first nine days of his contract, if any, is what the court must consider when deciding whether the delay worked a hardship on the innocent party. (D) is incorrect not only because it is not entirely true (*i.e.*, notification the day before performance was to begin probably did not give the circus manager time to procure a substitute performance), but also because notification of delay, while perhaps indicating absence of willful behavior, is not itself one of the factors courts consider in determining materiality of breach.

Answer to Question 123

(B) The witness's testimony is admissible to help prove that the defendant owned the lot. Under Federal Rule 407, subsequent repairs or precautionary measures following an injury (such as cutting down rotten limbs after one fell) are not admissible if offered to prove that the defendant was negligent (*e.g.*, in not cutting down the limbs sooner). This rule of exclusion is to encourage people to make such repairs. The evidence may be admissible, however, if it is relevant to some other issue in the case, such as ownership or control. Since the defendant's defense is that he did not own the property, the evidence would help establish ownership. People do not usually make repairs to property for which they have no responsibility. (A) is wrong because, as discussed above, the evidence would be inadmissible to help establish negligence. (C) is wrong because the evidence is not being offered to establish negligence; since it is offered only to show proof of ownership, it is admissible. (D) is wrong because it is not necessary that the evidence *prove* ownership. If the evidence *would help establish* ownership, it will be relevant.

Answer to Question 124

(B) The father validly assigned his right to receive the money to his friend. However, this assignment

was revocable, and it was revoked when the father accepted the money from his daughter. The father's right to receive the money from his daughter was a right that could be assigned. By telling her to pay the money to his friend, the father manifested an intent to transfer his rights completely and immediately to his friend. Neither a writing nor consideration was required for this assignment to be valid. However, these factors do affect revocability. This assignment was not given for consideration. Such a gratuitous assignment is generally revocable. Among the exceptions to this rule are situations where the obligor has already performed, or where the assignor is estopped from revoking by virtue of the fact that he should reasonably foresee that the assignee will change his position in reliance on the assignment and such detrimental reliance occurs. Here, the daughter (the obligor) has not already performed the terms of the assignment. On the contrary, she tendered performance directly to the original obligee. Also, there is no indication that the friend in fact changed his position detrimentally in reliance on the assignment. Consequently, the general rule of revocability of a gratuitous assignment applies. One way in which a gratuitous revocable assignment may be terminated is by the assignor taking performance directly from the obligor. By accepting the money from his daughter, the father (the assignor) took direct performance from the obligor, thereby revoking the assignment. As a result, his friend has no right to the money. (A) incorrectly fails to account for the fact that, although the father effectively assigned his right, he later revoked this assignment. (C) is incorrect because the daughter was indebted to her father's friend while the assignment was in effect. Although she did not herself incur the debt with the friend, a valid assignment that was not revoked would have obligated her to pay the friend. (D) is incorrect because these facts do not indicate that there has been a novation. There is a novation where a new contract substitutes a new party to receive benefits and assume duties that had originally belonged to one of the original parties under the terms of the old contract, who is thereby released. Here, the original agreement was between daughter and father. The daughter's payment of the money to her father and his acceptance thereof did not substitute any new parties or extinguish contractual duties as between the original contracting parties. Thus, there was no novation.

Answer to Question 125

(A) The homeowner cannot enforce the contract if she had reason to know that $4,400 was a mistake. When only one of the parties entering into a contract is mistaken about facts relating to the agreement, the nonmistaken party cannot "snap up" the offer if she knew or had reason to know of the mistake. Here, the bidder alone was mistaken as to the cost of the work; thus, there is a unilateral mistake, which ordinarily will not prevent formation of a contract. However, the court could find that, for a bid that was considerably lower than the six other bids ($800 lower than the next lowest bid), the homeowner should have known that it resulted from an error in computation. If the court does so, the homeowner cannot enforce the contract under the erroneous price. (B) is incorrect even though there is no evidence that the homeowner relied on the bid. While reliance on an erroneous bid may make it enforceable (such as when a general contractor submits a bid in reliance on a subcontractor's bid), it is not essential in the case of a unilateral mistake. The nonmistaken party may enforce the contract even without reliance unless she had reason to know of the mistake. (C) is incorrect even though it may be true here. Even when a unilateral mistake has a material effect on the agreed-on exchange, the nonmistaken party may enforce the contract absent reason to know of the mistake. (D) is incorrect because, even though the bidder assumed the risk of bid mistakes, he may avoid the contract under the condition stated in (A).

Answer to Question 126

(A) Even if the jury believes that the defendant did not intend to hit the park ranger with the arrow, the defendant nonetheless may be found guilty of murder. At common law, murder is the unlawful

killing of a human being with malice aforethought. Malice aforethought exists if the defendant has any of the following states of mind: (i) intent to kill; (ii) intent to inflict great bodily injury; (iii) reckless indifference to an unjustifiably high risk to human life (*i.e.,* an "abandoned and malignant" heart); or (iv) intent to commit a felony. Here, a jury could find that the act of shooting an arrow toward the close proximity of another person constituted a reckless disregard for a high risk of serious injury or death. (B) is incorrect because the facts do not support a conviction for voluntary manslaughter. An intentional killing is reduced from murder to voluntary manslaughter if it is committed under a provocation that would arouse sudden and intense passion in the mind of an ordinary person such as to cause him to lose self-control. Here, the park ranger merely called the defendant stupid. This would not be sufficient provocation so as to reduce an intentional killing to voluntary manslaughter. (C) is incorrect because it is possible for the defendant to be convicted of a more serious crime than involuntary manslaughter. Criminal negligence requires a substantial deviation from the standard of care that a reasonable person would exercise under the circumstances. Although a jury could easily find that shooting an arrow in the direction of another constitutes criminal negligence, thus making conviction for involuntary manslaughter possible, it is not the ***most serious*** crime for which the defendant might be liable. As discussed above, the jury could convict the defendant for murder for acting in reckless disregard of a high risk of serious injury or death. Similarly, (D) is incorrect. Even if shooting an arrow in a public park is a misdemeanor that would serve as the basis for a misdemeanor-manslaughter charge, murder would still be a more serious crime.

Answer to Question 127

(B) The client's motion should be denied because the seizure of the marijuana was properly within the scope of the stop and frisk. A police officer may stop a person without probable cause for arrest if she has an articulable and reasonable suspicion of criminal activity. [Terry v. Ohio (1968)] In such circumstances, if the officer reasonably believes that the person may be armed and dangerous, she may conduct a protective frisk. The scope of the frisk is limited to a patdown of the outer clothing for concealed instruments of assault, but the officer may reach into the suspect's clothing and seize any item that the officer reasonably believes, based on its "plain feel," is a weapon ***or contraband***. [Minnesota v. Dickerson (1993)] Here, the officer believed that the client put a weapon in his jacket as he was leaving a place where weapons and ammunition were being sold illegally; thus, she had reasonable grounds to conduct both a stop and a frisk. If the court accepts the officer's testimony that she instantly recognized the marijuana cigarettes ***based on the patdown only*** without any further conduct, they were properly seized and can be admitted into evidence. (A) is incorrect because the client was not under arrest at the time the patdown disclosed the marijuana. While the police may conduct a full search incident to a lawful arrest, they had only detained the client for purposes of an investigatory detention at the time of the seizure. (C) is incorrect because, as discussed above, a frisk for weapons also allows an officer to seize contraband if she immediately recognizes it as such. (D) is incorrect because the police did not need to rely on the search warrant to search the client; for the limited stop and frisk that occurred here, the police need only a reasonable suspicion of criminal activity and a reasonable belief that the suspect is armed and dangerous.

Answer to Question 128

(C) The defendant's motion should be denied because his constitutional rights were not violated by the search and seizure of the bookie's home based on an invalid warrant. To have a Fourth Amendment right to be free from unreasonable search and seizure, a person must have a reasonable expectation of privacy in the place searched or the item seized. Standing to challenge a search on Fourth Amendment grounds does not exist merely because a person will be harmed by introduction

of evidence seized during an illegal search of a third person's property; the defendant's *own* expectation of privacy must be violated. Here, the defendant had no right of possession of the place searched and no property interest in the items seized; thus, he had no standing to object to the search of the bookie's home and the seizure of the betting slips and check. (D) is incorrect because the defendant's motion should be denied regardless of the reasonableness of the police reliance on the search warrant. Under *United States v. Leon* (1984), a finding that a warrant was invalid because it was not supported by probable cause will not entitle a defendant to exclude the evidence obtained thereby if the police reasonably relied on a facially valid warrant. However, that determination does not need to be made with regard to the defendant because his constitutional rights were not violated by the defective warrant. (A) and (B) are incorrect because, as discussed above, the search was unlawful only with regard to the bookie's rights; the evidence may be used against the defendant because he had no expectation of privacy in the place searched.

Answer to Question 129

(D) The tenant is bound to a year-to-year tenancy at $600 per month, which, absent six months' notice to terminate, will automatically renew on the following September 30. When a tenant continues in possession after the termination of his right to possession, the landlord may evict him or bind him to a new *periodic* tenancy. In a commercial lease, if the original lease term was for a year or more, a year-to-year tenancy results. If, prior to the termination of the original tenancy, the landlord notifies the tenant that occupancy after termination will be at an increased rent, the tenant will be held to have acquiesced to the new terms if he does not surrender. A periodic tenancy is automatically renewed until proper notice is given. Proper notice for a year-to-year tenancy is six months' notice. In this case, the tenant's lease expired on September 30. Prior to that expiration, the landlord notified him that any continued tenancy would be at $600 per month. Thus, when the tenant remained in possession after September 30, the landlord could choose to hold him to a year-to-year tenancy (because the original term was five years) at $600 per month. Because the new tenancy is a periodic tenancy, it will be automatically renewed on the following September 30 unless one of the parties gives six months' notice of termination. (A) is wrong for two reasons: (i) the new tenancy is year-to-year, and (ii) the rent is $600 per month. (B) is wrong because the new tenancy is year-to-year, not month-to-month. (C) is wrong because the tenant had notice that if he stayed beyond September 30, the rent would be $600. Thus, the tenant is bound to the $600 rent. Note that the landlord's depositing of the tenant's check would not create an accord and satisfaction even though it was marked as rent payment. In addition to the requirement that a bona fide dispute must exist as to the amount owed, the check must conspicuously state that it is in full satisfaction of the debt before an accord and satisfaction can occur.

Answer to Question 130

(C) Because the federal legislation merely allows the district court to issue a "recommendation," the legislation permits the rendition of advisory opinions. Article III of the United States Constitution establishes the basis for the judicial power of federal courts. It provides that the judicial power extends to "cases and controversies." Although Congress has plenary power to delineate the jurisdictional limits of Article III courts, it is bound by the standards of judicial power set forth in Article III as to subject matter, parties, and the requirement of "case or controversy." Thus, Congress cannot require these courts to render advisory opinions or perform administrative or nonjudicial functions. The federal orange marketing legislation at issue here does not give federal district courts the authority to render binding decisions in final resolution of a controversy. Rather, the legislation simply allows the courts to make a recommendation as to confirmation, modification, or rescission of a challenged marketing order. This recommendation is apparently nonbinding on the parties and is followed by a re-vote of the marketing council. These circumstances indicate that, under this federal legislation, an Article III federal court would be rendering an advisory opinion in violation of the Constitution. It is true that, as (A) states, the federal government may properly regulate items in interstate commerce. This commerce power permits congressional regulation of any activity, local or interstate, that either in itself or in combination with other activities has a substantial economic effect upon interstate commerce. This power would permit federal legislation of the marketing and sale of oranges. However, the validity of the legislation under the commerce power does not make it immune from constitutional challenge on other grounds. Because the legislation calls for the rendition of advisory opinions, it is unconstitutional. (B) is likewise incorrect, although it states a valid general proposition of law. Congress does possess auxiliary powers that are "necessary and proper" for carrying out all powers vested in the federal government. "Necessary and proper" includes anything that is appropriate to achieve a legitimate end, but a provision that violates a specific constitutional provision is not an "appropriate" means of achieving the end. Hence, the marketing order system is not valid under the Necessary and Proper Clause because it provides for advisory opinions. (D) is incorrect because the grower is not being deprived of property without due process. The facts do not indicate that the grower is without sufficient procedural safeguards to afford him protection against arbitrary governmental deprivation of his property. Fair procedure requires at least an opportunity to present objections to the proposed action to a fair, neutral decisionmaker. The grower could argue that he does not have the opportunity to object to a neutral decisionmaker, because the district court will not be rendering a "decision." However, this is a debatable proposition, whereas it is clear that the legislation allows for impermissible advisory opinions. Therefore, (C) is a better answer than (D).

Answer to Question 131

(B) The merchant has standing to challenge the ordinance because her business will be harmed by it, and this will adversely affect her relationship with those who would buy and rent her equipment, resulting in an indirect violation of their rights. A person who challenges a government action must have standing to raise the constitutional issue. A person has standing only if she can demonstrate a concrete stake in the outcome of a controversy and that the governmental action at issue impairs her own rights. A plaintiff may assert third-party rights if she has suffered injury and that injury adversely affects her relationship with third parties, resulting in an indirect violation of their rights. Enforcement of the ordinance at issue will effectively destroy 70% of the merchant's business. Thus, the merchant is faced with an immediate and direct threat of injury to her livelihood as a result of the ordinance. This injury will also adversely affect her relationship with those persons at the beach areas of the city who would normally buy and rent her equipment, because they will now be prohibited from roller skating on the beaches between the hours of 7 a.m. and 9 p.m. This will, in turn, cause a potential violation of the rights of such third parties (e.g., the law might violate their First Amendment right to join with other persons for expressive activity). Consequently, the merchant is deemed to have standing to challenge the ordinance, and the court will reach the merits of the challenge. (A) is incorrect. The right to associate for expressive purposes is not absolute and generally does not encompass the right to secure patrons for one's business. Also, to the extent that the ordinance might interfere with the skaters' right of free association, that is an issue going to the merits of the challenge, which will not be reached until the matter of the merchant's standing is resolved. (C) is incorrect because, although the ordinance does not prohibit the merchant from renting skating equipment, it immediately and directly threatens her livelihood by prohibiting people who comprise 70% of her business from skating on public property during daytime hours. Hence, she will have standing to bring the challenge. (D) is incorrect because the facts stated in that choice are relevant only as a defense on the merits of the ordinance, rather than as factors on the issue of the merchant's standing; they would not constitute grounds for the court to decline to hear the case.

Answer to Question 132

(B) The landowner can recover against the grocer and the florist jointly and severally for $10,000 and against the grocer and the barber jointly and severally for $10,000. If a tenant makes a complete transfer of the entire remaining term of his leasehold interest, he has made an assignment. In an assignment, the assignee and the landlord are in privity of estate, and each is liable to the other on all covenants in the lease that run with the land. Because the covenant to pay rent runs with the land, an assignee owes the rent directly to the landlord during the time that she is in privity of estate with the landlord. If the assignee reassigns the leasehold interest, her privity of estate with the landlord ends, and she is not liable for the subsequent assignee's failure to pay rent. Hence, the florist is liable to the landowner for the one year of rent while she was in privity of estate with her, but not for the year that the barber did not pay rent. The barber is liable for the one year of rent while he was in privity of estate with the landowner. The grocer continues to be liable for rent, even though he is no longer in privity of estate with the landowner, based on the contractual obligation in the lease to pay rent, *i.e.,* on privity of contract grounds. For each of the two years of rent, the two liable parties are jointly and severally liable for the rent because the landowner can choose to collect all of it from one party or some of it from one party and some from the other party. (A) is wrong because, as discussed above, the barber also is liable for the final year of rent payments because he was in privity of estate with the landowner. (C) is wrong because there is no basis for holding the florist liable for the second year that rent was not paid. She was not in privity of estate with the landowner at that time, and there is no indication that the florist specifically promised the landowner that she would be liable for the rent for the remainder of the lease term (which would have given the landowner a privity of contract basis for holding the florist liable). Also, the facts indicate that there was no specific promise in the agreement between the grocer and the florist regarding payment of rent, so the landowner has no third-party beneficiary grounds to sue the florist for the second year of rent. (D) is wrong because it states the result if the barber had only obtained a sublease from the florist rather than an assignment. If that were the case, the florist rather than the barber would be liable for the second year of rent because the barber would be in neither privity of contract nor privity of estate with the landowner. However, because the florist retained no part of the remaining term when she transferred her interest to the barber, the transfer was an assignment rather than a sublease, and the barber rather than the florist is in privity of estate for that period.

Answer to Question 133

(A) If the car owner prevails, it will be because the boy did not conform to the standard of care of a child of like age, education, intelligence, and experience. When the tortfeasor is a child, the standard of care generally imposed by the courts in negligence actions is that of a child of like age, education, intelligence, and experience. This permits a subjective evaluation of these factors. If the boy failed to act according to the standard of care of a 12-year-old child who had flown model airplanes before, he has breached his duty to the car owner, who was a foreseeable plaintiff because his car was parked nearby. This breach was the actual and proximate cause of damages to the owner's car, completing the prima facie case for negligence. (B) is incorrect because it applies the adult reasonable person standard; this standard has been applied to children only when they are engaged in activities that normally only adults engage in, such as driving an automobile or piloting an actual airplane. (C) is incorrect because the warning in the instruction manual may be a factor in establishing whether the boy breached the standard of care applicable to him, but it is not determinative. Even if the instruction manual were silent about flying the airplane in the rain, the boy may have been negligent by continuing to fly it when he had trouble controlling it. (D) is incorrect because trespass to chattels requires an intent to do the act that causes the damage to another's chattels. The boy did not intend to fly the airplane at the owner's car; hence, he is liable only if he acted negligently.

Answer to Question 134

(A) Both the kidnapper and the cohort are guilty of conspiracy. At common law, a conspiracy was an agreement between two or more persons to commit an unlawful act or to commit a lawful act in an unlawful manner. The elements are: (i) an agreement between two or more persons; (ii) the intent to enter into an agreement; and (iii) the intent to achieve the objective of the agreement. When the kidnapper and the cohort decided to kidnap the wealthy man's son, they were guilty of common law conspiracy. Although a majority of states now require an overt act in furtherance of the conspiracy, mere preparation, such as the surveillance here, suffices. (B) is wrong for two reasons: If a person withdraws from a conspiracy, he is no longer liable for future crimes committed in furtherance of the conspiracy, but he remains liable for the crime of conspiracy, which was complete at the time of the agreement. Second, to have a successful withdrawal, a person must communicate the withdrawal to his co-conspirators, which the cohort did not do. (C) is also wrong for two reasons: First, the cohort is still liable for conspiracy. Second, even if his withdrawal relieved him from liability for subsequent offenses, the kidnapper could still be convicted of conspiracy. (D) is wrong because, at common law, both parties must have the intent, at the time of the agreement, to commit the unlawful act. Given that the butler did not have the necessary intent, neither he nor the kidnapper can be convicted of conspiracy with respect to their conversations.

Answer to Question 135

(A) The most accurate statement is that the brother will be found guilty of attempted murder. Attempt requires a specific intent to commit the crime and an act beyond mere preparation in furtherance of the crime. The Model Penal Code and most state criminal codes require that the act or omission constitute a substantial step in a course of conduct planned to culminate in the commission of the crime. In addition, an act will not qualify as a substantial step unless it is strong corroboration of the actor's criminal purpose. Here, the brother had the specific intent to commit murder, and took a substantial step toward committing the offense by paying the hit man, an act that strongly corroborates his intent. Hence, he can be found guilty of attempted murder. (B) is incorrect because the conspiracy does not automatically result in attempt liability. For attempt, specific intent and a substantial step corroborative of intent must be established. Furthermore, under the modern (Model Penal Code) rules for attempt, the sister can raise withdrawal (renunciation) as a defense to attempt, because she voluntarily and completely abandoned her efforts to commit the crime (and took steps to prevent its commission) as a result of her "change of heart." (C) is incorrect because the hit man's response to the brother is irrelevant for attempt. Because the brother had the requisite intent and took a substantial step toward committing the offense by contacting the hit man, the brother can be found guilty of attempted murder. (D) is incorrect. The brother and sister did have the mental state necessary for attempt because they had the specific intent to kill the parents.

Answer to Question 136

(B) The homeowner prevails because the painter gave no consideration for the purported modification of the contract. Terms of a contract may be modified by the parties to the contract. However, consideration generally is necessary to modify a contract (in other words, the modification must have a bargained-for exchange with some element of legal value to the parties). Where a modification would operate to the benefit of only one of the parties, it will be unenforceable unless

some consideration is being given to the other party. Under the preexisting legal duty rule, the promise to perform or the performance of an existing legal duty will not be sufficient consideration. Here, the homeowner and the painter have attempted to modify their contract so that the homeowner will pay the extra $600. Because this modification would work to the painter's benefit only, it is unenforceable because the painter has not given any consideration to the homeowner for the modification. The painter was already under a binding contract to repaint the homeowner's house for $8,000. Thus, the painter's performance of a duty that he was already obligated to perform does not constitute sufficient consideration to support the modification. Consequently, the homeowner is obligated to pay only the originally agreed-upon $8,000. (A) is incorrect, because the homeowner's promise to pay the additional money need not be in writing to be enforceable. Under the Statute of Frauds, a writing signed by the party sought to be bound is required for: (i) a promise by an executor or administrator to pay the estate's debts out of her own funds; (ii) a promise to answer for the debt of another; (iii) a promise made in consideration of marriage; (iv) a promise creating an interest in land; (v) a promise that by its terms cannot be performed within one year; and (vi) a promise for the sale of goods of $500 or more. Because the homeowner's promise does not come within any of these categories, it need not be in writing. (C) is incorrect because, in repainting the homeowner's house, the painter was simply fulfilling his contractual obligation, rather than acting to his detriment in reliance on the homeowner's promise to pay the additional money. Even where unsupported by consideration, a promise is enforceable under the promissory estoppel doctrine to the extent necessary to prevent injustice if: (i) the promisor should reasonably expect to induce action or forbearance of a definite and substantial character; and (ii) such action or forbearance is in fact induced. The painter was legally bound to perform the work on the homeowner's house regardless of whether the homeowner agreed to pay the extra $600. Thus, it cannot be said that the painter incurred a detriment in reliance on the homeowner's promise. (D) is incorrect because there was no good faith dispute between the parties. An exception to the preexisting legal duty rule provides that, if the scope of the legal duty owed is the subject of honest dispute, a modifying agreement relating to it will be given effect. Here, the parties' legal duties were clearly specified: The painter was to repaint the homeowner's house, and the homeowner was to pay $8,000. There is no indication that the painter believed in good faith that he had legal grounds for avoiding the original contract because he could not otherwise make a profit. Therefore, the homeowner's promise to pay the extra money was not the settlement of a good faith dispute.

Answer to Question 137

(D) As an expert witness, the engineer may base her opinion on facts not in evidence that were supplied to her out of court, and that are of a type reasonably relied upon by experts in that particular field in forming opinions on the subject. In this case, expert testimony is admissible because its subject matter (*i.e.,* whether the closures caused the deflation panel to give way) is one where specialized knowledge will assist the trier of fact in determining a fact in issue. A structural engineer possesses the special knowledge and training sufficient to qualify her as an expert. An expert may base her opinion on facts not known personally but supplied to her outside the courtroom (*e.g.*, reports of technicians or consultants). Such facts need not be in evidence or even of a type admissible in evidence as long as they are of a kind reasonably relied upon by experts in the particular field. [Fed. R. Evid. 703] Consequently, the engineer's testimony should be admitted because it is based on the laboratory reports, and it is industry practice to rely on such reports. (A) is incorrect because, as noted above, the engineer may base her opinion on facts not known personally to her. Thus, the admissibility of the engineer's testimony does not require that she have personally performed the tests on which the lab reports are based. (B) is incorrect because the facts upon which the engineer bases her opinion need not be of a type admissible in evidence. Thus, although the lab reports might be inadmissible hearsay, the engineer may base her testimony on them. (C) is incorrect because the engineer may base her opinion on facts that are not in evidence. Furthermore, while the engineer may be required to disclose the underlying facts on cross-examination, they may not be disclosed to the jury on the balloonist's direct examination unless the court determines that their probative value in assisting the jury evaluate the expert's opinion substantially outweighs their prejudicial effect.

Answer to Question 138

(B)   Testimony as to the date of purchase of the sculpture should not be admitted because its minimal relevance is substantially outweighed by considerations of waste of time and confusion of the issues under Rule 403. Whether the plaintiff actually purchased the sculpture one week sooner than the date testified to by him has no bearing on the amount he should have been charged, which is the issue in controversy. The only relevance of the clerk's testimony is to cast doubt on the plaintiff's credibility, but it is not admissible for impeachment purposes either. When a witness makes a statement not directly relevant to the issues in the case, the rule against impeachment on a collateral matter bars his opponent from proving the statement untrue either by extrinsic evidence or by a prior inconsistent statement. As noted previously, the plaintiff's statement as to the date on which he purchased the sculpture is not directly relevant to any other issue in the case. Thus, the defendant is not permitted to prove the statement untrue by means of the clerk's testimony that the plaintiff made the purchase on a different day. (D) is incorrect even though it is true that the clerk's testimony tends to prove that the plaintiff purchased the sculpture on a date other than that to which he testified. As detailed above, the limited relevance of the date for impeachment purposes is outweighed by considerations of waste of time and confusion of issues. (A) is incorrect because the clerk is not testifying to the content of the purchase order. Rather, she is simply testifying to the date of purchase from her own memory. Thus, the hearsay nature of the contents of the purchase order is not at issue. (C) is incorrect. Under the past recollection recorded exception to the hearsay rule, where a witness states that she has insufficient recollection of an event to enable her to testify fully and accurately, even after she has consulted a writing given to her on the stand, the writing itself may be introduced into evidence if: (i) the witness at one time had personal knowledge of the facts recited in the writing; (ii) the writing was timely made when the matter was fresh in the witness's mind; (iii) the writing was made by the witness or under her direction or adopted by her; and (iv) the witness is presently unable to remember the facts. Here, the clerk has not stated that she has insufficient recollection of the events to which she is testifying, and the defendant is not even attempting to introduce the purchase order into evidence. She is fully able to testify as to the date on which the plaintiff purchased the sculpture, and is simply referring to the purchase order because of having seen the plaintiff's unusual signature on it. Thus, the purchase order does not constitute a past recollection recorded.

Answer to Question 139

(B)   The nephew has ownership of the land because he has exercised his power to terminate the developer's fee simple subject to condition subsequent in the land. A fee simple subject to a condition subsequent is created when the grantor retains the power to terminate the estate of the grantee on the happening of a specified event. On the happening of that event, the estate of the grantee continues until the grantor exercises her power of termination (right of entry) by bringing suit or making reentry. Here, the landowner conveyed a fee simple subject to a restriction against constructing multi-family dwellings, retaining a right of entry. She devised this interest to the nephew in her will, as the statute permitted, and the nephew exercised this right by bringing an ejectment action against the developer after the condition was violated. Hence, the nephew will

have ownership of the land. (A) is not as good a choice as (B) because the developer's interest in the land was not automatically terminated once he violated the condition; it continued until the nephew took action to terminate it. Absent the nephew bringing an ejectment action, the developer would have superior rights in the land. (C) is incorrect because the Rule Against Perpetuities does not apply to a right of entry. A right of entry is a reversionary interest of the transferor, which is not subject to the Rule Against Perpetuities because it is vested. It retains its status as a reversionary interest even when it is transferred to a third party. Thus, the nephew had the power to exercise the right of entry. (D) is incorrect because the transaction was a valid conveyance of a defeasible fee simple. Restraints on alienation refer to restrictions in transferring property to others. There was nothing in the conveyance preventing the developer from transferring his interest to a third party. The restriction on the use of the property was a valid condition subsequent.

Answer to Question 140

(C) The testimony of the witness is inadmissible because it does not tend to prove or disprove any trait of the defendant that is pertinent to the case. To be admissible, evidence must be relevant, *i.e.,* it must have some tendency to make the existence of any fact that is of consequence to the determination of an action more probable than it would be without the evidence. In a criminal case, the prosecution cannot initiate evidence of the bad character of the defendant merely to show that he is more likely to have committed the crime of which he is accused. However, the defendant may introduce evidence of his good character to show his innocence of the alleged crime. [Fed. R. Evid. 404(a)(1)] This is done by calling a qualified witness to testify to the defendant's good reputation for *the trait involved in the case*, or to give his personal opinion concerning that trait. [Fed. R. Evid. 405] The defendant is charged with assault with a deadly weapon. There is no indication that the defendant's honesty is at issue; rather, any traits of violence are at issue and are pertinent to the crime of which the defendant is accused. Because the testimony of the witness relates to the defendant's honesty, which is of no consequence to the determination of this criminal proceeding, such testimony is inadmissible as being irrelevant. (A) is incorrect because reputation evidence is not always admissible to establish a character trait. The trait sought to be established must be pertinent to the crime that is charged. (B) is incorrect because only the criminal defendant can put his character in issue. The prosecution cannot initiate evidence of the defendant's character, and the mere filing of criminal charges against a person does not put that person's character in issue. (D) is incorrect because reputation of a person's character in the community is an exception to the hearsay rule. [Fed. R. Evid. 803(21)] Thus, the evidence offered here would not be excluded on the ground that it is inadmissible hearsay.

Answer to Question 141

(B) The court will allow the historian to testify as to the identity of the voice simply because he is familiar with the uncle's voice. Where the identity of a speaker is important, the oral statements require authentication as to the identity of the speaker. A voice, whether heard firsthand or through a tape recording, may be identified by the opinion of anyone who has heard the voice at any time. As long as such a foundation is laid to show familiarity with the voice, a lay opinion as to the identity of the speaker is permissible. Thus, because the historian became familiar with the uncle's voice when he made the tape recording, he will be permitted to testify that the voice on the tape was the uncle's. (A) is incorrect because, even assuming that the uncle is a party opponent, the historian is only testifying as to the identity of the speaker rather than any admissions that the uncle may have made. (C) is incorrect because, in contrast to the rule for handwriting

verification, a person can become familiar with a voice after litigation has begun and for the sole purpose of testifying. Hence, the fact that the historian became familiar with the uncle's voice before the dispute arose is not critical to admissibility of his testimony. (D) is incorrect because expert testimony is not required for identifying a voice on a tape recording. Because the historian's testimony is based on his previous familiarity with the uncle's voice and is needed to authenticate the tape recording, it will be admissible as opinion testimony under Federal Rule 701.

Answer to Question 142

(C) No contract was created because the supplier effectively revoked his offer. Under the U.C.C., an offer by a merchant to buy or sell goods in a signed writing that, by its terms, gives assurances that it will be held open is not revocable for lack of consideration during the time stated (not to exceed three months). If the term assuring that the offer will be held open is on a form supplied by the offeree, it must be separately signed by the offeror. Here, the school district supplied the form stating that the offer must be held open for four months. The supplier's verbal assent to that requirement was not sufficient to qualify as a firm offer under the U.C.C. Thus, he was free to revoke his offer. (A) is incorrect because the fact that a writing would not be required under the Statute of Frauds if a contract had been formed between the parties is irrelevant. A writing is required for a firm offer under the U.C.C. regardless of the value of the goods offered. (B) is incorrect because the school district lost its power of acceptance when the supplier revoked his offer, regardless of the fact that three months had not passed. As discussed above, the supplier's offer did not constitute a firm offer under the U.C.C. (D) is incorrect because the fact that the term of the firm offer was more than three months does not invalidate it. If the stated period extends beyond three months, the firm offer will stand, but it will only last for the three-month maximum.

Answer to Question 143

(A) The suspect's motion should be denied. As a general matter, to conduct a constitutionally valid search, the police must have a search warrant based on probable cause unless the case falls under one of the exceptions to the warrant requirement. One well-established exception to the warrant requirement is the automobile exception. If the police have probable cause to believe that an automobile contains contraband or evidence of a crime, they may search whatever area of the car that may contain the object of their search without having to get a warrant. Probable cause to search is defined as reasonable grounds for believing that a particular item of seizure is located at a particular place. From the facts given, the officers had reasonable grounds to believe that cocaine was in the trunk of the car. (B) is wrong. If the police make a valid arrest of the driver of the car, they can search the area within the immediate control of the driver as a search incident to an arrest. The area within the control of the driver would include the entire passenger area of the car, but not the trunk. The trunk cannot be searched as a search incident to an arrest. (C) is no longer the law. At one time, the officers were required to secure the closed container and then obtain a warrant. Under present law, the police can open the package if they have probable cause. (D) is wrong. Actual knowledge that it is the same package is not required. Probable cause—reasonable grounds to believe—is the criteria.

Answer to Question 144

(B) The driver's motion should be denied. As a general matter, to conduct a constitutionally valid search, the police must have a search warrant based on probable cause unless the case falls under one of the exceptions to the warrant requirement. A well-recognized exception to the general requirement of a search warrant is a search incident to a lawful arrest. If the police make a valid

arrest of the driver of the car, they may conduct a warrantless search of the entire passenger compartment of the car as a search incident to the arrest. A valid arrest requires probable cause to arrest—reasonable grounds to believe that the person being arrested has committed a crime—but does not require an arrest warrant. From the facts given, the police had plenty of probable cause to arrest the driver. Therefore, the search of the front seat where the open bottle of whiskey was found was valid. (A) is too broad a statement. Under the "automobile" exception, if the police have probable cause to believe that a car contains contraband or fruits, instruments, or evidence of a crime, they may search the car without a warrant. However, under the facts given, there are no indications that the officer had grounds to believe any of those items were in the car. (C) is wrong. Even though the police did not have probable cause to search the car, it could be searched as a search incident to an arrest. (D) is wrong. Even after the driver has been arrested and placed in a squad car, the search incident to an arrest can take place.

Answer to Question 145

(D) The seller is not entitled to specific performance because she is unable to furnish the buyer with such title to the land as to eliminate a reasonable probability that the buyer will be subjected to a lawsuit. Absent a provision to the contrary, a contract for the sale of land contains an implied promise by the seller that she will deliver to the buyer a marketable title at the time of closing. This promise imposes on the seller an obligation to deliver a title that is free from reasonable doubt; *i.e.,* free from questions that might present an unreasonable risk of litigation. Title is marketable if a reasonably prudent buyer would accept it in the exercise of ordinary prudence. An inability to establish a record chain of title will generally render the title unmarketable. If the buyer determines, prior to closing, that the seller's title is unmarketable, he must notify the seller and allow a reasonable time to cure the defect. If the seller is unable to acquire title before closing, so that title remains unmarketable, the buyer can rescind, sue for damages caused by breach, or obtain specific performance with an abatement of the purchase price. Here, the title search report fails to indicate how title to the land left the farmer and was conveyed to the landowner. This in turn indicates that some records are missing from the report. The fact that records are missing would create in a reasonably prudent buyer a doubt as to the probability of being subjected to a lawsuit by, *e.g.,* the farmer or someone else who might claim rightful title to the land on the basis of the landowner's conveyance to the seller being fraudulent or otherwise invalid. Consequently, the seller's title to the land was unmarketable. It is the seller's inability to make good her title by the closing date that permits the buyer to rescind the contract and prevents the seller from being able to specifically enforce the contract. It is true that, as (C) states, there is a gap in the title. However, this gap does not by itself render title unmarketable. Rather, it is the seller's inability to establish a record chain of title or otherwise satisfactorily explain the gap by the closing date, after being notified of it, that renders title unmarketable. Therefore, (C) is not as good an answer as (D). It is also true that, as (A) states, the uniqueness of land makes it a proper subject for specific performance. However, as explained above, the seller's breach of her promise to deliver marketable title prevents her from specifically enforcing the contract, and permits the buyer to rescind it. Thus, (A) is incorrect. (B) is also incorrect. Because the seller took title from the landowner by warranty deed, she has received some assurance either that the landowner had the authority to make the conveyance or that he will defend on her behalf against any lawful claims of title by a third party. However, even if such protections were extended to the buyer (as the seller's transferee), title would still be unmarketable. The buyer is not required to "buy a lawsuit," even if his ultimate success on the merits of such a suit seems likely.

Answer to Question 146

(A) The court will likely find the legislation to be a constitutional regulation of obscenity. Obscenity, which is not protected speech under the First Amendment, is defined by the Supreme Court as a description or depiction of sexual conduct that, taken as a whole, by the average person, applying contemporary community standards, appeals to the prurient interest in sex, portrays sex in a patently offensive way, and—using a national reasonable person standard—does not have serious literary, artistic, political, or scientific value. Thus, the legislation here is constitutional because it uses a reasonable person standard, rather than a community standard, for determining the value of the work. (B) is incorrect because while a statewide standard for determining whether the material is patently offensive is permissible, it is not mandatory. A state may use a "community standard" for making this determination. (C) is incorrect because, again, a statewide standard for determining whether the material is patently offensive is permissible. Only the "social value" element of the obscenity test requires a national standard. (D) is incorrect because the legislation is valid regardless of whether it is necessary to achieve the state's compelling interest in reducing violent crime. Speech that falls within the definition of obscenity is unprotected speech; the government does not need a specific compelling interest to ban it.

Answer to Question 147

(B) Because time was of the essence in the contract, the builder's tardiness in delivering the deed and certificate of completion was a material breach, thus excusing the buyer from her duty of performance. When a promisor is under an absolute duty to perform, and this duty has not been discharged, the failure to perform in accordance with the contract will constitute a breach of the contract. A minor breach (where the obligee gains the substantial benefit of her bargain despite the breach) affords a remedy to the aggrieved party but does not relieve him of his duty of performance under the contract. If the breach is material, the nonbreaching party may treat the contract as at an end (*i.e.,* any duty of counterperformance owed by him is discharged) and will have an immediate right to all remedies for breach of the entire contract. Generally, failure of a promisor to render timely performance, although a breach, will not be material. However, where the contract by its terms provides that time is of the essence, failure of timely performance will be a material breach. The contract between the buyer and the builder contained a clause stating that time was of the essence. Thus, when the builder failed to deliver the deed and certificate on time, as per his contractual duties, this failure constituted a material breach. Because the breach is material, the buyer may treat the contract as at an end, and the duty owed by him to pay the agreed-upon purchase price is discharged. Therefore, the builder will recover nothing. (C) is incorrect because, where time is of the essence, the shortness of the delay in performing will not render the breach minor. (D) is incorrect because, as explained above, the material breach by the builder discharges the buyer's duty of counterperformance. Therefore, even where the buyer suffered no damages as a result of the delay, the buyer may treat the contract as ended, and the builder can recover nothing from him. (A) is incorrect because there is no indication that preparing a certificate of completion requires that degree of personal judgment and skill as to make the duty nondelegable, nor is there any indication that the buyer even contracted for a specific architect to prepare the certificate.

Answer to Question 148

(C) Under Article 2 of the U.C.C., an offer to buy goods for current or prompt shipment is construed as inviting acceptance either by a promise to ship or by current or prompt shipment of conforming or nonconforming goods. While shipment of nonconforming goods ordinarily is an acceptance creating a bilateral contract as well as a breach of that contract, the result is different if the seller seasonably notifies the buyer that a shipment of nonconforming goods is offered only as an accommodation to the buyer. In that case, the shipment is a counteroffer rather than an acceptance, and the buyer is free to accept or reject it, as stated in (C). (A) and (B) are wrong because the store owner does not have any damage claim against the supplier, because his shipment of the gloves was a counteroffer rather than an acceptance and breach, and the store owner has the option to accept the offer on its terms or reject it, in which case no contract would be formed. (D) is wrong because, as discussed above, the shipment of the gloves did not constitute an attempted acceptance and performance of the store owner's offer but rather a counteroffer by the supplier. The store owner did not have the power to accept only part of the goods.

Answer to Question 149

(D) The court should rule for the sister because she has a valid right of first refusal that she is entitled to exercise. A joint tenancy is a type of concurrent ownership of a parcel of land that is distinguished primarily by the right of survivorship; *i.e.,* when one joint tenant dies, the property is freed of her concurrent interest and the survivor retains an undivided right in the property that is no longer subject to the interest of the deceased co-tenant. To create a joint tenancy, a grantor must explicitly indicate in the conveyance that the parties are to hold as joint tenants. If one joint tenant conveys her interest, the joint tenancy is severed. The new tenant holds as a tenant in common with the remaining joint tenant, so that there is no longer a right of survivorship. Here, the father, the grantor of the property, expressly indicated in the conveyance that the son and the daughter were to take the property as joint tenants with right of survivorship. When the daughter quitclaimed her interest in the property to the purchaser, the joint tenancy between the daughter and the son was severed (despite the fact that the son did not know of the conveyance to the purchaser). However, the daughter's conveyance triggered the sister's right of first refusal. A right of first refusal is a preemptive option that gives its owner the right to meet any offer to purchase real estate. Thus, the sister should have been given the opportunity to meet the purchaser's offer. Because the purchaser's interest in the property is no greater than the daughter's interest, the sister may enforce her right of first refusal against the purchaser. (A) is incorrect because the right of first refusal is a valid restraint on alienation if it is reasonable. Here, the right of first refusal is based on the sale price of the property, which would be deemed reasonable. (B) is incorrect because the joint tenancy was severed by the daughter's conveyance. (C) is incorrect because the right of first refusal here does not violate the Rule Against Perpetuities. Under the common law Rule Against Perpetuities, no interest in property is valid unless it must vest, if at all, within 21 years after a life in being at the time the interest is created. Because a right of first refusal is treated as a contingent future interest, it is subject to the Rule. Thus, if the right *might* be exercised beyond the perpetuities period, it is void. Here, the right of first refusal is limited to the son's and the daughter's lifetimes. As the son and the daughter were lives in being at the creation of the interest, the interest is valid.

Answer to Question 150

(B) The friend will have a fee simple determinable and the niece will have a possibility of reverter on the owner's death. A fee simple determinable is an estate that automatically terminates on the happening of a stated event and goes back to the grantor. The interest that is left in a grantor who conveys a fee simple determinable is a possibility of reverter, which arises automatically in the grantor and can be devised by will in almost all jurisdictions. Here, the friend has a fee simple that is subject to automatic termination if dogs are no longer kept on the property. As discussed below, the ASPCA's interest is stricken because it violates the Rule Against Perpetuities. This leaves a possibility of reverter in the niece as the owner's residuary devisee. (A) is incorrect because the friend's interest is a fee simple determinable (because it has "so long as" as part of the conveyance) that terminates automatically when the event occurs. In contrast, a fee simple

subject to a condition subsequent is created when the grantor retains the power to terminate the estate (the right of entry) on the happening of a stated event, but the estate continues until the grantor exercises the power. (C) is incorrect because the ASPCA's interest, if it were valid, would be an executory interest rather than a remainder. A remainder is a future interest that is capable of taking possession on the natural termination of the preceding estates created in the same disposition. Under modern law, this means that a remainder must always follow a life estate. If the present interest is a defeasible fee that has potentially infinite duration but can be cut short by the happening of a stated event, as in this question, the future interest created in a third party must be an executory interest. (D) is incorrect because the ASPCA's interest is void under the Rule Against Perpetuities and is stricken; the charity-to-charity exception to the Rule does not apply. The Rule Against Perpetuities provides that no interest in property is valid unless it must vest, if at all, not later than 21 years after one or more lives in being at the creation of the interest. It applies to executory interests created in third persons but not to reversionary interests of the grantor. Like any other gift, a gift for charitable purposes is void for remoteness if it is contingent on the happening of an event that may not occur within the perpetuities period. The only exception is when there is a gift to one charity followed by a gift over to another charity upon a possibly remote event (the charity-to-charity exception). Here, the first gift is to an individual and the gift over (a shifting executory interest) is to a charity; because the triggering event that will transfer the property (no dogs kept on the property) *may* occur more than 21 years after lives in being at the creation of the interest, the interest is stricken under the Rule Against Perpetuities.

Answer to Question 151

(C) The most likely basis for finding the waiting provision unconstitutional is that it improperly discriminates against the consultant's exercise of her fundamental right of interstate travel. An individual has a fundamental right to travel from state to state, and a state law that is designed to deter persons from moving into the state is likely to violate the Equal Protection Clause. When a state uses a durational residency requirement (a waiting period) for dispensing benefits, that requirement normally should be subject to the strict scrutiny test and will be found not to have satisfied that test. One such requirement that has been invalidated on this basis is a one-year waiting period for state-subsidized medical care. [Memorial Hospital v. Maricopa County (1974)] Thus, the most likely basis for the consultant to prevail is stated in (C). (A) is not correct because the validity of state residency requirements will not depend on whether they have some theoretical rational relationship to an arguably legitimate end of government. Because a fundamental right is burdened, a higher standard of review is employed. (B) is incorrect because the privileges and immunities protection of Article IV prohibits discrimination by a state against nonresidents when fundamental national rights are involved. Here, the consultant is a resident of the state whose legislation she is challenging; hence, the Equal Protection Clause will be the basis of her challenge. (D) is incorrect because a property interest entitled to protection under the Due Process Clause requires more than an abstract need or desire for the benefit. Here, the state is not attempting to take away from the consultant, without due process of law, a right for which she has already qualified; it is simply providing that the group to which she belongs (recent residents) is not entitled to certain benefits that are granted to other residents.

Answer to Question 152

(B) If the owner prevails, it will be because the mower clutch engaged because of some defect in manufacture. To recover in an action for indemnity, the owner must show that the manufacturer breached a duty that caused the injuries to the motorist. Indemnity involves shifting the entire loss between tortfeasors. One of the circumstances in which indemnity is available allows one

joint tortfeasor to recover against a fellow joint tortfeasor due to a considerable difference in degree of fault. Where the tortfeasor is a retailer or user of a product who negligently failed to discover or guard against a product's defect, he can receive indemnification from the manufacturer who was liable for the defect on either a negligence or a strict liability theory. Here, if the claim of the motorist was valid, then the owner must have been at fault in allowing the mower to reach the street. However, if the mower clutch engaged due to some defect in manufacture, then the manufacturer would be a joint tortfeasor. In such an instance, the manufacturer's conduct, either in negligently manufacturing the mower or in placing into commerce a mower that was so defective as to be unreasonably dangerous, actually and proximately caused the injuries suffered by the motorist. Such wrongful conduct on the part of the manufacturer is considerably more culpable than that of the owner, who apparently was merely careless in losing control of the mower. Consequently, under these circumstances, the owner is entitled to indemnity from the manufacturer, which is the "more wrongful" tortfeasor. (A) is incorrect because, as explained above, the owner is entitled to indemnity if his negligence is appreciably less than any wrongful conduct by the manufacturer. Thus, the owner's recovery of indemnity is not dependent on a finding that he exercised reasonable care in maintaining the mower. (C) is incorrect because the manufacturer would be liable even if it hired another company to manufacture or assemble the clutch assembly. The manufacturer would be liable for a defect in the clutch assembly because the manufacturer put the mower into the stream of commerce. (D) is incorrect because it would be a reason why the owner would not prevail. Most jurisdictions adopting comparative contribution, whereby damages are apportioned based on relative fault, no longer apply indemnity rules to cases based on differences in degree of fault.

Answer to Question 153

(B) If the passenger does not prevail, it will be because she did not suffer physical injury from her distress. The duty to avoid negligent infliction of emotional distress is breached when the defendant creates a foreseeable risk of physical injury to the plaintiff, either by causing a threat of physical impact that leads to emotional distress or by directly causing severe emotional distress that by itself is likely to result in physical symptoms. In either case, the emotional distress must cause some physical symptoms. Emotional distress without physical symptoms is insufficient in most jurisdictions for the tort of negligent infliction of emotional distress. Here, the tourist created a risk of physical injury (the contagious disease) to those around him, such as the passenger. She suffered distress as a result of the threat, but she cannot recover if her distress did not cause physical injury. (A) is incorrect because the tort of negligent infliction of emotional distress does not require that the defendant's conduct be extreme and outrageous. That is an element of *intentional* infliction of emotional distress, which also requires that the defendant intend that the plaintiff suffer severe emotional distress, or act in reckless disregard of a high probability that emotional distress will result. Here, the tourist had no such intent, nor is there evidence that he believed there to be a high probability that anyone would suffer emotional distress, given his efforts to keep his unauthorized travel quiet. (C) is incorrect because it is not necessary for the passenger to have contracted the disease to prevail. She can recover for negligent infliction of emotional distress as long as she suffered physical symptoms from her distress. (D) is incorrect because the fact that the tourist did not foresee a risk that anyone would suffer emotional distress does not preclude recovery. He created a foreseeable risk that the passenger would suffer physical harm as a result of contracting the tourist's disease, satisfying the breach of duty requirement for the tort.

Answer to Question 154

(B) The federal court will rule for the state. The President is empowered by the Constitution to grant reprieves and pardons for offenses against the United States, except in cases of impeachment. Here, the President seeks to pardon a person who has been convicted of a violent crime in a state. Thus, the President's pardon power does not extend to this prisoner, and the state will not be compelled to release him. (A) is incorrect because, pursuant to the Supremacy Clause of the Constitution, the Constitution, laws, and treaties of the United States take precedence over state laws. Any state law that is inconsistent with federal law will be superseded by the federal law. Although a state official may be acting pursuant to his state's constitution, that constitution may be in conflict with the United States Constitution or with other federal law. In such an instance, the state official will be required to abide by proper directives of a federal official issued in furtherance of the enforcement and execution of federal law. (C) is incorrect. As noted above, the President does have the power to pardon those convicted of federal offenses. Thus, an attempted pardon of a federal offender does not violate the President's sworn duty to see that the laws of the United States are faithfully executed; *i.e.,* the President is not "subverting" the law by issuing a pardon. It is in issuing a pardon for a crime that falls outside the scope of his pardon power that the President runs afoul of the Constitution. (D) is incorrect because the President's treaty power does not authorize his actions here. Although the Constitution gives the President the power to make treaties, he is not given the authority to use unconstitutional means to facilitate the making of a treaty. The President is acting here with the goal of advancing negotiations on a critical treaty. However, in doing so, the President may not disregard the Constitution by issuing a pardon that is outside the limits of his constitutionally derived pardon power.

Answer to Question 155

(B) The state has the burden of proving that the program is substantially related to an important government interest. When analyzing government action based on gender, the courts will apply an intermediate standard of review and strike the legislation unless it is substantially related to an important government interest. In these cases, the government bears the burden of proving this substantial relationship. Here, because the formula used to calculate termination of pension bene- fits depended on whether the surviving spouse was male or female, the legislation discriminates on the basis of gender. Thus, an intermediate scrutiny standard will be applied. (A) is wrong because the court will not apply the strict scrutiny standard in this case. A suspect class is not involved, and the program does not improperly burden a fundamental right. While marriage is a fundamental right, strict scrutiny applies only to legislation that directly and substantially inter- feres with the right to marry. Laws terminating certain benefits upon marriage do not directly and significantly interfere with that right, and thus are not subject to strict scrutiny. (C) is wrong because the government, rather than the challenger, bears the burden of proof in gender discrimi- nation cases. (D) is wrong for the same reason and also because it applies the incorrect standard; an intermediate scrutiny standard is applied rather than the minimal scrutiny of the rational basis test.

Answer to Question 156

(C) The plaintiff will prevail against the snowmobile manufacturer if the component manufacturer was negligent in not discovering and correcting the defect. To establish a prima facie case of negligence in a products liability case, the plaintiff must show: (i) the existence of a legal duty owed by the defendant to that particular plaintiff; (ii) breach of that duty; (iii) actual and proxi- mate cause; and (iv) damages. The duty of care arises when the defendant acts as a commercial supplier of products. A commercial supplier who assembles a product from components manu- factured by others is subject to the same liability as the manufacturer of the defective component. To prove breach of duty, the plaintiff must show (i) negligent conduct by the defendant that leads

to (ii) the supplying of a defective product. Here, because the snowmobile manufacturer assembled the snowmobile from component parts, including the steering mechanism manufactured by the component manufacturer, and sold the snowmobile as its own product, it will be liable for the negligence of the component manufacturer. Hence, if the steering mechanism was defective and the component manufacturer could have discovered and corrected the defect in the exercise of reasonable care, as (C) states, the snowmobile manufacturer has breached its duty to the plaintiff, and this breach of duty caused the plaintiff's injuries. (A) would be correct if the plaintiff were suing the snowmobile manufacturer on a strict liability theory, but the facts of the question indicate that the plaintiff is suing in negligence. *In products liability actions, always make sure you are applying the appropriate theory of liability.* (B) is incorrect because a commercial supplier of a defective product owes a duty of care to any foreseeable plaintiff; thus, the plaintiff could recover even if he were a bystander who had no relation to the purchaser of the snowmobile. (D) is incorrect even though the snowmobile manufacturer may have had a duty to inspect the steering mechanism before assembly. Nothing in (D) indicates that either the component manufacturer or the snowmobile manufacturer was negligent. The existence of a defect does not by itself establish negligence, and the snowmobile manufacturer's failure to inspect the mechanism before assembly is not actionable negligence if the defect would not have been discovered even with a reasonably careful inspection. Hence, (C) is a better choice because it supplies the negligence element.

Answer to Question 157

(D) While the facts do not indicate that a reasonable inspection by the machinery company would have disclosed any defects, even if an inspection would have disclosed the defect, the machinery company's failure to do so would have no legal effect on the electronics company's liability. Regardless of whether the technician's survivors are using a negligence theory or a strict liability theory (both theories must be considered because the call of the question does not supply the theory of liability), an intermediary's negligent failure to discover a defect is *not* a superseding cause, and the defendant who supplied the defective product will be held liable along with the intermediary. Thus, even if the machinery company's failure to inspect were negligent, it would not relieve the electronics company of liability. (A) is incorrect because it is a reversal of one of the situations in which indemnity is available. Where strict liability rules apply, each supplier of a defective product is liable to an injured person, but each supplier has a right of indemnification against all *previous* suppliers of the defective product in the distribution chain. Here, both the machinery company and the electronics company would be liable in a strict liability action as suppliers if they supplied a defective product. However, the electronics company, as the previous supplier in the chain, would be liable to the machinery company for indemnity, rather than the machinery company being liable to the electronics company for indemnity, as (A) states. (B) is incorrect because the failure of the machinery company to inspect is, at most, ordinary negligence. A superseding force is one that breaks the causal connection between the initial wrongful act and the ultimate injury. To be superseding, an intervening force must have been unforeseeable. Any ordinary negligence on the part of the machinery company was foreseeable and would not relieve the electronics company of liability for the consequences of supplying a defective product. (C) is incorrect because the machinery company and the electronics company do not have the type of relationship to which respondeat superior is applicable. Under the doctrine of respondeat superior, an employer is vicariously liable for tortious acts committed by his employee if such acts occur within the scope of the employment relationship. No facts suggest that the machinery company is an employee of the electronics company. The companies appear to be independent of each other; their only relationship is a contractual one. Therefore, any wrongful conduct committed by the machinery company will not result in the imposition of vicarious liability against the electronics company under respondeat superior.

Answer to Question 158

(D) State Beta need not give full faith and credit to the State Alpha judgment because it was not on the merits. Under the Full Faith and Credit Clause, a judgment that is valid in one state must be recognized by other states provided that: (i) the court that rendered the judgment had jurisdiction over the parties and the subject matter; (ii) the judgment was on the merits; and (iii) the judgment was final. Here, the State Alpha court had jurisdiction and entered a final judgment, but the judgment was not on the merits; *i.e.,* it was not based on the substance of the plaintiff's contract claim. (A) is incorrect because it is not enough that the court entered a judgment that was final. Rather, the judgment must also have been on the merits of the case. (B) is incorrect because forum shopping is not a factor used to analyze a Full Faith and Credit Clause issue. (C) is incorrect because, by its terms, the Full Faith and Credit Clause applies only to state matters.

Answer to Question 159

(C) The purchaser has title to the land because the merchant's fee simple determinable automatically terminated when she sold tobacco on the land. A fee simple determinable is created by the use of durational language such as "while" or "so long as" and is subject to automatic termination on the happening of the stated event. The corresponding future interest in the grantor, called a possibility of reverter, does not have to be expressly retained; it arises automatically when the determinable fee is created. In the majority of jurisdictions, a possibility of reverter can be transferred inter vivos or devised by will. Here, the owner retained a possibility of reverter when he made the conveyance to the merchant, and it was transferred to the friend when the owner devised all of his real property interests to the friend. The friend transferred the future interest to the purchaser by quitclaim deed, and it became a present possessory interest when the merchant's fee simple determinable automatically ended. (A) is incorrect because the Rule Against Perpetuities does not apply to a possibility of reverter created in the grantor, regardless of whether the grantor later transfers or devises it to a third party. (B) is incorrect because, as discussed above, in most states the possibility of reverter is freely transferable inter vivos. (D) is incorrect because the merchant's interest was a fee simple determinable rather than a fee simple subject to a condition subsequent. In the latter interest, the grantor retains the power to terminate the estate upon the happening of a specified event, but the estate will continue until the grantor exercises his power of termination (right of entry). In contrast, the fee simple determinable ends automatically when the event occurs.

Answer to Question 160

(D) The defendant's wife can testify about the drug sale in 2008 if she wants to. The federal courts recognize two separate and distinct spousal privileges. First, in a criminal case, a spouse can testify if she wants to testify, but the spouse cannot be compelled to testify. The privilege applies to all information that the spouse has gained before or during the marriage. This privilege ends when the marriage ends. Second, in any type of case, a spouse can refuse to disclose, or prevent a spouse from disclosing, confidential communications made between the spouses during the marriage. While the defendant can object to his wife's testimony concerning confidential communications during the marriage, he has no privilege to object to other testimony by her. It is clear that the 2008 drug transaction was not a confidential communication, since the defendant was not aware of her presence. (A) is incorrect because the defendant's wife cannot testify to his 2008 statements that were made during the marriage unless he does not object. (B) is incorrect because the defendant's wife cannot be compelled to testify against him even with respect to information received before they were married. (C) is incorrect because, while the defendant can

object to his wife's testimony concerning confidential communications during the marriage, she can testify to his 2007 statements if she desires, because they were not communications made during the marriage.

Answer to Question 161

(A) The statements that the onlooker gave to the homicide detective most likely will not be suppressed due to a failure to provide a *Miranda* warning. Prior to custodial interrogation, the person being questioned must be informed that he has the right to remain silent, that anything he says can be used against him in court, that he has the right to the presence of an attorney, and that, if he cannot afford an attorney, one will be appointed for him if he so desires. The interrogation must take place in a custodial setting. The test to determine whether a person is in custody is an objective test; the subjective beliefs of the interrogator or the accused are not determinative. Essentially, the question boils down to whether the person's freedom is being constrained in a significant way. Here, the onlooker had not been arrested, had not been placed in handcuffs, nor was he even at a police station. Being unconstrained at a crime scene probably would not constitute being "in custody"; as a result, *Miranda* warnings were not required and (A) is correct. (B) is incorrect because who initiates the contact is not really relevant to determine whether the person is "in custody," although it may be a factor to be considered when determining whether the defendant was free to leave. (C) is incorrect because it falsely states that the test for custody is a subjective one. The test is an objective test. (D) is also incorrect. *Miranda* warnings are required prior to custodial interrogation. The subjective beliefs of the interrogator as to who may have committed the crime are irrelevant.

Answer to Question 162

(A) The court should admit the coat based on the plaintiff's testimony. Federal Rule of Evidence 402 provides that all relevant evidence is admissible unless a specific rule keeps the evidence out or limits its admissibility. In the case of real evidence, the object at issue is presented for inspection by the trier of fact. Such evidence can be presented to any of the senses of the jury from which the jury can obtain relevant information. Clearly the odor of the coat is a central issue in the case and the jury would obtain relevant evidence on that issue by smelling the coat. Admitting the coat for the stated purpose would violate no other rules of evidence. (B) is wrong because the plaintiff's testimony is sufficient authentication. Federal Rule 901 does require, as a prerequisite to the admission of real proof, evidence sufficient to support a finding that the item is what the proponent claims. However, real evidence is commonly authenticated by recognition testimony, such as in the case here. Thus, Rule 901 has been satisfied by the plaintiff's testimony, and additional evidence would not be required. (C) is incorrect because the fact that the plaintiff had not been impeached would not matter. The coat is being offered for the purpose of having the jury smell it, because that is direct evidence of her claim; it is not being offered as evidence to bolster credibility. (D) is not as good a choice as (A). While it is true that, under Federal Rule of Evidence 403, the coat could be rejected if the judge determined that its probative value was substantially outweighed by unfair prejudice, it is difficult to see any substantial prejudice that would result from smelling the coat.

Answer to Question 163

(B) The ranger's strongest argument, although by no means guaranteed of success, is that the height restriction is a gender-based classification that is not substantially related to important governmental interests. The Due Process Clause of the Fifth Amendment protects against action by the federal government. Although not expressly stated, this clause also provides an equal protection guarantee against federal action that generally applies to the same extent that the Fourteenth Amendment Equal Protection Clause applies to the states. If the ranger can show that the Park Service restriction actually establishes a classification of eligibility for the new position based on gender, then the restriction will be found to violate the Fifth Amendment Due Process Clause unless the government has an exceedingly persuasive justification that the restriction is substantially related to important governmental interests. However, if the ranger is only able to show that the restriction has a discriminatory impact without being able to prove discriminatory intent, the court will not treat it as a gender-based classification and the ranger will not be successful. Despite the difficulty of success, however, (B) is the correct answer because it provides the best possibility of a winning argument for the ranger. ***Remember that "best of the lot" questions are sometimes "best of a bad lot." You might need to work through all of the alternatives and arrive at the best answer by process of elimination.*** (A) is the most clearly incorrect, because it relies on the Equal Rights Amendment ("ERA"). The ERA was not ratified by the requisite number of states; thus, it has not become part of the Constitution and would provide no basis for arguing against the validity of the restriction at issue. (C) is incorrect because the Fourteenth Amendment is applicable only to states and not to the federal government. Because an agency of the federal government is being sued, the ranger must rely on the Fifth Amendment. (D) is incorrect because there is no evidence that the ranger has a property right in the newly created position in the Park Service. The Due Process Clause of the Fifth Amendment provides procedural safeguards against arbitrary deprivation by the government of a person's life, liberty, or property. One might have a property right in continued public employment if a statute creates a public employment contract. Here, the ranger is not being threatened with loss of the federal employment she currently holds, nor is there any statute or agreement from which she can derive an interest in or legitimate claim to the newly created position. Because the ranger does not have a property right in the newly created position, she cannot rely on her procedural due process rights. This leaves (B) as the only possible correct answer.

Answer to Question 164

(B) It would be least helpful to a kidnapping participant's defense if kidnapping were a general intent crime in the jurisdiction. Although courts have not always clearly defined "general intent," the mental state required for the material elements of the offense are analogous to "recklessness" under the Model Penal Code: conscious disregard of a substantial or unjustifiable risk that the material element exists or will result from his conduct. Thus, the defendant need not be certain that his conduct will cause the result or that the attendant circumstances required by the crime exist; it is enough if he is aware of a high likelihood of that result or circumstance. In contrast, a specific intent crime requires the doing of an act with a conscious intent or objective. Most importantly for the participant's purposes, defenses such as voluntary intoxication and unreasonable mistake of fact are not recognized as defenses to general intent crimes, but are for specific intent crimes. If the jurisdiction treats kidnapping as a specific intent crime, the participant's intoxication could be used to show that he was incapable of forming the requisite intent or that he mistakenly believed that the groom had consented to being left on the island. For specific intent crimes, any mistake of fact, even if unreasonable, is a defense. In contrast, voluntary intoxication is not a defense to a general intent crime, and any mistake of fact offered to negate a general intent must be reasonable to be valid. Hence, it would be helpful to the participant's defense if the jurisdiction treated the offense as a specific intent crime, but not if it were treated as a general intent crime. Thus, (B) is correct because it is not helpful, and (C) is incorrect because it is helpful. (D) is incorrect because that fact may be helpful to the participant's defense. If he believed that the groom wanted to be left on the island, he may not have had the intent required for

the offense. (A) is incorrect because it is helpful to the participant's defense. The offense is defined as the unlawful movement or concealment of a person without his consent. If the participant was not legally intoxicated, his consent would be a valid defense; if he was legally intoxicated, it could be argued that he was incapable of consenting, thus negating the participant's defense.

Answer to Question 165

(B) The landowner will prevail regardless of whether the motorist was exercising due care because the motorist intentionally entered onto the landowner's property and had only a qualified privilege to do so. The elements of trespass to land are: (i) an act of physical invasion of plaintiff's real property by defendant, (ii) intent on defendant's part to bring about the physical invasion of plaintiff's property, and (iii) causation. Here, although the motorist did not intend to harm the landowner's land, he intended to enter upon it, and thus would have committed a trespass absent the privilege of necessity. A person may interfere with the real or personal property of another when the interference is reasonably and apparently necessary to avoid threatened injury from a natural or other force, as long as the threatened injury is substantially more serious than the invasion that is undertaken to avert it. However, when the act is solely to benefit a person or to protect a property from destruction or serious injury, this is considered private necessity and the defense is qualified; *i.e.,* the actor must pay for any injury that he causes. Hence, even though the motorist had a privilege to enter onto the landowner's property (that superseded the landowner's privilege of defense of property), he remains liable for any damages he caused on the land. (A) is wrong because the landowner's damage action is based on the motorist's intentional entry onto the landowner's land; therefore, he does not need to establish lack of due care to recover. (C) is wrong because, as discussed above, the motorist's defense of necessity is not an absolute defense and he must pay for the damages caused by his entry on the landowner's land. (D) is wrong because it is not relevant as a defense to the motorist's trespass to land. The motorist is not being sued for his negligence in driving too fast (and even if he were, it is doubtful that the tree in the road would be so unforeseeable as to qualify as a superseding force to cut off his liability); he is being sued for intentionally driving onto the landowner's property to avoid hitting the tree. Thus, while the existence of the tree in the road may help establish the qualified defense of necessity, it does not cut off the motorist's liability for the damage to the landowner's property.

Answer to Question 166

(B) The court should not grant the directed verdict because the jury could find that it was foreseeable that the son might cause damage to cars in the parking lot if he was left unattended. The common law rule is that a parent is not vicariously liable for the tortious conduct of her child. However, the parent may be held liable for her own negligence in allowing the child to do something that injures another's person or property. Under ordinary negligence principles, the mother owed a duty to the owners of other cars in the parking lot if it was foreseeable that her son might cause damage to them if left unattended. It is a question of fact for the jury whether she breached her duty to the other car owners by leaving her son unattended, and whether her conduct was an actual and proximate cause of the damage to the shopper's car. (A) is incorrect because it is doubtful whether the mother's violation of the statute is applicable here. The precise standard of care in a common law negligence case may be established by proving the applicability to that case of a statute providing for a criminal penalty. If that is done, the statute's more specific duty will replace the more general common law duty of care. Violation of the statute establishes negligence per se—a conclusive presumption of duty and breach of duty; plaintiff must then establish causation and damages to complete the prima facie case of negligence. In proving the availability of the statutory standard, plaintiff must show that (i) she is in the class intended to be protected by the statute, and (ii) the statute was designed to prevent the type of harm that she suffered. Here, it is more likely that the statute was designed to protect small children from harm if left unattended in a car, as (C) states, and the shopper would not be in the class intended to be protected by the statute. (C) is incorrect because it is not necessary for the statute to apply to find negligence on the part of the mother. As (B) states, the jury could find that the mother should have known that her son might cause damage to cars if left unattended, making her liable under ordinary negligence principles without resort to the statute. (D) is incorrect even though it is a true statement at common law. The shopper is not relying on vicarious liability to hold the mother liable but rather on the mother's own negligence in leaving her four-year-old son unattended.

Answer to Question 167

(C) The landowner can recover $50,000, which is the amount above the contract price that it will cost to get the building completed. In construction contracts, the standard measure of damages when the builder breaches will depend on when the breach occurred. If the builder breaches after partially performing, the owner is entitled to the cost of completion plus reasonable compensation for any delay in performance (unless completion would involve undue economic waste). Most courts will allow the builder to offset or recover for work performed to date if necessary to avoid the unjust enrichment of the owner. Here, the cost of completion (the amount above the contract price that it will cost to get the building completed) is $50,000, which was a reasonable price considering the deadline. Hence, that is what the landowner can recover. (A) and (B) are incorrect because the landowner is not being unjustly enriched by the additional amount that the builder expended in performance over the progress payments that it received. The landowner still had to pay $50,000 more than the contract amount for completion of the warehouse because of the builder's breach; thus, that is the landowner's recovery. (On the other hand, if the cost of completing the building to specifications were only $150,000 after the builder's breach, the builder could recover $50,000 in restitution from the landowner in a quasi-contract action because the landowner would have been unjustly enriched from the builder's breach.) (D) is incorrect because the cost of completion is determined from the perspective of the landowner, *i.e.,* how much additional he has to pay to have the building completed. The landowner would be unjustly enriched if he could recover $50,000 more than the damages he incurred.

Answer to Question 168

(D) The appliance company will win because it has a valid security interest in the oven, and no other party has a superior interest. In a fixture case involving divided ownership, the majority rule is that, absent an agreement to the contrary, a tenant may remove a chattel that he has attached to the demised premises as long as the removal does not cause substantial damage to the demised premises or the virtual destruction of the chattel. Furthermore, if the landowner mortgages her land to a mortgagee and then leases it to a tenant who annexes a chattel to the premises, the mortgagee has no greater rights in the chattel than the mortgagor, provided that the original sufficiency of the security is not impaired (*e.g.,* removal would not cause substantial damage to the premises). Finally, as between the tenant-purchaser of the chattel and the holder of a properly created security interest, the holder of the security interest can reclaim possession of the chattel on the purchaser's default according to the terms of the security agreement. Therefore, the appliance company has a claim to the oven that is superior to the other listed parties. (A) is wrong because it states the rule applicable to common ownership cases, *i.e.,* cases in which the person who brings the chattel onto the land owns both the chattel and the real estate. To the extent that the owner of the real estate mortgages the realty, the mortgage attaches to all fixtures on the real

estate in the absence of an agreement to the contrary. In that case, the appliance company's failure to make a fixture filing for its purchase money security interest would have caused it to lose priority. However, as discussed above, this rule does not apply in divided ownership cases where the tenant brings the chattel onto the premises. (B) is wrong because the tenant's rights are superior to those of the homeowner and the bank, but not the appliance company. Absent the security agreement with the appliance company, the tenant would have been free to remove the oven that he purchased and retain possession of it because its removal would not substantially damage the leased premises. (C) is wrong because, as discussed above, the landlord would not prevail against a tenant who brought the chattel onto the leased premises, as long as the chattel can be removed without substantial damage to the premises.

Answer to Question 169

(A) The wife's conveyance of her interest in the property to the purchaser severed the joint tenancy between the husband and the wife, leaving the husband and the purchaser holding the entire parcel as tenants in common. A joint tenancy is a type of concurrent ownership of a parcel of land that is distinguished primarily by the right of survivorship; *i.e.,* when one joint tenant dies, the property is freed of her concurrent interest and the survivor retains an undivided right in the property that is no longer subject to the interest of the deceased co-tenant. To create a joint tenancy, a grantor must explicitly indicate in the conveyance that the parties are to hold as joint tenants. If one joint tenant conveys her interest, the joint tenancy is severed. The new tenant holds as a tenant in common with the remaining joint tenant, so that there is no longer a right of survivorship. Here, the mother, grantor of the property, expressly indicated in her will that the husband and the wife were to take the parcel of property as joint tenants with right of survivorship. When the wife quitclaimed her interest in the property to the purchaser, the joint tenancy between the husband and the wife was severed (despite the fact that the husband did not know of the conveyance to the purchaser). This left the husband and the purchaser holding the property as tenants in common, with no right of survivorship. The husband and the purchaser each own an undivided one-half interest in the property, and the purchaser will succeed in his suit to partition the property to reflect the respective interests of the co-tenants. (B) is incorrect. Although under modern law, when two or more persons take property by a single conveyance a tenancy in common is presumed, a clear expression of intent to create a right of survivorship (*e.g.,* "as joint tenants with right of survivorship") results in a joint tenancy. Here, the husband and the wife did take as joint tenants, but the wife's conveyance of her interest to the purchaser severed the joint tenancy, thus eliminating the right of survivorship. Thus, the basic premise of (B)—that the purchaser cannot prevail if the husband and the wife took as joint tenants because the husband would take the entire property by right of survivorship on the death of the wife—is incorrect. (C) is a trap for the unwary, because it implies that the marital status of the husband and the wife is relevant to the ownership of this property. Under the common law, a grant to husband and wife resulted in the creation of a tenancy by the entirety, which carried with it a right of survivorship that would not be eliminated by a conveyance to an outsider by one spouse alone. Divorce can terminate a tenancy by the entirety (leaving the parties as tenants in common with no right of survivorship), but separation does not terminate the estate. Hence, if this were a tenancy by the entirety, the husband would prevail rather than the purchaser. However, most states do not recognize a tenancy by the entirety. As noted above, the husband and the wife took the property as joint tenants. The husband and the wife did not receive this status by virtue of the fact that they were married, nor is their continuation in such status dependent on their remaining married. The wife's conveyance of her interest to the purchaser severed her joint tenancy with the husband and eliminated the right of survivorship, regardless of whether she and her husband were legally separated at the time. (D) is incorrect because the husband no longer had a right of survivorship after the joint tenancy with the wife was severed. Thus, the wife's death is irrelevant to the current ownership interests in the property.

Answer to Question 170

(C) The Commerce Clause provides the strongest support for the computer store owner's position, because the state legislation discriminates against out-of-state goods. A state may regulate local aspects of interstate commerce if such regulation is not in conflict with federal regulations and if: (i) the subject matter of the regulation does not require nationally uniform regulation; (ii) the regulation does not discriminate against out-of-state competition to benefit local economic interests; and (iii) any incidental burden on interstate commerce of the nondiscriminatory regulation does not outweigh the legitimate local benefits produced by the regulation. Laws that are designed to protect local businesses against interstate competition generally will be invalidated. Here, the state legislation discriminates against out-of-state manufacturers to protect local businesses by limiting the amount of units that can be sold by retailers of electronic products containing microprocessors manufactured out of state. There is no such limit on units that can be sold that utilize locally manufactured microprocessors. This law was enacted to encourage the development of local manufacturing operations. Because this law is designed to protect local businesses against interstate competition, it should fail a challenge under the Commerce Clause. (D) is incorrect because the Privileges and Immunities Clause of Article IV, which prohibits discrimination by a state in favor of its own citizens, applies only when citizens of other states are denied, without substantial justification, basic rights or the pursuit of essential activities. Although the state legislation does discriminate in favor of that state's manufacturers (and commercial activities are protected by the clause), the store owner is probably a resident of that state. Any burden that the legislation places on him is not based on his citizenship status but rather on the location of the supplier of his products. Hence, the Article IV Privileges and Immunities Clause does not provide the strongest support for his position. (A) is incorrect because, under the Fourteenth Amendment Equal Protection Clause, the validity of a classification that relates only to matters of economics or social welfare is determined by the rational basis test. Under this test, the store owner would have the burden of proving that the classification differentiating between resident and out-of-state manufacturers does not have a rational relationship to a legitimate governmental interest. Because this is a difficult burden to meet, the equal protection argument is not the store owner's strongest. (B) is incorrect because economic legislation such as this, which does not limit a fundamental right, will be sustained against a due process challenge as long as it is rationally related to a legitimate end of government. As with the Equal Protection Clause, relying on the Due Process Clause would impose on the store owner a heavy burden of proving the invalidity of the legislation.

Answer to Question 171

(B) The court should permit the decorator to introduce evidence of trade usage to support its definition of "Oriental rug." Under the U.C.C., which governs contracts for the sale of goods, the parol evidence rule does not bar the introduction of evidence based on course of dealing, usage in the trade, or course of performance to explain or supplement a contractual term. Here, the decorator is claiming that the parties understood the term "Oriental rug" to have a narrower definition than a layperson's understanding of the term (with the latter typically defining the term based on appearance or pattern rather than country of origin). Pursuant to U.C.C. section 2-202, evidence that the term was used in the trade as the decorator used it is admissible to support the decorator's claim. (A) is incorrect because a latent ambiguity occurs where the expression of the parties' agreement appears perfectly clear at the time the contract is formed, but because of subsequently

revealed facts, it may be reasonably interpreted in either of two ways. However, rather than using an objective test, the courts look to the subjective intention of the parties in determining whether an ambiguity existed. Here, the decorator is claiming that both parties subjectively understood the meaning of the term "Oriental rug" in the context of the contract and that both parties intended the term to mean what the decorator is claiming; hence, the decorator's argument is that, as between the parties, there was no ambiguity as to the term. (C) and (D) are incorrect because, although there is a general rule providing that a writing that is a complete integration or a final expression of the parties' agreement cannot be contradicted or supplemented by additional terms, the U.C.C. permits extrinsic evidence that explains or supplements a term through course of dealing, usage in the trade, or course of performance, even when the writing is otherwise a complete integration or final expression of the parties' agreement. Here, the decorator wants to introduce parol evidence of trade usage for the sole purpose of explaining the term "Oriental rug," and such parol evidence would be admissible, notwithstanding the fact that the writing was otherwise a complete integration or final expression of the parties' agreement.

Answer to Question 172

(D) The pet food manufacturer must allow the farming concern until November 15 to ship cornmeal that conforms to the contract because that is the original date when performance was due. Under the U.C.C., if a buyer has rejected goods because of defects, the seller may within the time originally provided for performance "cure" the defective tender by giving reasonable notice of its intention to do so and making new tender of conforming goods, which the buyer must then accept. Here, the farming concern promised to deliver cornmeal that conforms to the contract by the original date of performance. Thus, the pet food manufacturer cannot declare the contract to be in breach and must accept the farming concern's delivery of conforming goods if it occurs by November 15. (A) is incorrect not only because the farming concern has the right to cure until November 15, but also because for contracts authorizing deliveries in separate installments, the buyer may declare a total breach only if the defects are such as to substantially impair the value of the entire contract. Hence, even if there were a specified time for the first shipment of corn-meal and it had expired, the pet food manufacturer would not be entitled to declare a total breach of contract. (B) is incorrect because, as discussed above, the farming concern has the right to cure the defective tender of the 50 tons by November 15, the date when performance is due under the contract. (C) is incorrect because it does not state the correct standard for determining when the defective tender can be cured in this case. Ordinarily, the seller has no right to cure beyond the original contract time. However, when the buyer rejects a tender that the seller reasonably believed would be acceptable, the seller, on reasonable notification to the buyer, has a further reasonable time beyond the original contract time within which to make a conforming tender. This situation is not applicable here, however. In this case, the time for performance under the original contract has not expired and the farming concern has promised to perform within that time. Furthermore, there is nothing in the facts to suggest that the farming concern believed its original shipment was reasonable; the farming concern acknowledged that the shipment did not conform to the contract and there was no indication that the pet food manufacturer had previously accepted nonconforming goods.

Answer to Question 173

(A) The defendant will not prevail in his double jeopardy challenge. The Fifth Amendment provides that one may not be twice put in jeopardy for the same offense. Under the *Blockburger* test, two crimes do not constitute the same offense if each crime requires proof of an additional element that the other crime does not require, even though some of the same facts may be necessary to prove both crimes. Under *Blockburger*, reckless homicide and driving while intoxicated are separate offenses because the first requires proof that someone died, while the second requires proof that the defendant was intoxicated (and recklessness for the homicide offense can be shown by evidence other than intoxication). Thus, prosecution for the reckless homicide charge did not violate double jeopardy. (B) is incorrect. Although imposition of cumulative punishments may be permissible even if two crimes constitute the same offense under *Blockburger* as long as this result was intended by the legislature, this situation applies only when the punishments are imposed at a single trial. Conversely, because the two charges are separate offenses, they could be tried together and cumulative punishments imposed without violating double jeopardy. (C) is incorrect because the fact that the two charges require proof of the same conduct is no longer relevant for purposes of double jeopardy. The *Blockburger* test governs regardless of whether the punishments are imposed at a single trial or multiple trials. [United States v. Dixon (1993)] (D) is incorrect because it is irrelevant that the sentences were of different lengths and not concurrent. If the two charges had constituted the same offense, imposition of multiple punishments would be prohibited even if the two sentences had run concurrently. [Rutledge v. United States (1996)]

Answer to Question 174

(D) The transaction described in (D) does not present the problem of potentially unconstitutional state regulation of interstate commerce, state regulation of foreign commerce, or state regulation of federal government activities, as do (A), (B), and (C), respectively. (A) involves a sale to a manufacturer whose plant is located out of state. Because this law requires the out-of-state manufacturer to pay the government-set price for cheese even if the overall market price for cheese is lower, the law burdens interstate commerce even though it is nondiscriminatory. If this burden on interstate commerce outweighs the promotion of legitimate, nondiscriminatory local interests, the state law will violate the Commerce Clause. (B) involves a restriction on the price of cheese that was made in a foreign country and is being sold by a citizen of that country. This is a regulation of foreign commerce. The power to regulate foreign commerce lies exclusively with Congress. Thus, (B) presents a situation in which the statute would not be constitutionally applied. In (C), a sale is being made to an agency of the federal government. Application of the state statute to such a sale would result in state regulation of the federal government. The federal government and its agencies and instrumentalities are immune from state regulation that interferes with federal activities, functions, and programs. Thus, it would be impermissible for the state to attempt to compel the Air Force to comply with a state statute setting a minimum price for cheese. The transaction in (D) involves no contact with foreign commerce or with the federal government. In addition, the transaction is entirely intrastate and does not appear to involve an undue burden on interstate commerce. Therefore, (D) is most likely to be constitutionally applied.

Answer to Question 175

(B) The niece has a life estate because of the rule of convenience, and the landowner's heirs have a reversion because of the Rule Against Perpetuities. When a gift is made to a group of persons generically described as a class, such as to someone's "nieces and nephews," the rule of convenience provides that the class closes when some member of the class can call for a distribution of her share of the class gift. Persons born after that date are excluded from the class. Here, the class of the landowner's nieces and nephews entitled to the life estate closed when they became entitled to take, which was at the termination of the preceding estate (the husband's life estate). Because the nephew was not yet born at the time the class closed, he is not entitled to a share of the life estate. Thus, (C) and (D) are wrong. The landowner's heirs have a reversion because the

remainder to the children of the nieces and nephews violates the Rule Against Perpetuities. Viewed at the time the perpetuities period begins to run, which is at the landowner's death, the niece alive at that time, as well as her son, could die and another niece or nephew not yet born could hold the life estate for more than 21 years after the death of the husband (the only other life in being at the time of the landowner's death). Hence, the surviving children of the nieces and nephews would not take within the perpetuities period. Because their interest is void, the landowner's heirs have a reversion, making (A) and (C) wrong.

Answer to Question 176

(C) The seller's mortgage remains on the property and the bank's mortgage is extinguished, and the buyer is personally liable to the bank for the deficiency. As a general rule, the priority of a mortgage is determined by the time it was placed on the property. When a mortgage is foreclosed, the purchaser at the sale will take title as it existed when the mortgage was placed on the property. Thus, foreclosure will terminate interests junior to the mortgage being foreclosed but will not affect senior interests. The proceeds of the foreclosure sale are used first (after expenses and fees) to pay the principal and accrued interest on the loan that was foreclosed, and then to pay off any junior interests in the order of priority. Where the proceeds of the sale are insufficient to satisfy a mortgage debt, the mortgagee can bring a personal action against the mortgagor/debtor for the deficiency. Here, foreclosure by the credit union leaves the seller's senior purchase money mortgage interest intact on the property; the purchaser at the foreclosure sale takes the property subject to that mortgage. On the other hand, the bank's mortgage interest, because it was junior to the credit union's interest, was extinguished by the credit union's foreclosure action. After the credit union's loan is paid off, the $20,000 that remains is used to reduce the amount of the debt owed to the bank. The bank can recover the balance against the buyer personally in a deficiency action. (A) is wrong because the seller's mortgage and the bank's mortgage are treated differently because of their priority in relation to the credit union's mortgage. (B) states the opposite of the actual result—the seller's mortgage (the senior interest) remains on the property and the bank's mortgage (the junior interest) is extinguished. (D) is wrong because, as discussed above, the seller's mortgage remains on the land; thus, all of the remaining proceeds from the foreclosure sale after the credit union's mortgage debt is satisfied go towards reducing the debt owed to the bank.

Answer to Question 177

(A) The child will prevail because he suffered physical injury as a result of the chemical company's engaging in an activity that involves a substantial risk of serious harm no matter how much care is exercised. A prima facie case for strict liability consists of: (i) an absolute duty on the part of the defendant to make safe; (ii) breach of that duty; (iii) such breach actually and proximately caused plaintiff's injury; and (iv) damage to the plaintiff's person or property. An activity is abnormally dangerous if it: (i) creates a foreseeable risk of serious harm even when reasonable care is exercised by all actors; and (ii) is not a matter of common usage in the community. In such cases, the duty owed is an absolute duty to make safe the dangerous activity or condition, and liability is imposed for injuries to persons or property resulting from the danger. The duty is owed to persons to whom a reasonable person would have foreseen a risk of harm under the circumstances. The harm must result from the kind of danger to be anticipated from such abnormally dangerous activity. The chemical company's maintenance of a deadly nerve gas system involves a risk of serious harm to persons and property through the release of harmful gas and heat, and cannot be undertaken without risk of serious harm no matter how much care is taken by the chemical company. Also, it is not common to maintain such a system in an urban area. Thus, this is an abnormally dangerous activity, imposing on the chemical company an absolute duty to make it safe. When the chemicals leaked, generating dangerous amounts of heat from the initiation of the chemical reaction, the duty was breached. This breach actually and proximately caused the child's cut leg, which was injured as he was fleeing from the danger. Harm to a person fleeing from the danger created by the activity is one of the kinds of danger to be anticipated from the activity. Thus, the chemical company is liable to the child for his injuries. (B) is incorrect because there is no indication that the chemical company was negligent with regard to the leakage of the chemicals. Apparently, the chemical company took all reasonable precautions under the circumstances. Thus, liability will be predicated on strict liability rather than on negligence. (C) is incorrect because, as explained above, injury to a person that is caused while fleeing from the immediate vicinity of a chemical leak is a kind of danger to be anticipated from maintaining a nerve gas system in an urban area. Thus, the harm incurred by the child flows from the normally dangerous propensity of the activity engaged in by the chemical company. In addition, even though the chemical company may not have known that children played in the chamber, a risk of harm is foreseeable to anyone (such as a city employee) who might enter the chamber. Hence, the child was within the "zone of danger" from the chemical company's activity. (D) is incorrect because the fact that the child was injured on property owned by the city is irrelevant to the chemical company's strict liability. The danger created by the chemical company's breach extended to the adjoining property, so the chemical company will be liable for injuries occurring there that were caused by the danger.

Answer to Question 178

(C) The court should deny the motion because the jury could find that the processor was negligent on the evidence presented. To prove breach of duty in a products liability case based on negligence, the plaintiff must show (i) negligent conduct by the defendant leading to (ii) the supplying of a defective product by the defendant. Defective food products are treated as manufacturing defects—the product is defective if it is dangerous beyond the expectation of the reasonable consumer. To show negligence in a manufacturing defect case, the plaintiff may invoke res ipsa loquitur against the manufacturer if the error is usually something that does not occur without the negligence of the manufacturer. Here, the jury could find that a piece of bone over an inch long in ground beef was a dangerous defect that would not have occurred without negligence on the part of the meat processor. Hence, the processor's motion should be denied and the case sent to the jury. (A) is wrong because, as discussed above, the plaintiff may rely on res ipsa loquitur to establish negligence. (B) is wrong because, even if the restaurant employees were negligent in not finding the bone, an intermediary's failure to discover a defect is not a superseding cause, and the defendant who created the defect will remain liable. (D) is wrong because the relative fault of the joint tortfeasors is not a basis for denying a directed verdict motion. The processor would be liable even if it were less at fault than the restaurant; the basis for denying its motion is to allow the jury to determine whether, and to what extent, it was at fault.

Answer to Question 179

(C) The court should rule that the officer's testimony is admissible as circumstantial evidence that the defendant was a member of a rival gang. Circumstantial evidence is evidence of a subsidiary or collateral fact from which, alone or in conjunction with a cluster of other facts, the existence of a material issue can be inferred. Under the Federal Rules, circumstantial evidence in the form of opinion testimony by a lay witness is admissible when it is: (i) rationally based on the perception of the witness, (ii) helpful to a clear understanding of his testimony or to the determination of a fact in issue, and (iii) not based on scientific, technical, or other specialized knowledge. Here, the

officer's testimony is based on his observation of the tattoo and his recognition, based on his experience, that it is worn by members of a gang that was a rival of the victim's gang. It is helpful to the determination of a fact in issue because it is circumstantial evidence contradicting the defendant's claim that he was not a member of the rival gang and tending to support the prosecution's theory of first degree murder. It is not based on scientific, technical, or similar specialized knowledge. Hence, (A) is incorrect because the officer does not need to know that the defendant is a member of the gang to testify that, based on his observation and experience, the defendant's tattoo was the gang's symbol. (B) is incorrect because the officer does not need to be qualified as an expert to testify as he proposes. His personal observation of tattoos on gang members makes his testimony, even if considered an opinion, sufficiently helpful to the trier of fact to make it admissible without him having to qualify as an expert on gangs. (D) is incorrect because the availability of the tattoo for display does not affect whether the officer's testimony is admissible. The only context in which a preference is expressed for the "original" piece of evidence is the best evidence or original document rule, which applies when the terms of a writing are sought to be proved. Here, even assuming that the tattoo would constitute a writing under the broad definition in the Federal Rules, the witness is not attempting to prove any terms or content of the "writing" that could be gleaned from the writing itself; thus, the rule does not apply.

Answer to Question 180

(D) Because the security chief's actions were merely part of a mock robbery, and the security chief had every reason to believe that the teller was aware of this, the security chief lacked the intent necessary to commit any of the crimes listed. Robbery is a taking of personal property of another from the other's person or presence by force or intimidation, with the intent to permanently deprive him of it. In taking from the teller the money, wallet, and wristwatch, the security chief simply intended to simulate the conditions of a bank robbery in as realistic a fashion as possible. The security chief did not intend to permanently (or even for any appreciable length of time) deprive the teller of any of his property. Because the intent required for robbery is missing, (A) is incorrect. Larceny is the taking and carrying away of tangible personal property of another by trespass with intent to permanently (or for an unreasonable time) deprive the person of his interest in the property. As explained above, the security chief lacked the intent to permanently deprive the teller of the property that was taken. In addition, the taking was not trespassory, because the security chief justifiably believed that the teller knew what was actually happening and that the taking was therefore consented to by the teller. Because of the absence of these elements of larceny, (B) is incorrect. An assault is either: (i) an attempt to commit a battery (*i.e.,* to unlawfully apply force to the person of another resulting in bodily injury or an offensive touching); or (ii) the intentional creation, other than by mere words, of a reasonable apprehension in the mind of the victim of imminent bodily harm. The security chief was not attempting to commit a battery, because at no time did he intend to apply force to the teller or otherwise cause the teller any injury. Although the teller may have had a reasonable apprehension of being shot, the security chief did not intend to create such an apprehension. The security chief was entitled to assume that the teller knew that this was merely a staged robbery, and that therefore there was no danger to the teller. Thus, under either definition of assault, the security chief is not guilty of this crime.

Answer to Question 181

(B) The husband's testimony is admissible as evidence of habit. Habit describes one's regular response to a specific set of circumstances. Evidence of the habit of a person is relevant to prove that the conduct of the person on a particular occasion was in conformity with the habit. [Fed. R. Evid. 406] Testimony that, every morning for the past seven years, the plaintiff has turned off the electric blanket immediately upon awakening describes her regular response to a repeated specific situation. Thus, the husband's testimony is evidence of habit. Such evidence is relevant to show that, on the day of the fire, the plaintiff's conduct was in conformity with this habit (*i.e.,* that she turned off the blanket before leaving for work). Therefore, the husband's testimony should be admitted. (A) misstates the rule as to admissibility of habit evidence. Evidence of habit is used to show that particular conduct conformed with such habit. However, evidence of prior conduct is not used to show conformity with habit. The husband's testimony is admissible because it is evidence of what the plaintiff probably did the morning of the fire, not because it is evidence of what she did on prior occasions. (C) is incorrect because habit, as a regular response to specific circumstances, is in fact proved by evidence of specific conduct rather than by opinion or reputation evidence. (D) is incorrect because there is no requirement under the Federal Rules that habit evidence be corroborated to be admissible.

Answer to Question 182

(D) The nephew, as the holder of a vested remainder, could ordinarily prevent the life tenant (the wife) from mining the property. However, the open mines doctrine permits the wife to continue to operate the mine because it was in operation at the time of the conveyance. The nephew's future interest is a remainder, because it is capable of becoming a present interest on the natural termination of the wife's preceding life estate. More particularly, the nephew has a *vested* remainder, because his remainder is certain to become a present interest on termination of the wife's estate, it is not subject to being defeated, and it is not subject to being diminished in size. According to the general rule, the wife (as the life tenant) would not be permitted to mine the property absent an express conferral of such a right by the miner, the grantor. This would allow the nephew, the remainderman, to successfully maintain an action enjoining the wife from operating the mine. However, the open mines doctrine allows the life tenant to continue to operate a mine that was open at the time of conveyance. The property containing the mine was conveyed to the wife on the miner's death, at which time the mine was already in operation. Therefore, under the open mines doctrine, the wife will be permitted to continue to operate the mine and the injunction will be denied. (A) incorrectly characterizes the nephew's vested remainder as subject to partial divestment. Such a remainder (also called a vested remainder subject to open) is a vested remainder created in a class of persons (*e.g.,* "children," "brothers and sisters") that is certain to take on the termination of the preceding estates, but is subject to diminution by reason of other persons becoming entitled to share in the remainder. The remainder here was created in the nephew, not in a class of persons, so that the nephew's remainder cannot be diminished as a result of other persons becoming entitled to share in the remainder. Therefore, the nephew does not have a vested remainder subject to partial divestment; he has an indefeasibly vested remainder that is certain to become possessory in him (or his heirs) when the wife dies. (B) is incorrect because, although the nephew's status as the holder of a vested remainder would ordinarily provide the basis for a successful action seeking to enjoin the wife's operation of the mine, (B) fails to take into account the open mines doctrine, pursuant to which the nephew's action will be defeated. (C) is incorrect because whether the wife's estate is a freehold estate is irrelevant to this analysis.

Answer to Question 183

(D) The homeowner cannot claim any right on title to the land over which the electrical wires were laid. The homeowner has not acquired a prescriptive easement because the neighbor consented to the wiring crossing his land. The holder of an easement has the right to use a tract of land for a special purpose, but has no right to possess and enjoy the tract of land. The neighbor's oral

consent to the wiring's crossing his land was not effective to create an easement. The Statute of Frauds requires that any conveyance of an easement interest of greater than one year in duration must be in writing to be enforceable; an oral attempt to create an easement results in a revocable license. What the neighbor's consent did, however, was to make it impossible for the homeowner to acquire an easement by prescription. As with adverse possession, an easement by prescription requires that the use be open and notorious, adverse, and continuous and uninterrupted for the statutory period. Because the neighbor consented to the homeowner's running of the wires, the homeowner's use of the land was not adverse, and thus did not ripen into a prescriptive easement before the neighbor's conveyance to the purchaser. (B) is therefore incorrect. (A) is incorrect because acquiring title by adverse possession requires that the possessor's actions amount to exclusive possession of the land, rather than a use of the land that does not exclude other uses. Running electrical wires across land could at most create a prescriptive easement. (C) is incorrect because the continuous use requirement does not require a constant use; it merely precludes sporadic and occasional trespasses from ripening into prescriptive easements. As with the continuous possession requirement for adverse possession, a seasonal use is sufficient if it is a use that the owner might make of the property under the circumstances.

Answer to Question 184

(D) The landowner is not likely to prevail because the statute does not constitute a total taking of his property and greatly promotes public welfare. If a government regulation denies a landowner all economic use of his land, the regulation may constitute a "taking" requiring the payment of "just compensation" under the Fifth Amendment. However, regulations that merely decrease the value of property do not necessarily result in a taking as long as there remains an economically viable use for the property. The court will consider the economic impact on the claimant and whether the regulation substantially interferes with distinct, investment backed objectives. Here, the statute promotes the important public purpose of trying to reduce mudslides and flooding, and does not totally ban the landowner from using his property for harvesting the plant. Thus, the regulation does not constitute a "taking" of private property in violation of the Fifth Amendment. (A) is incorrect because even a substantial impairment of economic value does not necessarily constitute a taking. As long as there is some economically viable use for the property, the court will use the above test. (B) is incorrect because, as discussed above, the statute does not result in a taking of private property. (C) is incorrect because it does not accurately state the test used by the Supreme Court for determining whether a regulation constitutes a "taking," but instead states the test for determining whether a particular use is a "public use" for purposes of applying the "Taking" Clause.

Answer to Question 185

(D) Direction (iv) needs to be corrected in its course but not its distance. In land contracts and deeds, property may be described in various ways as long as the description is unambiguous. From a designated starting point that can be identified by reference to a government survey or a natural or artificial monument, the boundaries of the property can be described by successive calls of courses (*e.g.*, angles) and distances until returning to the starting point. A course is a statement of direction generally stated as some number of degrees east or west of due north or south. In each call a distance must be stated together with the course. Thus, the boundary in direction (iv) runs at an angle 45 degrees east of due south (*i.e.*, southeast) for a distance of 100 feet. However, because direction (i) went southeast, direction (ii) went southwest, and direction (iii) went northwest, the fourth direction has to be northeast for a distance of 100 feet to bring the final boundary back to the starting point. (In this type of question, diagram the boundaries as shown below to help you visualize the property.) Therefore, the correction in choice (D) is correct. (A), (B), and (C) are incorrect because none of those proposed changes in distance or direction would be sufficient to bring the final call back to the starting point.

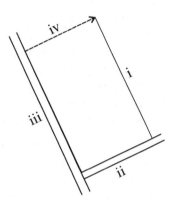

Answer to Question 186

(D) The reasonableness of the collector's belief that the length of his rifle did not violate the statute provides no defense to the crime charged. Unless the collector can establish a valid defense, he will be liable for violating the statute because he possessed a rifle less than 24 inches long. It is not a defense to a crime that the defendant was unaware that his acts were prohibited by the criminal law or that he mistakenly believed that his acts were not prohibited, even if such ignorance or mistake was reasonable. Here, the collector knew that the rifle he was purchasing was 22 inches long, but he was unaware that the statute prohibited possession of a rifle whose length was less than 24 inches. Such ignorance of the prohibition of the statute will not constitute a defense to the charge of possession of a sawed-off rifle, even if such ignorance remained after a reasonable investigation by the collector. (A) is incorrect because it would allow ignorance of the law to constitute a defense to a crime; *i.e.*, the collector would be acquitted because he did not know that the statute prohibited the possession of a rifle that is less than 24 inches in length. Where a statute requires knowledge of some other aspect of law, ignorance of that aspect of law might negate a mens rea element of the offense, but here, even if the statutory language prohibited only a "knowing" possession of the weapon, it would not require knowledge of the statute. (B) is incorrect because the collector's ignorance of the law will not be deemed a valid defense merely because he conducted a reasonable investigation to ensure compliance with the statute. The statute is clear in its terms, and was reasonably available for the collector's perusal. The fact that he personally measured the rifle to confirm that its barrel was at least 16 inches long, so as to assure conformity with the part of the statute of which he was aware, does not excuse his failure to be aware of the rest of the statute. (C) incorrectly states that ignorance of the law is a defense if such ignorance is reasonable. As noted above, the reasonableness of the mistake or ignorance does not render it a valid defense.

Answer to Question 187

(A) The court will admit rehabilitation testimony of the witness's good reputation for truthfulness if her credibility was attacked by conviction of a felony. Under Federal Rule of Evidence 608, when the witness's general character for truth and veracity has been attacked, the party for whom the impeached witness has testified may call other witnesses to testify to the good reputation for truth of the impeached witness or to give their opinion as to the truthfulness of the impeached witness. The attack on the witness's veracity may have been not only by reputation or opinion evidence, but also by conviction of a crime under Rule 609. Here, the plaintiff's witness was

impeached by conviction of a recent felony. (Because it is a felony, the crime does not have to involve dishonesty or a false statement.) This constitutes an attack on her general character for truth and veracity, allowing the plaintiff to present reputation or opinion evidence as to her truthfulness. (B) and (D) are both incorrect because impeachment by showing bias can be rebutted, but generally not by testimony as to the witness's overall good reputation for truthfulness (because showing bias usually is deemed not to be a broad attack on the witness's overall character for veracity). [*See* comments to Fed. R. Evid. 608] (C) is similarly not as good a choice as (A) because impeachment by showing a witness's sensory deficiencies usually does not constitute a general attack on the witness's character for truthfulness but rather is offered to show that the witness was mistaken as to her perception; hence, testimony as to the witness's good reputation for truthfulness probably would not be allowed under the circumstances here.

Answer to Question 188

(B) The roommate is likely to prevail because the woman acted in reckless disregard of a high probability that emotional distress would result. To establish a prima facie case for intentional infliction of emotional distress, plaintiff must show: (i) an act by defendant amounting to extreme and outrageous conduct, (ii) intent on the part of defendant to cause plaintiff to suffer severe emotional distress, or recklessness as to the effect of defendant's conduct, (iii) causation, and (iv) damages—severe emotional distress. Here, the woman's conduct was extreme and outrageous, and she caused the roommate to suffer severe emotional distress. The facts indicate that she wanted to make a lasting impression on her roommate, so she knew that there was a high likelihood that the roommate would suffer severe distress; hence, she has acted with the mental state of recklessness, and the roommate can establish the prima facie case for this tort. (A) is wrong because it does not suffice for intentional infliction of emotional distress to show only that it was foreseeable that emotional distress would result, which is a negligence standard; at a minimum, a reckless disregard of a high probability that emotional distress would result is required. (C) is incorrect because there is no physical injury requirement for intentional infliction of emotional distress; severe emotional distress is sufficient. Physical injury is an element of negligent infliction of emotional distress, but that tort only arises when the defendant negligently creates a foreseeable risk of physical injury to plaintiff, typically through threat of physical impact; it is not applicable to these facts. (D) is incorrect because that factor would only be relevant if the roommate were trying to recover for her emotional distress caused by physical harm inflicted on her boyfriend. Here, the woman's conduct was directed at the roommate rather than her boyfriend and is actionable because the woman knew that it was very likely that the roommate would suffer severe emotional distress.

Answer to Question 189

(D) The statement is inadmissible because it is hearsay not within any exception. It is an out-of-court statement being offered for the truth of the matter asserted, *i.e.,* that the victim's assistant committed the crime. As will be explained below, the statement does not qualify for exception either as a dying declaration or as a declaration of the victim's state of mind. In addition, the statement does not constitute an excited utterance. Despite the fact that the declaration was made while the victim was still under the stress of a startling event, the statement does not qualify under the exception because it does not concern the immediate facts of the startling occurrence. The fact that the victim believes that her assistant would kill for her job does not concern what is happening to her at that moment except to give her opinion of who did the deed. (A) is wrong for the same reason. The statement does not appear to concern the *facts* of the cause or circumstances of what she believed to be her impending death. A declaration of mere opinion that is not based on firsthand knowledge is inadmissible. While an argument could be made either way on this issue, a more certain reason why the statement is inadmissible as a dying declaration is that the assistant is being tried for *attempted* murder. Use of dying declarations *in criminal prosecutions* is limited to homicide cases. (B) is wrong because the state of mind exception covers statements of the declarant's then-existing state of mind, emotion, sensation, or physical condition, and is applicable only to show the declarant's state of mind when it is directly in issue or to show subsequent acts of the declarant. Neither of these situations is present here. Thus, this exception is inapplicable. (C) is wrong because it is too broad. While the use of dying declarations in a criminal prosecution is limited to homicide cases, a dying declaration is admissible in a civil action even though the declarant did not die.

Answer to Question 190

(C) The manufacturer's best defense is that the son's riding on a ledge at the bottom of the trolley constituted a misuse of the trolley that was not reasonably foreseeable, thus relieving the manufacturer of any potential strict liability. A prima facie case in products liability based on strict liability in tort consists of: (i) a strict duty owed by a commercial supplier; (ii) breach of that duty; (iii) actual and proximate cause; and (iv) damages. Breach of duty is established by showing that the defendant sold or produced a product in a defective condition unreasonably dangerous to users. Some products are safe if used as intended, but may pose serious dangers if used in other ways. Thus, suppliers must anticipate reasonably foreseeable uses (even if they are misuses) of the product. Here, the trolley was designed to seat four children. If so used, there is no indication that the trolley was unsafe. The son's injury resulted from his losing his grip on the edge of the trolley. Because the operator of the ride would be monitoring it to ensure that only children who had paid admission would ride, the manufacturer has a strong argument that it was not reasonably foreseeable that a child would ride the trolley by holding onto an outer edge and riding on the outside. Thus, the manufacturer was not required to anticipate and guard against such a misuse of the trolley. Consequently, the trolley was not so defective as to be unreasonably dangerous. (A) is incorrect because privity is not required to apply the protection of strict liability. The strict duty is owed not only to buyers but also to family, guests, friends, and employees of the buyer, as well as foreseeable bystanders. Thus, the manufacturer will be unable to avail itself of the lack of contractual privity between itself and the son. (B) is incorrect because ordinary contributory negligence is not a defense to a strict products liability action in contributory negligence jurisdictions. Only voluntarily and unreasonably encountering a known risk or misusing the product in an unforeseeable manner (as (C) states) would serve as a defense. (D) is incorrect because, even if the father were negligent in his supervision of the son, such ordinary negligence will not be deemed to be a superseding intervening force that breaks the causal connection between any initial wrongful conduct by the manufacturer and the ultimate injury. Thus, any negligence on the part of the father will not relieve the manufacturer of liability for any consequences of its supplying a defective product.

Answer to Question 191

(A) The writer is entitled to keep the $10,000 as liquidated damages. A liquidated damages clause will be enforceable if: (i) damages are difficult to ascertain at the time of the making of the contract, and (ii) the damages are a reasonable forecast of compensatory damages. The test for reasonableness is a comparison between the amount of damages prospectively probable at the time of contract formation and the liquidated damages figure. Here, the damages were difficult to ascertain at the time the contract was entered into, but $50,000 appears to be a reasonable forecast of damages by the writer given the amount of the advance. Thus, the writer is contractually

entitled to keep the $10,000 as part of his liquidated damages. (B) is incorrect because "impossibility" will discharge a contract only when performance cannot be accomplished by anyone. Here, the publisher may have been required to find other resources to get the book published or subcontract the job to another publisher. Thus, it likely was not impossible to publish the book. (C) is incorrect because the contractual condition for the agent's payment was not met: She was to receive 20% of the amount of money the writer earned from the sales of his book if the book was published, and the book was not published or sold. (D) is similarly incorrect because the agent was entitled under her contract to receive proceeds from the sales of the book if it were published; the book was not published and the $10,000 was liquidated damages and not proceeds from sales.

Answer to Question 192

(C) The pedestrian can recover $75,000 from the motorist, but the motorist can recover $30,000 from the shopping mall in contribution. Under pure comparative negligence, an injured plaintiff may recover damages from a negligent defendant no matter how great his own negligence was. Hence, the pedestrian is entitled to recover $75,000 of his $100,000 in damages because he was 25% at fault. The pedestrian may recover the entire $75,000 from the motorist under joint and several liability rules. Under joint and several liability, when two or more tortious acts combine to proximately cause an indivisible injury to the plaintiff, the plaintiff can recover the entire judgment from any defendant. However, the motorist can recover $30,000 from the shopping mall because the jurisdiction uses a comparative contribution system. Under the rule of contribution, any defendant required to pay more than her share of damages has a claim against the other jointly liable parties for the excess. In jurisdictions that have adopted a comparative contribution system, nonpaying tortfeasors are required to contribute only in proportion to their relative fault. Thus, the motorist can recover $30,000 from the shopping mall because it was found to be 30% at fault. (A) is incorrect because the jurisdiction retains joint and several liability, so the motorist can be required to pay all but 25% of the pedestrian's damages. (B) is incorrect—even though the dollar amount is correct—because the rationale is wrong. As stated above, an injured plaintiff can recover in a *pure* comparative negligence state even if his fault is greater than the fault of a negligent defendant. (Hence, the pedestrian found to be 25% at fault could recover $75,000 against the motorist even if the motorist were only 20% at fault and the shopping mall 55%.) Therefore, the fact that the pedestrian's fault was less than the motorist's fault is irrelevant. (D) is incorrect because comparative contribution rules do not have a threshold requirement. The motorist can recover from another jointly liable tortfeasor even though her fault is greater than that of the other tortfeasor.

Answer to Question 193

(D) The cocaine will not be suppressed. The issues are whether the defendant was unlawfully seized, thus making the cocaine the fruit of an illegal seizure of the person, whether the trooper needed a warrant before searching the baggage, and whether the trooper was required to advise the defendant of his rights under *Miranda* prior to asking him if the bag belonged to him. Whether a seizure occurs depends on whether a reasonable person would believe that he is not free to leave. The test is whether, under the totality of the circumstances, a reasonable person would feel free to decline the officers' requests or otherwise terminate the encounter. In fact, the Supreme Court has held that an officer boarding a bus does not constitute a seizure of the person so long as a reasonable person would believe that he was free to leave. In the instant case, the trooper boarded the bus, explained that the passengers were free to leave if they so desired, and then moved to the back of the bus to avoid blocking the aisle. Under Supreme Court precedent, this would not constitute a seizure of the person, as a reasonable person would know that he is free to leave. Thus, the cocaine will not be suppressed as the fruit of an illegal seizure of the person. The next issue is whether the trooper needed a warrant before conducting a search of the defendant's luggage. To be reasonable under the Fourth Amendment, most searches must be pursuant to a warrant. A search conducted without a warrant will be invalid (and evidence discovered during the search must be excluded from evidence) unless it is within one of the permissible warrantless searches. One such exception is when the officers conducting the search have voluntary and intelligent consent to do so. In the instant case, the officer informed all bus passengers that he might ask them to open up their luggage, and he informed them of their right to decline. Thus, the defendant's consent should be deemed "voluntary and intelligent." As a result, no violation of the Fourth Amendment occurred, which makes (A) and (C) incorrect answers. As to the Fifth Amendment argument, a person *in custody* must be informed that: (i) he has the right to remain silent; (ii) anything he says can be used against him in court; and (iii) if he cannot afford an attorney, one will be appointed for him if he so desires. The threshold requirement is that a person be in custody before the Fifth Amendment privilege against compelled self-incrimination is triggered. In the instant case, the trooper made it clear that each passenger was free to leave, and the trooper took steps not to block the exit. Thus, the defendant here was not in custody, and no *Miranda* warnings were required. Thus, even assuming that a court would exclude evidence under the fruits of the poisonous tree doctrine (and it is not clear that they would have to do so) based on a failure to give *Miranda* warnings, the warnings were not required under these facts. Thus, (B) is incorrect, and this provides another reason for (C) being incorrect.

Answer to Question 194

(B) Of all the alternatives, statement (B) most accurately reflects the balance between the scope of First Amendment protection for the dissemination of truthful commercial speech and the state's ability to enact narrowly drawn regulations to advance substantial governmental interests. Although commercial speech is protected by the First Amendment, it is subject to significant regulation. A state may outlaw commercial speech that proposes an unlawful transaction or that is misleading or fraudulent. If commercial speech concerns a lawful activity and is not misleading or fraudulent, the government regulation, to be valid, must directly advance a substantial governmental interest and must be no more extensive than necessary to serve that interest. The regulation must be narrowly drawn and there must be a reasonable fit between the legislation's end and the means chosen. If, as (B) states, the legislation here at issue does not prohibit the dissemination of truthful information about prices and product availability, and is otherwise narrowly tailored to serve a substantial state interest, the legislation probably will constitute a valid regulation of commercial speech. (A) is incorrect because it would overly limit the ability of the state to reasonably regulate commercial speech. This legislation does not necessarily violate auto dealers' rights of free speech. If it does not prohibit the dissemination of truthful information and is otherwise reasonable, the legislation is sufficiently narrow to pass constitutional muster. (C) incorrectly implies that the state's police power is broader than it actually is. This legislation does in fact potentially infringe the federal constitutional right of free speech (which extends to commercial speech). If the legislation does not satisfy the test for reasonable regulations of commercial speech, the police power of the state would not save it from being found invalid. (D) is a misstatement of the law. The Constitution prohibits any state from passing any law impairing the obligation of contract. This Contract Clause prevents state destruction of all rights or all enforcement of existing contracts. (D) refers to infringement of the right to enter into a contract rather than impairment of a currently existing contract. This is outside the purview of the Contract Clause.

Answer to Question 195

(A) The contractor has not breached the contract, and the chef need not make the first payment. The contractual term as to the contractor's beginning construction on April 15 is a condition rather than a promise, and failure of occurrence of a condition is not a breach of contract. A promise is a commitment to do or refrain from doing something. A condition is an event, other than the passage of time, the occurrence or nonoccurrence of which will create, limit, or extinguish the absolute duty to perform in the other contracting party. There is no breach of contract until the promisor is under an absolute duty to perform. Failure of a condition is not a breach of contract, but it discharges the liability of a party whose obligations on the conditional promise never mature. Here, the term regarding the beginning of construction of the restaurant on April 15 merely fixes a tentative time of the start of performance, and does not involve an absolute promise by the contractor to commence performance on April 15. This term is a condition, because its occurrence will create in the chef the absolute duty to make the initial $20,000 payment. Because the contractor was under no absolute duty to commence construction on April 15, his failure to do so does not constitute a breach of the contract. However, this failure does mean that the condition that governs whether the chef has an absolute duty to pay has not yet occurred. Consequently, the chef need not make the initial payment. (B) is incorrect because, with the failure to satisfy the condition, the chef is not yet contractually obligated to make the initial payment. (C) and (D) are incorrect because the contractor's failure to commence construction on April 15 is not a breach. As explained above, there can be no breach until there is an absolute duty to perform, and the contractor had not absolutely promised to commence construction on April 15. An additional note: (C) states that, if the contractor has breached the contract in a nonmaterial manner, then the chef need not make the initial payment. Actually, the usual effect of a minor breach would be simply to provide a remedy to the aggrieved party; the aggrieved party would not be relieved of her duty of performance under the contract. Only if the promise that is breached is also a condition for the aggrieved party's performance would the breach relieve the party's duty to perform. Hence, even if the contractor's failure to begin on time were a minor breach, that fact alone would not have allowed the chef to suspend his performance.

Answer to Question 196

(C) The contractor will recover the balance owing on the contract because he did not intend to assume the risk of the theater not making a profit. Once again, distinguishing between a promise and a condition is critical. If the provision regarding payment once the theater became profitable is a condition, its failure to occur will extinguish the consortium's duty to pay the contractor what it promised under the contract. The basic test of whether a contractual provision is a promise or a condition is the intent of the parties. Courts will examine the words of the agreement, prior practices of the parties, custom, and whether fulfillment of the provision is to be rendered by the promisee (in which case it is more likely to be a condition) or by the promisor. Under a provision that a duty is to be performed "once" an event occurs, if the event is not within the control of the promisee, it is less likely that he will have assumed the risk of its nonoccurrence and therefore less likely to be a condition of the promisor's duty to perform. In doubtful situations, courts will more likely hold that the provision is a promise rather than a condition because it supports the contract and preserves the reasonable expectations of the parties. Here, there is no evidence that the contractor was agreeing to a joint venture with the consortium whereby he would not get paid if the consortium did not do well but would not receive any extra if it was very successful. Whether the theater made a profit was more within the control of the consortium than of the contractor; he was assuming nothing more than a risk of delay in receiving payment to allow the consortium a chance to begin making a profit. His reasonable expectation was that ultimately he would be paid

the balance owing on the contract, and the sale of the theater by the consortium gives it the ability to pay him. (A) is incorrect because the provision governing payment is not a condition excusing the absolute duty of the consortium to perform under the contract. The court will imply a promise to pay the balance after a reasonable time if the timing provision in the contract is not triggered. (B) incorrectly suggests that the contractual duty of the consortium was discharged by frustration of the contract's purpose. Frustration exists if: (i) some supervening act or event occurs that was not reasonably foreseeable at the time of entering into the contract; (ii) the act or event has completely or almost completely destroyed the purpose of the contract; and (iii) both parties realized the purpose of the contract at the time of making it. Here, the failure to earn a profit from a new theater was certainly not unforeseeable; in fact, the timing provision indicates that the parties realized at least some uncertainty as to the theater's profitability. (D) is not as good a choice as (C) even though it may be a true statement. While the contractor's completion of the theater is not only a promise by him but also a condition precedent to the consortium's duty to pay (and this condition has occurred), the issue in this question is whether the payment provision is a condition or merely a promise as to the timing of the monthly payments, and (C) specifically addresses that issue.

Answer to Question 197

(C)   The fare increase probably will be upheld because the action undertaken by the city council will not require strict scrutiny. The Equal Protection Clause of the Fourteenth Amendment prohibits states from denying persons equal protection of the laws. Whenever a law treats certain classes of people differently from others, a potential equal protection issue is raised. If the governmental action classifies persons based on a suspect classification (such as race), a strict scrutiny standard will be applied and the action will be struck down unless the government proves that it is necessary to achieve a compelling interest. On the other hand, most classifications, including those based on income level, are reviewed under the rational basis standard and will be upheld unless they bear no rational relationship to any conceivable legitimate government interest. Here, the fare increase could be challenged on the ground that a suspect classification (race) is involved. However, the mere fact that a governmental action has a discriminatory effect is not sufficient to trigger strict scrutiny. There must be *intent* to discriminate on the part of the government. When the law does not discriminate on its face and is not applied in a discriminatory manner, a suspect classification will be found only if the lawmaking body enacted or maintained the law for a discriminatory purpose. While statistical evidence is admissible that the law has a disproportionate impact on one class of persons, such evidence will almost never be sufficient by itself to prove that the government had a discriminatory purpose in passing a law. In this case, the fare increase does not discriminate on its face and is not applied just to some classes of bus riders and not others. While the fare increase has a disproportionate impact on members of a minority group because they rely more heavily on the bus lines, there is no evidence that the increase was motivated by any other purpose than eliminating the operating deficit of the bus lines. Hence, the fare increase will be held not to involve a suspect classification based on race. The other group for which the fare increase creates a disproportionate impact is the poor. However, the Court has never held that wealth alone is a suspect classification. Unless a governmentally required fee deprives a person of a fundamental constitutional right, it will be judged under the rational basis standard (*i.e.,* it will be upheld if it is rationally related to a legitimate government interest). Here, the fare increase does not deprive poor persons of any fundamental right and it is rationally related to the legitimate purpose of reducing the operating deficit of the bus system. Therefore, the fare increase will be held constitutional. (A) is incorrect because there is no evidence that the voting system established for the election of city council members violates the Equal Protection Clause, which prohibits state dilution of the right to vote. In the absence of such evidence, the

action of the city council cannot be challenged on the basis of inadequate representation. (B) is incorrect because, as discussed above, the existence of a disparate impact on a suspect class is not sufficient by itself to trigger strict scrutiny; thus, the city will **not** need to show that the fare increase is necessary for a compelling state interest. (D) is incorrect because political questions are limited to those issues committed by the Constitution to another branch of government and those issues inherently incapable of resolution and enforcement by the judicial process. The fare increase is not a political question and will be subject to review by the courts, even though only the rational basis standard will be applied.

Answer to Question 198

(A) The court is likely to rule that the library board's meeting room policy is valid because it is reasonably related to a legitimate government interest. The library board, as a government body, may reasonably regulate speech-related conduct in public forums and designated public forums through reasonable time, place, and manner regulations. Some public property, such as streets, sidewalks, and parks, is so historically associated with the exercise of First Amendment rights that it is categorized as a traditional public forum. Other public property may become a designated public forum when the government, by policy or practice, opens it for expressive activity. However, most locations other than streets, sidewalks, and parks are not public forums and may be reserved by the government for their intended activity. When a nonpublic forum is involved, government regulations designed to reserve the forum for its intended use will be upheld if they are (i) viewpoint neutral, and (ii) reasonably related to the intended purpose of the nonpublic forum (which must be a legitimate government purpose). Here, a library meeting room is not a traditional public forum, and the library board has not designated it as a public forum because its use is limited to library groups for library purposes. Thus, the court would likely characterize it as a nonpublic forum. The restriction is viewpoint neutral (*i.e.*, it is not an attempt to limit the presentation of issues to only one viewpoint), and it is rationally related to the legitimate objective of alleviating the staff's scheduling burden. Hence, the library's policy would probably be upheld by the court. (B) is incorrect because it states part of the standard for restricting speech in public forums. Speech in public forums may be regulated by reasonable time, place, and manner regulations if the regulation (i) is content neutral (*i.e.*, subject matter neutral and viewpoint neutral), (ii) is narrowly tailored to serve a significant government interest, and (iii) leaves open alternative channels of communication. Here, as discussed above, the library meeting room probably would not be characterized as a public forum. (C) is incorrect because the library, as a nonpublic forum, is permitted to restrict speech based on content (*i.e.*, subject matter) as long as the restriction is not based on the viewpoint of the speech. (D) is incorrect because the requirement of alternative channels of communication is a component of the public forum standard. Here, because the library meeting room is not a public forum, the policy is valid regardless of the availability of alternative meeting facilities.

Answer to Question 199

(B) The thief can be convicted of burglary and robbery. At common law, the elements of burglary are: (i) a breaking (ii) and entry (iii) of the dwelling (iv) of another (v) at nighttime, (vi) with the intent to commit a felony therein. Here, the thief has committed a constructive breaking because she gained entry by means of a fraud. The hotel room constitutes a dwelling for purposes of burglary, and the thief apparently had the intent to commit larceny when she entered the room. The thief has also committed robbery, which is defined as (i) a taking (ii) of personal property of another (iii) from the other's person or presence (iv) by force or intimidation, (v) with the intent to permanently deprive the other of the property. The thief used the threat of force against the victim to obtain the property, and obtained it while in the victim's presence. Thus, she can be convicted of both burglary and robbery, making (C) and (D) incorrect. (A) and (C) are incorrect because the elements of larceny are contained within the more serious offense of robbery, which is basically an aggravated form of larceny.

Answer to Question 200

(C) A record of an arrest, even for a crime such as embezzlement, cannot be used to impeach the credibility of a witness. Since there was no criminal conviction, this would be classified as evidence of a prior bad act that demonstrates dishonesty. Federal Rule of Evidence 608 would allow an inquiry into such a prior bad act during cross-examination of the witness being impeached, but extrinsic evidence of such acts is not allowed under Rule 608, even if the witness denies the act on cross-examination. (A) might be admissible to impeach. Under Federal Rule 609, a prior felony conviction for crimes that do not involve dishonesty can be used to impeach if the trial judge determines that the probative value of the evidence is not substantially outweighed by prejudice or other Rule 403 considerations. (B) represents an acceptable method of impeachment. Prior inconsistent statements can be introduced to show that the witness is not always truthful. (D) is an acceptable impeachment method. Under Rule 608, a witness may be interrogated on cross-examination with respect to any act of misconduct that is probative of truthfulness (*i.e.*, demonstrates dishonesty). Lying on an expense report would be such an act.

Lecture Handout

CONSTITUTIONAL LAW

Question 2

One of the provisions of federal anti-smoking legislation imposes restrictions on federal economic development grants, which were awarded to states to promote and assist small businesses in urban areas. The legislation mandates that grants will be reduced by 10% for any state that fails to require businesses engaged in the sale of cigarettes to take steps to avoid sales to minors, including checking drivers' licenses or photo ID cards. A tobacco-growing state that receives several million dollars under the federal grant program challenged the constitutionality of the provision in federal district court. The state established that the federal provision affects businesses that do not operate in interstate commerce.

Should the court uphold the federal provision?

(A) No, because the federal provision affects state regulation of businesses that do not operate in interstate commerce.

(B) No, because state distribution of economic development funds is an integral government function.

(C) Yes, because Congress may condition grants of money under its spending power.

(D) Yes, because the provision is substantially related to the important government interest of restricting minors' access to cigarettes.

Question 85

Congress enacted a statute that provided for direct money grants to the various states to be distributed by them to police agencies within their jurisdictions for the purpose of purchasing gas-efficient patrol vehicles. One of the objectives of the statute was to help reduce the dependency of the United States on imported oil.

Which of the following would provide the best constitutional justification for the statute?

(A) The Commerce Clause.

(B) The power to tax and spend for the general welfare.

(C) The Necessary and Proper Clause.

(D) The power to conduct the foreign relations of the United States.

Question 74

In connection with its agricultural products price support program, the United States Department of Agriculture regularly sent marketing and price information via email to its numerous field offices in various states. Recently, sophisticated criminals began using electronic devices to intercept the transmitted information, which they then used to gain an unfair advantage over other traders in the nation's commodities markets. To alleviate the problem, Congress enacted legislation making it a criminally punishable offense to "intercept marketing and/or price information in any fashion or to transmit such intercepted information to any other person in any fashion." A citizen opposed to the federal agricultural price support program learned the identity of the individuals who are intercepting the Department of Agriculture transmissions and, in exchange for not revealing their identities, obtained copies of every transmission they intercepted. He published these in his weekly newsletter.

If the citizen is prosecuted for violation of the federal statute prohibiting transmission of intercepted marketing or price information, what is his strongest argument that the statute is unconstitutional as applied to him?

(A) The statute denies him the equal protection of the law as guaranteed by the Fourteenth Amendment.

(B) The statute violates his right not to be deprived of liberty without due process of law.

(C) The statute violates his First Amendment right to free speech.

(D) The statute is an undue burden upon interstate commerce.

Question 89

As permitted by state law, a large city in the state adopted an ordinance legalizing slot machines in shopping malls within the city. Several prominent city residents were upset by the new ordinance because gambling violates one of the main tenets of their religion. Seeking relief, the citizens contacted their representative in Congress and asked the representative to sponsor a bill making it illegal to place gambling machines in shopping malls throughout the country. The representative sponsored such a bill. Congress made a factual finding that the activity regulated has a substantial economic effect on interstate commerce and passes such a statute.

If the statute banning gambling machines in shopping malls is challenged on constitutional grounds by a proper plaintiff in federal court, would the court likely uphold the statute?

(A) No, because it was based on the citizens' religious tenets and so violates the First Amendment Establishment Clause.

(B) No, because the statute does not regulate the channels or instrumentalities of interstate commerce.

(C) Yes, because Congress has made a factual finding that the activity regulated has a substantial economic effect on interstate commerce.

(D) Yes, because there is a conceivable rational basis for concluding that the activity regulated, in aggregate, substantially affects interstate commerce.

Question 94

One provision of a federal law provided that state governments may enact legislation regulating any form of pinball machine or video game, including location and hours of operation. In response, a Western state enacted legislation providing, among other things, that any video game sold or operated within the state use a particular LCD screen designed to minimize eyestrain.

A corporation that designs and manufactures video games for sale throughout the United States and in Europe is based in the Midwest. Approximately 10% of its gross sales are made in the Western state that has regulated the LCD screens. The corporation's machines are not manufactured using the special eye-protecting LCD screens; to install such screens in all machines manufactured would cause the price of the machines to increase by 20%, and to use the screens in machines sold only in the Western state would increase the cost of those machines by 50%. The corporation files suit in federal court to enjoin enforcement of the state video game statute.

How should the court rule?

(A) For the state, because the challenged legislation is within the powers specifically reserved to the states by the Tenth Amendment.

(B) For the state, because Congress has acted within its power to authorize video game regulation by the states.

(C) For the corporation, because the challenged statute violates the Commerce Clause.

(D) For the corporation, because the challenged statute is overbroad and exceeds the permissible bounds of regulation as authorized by Congress.

Question 170

To encourage the development of local integrated circuit manufacturing operations, a state enacted legislation requiring that at least 50% of the units sold by electronic products retailers within the state incorporate locally manufactured microprocessors. The owner of a chain of computer stores in the state sells electronic devices manufactured entirely in other states.

If the computer store owner attacks the state legislation on constitutional grounds, which of the following would provide the strongest support for his position?

(A) The Equal Protection Clause of the Fourteenth Amendment.

(B) The Due Process Clause of the Fourteenth Amendment.

(C) The Commerce Clause.

(D) The Privileges and Immunities Clause of Article IV.

Question 174

A state's Commercial Code provides, in part, that "the minimum price of cheese sold in this state shall be $2.50 per pound."

As to which of the following persons would the state statute be most likely constitutionally applied?

(A) A resident of the state selling cheese in that state to a manufacturer of snack foods whose plant is located in a neighboring state.

(B) A resident of Canada selling cheese made in Canada to the citizens of the state.

(C) A resident of the state selling cheese to the Commissary at the United States Air Force base in the state.

(D) A resident of the state selling cheese to the state Department of Education for its use in its school lunch program.

Question 36

A state statute prohibited the sale or possession of any food product containing more than one part per billion of a dangerous pesticide. An out-of-state driver taking her recreational vehicle through a corner of the state was stopped at a state inspection station. When the state trooper learned that the pantry of her RV was stocked with food, he asked to test a few samples of her baked goods. The samples contained about 600 parts per billion of the prohibited pesticide, and all of the other baked goods in her possession were tested and found to have the same level of pesticide. All of her baked goods, worth about $150, were confiscated and destroyed.

The state in which the driver lived has no laws governing the pesticide level of baked goods. A federal law designed to protect agricultural workers requires that any food product containing more than 500 parts per billion of the toxic pesticide must be labeled as such and be in special containers. The driver brings an action in federal court asserting that the state statute is invalid because it is preempted by the federal law.

How should the court rule as to this claim?

(A) For the state, because the purposes of the federal law are different from those of the challenged statute.

(B) For the state, because regulation of food quality is a power reserved to the states by the Tenth Amendment.

(C) For the driver, because the federal law does not expressly permit states to enact more stringent pesticide level controls.

(D) For the driver, because the federal law and the state statute regulate the same subject matter.

Question 116

A state prohibited the sale of heated grips for motorcycles within its borders to discourage motorcyclists from riding in dangerously cold conditions. The owner of a cycle shop that sells heated grips within the state that are purchased from an out-of-state manufacturer seeks an injunction in state court prohibiting the state from enforcing its statute. The owner claims that the statute unreasonably interferes with interstate commerce.

If the state court rules that the relevant statute is valid and denies injunctive relief, which of the following is the proper next step for the corporation to take to obtain review of the state court decision?

(A) Appeal to the state appellate courts.

(B) Petition for removal to the federal district court within the state.

(C) Appeal to the federal circuit court of appeals with jurisdiction over cases from the state.

(D) Petition for certiorari to the Supreme Court of the United States.

Question 117

The owner of a chain of natural food stores located within a particular state contracted with landowners and construction firms in a neighboring state in preparation for the opening of several new stores in the neighboring state. The chain's products are stored and sold in bulk within the stores. Consumers remove the amount of product they want from bins within the stores, place the product in plastic bags, and then present their bags at a checkout counter. Statutes in the neighboring state in which the chain owner would like to open his new stores prohibit the sale of food in bulk due to the health hazards

associated with bulk storage and contamination from consumer access to food sold from bins. The state has prosecuted other grocers' violations of the statute in the past.

If the chain store owner seeks an injunction against state officials in the federal district court with jurisdiction over the matter and the state officials seek dismissal on the ground that the corporation lacked standing to sue, what would be the probable outcome?

(A) The suit would be dismissed, because the owner has suffered no injury.

(B) The suit would be dismissed, because the challenged state legislation has no effect on civil liberties.

(C) The federal court would hear the suit, because a federal question—interstate commerce—is involved.

(D) The federal court would hear the suit, because the owner has undertaken substantial steps to open outlets in the state.

Question 110

Recently enacted legislation required farmers in certain counties of a western state to use drip irrigation systems instead of traditional methods in order to conserve water for agricultural and other uses. A farmer who refused to use the drip system was charged pursuant to the enforcement provisions of the legislation. A state court enjoined him from using other irrigation methods and fined him.

The farmer appealed to the state supreme court, renewing his trial court claims that the irrigation legislation violated a state constitutional provision prohibiting certain governmental intrusions into private commercial activities and that it was preempted by federal water management statutes. The state supreme court held that the state constitution prohibited the challenged legislation, and construed the relevant statutes as being within the parameters of the federal statutes, and thus preempted.

If the state petitions for certiorari to the United States Supreme Court, how should the Court rule on the petition?

(A) Grant the petition, to determine whether the state court's interpretation of the scope of the federal statutes was incorrect.

(B) Grant the petition, because, under principles of federalism, a state court cannot be the final arbiter of the validity of its own legislation when it is alleged to be in conflict with federal law.

(C) Deny the petition, because there is no substantial federal question that is dispositive of the case.

(D) Deny the petition, because a state government may not seek review of decisions of its own courts in the United States Supreme Court.

Question 130

Federal legislation provided that the marketing and sale of oranges was subject to the control of a local marketing authority. The marketing authority determined what quantity of oranges could be sold by each grower, the price, and the location of sale. These decisions were made by a council of local growers whose members were selected by the federal Department of Agriculture. The applicable federal legislation provided, in part, that when any grower subject to a marketing order challenged the propriety of that order, the council of the marketing authority must submit the controversy to the United States district court with geographical jurisdiction for a recommendation as to whether the order should be confirmed, modified, or rescinded. After the hearing in district court, the council must revote on the challenged marketing order.

A citrus grower brings suit in United States district court, seeking on constitutional grounds to enjoin enforcement of the federal legislation providing for the marketing order that the council issued with regard to his orange crop.

If the court rules on the constitutional issue, the grower will probably:

(A) Lose, because the federal government may properly regulate items in interstate commerce.

(B) Lose, because the marketing order system is a necessary and proper means of effectuating the commerce power.

(C) Win, because the federal legislation permits the federal district court to give an advisory opinion.

(D) Win, because the federal legislation deprives the grower of his property without due process of law.

Question 131

A merchant owned a skate rental business that she operated out of a specially equipped van. She would drive to various parks and public beaches within her home state and rent roller skates, related safety equipment and lightweight stereo/earphone sets to passersby on an hourly basis. She also sold skates and skating equipment. About 50% of the merchant's time is spent in a single city, and she earns about 70% of her gross rental and sale income at that city's beach areas. After receiving numerous complaints from beachgoers about the sidewalks

congested with roller skaters, the city council passed an ordinance prohibiting roller skating on public property between the hours of 7 a.m. and 9 p.m.

If the merchant seeks to enjoin enforcement of the ordinance in federal district court on the basis that it is unconstitutional, that court will probably:

(A) Reach the merits of the merchant's challenge to the ordinance, because it interferes with his right to free association.

(B) Reach the merits of the merchant's challenge, because enforcement of the ordinance will harm her business and the rights of the public are linked to her rights.

(C) Decline to hear the case, because the ordinance does not prohibit the rental of skating equipment.

(D) Decline to hear the case, because skating is not prohibited on private property, nor on public property from 9 p.m. to 7 a.m.

Question 59

A state legislature was concerned about the number of households headed by single teenage mothers and the deleterious effects of overpopulation. It enacted legislation requiring any person under the age of 25 to obtain a certificate of responsibility before having children. Under the statutes, any fetus whose parents do not both have a certificate of responsibility is required to be aborted, and any child born into the same circumstances is required to be placed up for adoption. Parents who violate the statute are subject to fine, imprisonment, or both.

A 22-year-old male resident of the state brings an action in federal court seeking to enjoin enforcement of the legislation on the ground that it violates his constitutional rights. In his complaint, he alleges that he plans to marry and father children before he is 25.

Which of the following provides the strongest justification for dismissing the action?

(A) It involves a nonjusticiable political question.

(B) It is not ripe for adjudication.

(C) There is no substantial federal question involved.

(D) The 22-year-old's future wife is not also a party to the action.

Question 158

A lawsuit involving a contract dispute between a resident of State Alpha and a resident of State Beta was properly filed by the State Alpha party in a State Alpha district court. The court dismissed the action because the statute of limitations had run. On learning that State Beta had a longer limitations period that would not have run, the plaintiff promptly filed an identical action in the appropriate State Beta court. However, on the defendant's motion, the State Beta court dismissed the action on the sole ground that it was obligated to accept the judgment of the State Alpha court under the Full Faith and Credit Clause of the federal Constitution.

Assuming that both courts had jurisdiction over the parties and the subject matter, was State Beta required to give full faith and credit to the judgment of the State Alpha court?

(A) Yes, because the State Alpha court had entered a final judgment in an identical case.

(B) Yes, because the defendant should not be penalized for the plaintiff's forum shopping.

(C) No, because the Full Faith and Credit Clause applies to judgments rendered by a federal court, not a state court.

(D) No, because the State Alpha court did not make a ruling on the merits of the case.

Question 90

During a nationwide trucker's strike, striking drivers committed repeated acts of violence against independent truckers and railroad shipments that had replaced truck transportation. This prompted Congress to enact an emergency measure directing the President to dispatch United States Army troops to specified cities and rail and highway locations to preserve order and ensure the continued flow of commerce.

This enactment is probably:

(A) Unconstitutional, because it infringes on the President's authority to faithfully execute the laws of the United States.

(B) Unconstitutional, because it infringes on the President's authority as Commander in Chief of the armed forces.

(C) Constitutional, under Congress's power to regulate commerce.

(D) Constitutional, under Congress's power to raise and support the armed forces.

Question 154

To gain progress on critical treaty negotiations with another country, the President issued an official pardon to the leader of a radical group who was in a state prison after being convicted of a violent crime in the state. The President directed the governor of the state to free the

leader but the governor refused. The Justice Department brought an action in federal district court seeking an order compelling his release.

The federal court most likely will rule:

(A) For the state, because a state official acting pursuant to his state's constitution need not obey inconsistent orders from a federal official.

(B) For the state, because the President's constitutional power to pardon prisoners extends only to those convicted of federal offenses.

(C) For the state, because the President's order and the pardon given the convicted leader violate his duty to see that the laws of the United States are faithfully executed.

(D) For the federal government, because the President's actions are authorized by his power to enter into treaties with other nations.

Question 184

After a recent rainy season, a number of the communities in a western state suffered flooding and mudslides. A study commissioned by the state legislature determined that the extensive removal of a certain plant from hillsides within the state contributed significantly to the flooding and mudslides. The plant had an extensive root system that helped hold hillside soil in place, and it was being rapidly removed because its roots had recently gained national favor as a powerful herbal remedy. As a result, the legislature passed a statute prohibiting the removal of more than 50% of such plants from any hillside within the state.

A landowner within the state challenged the statute on federal constitutional grounds, alleging that he had regularly harvested substantially more than 50% of the plants from his property and needed to do the same this year to meet the demand for the root.

Is he likely to prevail in his challenge?

(A) Yes, because the statute substantially impairs the economic value of the landowner's property.

(B) Yes, because the statute effects a taking of private property for public use without just compensation.

(C) No, because the statute is rationally related to the legitimate government interest of preventing flooding damage to property.

(D) No, because the statute promotes a legitimate public purpose and permits the continued use of the landowner's property.

Question 10

A state statute prohibited the state and any county, municipality, or other governmental unit within the boundaries of the state from hiring as a civil engineer any person who is not a citizen. A well-qualified engineer who is not a United States citizen read that the state's department of transportation needed a new drafting engineer. The foreign engineer applied for the position and had the required qualifications. However, the hiring official turned down the engineer's application, explaining that he could not hire her because of the state statute. The engineer filed suit in federal court, claiming that the statute violates her right to equal protection under the Fourteenth Amendment.

If the engineer prevails, it will most likely be because:

(A) The engineer proved that the statutory provision is not necessary to achieve a compelling government interest.

(B) The engineer proved that the statutory provision is not rationally related to a legitimate government interest.

(C) The state has failed to prove that the law is necessary to achieve a compelling government interest.

(D) The state has failed to prove that the law is substantially related to an important government interest.

Question 31

After a widely publicized accident in which an elderly motorist drove onto the sidewalk and struck and killed several pedestrians, the state legislature revised its motor vehicle statutes. The new legislation required motorists over the age of 70 to undergo more frequent and more thorough testing to maintain their driver's licenses. A 75-year-old former race car driver who was required by the new legislation to be tested every year to maintain his driver's license brought suit in the federal district court in the state, alleging that the legislation results in unconstitutional age discrimination.

Which of the following statements best reflects the burden of persuasion that the court will apply in the driver's suit?

(A) The state must show that the law is substantially related to an important government purpose.

(B) The state must show that the law is rationally related to a legitimate government interest.

(C) The driver must show that the law is not rationally related to a legitimate government interest.

(D) The driver must show that the law is not substantially related to an important government purpose.

Question 155

A state's pension program provided supplemental state pension benefits to surviving spouses and children of state employees. The program provided that when the spouse remarried, that spouse's benefits would be gradually terminated based on a statutory formula. Because of statistics showing past disparities between the household income levels of male surviving spouses and female surviving spouses, different formulas were used for the termination schedule depending on whether the surviving spouse was male or female.

A widower of a state employee was informed after he remarried that his pension benefits would be terminated in 90 days according to the applicable formula. Upon learning that a similarly situated widow would have continued to receive benefits for six months after remarrying, the widower decided to file suit in federal court, alleging that the state program is unconstitutional because it is discriminatory and it unfairly burdens his right to marry.

Which of the following best states the burden of persuasion in this case?

(A) The state must demonstrate that the program is narrowly tailored to achieve a compelling government interest.

(B) The state must demonstrate that the program is substantially related to an important government interest.

(C) The widower must demonstrate that the program is not substantially related to an important government interest.

(D) The widower must demonstrate that the program is not rationally related to a legitimate government interest.

Question 73

Concerned about the rising death toll on the state's highways, a state legislature enacted a statute providing for a summary one-year suspension of the driver's license of any person convicted of three speeding violations within a 12-month period. The statute provided that an administrative hearing is immediately available upon request. However, that hearing is limited to a determination of whether the licensee is the same person who was convicted of the speeding violations.

A driver received three speeding citations in a three-week period and was convicted of all three charges. Her license was promptly suspended under the authority of the state statute. Without first seeking an administrative hearing, the driver files a suit in federal district court challenging the constitutionality of the statute.

The court should rule that the state law is:

(A) Constitutional, because driving an automobile on the state's highways is a privilege and not a right.

(B) Constitutional, because the state's interest in promptly removing unsafe drivers from its roads outweighs the driver's right to a prior hearing under these circumstances.

(C) Unconstitutional, because the law creates an irrebuttable presumption that all drivers falling within the ambit of the statute are unsafe.

(D) Unconstitutional, as a denial of due process without a prior hearing.

Question 20

A certain city was the county seat and had a population of about 250,000. The city council consisted of 20 members, each of whom was elected at large. Although at one time the city had individual member districts, the city charter was revised in 1954 to provide for at-large election of all council members. The political life of the city had been dominated by members of the Alpha Party, and its full slate of candidates almost always won election. During the long period that the city had used the at-large election system, only one African-American had ever been elected to the city council, and only because of the support of the Alpha Party. When he ran for reelection, he did not receive the Alpha Party's support because he raised concerns of minority voters. He was soundly defeated, even though he received 95% of the African-American vote. Since then, no member of a minority group has served on the city council, nor has a member of a minority group been slated as a candidate by the Alpha Party. Among the population of the city are now 60,000 African-Americans, 20,000 Hispanics, 3,000 Asians, and 2,000 Native Americans.

If a minority coalition association brings suit to compel the city to provide for single member districts, it would be most likely to win its case with arguments based on which of the following provisions of the United States Constitution?

(A) Equal Protection Clause.

(B) Due Process Clause.

(C) The Fourteenth Amendment Privileges or Immunities Clause.

(D) Article I, Section 2, Clause 4.

Question 151

A state provided generous state-subsidized health benefits to all residents who did not have an employer-funded program that met specified minimum requirements.

To alleviate the burden on the state's budget, the legislation provided that a person must have resided in the state for at least one year to be entitled to any health benefits provided by the state. A consultant moved to the state last month to take a consulting job. The position does not provide health benefits, so she sought coverage through the state program and was denied. She then filed suit in federal district court, challenging the denial of the state benefits to her.

If the court finds in favor of the consultant, it will most likely be because:

(A) The restriction does not have a rational relationship to a legitimate state interest as required by the Equal Protection Clause of the Fourteenth Amendment.

(B) The restriction deprives the consultant of certain privileges and immunities in violation of the Interstate Privileges and Immunities Clause of Article IV, Section 2.

(C) The restriction improperly burdens the fundamental right of interstate travel in violation of the Equal Protection Clause of the Fourteenth Amendment.

(D) The restriction deprives the consultant of a property interest without due process of law in violation of the Due Process Clause of the Fourteenth Amendment.

Question 21

A philanthropist told his friend, who was a state governor, that he planned to build a museum. The governor thought that the museum would bolster the state's tourism industry and offered to arrange to have the state purchase land and grant it to the museum to enable the philanthropist to build a bigger museum with his money than originally planned. The philanthropist agreed and the museum was built.

The philanthropist undertook the hiring of the museum's senior staff. He was of German descent and was ashamed of Germany's actions during World War II. To assuage his own conscience, he refused to hire anyone whom he believed to be of German descent. A restoration expert applied for a job as chief curator of the museum, but the philanthropist refused to hire him because of his German background. The restoration expert discovered the philanthropist's rationale and brings suit against the museum, claiming that the hiring practice violates his constitutional rights.

The court will most likely find that the philanthropist's hiring policy is:

(A) Constitutional, because the museum is a private entity and so may constitutionally hire and fire as it desires.

(B) Constitutional, to the extent necessary to remedy past discrimination.

(C) Unconstitutional under the Equal Protection Clause, because the grant of the land is sufficient state involvement to render the museum's actions state action.

(D) Unconstitutional under the Equal Protection Clause, because the state will benefit from the museum and this creates a sufficient nexus to find state action.

Question 163

The National Park Service recently created a new personnel level for field employees, which became the highest salaried position available to Park Service field employees. The position is restricted to employees over six feet in height. A female ranger who is five feet, three inches tall seeks your advice as to whether she can challenge the validity of the height restriction in federal court.

If you decide to file suit on her behalf, which of the following would be your strongest argument against the validity of the restriction?

(A) Because most women are less than six feet tall, the restriction is unconstitutional as a violation of the Equal Rights Amendment.

(B) Because most women are less than six feet tall, the restriction is an invalid discrimination on the basis of gender in violation of the Due Process Clause of the Fifth Amendment.

(C) Because most women are less than six feet tall, the restriction is an invalid gender-based discrimination in violation of the Equal Protection Clause of the Fourteenth Amendment.

(D) The restriction denies the ranger a property right without an opportunity for a hearing before a neutral decisionmaker, in violation of the Due Process Clause of the Fifth Amendment.

Question 197

An industrial city in the Midwest had approximately 300,000 inhabitants, and about half of them were members of a recognized racial minority. The latest census figures indicated that 33,501 minority residents of the city could be classified as "poor" under federal poverty guidelines. In contrast, only 7,328 of the approximately 150,000 nonminority residents of the city could be classified as "poor." To combat a budget deficit, the city's 10-member city council, including no minority members and no poor members, decided to raise bus fares during rush hour periods from 80¢ to $1. Because poor people and members of minority groups placed greater reliance on the city's bus lines than did the bulk of the nonpoor

and nonminority population (many of whom drove to work), the effect of the transit fare increase was hardest on the poor and minority communities. Several activist groups representing the poor, various minority organizations, and some community action coalitions vowed to fight the fare increase in federal court.

Which of the following statements most accurately describes the constitutional status of the fare increase?

(A) The fare increase is unconstitutional because the city council is composed solely of nonpoor and nonminority members who cannot adequately represent the interests of poor persons, who need low bus fares to survive.

(B) The fare increase is unconstitutional, because the city cannot show that the resulting disparate impact of the fare increase is necessary for a compelling state interest.

(C) The fare increase is constitutional, because there is no evidence that the city council acted irrationally or was motivated by an intent to discriminate on the basis of race.

(D) The fare increase is constitutional, because a political question is involved and fares and fees may be increased if the city council deems such increases appropriate to cure deficits.

Question 8

To encourage minority business and foster pride in minority heritage, a state adopted legislation exempting magazines and other periodicals from the state's receipts tax if 20% of the magazine is devoted to articles concerning minorities (a commission was set up to sample magazines to determine on a yearly basis whether they should be exempt). A publisher produced a sports magazine in the state that occasionally contained articles about minority athletes, but the commission determined that the publisher's magazine was not eligible for the receipts tax exemption. After paying the tax assessed on her magazine, the publisher sued for a refund.

The court will most likely rule:

(A) Against the publisher, because taxpayers do not have standing to challenge tax exemptions.

(B) Against the publisher, because the state has a compelling interest in encouraging minority business.

(C) In favor of the publisher, because the tax violates the Equal Protection Clause.

(D) In favor of the publisher, because the tax violates the First Amendment freedoms of speech and press.

Question 146

Based on recommendations of a state commission studying the effect of pornographic films on violent criminal activity, a state adopted legislation banning films intended for commercial distribution that appealed as a whole to the prurient interest in sex of the average person in the community, portrayed sex in a patently offensive way to citizens of the state, and which a reasonable person in the United States would find had no serious literary, artistic, political, or scientific value.

In ruling on a constitutional challenge to the legislation from a film distributor in the state who was convicted of distributing films in violation of the legislation, the federal court will likely find the legislation:

(A) Constitutional, because it uses a national "reason-able person" standard for determining the social value of the work.

(B) Constitutional, because it uses a statewide standard rather than a community standard for determining whether the material is patently offensive.

(C) Unconstitutional, because it uses a statewide standard rather than a national standard for deter-mining whether the material is patently offensive.

(D) Unconstitutional, unless the court finds that the legislation is necessary to advance the state's compelling interest in reducing violent criminal activity.

Question 194

The legislature of a state was concerned that the numerous and strident television, radio, and newspaper advertisements by auto dealerships annoy and mislead the public. Therefore, it enacted comprehensive legislation regulating the timing and content of such ads, limiting their duration, frequency, and the types of claims and information made and given.

Which of the following statements is most accurate as to the constitutionality of the state's ad regulation?

(A) It is unconstitutional, because it infringes on the First and Fourteenth Amendment rights of auto dealers to free speech.

(B) It is constitutional if it does not prohibit the dissemination of truthful information about price and the availability of products, and is narrowly tailored to serve a substantial government interest.

(C) It is constitutional, because it is within the police power of the state and no federal constitutional rights are infringed.

(D) It is unconstitutional, because it infringes on the rights of the auto dealers to enter into contracts for advertising.

Question 198

On completion of a major expansion project, a city's public library board adopted a usage policy for the new meeting room that was added to the facility. To alleviate the scheduling burden on the staff if the meeting room were open to all groups, the policy provided that the meeting room was to be used only for "library purposes" by the library staff, the library board, or groups affiliated with the library, such as the library's teen advisory group or volunteer "Friends of the Library" group. A local organization that promoted the political interests of an ethnic minority in and around the city requested use of the meeting room for an informational meeting that would be open to the public. Although no other event was scheduled for the meeting room at the time requested, the library director declined the organization's request, citing the meeting room policy adopted by the library board. The organization filed suit in federal district court, challenging the library's policy and seeking access to the meeting room. How is the court likely to rule?

(A) The library's policy is valid, because limiting the meeting room's use to library purposes is reason-ably related to a legitimate government purpose.

(B) The library's policy is valid, because limiting the meeting room's use to library purposes is narrowly tailored to serve a significant government interest.

(C) The library's policy is not valid, because limiting the meeting room's use to library purposes is restricting speech based on its content.

(D) The library's policy is not valid unless there are alternative facilities in the area available for groups to hold meetings.

Question 77

To combat fraud and misuse of driver's licenses, a state's department of motor vehicles enacted new regulations for the issuance of driver's licenses. One of the regulations, which were authorized by state law, required for the first time that driver's licenses display a photograph of the person whose name is on the license. The regulations did not provide for any exemptions from this requirement. Living entirely within the state was a religious sect whose followers devoutly believed that allowing oneself to be photographed was sinful. How-ever, because much of the state was rural and sparsely populated, members of the sect needed to travel by automobile to obtain necessary services and to gather for worship. A member of the sect who was refused a

driver's license because he would not allow himself to be photographed challenged the state regulation in federal court.

Is the court likely to uphold the application of the regulation to the religious group?

(A) Yes, because exempting the church's members from the regulation would not have a secular purpose and would constitute improper state advancement of, and entanglement with, religion.

(B) Yes, because enactment of the regulation was not motivated by a desire to interfere with religion.

(C) No, unless the state shows that the regulation is necessary to promote a compelling governmental interest.

(D) No, because the opposition to the regulation arises from a sincerely held religious belief.

Question 70

A state legislature enacted a program by which students in the public schools could request instruction as to specific religions and religious beliefs, and thus participate in public school programs in which leaders of the religions involved gave religious instruction and performed religious practices on school grounds. The program provided instruction on any religion requested by a student.

Which of the following would *not* be relevant in assessing the constitutionality of the state religious instruction program?

(A) The substantial effect of the legislation is to promote the religions studied.

(B) The primary purpose of the statute is to foster belief in the religions studied.

(C) The state does not have a compelling interest in instructing public school students about specific religions.

(D) The legislation requires that religious leaders and school officials interact constantly and frequently.

CONTRACTS

Question 14

A jogger found a stray dog in the park. She took the dog home with her and placed an ad in the paper to try to find the dog's owner. Soon thereafter, the owner of the dog contacted the jogger. He came to the jogger's home and identified the dog as his. He offered to pay the jogger a $200 reward at the end of the week. The jogger thanked the dog owner but turned down the reward.

At the end of the week, however, the jogger changed her mind, so she called the dog owner and told him that she would like the reward after all. He refused to pay her, and she sues him for breach of contract.

What will the jogger recover?

(A) Nothing, because she rejected the dog owner's offer.

(B) Nothing, because there was no consideration to support a contract.

(C) $200, because the technical defense of the Statute of Frauds will be overcome by the dog owner's moral obligation to pay.

(D) $200, because the dog owner could not have revoked his offer until the end of the week, and he failed to do so before the jogger accepted.

Question 47

The food and beverage manager of an exclusive country club received a letter in the mail dated December 3 and signed by the sales director of a distiller, offering to meet the club's requirements for vodka for the next calendar year. The offer provided for delivery on the 15th of each month at $120 per case. The manager promptly wrote back, accepting the offer per the terms provided in the letter. At the same time, the manager placed a modest order for the distiller's vodka, which was duly delivered at the stated price on January 15. The manager placed orders of similar size throughout the rest of the year, and they were delivered at the stated price.

The agreement between the distiller and the club is best described as:

(A) A single bilateral contract.

(B) A series of unilateral contracts.

(C) A series of option contracts.

(D) Not an enforceable contract.

Question 142

On March 1, the purchasing agent for a suburban school district faxed a "quotation request form" to a supplier of school furniture requesting an offer for the sale of 20 student chairs. The form was on school district letterhead and signed by the purchasing agent. It specified that the offer must be held open for four months and that the price term must be no higher than $30 per chair. The supplier telephoned the purchasing agent and told him that he would sell the school district 20 chairs at $20 per chair. He also agreed to hold the offer open for four months. The purchasing agent thanked the supplier for the offer and indicated that he would get back to him within that time period. On May 1, before the purchasing agent had responded to the supplier's offer or taken any action in reliance on it, the supplier faxed a letter to the purchasing agent stating that demand for student chairs had been higher than expected and that the offer was terminated. On May 2, the purchasing agent called the supplier, told him that the school district was treating his offer as still being open, and accepted it on its terms.

Did the purchasing agent's call on May 2 create a legally enforceable contract with the supplier?

(A) Yes, because the contract is for the sale of goods valued at less than $500.

(B) Yes, because the school district accepted the offer within three months.

(C) No, because the supplier did not sign the form specifying the length of time that the offer would be held open.

(D) No, because a firm offer under the U.C.C. is not effective if its term is more than three months.

Question 28

The owner of a restored 1957 Chevrolet told his neighbor that he was interested in selling his car but did not know what price to ask. The neighbor said that he would pay $12,000 for the car "if he could get the financing." The car owner hesitated, and the neighbor suggested that the car owner give him 10 days to obtain financing. The car owner agreed and promised, in writing, that he would sell the car to the neighbor if he came up with $12,000 within 10 days.

Which of the following best describes the agreement between the car owner and the neighbor?

(A) A promissory estoppel situation.

(B) A quasi-contract.

(C)   An offer for a unilateral contract.

(D)   An option contract.

Question 29

A quilter who had restored a rare Civil War-era quilt spoke with an old friend whose business was selling new and vintage quilts. When the friend learned of the quilter's latest restoration, she told her that for 15% of the gross, she could find her a buyer who would pay at least $5,000 for it. The quilter said nothing in reply. The next morning, the friend telephoned the quilter and told her that she had a prospective buyer who was willing to pay $5,200 for the quilt, sight unseen. The quilter asked for the buyer's phone number, which the friend gave to her, and then called the buyer and arranged a sale. The quilter refused to pay her friend the 15% commission, disclosing to her that another party had expressed interest in the quilt and she instead could have sold it to that party for at least $5,200. The friend sues the quilter for breach of contract, seeking her 15% sales commission.

What will be the probable outcome?

(A)   The quilter will win, because 15% is unconscionably large as a finder's fee in such a transaction.

(B)   The quilter will win, because there was no consideration for any promise to pay that might have been implied from her conduct.

(C)   The quilter will win because she could have sold the quilt to another party who would pay at least $5,200 for it.

(D)   The friend will win, because she obtained a buyer for the quilt and a purchase price over $5,000 was paid.

Question 41

A homeowner offered to pay a roofer $500 to replace the bad shingles on his roof, provided the roofer could finish the job by October 1. The roofer told the homeowner he would get back to him after he had checked out prices at a local supply store. The next day, the roofer phoned the homeowner, who was not at home, and left a message on his answering machine that he could not do the work for less than $650. The roofer did not hear from the homeowner for several days. Because October 1 was still two weeks away, the roofer phoned the homeowner again and left another message on his answering machine stating that he would do the job for $500 and that he would do the work the next weekend unless that would be inconvenient for the homeowner. The homeowner replayed the second message just as he was leaving town on a business trip and did not contact the roofer. That weekend, unbeknownst to the homeowner, the roofer went to the homeowner's house and repaired the roof. When the homeowner returned home, the roofer presented him with a bill for $500, which represented the actual value of the work done. The homeowner refused to pay the bill.

If the roofer sues solely for breach of contract, who will likely prevail?

(A)   The roofer, because he accepted the homeowner's offer before the latter materially changed his position in reliance on the first telephone message.

(B)   The roofer, because the work he did was actually worth $500.

(C)   The homeowner, because he was unaware that the roofer was doing the roof repair while he was out of town.

(D)   The homeowner, because he did not accept the roofer's offer to do the roof repair for $500.

Question 102

On July 26, a manufacturer of computer accessories received a purchase order form from a retailer who ordered 2,000 ergonomic mouse pads for delivery no later than September 1 for a total price of $10,000, as quoted in the manufacturer's current catalog. Two days later, the manufacturer faxed its own purchase order acceptance form to the retailer, who was a first-time customer. This form stated that it was an acceptance of the specified order, was signed by the manufacturer's shipping manager, and contained all of the terms of the retailer's form, but it also contained an additional printed clause stating that all disagreements under this sale are subject to arbitration by the American Arbitration Association.

Assuming no further communication between the parties, which of the following is an accurate statement of the legal relationship between the manufacturer and the retailer?

(A)   There is an enforceable contract between the parties whose terms do not include the arbitration clause in the manufacturer's form.

(B)   There is an enforceable contract between the parties whose terms include the arbitration clause in the manufacturer's form.

(C)   There is no enforceable contract between the parties because the manufacturer's form constituted a rejection of the retailer's offer and a counteroffer by the manufacturer.

(D)   There is no enforceable contract between the parties because the manufacturer's form added an additional term that materially altered the terms of the retailer's offer.

Question 148

The owner of an apparel store faxed an order to her regular supplier for 100 pairs of wool gloves at $10 a pair, the supplier's list price. The supplier checked his inventory and discovered that he had only 90 pairs of wool gloves, which he shipped to the store owner along with 10 pairs of wool blend gloves that also had a list price of $10 a pair. The supplier also enclosed a note to the store owner explaining that he did not have enough stock of wool gloves to fill her order, and that, in the hopes she could use them, he was sending wool blend gloves at the same list price to make up the balance of the shipment.

On receipt of the shipment and note, what are the store owner's options?

(A) The store owner may accept the shipment, in which case she must pay the supplier $1,000 less any damages sustained because of the nonconforming shipment, or she may reject the shipment, in which case she has no further remedy against the supplier.

(B) The store owner may accept the shipment, in which case she must pay the supplier $1,000, or she may reject the shipment, in which case she may recover against the supplier for breach of contract.

(C) The store owner may accept the shipment, in which case she must pay the supplier $1,000, or she may reject the shipment, in which case she has no further remedy against the supplier.

(D) The store owner may accept the conforming part of the shipment and reject the nonconforming part, in which case she must pay the supplier $900 less any damages sustained because of the nonconforming part of the shipment, or she may reject the entire shipment, in which case she may recover against the supplier for breach of contract.

Question 15

Two brothers who were certified public accountants were in business together practicing their chosen profession. The older brother was concerned about his younger brother's apparent inability to show up at his job by 9 a.m. each morning, sober and clear-eyed. One day, after the younger brother showed up late for work yet again, the older brother told him that if he would show up at the office sober and ready to work by 9 a.m. each morning for the next 10 months, he would pay him $15,000 at the end of that time. The younger brother accepted the offer, and complied with its terms from that day forward. Nine months later, the older brother died unexpectedly. One month after that, the younger brother filed a claim with his brother's estate for the $15,000.

Will the younger brother prevail in his claim?

(A) No, because he will be unable to prove the terms of the oral contract between him and his brother, because his brother is dead.

(B) No, because his brother's offer to pay was terminated on his death.

(C) Yes, because he has performed under a valid contract, and thus his brother's estate must now perform.

(D) Yes, because he changed his position for the worse in reliance on his brother's promise, and thus his brother's executor is estopped from denying that the contract existed.

Question 48

A father wanted his adult daughter to stop smoking, and one day he told her that if she gave up smoking for the next 12 months, at the end of that time he would give her $10,000. She agreed to stop smoking, but later that day had doubts about whether her father would actually pay up if she complied. She contacted her stepmother, who told her to go ahead and quit smoking, and she would make good on the father's promise to pay her if he refused to do so. That very day, the daughter quit smoking and never smoked again. Eleven months after his conversation with his daughter, the father died.

One month later, the daughter sought payment of the $10,000 from her father's estate, which refused to pay. The daughter then asked her stepmother for the $10,000 but the stepmother also refused to pay. The daughter filed a claim against her stepmother for $10,000. She proves at trial that she has submitted a claim for $10,000 to the executor of her father's estate and has been refused payment.

What is the best argument for the court's rejecting this claim against her stepmother?

(A) The contract between the daughter and her stepmother was illusory.

(B) The daughter has not been damaged by any breach because the only effect—that she quit smoking—was salutary.

(C) The contract between the daughter and her stepmother was oral.

(D) No consideration flowed to the stepmother under the contract.

Question 24

A nephew asked his uncle, who like him was a farmer, to guarantee a loan to buy a new tractor. The local bank

had already refused to extend credit to the nephew alone to buy the tractor. The uncle was inclined to refuse, but then decided that he could benefit from his own use of the tractor, so he told his nephew that he would guarantee the loan if he could use the new tractor without cost for 10 days during his harvest season. The nephew agreed to his uncle's proposal. The uncle went to the bank and told the loan officer that he was willing to guarantee the proposed loan to his nephew. This prompted the loan officer to agree to extend the requested credit to the nephew. Although the loan officer did not make the uncle sign any papers, the uncle provided consideration and the bank issued the nephew a loan commitment statement. That evening, the uncle had a change of heart. The next day, he telephoned the loan officer and told him to forget about his guaranteeing any loan to his nephew. Despite the uncle's phone call, the loan officer did not stop the check from being issued, and the nephew received the money to purchase the tractor. He drove the tractor over to the uncle's farm and delivered it for the uncle's 10-day use, as promised. The uncle told his nephew that he did not want to use the tractor and that he was not guaranteeing his loan. Within six months, it became clear that the nephew could not make good on the loan.

If the bank sues the uncle for the unpaid portion of the loan:

(A) The bank will win, because the suretyship agreement was supported by consideration between the bank and the uncle.

(B) The bank will win, because the uncle's main purpose in making the agreement with the bank was to benefit himself, not his nephew.

(C) The uncle will win, because the suretyship agreement was not in writing.

(D) The uncle will win, because he withdrew his promise before the nephew received the money or the tractor.

Question 125

A homeowner wanted to have his driveway resurfaced. He called seven resurfacing companies and received one bid for $4,400 and six other bids ranging from $5,200 to $6,000. The homeowner entered into a contract with the low bidder to have the driveway resurfaced. Shortly before the low bidder was scheduled to begin work, he called the homeowner and told him that his secretary made a mistake in adding figures and he could not possibly do the work for less than $5,400.

Can the homeowner enforce the contract for $4,400?

(A) No, if the court finds that the homeowner had reason to know of the mistake.

(B) No, because the homeowner has not relied on the bid to her detriment.

(C) No, because the $1,000 error has a material effect on the agreed-on exchange.

(D) Yes, because the low bidder assumed the risk of bid computation errors.

Question 136

A homeowner wanted to have his house repainted. He called a number of house painters and received bids ranging from $8,500 to $9,000. A local painter submitted a bid to do the work for $8,000, and the homeowner entered into a contract with him to have the house repainted. Shortly before the painter was scheduled to begin work, he discovered that he could not make a profit if he were paid less than $8,600. He called the homeowner with this information. The homeowner agreed to pay him the extra $600. After the painter finished the job, the homeowner handed him $8,000 in cash, saying that that was all he was going to pay him because he had no right to raise the price.

If the painter sues the homeowner for the additional $600, who will prevail?

(A) The homeowner, because the promise to pay the additional money was not in writing.

(B) The homeowner, because the painter was already under a preexisting duty to paint the house for $8,000.

(C) The painter, because he relied to his detriment on the homeowner's promise to pay the additional money.

(D) The painter, because the promise to pay the additional money was the settlement of a good faith dispute.

Question 171

An interior decorator entered into a detailed contract with a rug dealer to purchase an Oriental rug for a law firm's reception area. On the date specified in the contract, the rug dealer brought the rug to the law firm, where the decorator was waiting. On inspecting the rug, the decorator was shocked to discover that it was made in a factory just outside of town, albeit by weavers knowledgeable in the art of Oriental rugmaking. He rejected the rug because it was not an "authentic" Oriental rug.

The rug dealer filed a claim in equity court compelling the decorator to accept the rug. The decorator claims that both parties to the contract understood that the term "Oriental rug" meant only a rug meeting certain criteria established in the rug trade, including, most importantly,

that the rug be made in an Asian country by native artisans.

Will the court permit the decorator to introduce evidence of trade usage supporting that understanding of the term "Oriental rug"?

(A) Yes, because there was a latent ambiguity in the expression of the parties' agreement.

(B) Yes, because trade usage is admissible to explain or supplement the terms of a contract.

(C) No, because the writing was a complete integration.

(D) No, because there is no evidence that the writing was intended as anything other than a final expression.

Question 172

A large farming concern in the Midwest contracted with a pet food manufacturer to deliver 100 tons of processed cornmeal no later than November 15. The purchase price and delivery terms were specified in the contract, which permitted partial shipments. On November 1, the farming concern delivered 50 tons of cornmeal to the pet food manufacturer with the notification that the balance would be shipped by November 15. The pet food manufacturer rejected the shipment because the written documentation accompanying the shipment did not establish that the cornmeal came from an approved source, as required by the contract. The farming concern responded to this rejection by conceding that the shipment did not conform to the contract and promising to deliver all 100 tons of cornmeal by November 15 with proper documentation.

Which of the following best expresses the pet food manufacturer's options?

(A) The pet food manufacturer may notify the farming concern that the entire contract is terminated and that it is going to obtain the 100 tons of cornmeal from another source.

(B) The pet food manufacturer may notify the farming concern that the contract is terminated as to the 50 tons of cornmeal that was shipped and did not conform to the contract, but must accept the additional 50 tons when it is shipped if it conforms to the contract.

(C) The pet food manufacturer must allow the farming concern a commercially reasonable time to ship cornmeal that conforms to the contract before it can terminate the contract.

(D) The pet food manufacturer must allow the farming concern until November 15 to ship cornmeal that

conforms to the contract before it can terminate the contract.

Question 87

On August 5, the owner of a hot dog plant and the proprietor of a local ballpark concession stand entered into a written agreement providing, among other things, that if the local team wins the state championship, the plant owner will deliver to the proprietor 500 hot dogs on each of the following days: September 5, 7, and 9. The price was set at 25¢ per hot dog, with payment to be made on September 10 by the proprietor to a creditor of the plant owner. On August 15, the plant owner decided that he wanted to avoid his obligation to deliver the hot dogs. The creditor has not become aware of the agreement between the plant owner and the proprietor.

Which of the following is the most accurate statement?

(A) The plant owner cannot rescind the contract without the permission of both the proprietor and the creditor.

(B) The plant owner cannot rescind the contract without the permission of the proprietor.

(C) The plant owner can repudiate the agreement because the promise to perform by the proprietor is illusory.

(D) The plant owner can revoke the offer to sell hot dogs if the team does not win the state championship.

Question 35

On April 25, a smoothie stand operator and a fruit processor entered into a written contract providing that the processor would deliver to the operator each month 20 barrels each of bananas, strawberries, blueberries, and raspberries at a price of $25 per barrel, with the first barrels to be delivered on May 1, and the same number of barrels to be delivered on the first of each month thereafter for the next 11 months, with payment made on the 15th of each month to a creditor of the fruit processor. The parties had actually agreed that the contract price per barrel of fruit would be $15, but the manager of the fruit processor had inadvertently written $25 in the contract, and neither party noticed before signing. The creditor first learned of the agreement between the parties on April 27. The next day, the operator and the processor agreed that the contract price for the barrels of fruit would be $20 per barrel instead of $25 per barrel. The first delivery was made one day late, on May 2. On May 15, the operator refused to pay any money to the creditor, and the creditor filed suit against the smoothie stand for the first month's payment of $2,000.

Which of the following would *not* provide a partial defense for the smoothie stand operator in the litigation?

(A) The parties had agreed on April 28 that the contract price per barrel of fruit would be $20 instead of $25.

(B) The parties had originally agreed that the contract price per barrel of fruit would be $15, but the manager of the fruit processor had inadvertently written $25 in the contract, and neither party noticed before signing.

(C) The fruit processor owed its creditor only $1,800.

(D) The fruit processor was late with its first delivery.

Question 3

A large insurance company instituted a supplemental benefit plan for its own employees. Under the plan, any employee who had worked for the company for at least 25 years would be permitted to designate a charity to receive, on the employee's retirement, a donation in the employee's name of six months' worth of the employee's salary. The plan gave participating employees an unqualified right to change the beneficiary at any time before payment was made. An employee nearing retirement enrolled in the plan and named his favorite church as the beneficiary of the donation. The church received a letter from the company informing it that the employee had named it beneficiary of his plan and indicating the approximate amount that it would receive on the employee's retirement in 10 months. The letter did not inform the church of the employee's right to change beneficiaries before that time. Church elders, anticipating the gift, authorized restoration work to the church building, making plans to pay for the work with the funds from the employee's benefit program.

Six months later, the employee converted to a different religion and changed the beneficiary of his plan to his new church. When the employee retired, the company paid the benefit to his new church. His old church, which had paid for the restoration work on its completion, demanded payment of the benefit from the company. When payment was refused, the church sued the company to force payment.

The court should rule in favor of:

(A) The church, if the interests of justice require it.

(B) The church, because the employee did not have the power to change the beneficiary of his plan after the church's rights as third-party beneficiary had vested.

(C) The company, because the agreement between the employee and the company allowed the employee to change the beneficiary of the benefit plan.

(D) The company, because it had a duty to pay the employee's new church as the named beneficiary of his plan.

Question 34

A large Midwestern wheat producer and a large food distributor located on the Pacific coast entered into a contract calling for the wheat producer to sell and the food distributor to buy 10,000 bushels of winter wheat for $5 per bushel. The contract stated that the wheat producer would deliver the wheat "F.O.B. St. Louis Railroad depot." The wheat producer hired a trucking company to transport the wheat from its silos to the St. Louis Railroad depot, where the wheat would be loaded onto railroad hopper cars bound west. En route to St. Louis, the trucks carrying the wheat were stopped and the wheat was carried off by highway robbers. The wheat producer brings suit against the food distributor, which refused to pay for the wheat.

What will the wheat producer likely recover in damages?

(A) Nothing.

(B) The amount necessary to replace the stolen wheat.

(C) The full contract price.

(D) The profits it would have realized under the contract.

Question 88

A large-scale bakery in the South entered into a written contract with a commercial apple orchard in the upper Midwest to purchase 200 bushels of apples at a cost of $8 per bushel. The contract provided that the apple orchard would deliver the apples "F.O.B. Louisville Railroad Depot," where the apples would be loaded onto a train headed south. The orchard assigned all of its rights under the contract to a large produce distributor which, in turn, hired a trucking company to deliver the apples to Louisville. En route to Louisville, the truck skidded off the road due to inclement weather and overturned, and the apples were destroyed. The bakery brought suit against the apple orchard for breach of contract.

What will be the probable outcome of the litigation?

(A) The bakery will lose.

(B) The bakery will recover the amount necessary to replace the destroyed apples, over the contract price.

(C) The bakery will recover the full contract price.

(D) The bakery will be able to compel specific performance of the contract.

Question 124

A daughter owed her father $1,250. The father's best friend was having financial difficulties and the father wanted to help him, so the father told his daughter to pay the $1,250 to his friend when the debt came due in three days. Immediately after directing his daughter to pay his friend, the father called his friend and told him he should expect to get $1,250 from his daughter in three days. When the debt came due, the daughter tendered the $1,250 to her father instead of to his friend, and the father accepted the money. The friend sues the daughter for $1,250.

Which of the following is the most likely result?

(A) The friend will recover, because the father effectively assigned his right to collect the $1,250 to his friend.

(B) The friend will not recover, because the father's acceptance of $1,250 from his daughter revoked his gift to his friend.

(C) The friend will not recover, because the daughter was never indebted to him and cannot be forced to pay him.

(D) The friend will not recover, because the daughter's tender of $1,250 to her father, and her father's acceptance of the money, constituted a novation.

Question 108

A debtor owed a creditor $5,000, but the debt was barred by the applicable statute of limitations. The debtor agreed to assign to the creditor a $4,000 debt that was owed to him by a third party and was coming due in a week. The debtor called the third party to inform him of the assignment. When the debt became due, the third party refused to pay the creditor. The creditor brings an action to collect the debt against the third party.

Will the creditor likely prevail?

(A) Yes, because the creditor's agreement to accept a lesser amount than the original debt constituted consideration for the assignment.

(B) Yes, because an assignment need not be in writing to be enforceable.

(C) No, because the third party may raise the debtor's statute of limitations defense on the original debt.

(D) No, because a new promise to pay a legal obligation barred by law must be in writing.

Question 61

A debtor owed a creditor $1,200 on a promissory note that was due on August 1. After the debtor told the creditor that he might not be able to pay the note on its due date, the creditor agreed to extinguish the debt if the debtor, who was the manager of a discount electronics store, bought a new entertainment system that sold for $1,200 and had it delivered to the creditor's home by August 15. Because the debtor would have to pay only $600 for the system due to his manager's discount, he agreed and the parties signed a written contract on July 26.

Is the new agreement between the debtor and the creditor legally enforceable?

(A) No, because the debtor incurred no additional detriment that would serve as consideration for the new agreement.

(B) Yes, because it would have cost the creditor $1,200 to purchase the entertainment system himself.

(C) Yes, because the debtor incurred a different obligation than he originally had.

(D) Yes, because the new agreement between the debtor and the creditor is enforceable with or without consideration as long as it was made in good faith.

Question 62

A buyer of a new car owed the car dealership where she purchased the vehicle $1,000 on a promissory note that was due on December 30. The buyer determined that she would be unable to pay the note on its due date, and she informed the owner of the dealership of that fact. The owner told her that she would not have to pay the debt if she bought him four tickets to a popular concert on January 15 that had been sold out for weeks, because she worked as publicist for the concert venue. She agreed to do so, and the parties memorialized their agreement in a signed writing on December 18. On January 2, the dealership filed suit against the car buyer for failure to pay the $1,000 promissory note, before the car buyer had secured the concert tickets for the owner.

May the car buyer have this action enjoined by introducing evidence of the December 18 agreement?

(A) Yes, because the December 18 agreement between the parties suspended the car buyer's obligation on the promissory note.

(B) Yes, because the December 18 agreement between the parties discharged the car buyer's obligation on the promissory note.

(C) No, because the car buyer has not yet bought the concert tickets in reliance on the owner's promise to extinguish the debt.

(D) No, because the car buyer's only remedy is to sue for damages for breach of the December 18 agreement.

Question 105

On January 1, a singer entered into a written contract with the owner of a nightclub to sing nightly at the nightclub for a period of two years at $54,000 per year, commencing February 1. On January 25, the singer phoned the nightclub owner and told him that he had not finished relocating from out of state and might not be ready to start singing until February 10. Furious, the nightclub owner located a substitute act for the month of February.

Can the nightclub owner bring an immediate suit against the singer?

(A) Yes, because the singer's telephone call was a repudiation.

(B) Yes, because he changed his position in reliance on the singer's telephone call.

(C) No, because the singer's telephone call did not constitute a repudiation.

(D) No, because a repudiation must be in writing to be given effect.

Question 122

On November 1, a trapeze artist entered into a written contract with a circus manager to perform his act for the traveling circus for the upcoming season, commencing December 1. On November 30, the trapeze artist faxed the circus manager, stating that, due to circumstances beyond his control, he would not be able to start performing under their contract until December 10. The circus manager got the message the same day and was unfazed, because he had another performer who could take his place in the interim. However, when a tightrope walker approached the circus manager a couple of days later about a job, offering to work for significantly less money, the manager hired the newcomer to take the trapeze artist's place.

Can the circus manager cancel the contract with the trapeze artist?

(A) Yes, because the trapeze artist failed to begin performing on December 1, when performance was due.

(B) Yes, because having to go through with the contract when there was another trapeze artist willing to

work for significantly less money would create a hardship for the circus.

(C) No, because the breach was minor.

(D) No, because the trapeze artist notified the circus manager of his delay in performance in a timely fashion.

Question 107

On April 1, an acclaimed tennis instructor entered into a written contract with a country club owner, calling for the instructor to conduct lessons and clinics at the club six days per week for a period of one year, beginning May 1. The instructor would be paid $48,000 for the year's work. After the instructor failed to appear at the club on May 1, the club owner read in the newspaper that the instructor had been hit by a car and was expected to be in the hospital for two months. The club owner hired a retired tennis pro to conduct lessons at his club for two months at a salary of $6,000 per month.

Can the club owner recover from the instructor the additional $2,000 per month salary that he must pay the tennis pro?

(A) Yes, because the instructor failed to give the club owner timely notice of his hospitalization.

(B) Yes, because of the general rule that the non-breaching party may recover the expenses of mitigation from the breaching party.

(C) No, because the replacement instructor's salary was not reasonable.

(D) No, because in a personal services contract, performance is excused by illness of the party performing the personal service.

Question 195

A chef wanted to open his own restaurant and a contractor offered to build the place for $160,000. Their written contract provided that the chef would pay the contractor $60,000 in cash on commencement of construction, scheduled for April 15 after the spring thaw. On completion of the restaurant on September 30, the contractor would be paid the remaining $100,000. The region had a late spring, and on April 30 the contractor had not yet commenced construction of the restaurant.

The contractor has:

(A) Not breached the contract, and the chef need not make the initial $60,000 payment.

(B) Not breached the contract, but the chef must make the initial $60,000 payment.

(C) Breached the contract in a nonmaterial particular; thus, the chef need not make the initial $60,000 payment.

(D) Breached the contract in a material particular; thus, the chef may treat the contract as at an end and sue for damages.

Question 196

A consortium of actors decided to open a new theater and almost immediately raised $130,000 of the $250,000 needed to build it. The contractor whom the consortium hired to build the theater agrees to be paid $50,000 in cash on commencement of construction, another $80,000 when construction was completed, and the remaining $120,000 in monthly payments of $1,000 principal plus 12% annual interest on the outstanding balance, once the theater started earning a profit. Their agreement was reduced to a writing that the parties signed.

The first installment was paid, construction was completed on time, and the second installment was paid. The theater opened, but business was not good, and the theater did not make any profit. The consortium found a buyer who paid them $260,000 for the theater. The contractor sues the consortium for the remaining $120,000 owing on the contract.

Will the contractor recover?

(A) No, because the consortium never earned a profit from its operation of the theater.

(B) No, because the failure to earn profits from the operation of the theater was an unforeseeable intervening event.

(C) Yes, because the provision governing payment of the outstanding balance of the construction cost merely established the time frame in which payment was to be made.

(D) Yes, because all of the conditions precedent to the consortium's duty to pay had occurred.

Question 191

A writer contracted with a literary agent to obtain a publisher for his book. The parties' written agreement provided that the agent would receive 20% of what the writer earned from the sales of his book. The agreement also provided that the publisher procured by the agent would pay the writer an advance against royalties of at least $10,000.

The agent found a willing publisher who entered into a written contract with the writer providing for the standard royalty amount minus the $10,000 that the publisher promised the writer as an advance. The writer insisted

that a clause be added to the contract providing for liquidated damages of $50,000 if the publisher breached the contract. Although the writer was unsure what his actual damages would be, he thought he could make $50,000 in royalties. The writer and the publisher signed the contract, and the publisher paid the writer $10,000 per their agreement.

A few weeks later, the publisher notified the writer that, due to unexpected financial constraints, it was no longer possible for him to publish the book. The publisher requested that the writer return the $10,000 but the writer refused, so the publisher filed suit. The agent intervened in the suit, demanding the $10,000 from the writer as her 20% share of the expected royalties.

Regarding the $10,000, what are the parties contractually entitled to?

(A) The writer is entitled to keep the $10,000 because the liquidated damages clause is reasonable.

(B) The publisher is entitled to get the $10,000 returned to him because his contractual duties were discharged by impossibility.

(C) The agent is entitled to get the $10,000 because she performed her part of the contract by finding a publisher.

(D) The writer is entitled to keep $8,000 and the agent is entitled to get $2,000, because the liquidated damages clause was reasonable and the agent is entitled to 20% of whatever the writer gets from the deal.

Question 147

On March 1, a builder entered into a contract with a buyer to build a home on land the builder owned and then transfer it to the buyer for $350,000. The builder and the buyer agreed that construction would be completed on August 1, and that escrow would close on the transaction on August 15. The contract also contained a time-is-of-the-essence clause at the insistence of the buyer, whose lease on his current home was set to expire on September 1.

State law required that a home builder have an architect's certificate of completion before any residence could be conveyed to a purchaser. The builder employed his own architect to design and oversee construction of his custom homes. Construction of the buyer's house was not completed until August 5. On August 8, the builder discovered that his architect had left the country without preparing the certificate of completion for the home. The builder was not able to obtain the certificate until August 20. When the builder attempted to place the deed and certificate of completion into escrow, he learned that the

buyer had canceled escrow on August 16 and refused to proceed with the purchase.

The builder sold the home nine months later for its then reasonable market value of $330,000. He brings an action for damages against the buyer, seeking $20,000, the difference between the contract price and the amount he ultimately received for sale of the house.

Will the builder recover?

(A)   No, because the duty to certify completion of the home cannot be delegated to an architect unfamiliar with the construction.

(B)   No, because he was late in delivering the deed and certificate of completion into escrow.

(C)   Yes, because the short time the builder was late in delivering the deed was not a material breach of the contract.

(D)   Yes, because the buyer suffered no damages as a result of the delay.

Question 167

A builder entered into a contract with a landowner to build a warehouse for $500,000 by August 1. The agreement provided for five progress payments of $100,000 each at various stages of completion. On June 20, after the builder had spent $350,000 on performance and received $300,000 in progress payments, the builder notified the landowner that he was quitting the project. The landowner hired another contractor to complete the warehouse by August 1 for $250,000, which was a reasonable price given the short deadline.

Which of the following statements regarding the parties' remedies is correct?

(A)   The builder can recover $50,000, the difference between the amount he expended on performance and the amount he was paid, to prevent the land-owner's unjust enrichment.

(B)   Neither party can recover anything, because the $50,000 extra that the landowner had to pay to complete the building is offset by the $50,000 difference between the builder's expenditures and the payments the landowner made to him.

(C)   The landowner can recover $50,000, the difference between the contract price and the total amount he paid for completing the building.

(D)   The landowner can recover $100,000, the difference between the contract price and the total amount spent constructing the building.

Question 16

A distributor of bottled spring water sent a letter to the manager of an upscale fitness center offering to meet the fitness center's requirements for bottled water for the next 12 months, at a price of $80 per case. The fitness center manager accepted the distributor's offer and they entered into a written contract formalizing the terms of their agreement. Two months later, the distributor wrote to the manager, informing him that because of increased costs, it would be necessary to increase the price of the bottled water to $120 per case. The manager balked at the price increase, reminding the distributor that they had a contract for $80 per case. The distributor replied, "No we don't, and in any case there's no way I can supply the bottled water to you now at $80 per case." The manager ordered bottled water from one of the distributor's competitors at a price of $95 per case, the best price he could get. The competitor's bottled water proved to be far less popular than the distributor's brand, and bottled water consumption at the fitness center declined, as did profits from their sale. The fitness center sued the distributor for damages.

If the fitness center is successful in its suit, the court should award it:

(A)   Nominal damages.

(B) $15 times the number of cases of the competitor's bottled water purchased from the time of the seller's breach through the end of the contract period.

(C)   The lost profits resulting from the reduced sales of the bottled water.

(D) $15 times the number of cases of the competitor's bottled water purchased from the time of the seller's breach through the end of the contract period plus the lost profits resulting from the reduced sales of the bottled water.

Question 22

A retailer of personal watercraft agreed to sell to a buyer a speedboat for $10,000. The written contract specified delivery within 30 days and a down payment of $2,000, but did not contain a liquidated damages clause. Two weeks after making the down payment, the buyer told the retailer that he could not afford to go through with the purchase, and asked for his down payment back. The retailer, which could get as many of that model of speedboat as it required from the manufacturer for a wholesale price of $7,000, put the boat back in its inventory. The retailer then sold it to someone else for $9,500. The buyer sues the retailer to get back his deposit; the retailer counterclaims for damages.

Excluding incidental costs, which of the following amounts represents the most likely recovery?

(A)   The buyer will recover $2,000.

(B)   The buyer will recover $1,500.

(C)   The retailer will recover $3,000.

(D)   The retailer will recover $1,000.

CRIMINAL LAW

Question 23

A fleeing bank robber ran into a school and took the principal hostage at gunpoint. The police, who had received a detailed description of the clothing the robber was wearing, surrounded the school and demanded that the robber come out with his hands up. When it began to get dark, the robber ordered the principal to undress, and the robber switched clothing with the principal. He tied the principal's hands to his side and pushed the principal out the door first. Seeing that the first person out of the door did not emerge with hands up and that the person was wearing clothing the robber was described as wearing, a police sharpshooter shot and killed the principal. The robber was captured and put on trial for the murder of the principal.

The jury should find the robber:

(A) Guilty, because the police were justified in using deadly force under the circumstances.

(B) Guilty, because changing clothes with the principal was an act taken with extreme indifference to an unjustifiably high risk to human life.

(C) Not guilty, because it was not foreseeable under the circumstances that the police would use deadly force.

(D) Not guilty, because the robber was not responsible for the police shooting the principal.

Question 126

The defendant bought a new bow and arrow set at a local sporting goods store and went to a public park to try it out. Based on prior experience, the defendant knew that practicing his marksmanship at the park was a violation of park regulations and constituted a misdemeanor. Right at the moment that the defendant fired his first arrow, a park ranger yelled at him from a distance to "stop shooting, stupid." Perturbed that he was caught so early, the defendant decided to fire an arrow a couple of feet above the ranger's head. Unfortunately, the defendant's aim was slightly off, and the arrow struck the ranger right between the eyes, killing him instantly.

The defendant is charged with homicide for the park ranger's death. At trial, the jury was given instructions on common law murder and manslaughter.

If the jury believes the defendant's testimony that he did not intend to hit the park ranger with the arrow, the most serious charge for which the jury may find him guilty is:

(A) Murder.

(B) Voluntary manslaughter.

(C) Involuntary manslaughter based on criminal negligence.

(D) Misdemeanor manslaughter.

Question 49

The accused was driving his beat-up old car along a narrow road when he was passed by the victim in her new car. The victim's daughter was lying down in the back seat and could not be seen. The accused sped up, drew even with the victim, and repeatedly rammed his car into the side of the victim's car. After several collisions, the victim was forced off the road, rolling down a cliff for several yards. Due to the rolling, both the victim and her daughter were severely injured. The accused was charged with attempted murder of both of them. At his trial, he testifies that he was angry because of the cavalier way the victim passed him in her new car, and that his only intent in smashing into her car was to scratch and dent it so that she would not be so haughty in the future. Assuming that the jury believes this testimony, the accused may be convicted as to:

(A) The victim.

(B) The victim's daughter.

(C) Both the victim and her daughter.

(D) Neither the victim nor her daughter.

Question 38

The defendant became very intoxicated one night. As he was staggering home, he came upon a construction site in which several large pieces of heavy equipment were parked. Having had heavy equipment training in the military, the defendant decided it would be fun to rearrange all the machines so that the operators would be very surprised when they returned to work the next day. He started up the largest piece of heavy equipment and drove it toward the edge of the site, but because he was so intoxicated, he lost control of it, and it rumbled out into the street, weaved along for about a quarter mile, and then crashed into a house, flattening it. In this jurisdiction, it is a misdemeanor to tamper with heavy equipment on a construction site. The defendant is prosecuted on the tampering charge, as well as for reckless damage of the house.

Should he be convicted of the reckless damage charge?

(A) Yes, because he was tampering with heavy equipment on a construction site, in violation of law, when he damaged the house.

(B) Yes, because he was intoxicated while driving a huge piece of earthmoving equipment.

(C) No, because at most he could be found guilty of criminal negligence.

(D) No, because he must have been aware that his conduct would cause damage to the house in order to be found guilty of reckless damage.

Question 39

A computer programmer sent a computer virus anonymously via e-mail to a business. The programmer believed that the virus would just disable the business's e-mail program for a short time without causing any additional damage, although he was aware that it very infrequently caused widespread damage to the infected computer. However, because of a hidden bug in the business's e-mail program, the virus infected the computer's entire hard drive, eventually rendering it unusable. Not only did the business lose important data, it also had to replace the computer, at a cost of over $1,000. The jurisdiction in which this occurred has a modern criminal code patterned after the Model Penal Code. One of its statutes makes it a criminal offense to "knowingly cause over $200 in damage to another's property." May the programmer be found guilty of violating the statute?

(A) No, because the programmer did not know that the virus would cause damage to the computer's hard drive.

(B) No, because the programmer did not intend to cause the damage to the computer's hard drive.

(C) Yes, because the programmer knew that he was sending a virus to the business's e-mail program.

(D) Yes, because the programmer was aware that in a very small percentage of cases the virus could cause widespread damage to a computer system.

Question 186

A gun collector ordered a rifle from a gun catalog. The rifle had a barrel 16 inches long and a pistol-type grip instead of the more usual rifle stock, so that the entire weapon was only 22 inches long. The collector was aware of a state penal statute that prohibited the possession of "any sawed-off shotgun or rifle." He was also aware that another statute defined sawed-off shotgun or rifle so as to include any such weapon whose barrel was less than 16 inches in length. He was unaware that the same statute also included in its definition of the prohibited weapons any shotgun or rifle whose overall length was less than 24 inches. When the rifle he had ordered arrived in the mail, he carefully measured it to confirm that its barrel was exactly 16 inches in length.

While driving to the target range one day, the collector was stopped for having a defective taillight, and the traffic officer saw the rifle he had ordered lying on the back seat of his car in plain view. The collector was arrested and subsequently prosecuted for possession of a sawed-off rifle.

What will be the probable outcome of the trial?

(A) He will be acquitted, because he honestly did not know that a weapon with an overall length of less than 24 inches was in violation of the statute.

(B) He will be acquitted, because he conducted a reasonable investigation to ensure that he was in compliance with the statute.

(C) He will be convicted, unless the trier of fact determines that his failure to realize that the overall length of the weapon was in violation of the statute was reasonable.

(D) He will be convicted, because his reasonable investigation does not vitiate violation of the statute arising from a mistake of law.

Question 67

A state statute prohibited, under criminal penalties, the sale or furnishing of any alcoholic beverage to a minor. A 16-year-old minor went to his neighborhood liquor store and asked a patron who was about to enter if the latter would purchase some beer for him. The patron agreed, took the minor's money, and returned with a six-pack of beer. At the moment that the beer changed hands, an official of the State Bureau of Alcohol Control leapt from behind a nearby car and announced that both the patron and the minor were under arrest. The patron ran to his car and escaped. The minor is now being prosecuted under the statute as having aided and abetted the patron in its violation.

Which of the following is his best argument in defense?

(A) He cannot be convicted as an aider and abettor unless the principal is first convicted.

(B) He cannot be convicted as an aider and abettor of violating a statute designed to protect the class of which he is a member—minors.

(C) He cannot be convicted of aiding and abetting any crime because he is a minor.

(D) He cannot be convicted alone of committing a crime that requires at least two parties to commit a violation.

Question 53

After a long period of marital problems, a wife told her husband that she was going to file for a divorce. Because the wife had recently inherited a large sum of money, the husband was determined not to let her go through with the divorce. He contacted an ex-convict and offered him $10,000 if he would kill his wife. The ex-convict agreed and they picked a time when the wife would be in the house by herself. When the ex-convict broke into the house, however, the wife called the police and fled out the back door. The ex-convict shot and wounded the wife as she was running away, but he was apprehended by the police before he could do any further harm.

After the ex-convict implicated the husband, both were charged with attempted murder and conspiracy to commit murder, and the husband was also charged with solicitation of murder. As part of a plea bargain, the ex-convict agreed to testify against the husband and plead guilty to aggravated battery in exchange for the attempted murder and conspiracy to commit murder charges being dropped.

Which of the following best states the crimes for which the husband can be convicted?

(A)   Solicitation, attempted murder, and conspiracy to commit murder.

(B)   Attempted murder and conspiracy to commit murder.

(C)   Solicitation and attempted murder.

(D)   Attempted murder only.

Question 63

A petty thief and a felon decided to meet at the mall, armed with a gun or knife, to look for elderly women wearing expensive jewelry, intending to follow them home and rob them. The thief began to have second thoughts when he considered that the felon had already done time for armed robbery and assault with a deadly weapon, and that he had vowed that he would never "do time" again because "somebody finked to the cops." The thief told the felon when they met at the mall that he had changed his mind and wanted no part of the action, and went home. That evening, the felon robbed and beat an elderly woman returning home from the mall. Because of her ill health and age, the woman had died as a result of the beating.

The thief is guilty of:

(A)   No crime.

(B)   Conspiracy.

(C)   Murder.

(D)   Murder and conspiracy.

Question 199

A thief looking for targets in a hotel lobby one evening spotted the victim wearing what appeared to be expensive jewelry as she checked into the hotel. After finding out the victim's room number, the thief broke into a supply room and put on a bellhop's uniform. She then grabbed some flowers from a vase in the hall and knocked on the door to the victim's room, announcing the delivery of a bouquet of flowers. After the victim let her in, the thief scanned the room for the jewelry while putting the flowers in a vase. When she did not see the jewelry, she pulled out a knife and forced the victim to reveal the whereabouts of the jewelry, which turned out to be the hotel's safe. The thief made the victim call the front desk and ask that someone bring the jewelry to the room. The thief then locked the victim in the bathroom, changed out of the bellhop's uniform, and accepted the jewelry when it was brought to the room. She was apprehended a few days later trying to sell the jewelry.

Under these facts, what are the most serious crimes the thief can be convicted of?

(A)   Burglary and larceny.

(B)   Burglary and robbery.

(C)   Larceny only.

(D)   Robbery only.

Question 19

The defendant, a player for a professional ice hockey team, had a reputation for being a dirty, vicious player. During a game, a player for the opposing team skated toward the defendant at a high rate of speed; his hockey stick was raised in a threatening manner. The player did not intend to actually harm the defendant, but wanted to show him how it felt to be threatened by a large man traveling at a high rate of speed with a hockey stick. As the player approached the defendant, the defendant smashed his stick into the other player's face, causing a serious injury.

If the defendant is charged with the crime of battery and found not guilty, it will be because:

(A)   He did not intend to injure the other player.

(B)   Professional hockey players consent to being hit by hockey sticks during a game.

(C)   He reasonably believed that he was under attack and his actions were reasonable.

(D)   The other player was the original aggressor.

Question 180

The manager of a bank branch announced to bank employees at a meeting that the corporate security staff would be staging a mock bank robbery that evening just at closing time, so that the employees could learn the proper responses to such a stressful situation and view bank security measures. At closing time that evening, the main bank's security chief, dressed in grubby clothes, entered the bank with an assistant and pointed his empty handgun at a bank teller, shouting, "Put all your money in this bag now! Get moving or I'll blow your head off!" The teller, who had been too busy with a crossword puzzle to listen to the manager's announcement at the meeting, thought that a real robbery was in progress. He nervously attempted to stuff the contents of his cash drawer into the bag while the security chief was threatening him and waving the gun at him. Believing that the teller was playing along, the security chief then demanded the teller's wallet and wristwatch, threatening to shoot the watch off if he did not hurry up. After giving the security chief what he wanted and watching him exit, the teller collapsed into a chair and suffered a mild heart attack before the security chief could return with his "loot" to discuss the exercise with the bank employees.

Which of the following crimes has the security chief committed with regard to the teller?

(A) Robbery.

(B) Larceny.

(C) Assault.

(D) No crime.

Question 164

After drinking heavily at his bachelor party at a beachfront resort, the groom was helped into a speedboat by a few of his friends and transported to a small island off the coast as a joke. They left him on the island, which had a small shelter but no communication facilities, without telling anyone else. As a result, the groom missed his wedding the next day. One of the participants was charged with kidnapping, which is defined in the jurisdiction as the unlawful movement or concealment of a person without his consent. In his defense, the participant claims that he was so intoxicated that he did not realize what he was doing, and that the groom had consented to being left on the island.

Which of the following would ***not*** be helpful to his defense?

(A) The groom was not legally intoxicated that evening.

(B) Kidnapping is a general intent crime in the jurisdiction.

(C) Kidnapping is a specific intent crime in the jurisdiction.

(D) The participant had overheard the groom say that he was not sure about going through with the wedding.

Question 109

A homeowner decided to destroy his home by fire in order to collect the insurance. A neighbor's house was located a short distance from the homeowner's home. The homeowner knew that there was a strong wind blowing towards the neighbor's home; while he did not want to burn the neighbor's home, he nevertheless set fire to his own home. The fire department was unable to save the homeowner's house. They did manage to put out the fire moments before it spread to the neighbor's home, which suffered damage from smoke and soot. The jurisdiction's arson statute covers burning one's own dwelling as well as the dwelling of another, but is otherwise unchanged from the common law.

If the homeowner is charged with attempted arson of the neighbor's home, he will most likely be found:

(A) Not guilty, because he did not intend to burn the neighbor's house.

(B) Not guilty, because the fire was put out before any part of the neighbor's home was burned.

(C) Guilty, because he intended to burn his own home and took a substantial step toward burning the neighbor's house.

(D) Guilty, because he acted with malice and took a substantial step toward burning the neighbor's house.

Question 134

A kidnapper and his cohort hatched a scheme to kidnap the son of a wealthy man and hold him for ransom. After conducting a surveillance of the wealthy man's home, they decided that they would have to have inside help to disable the alarm at the home. They agreed that the kidnapper would contact the man's butler, who they learned was heavily in debt and frequented a local racetrack during his time off. The butler would be offered money to disconnect the alarm on the night of the planned kidnapping. Shortly before the kidnapper was to go to the track to make contact with the butler, the cohort had a change of heart about the scheme and contacted the butler. He warned the butler not to have anything to do with the kidnapper. The butler met with the kidnapper anyway and pretended to go along with his proposal, accepting the down payment that the kidnapper offered. After meeting with him, the butler contacted the authorities.

The kidnapper and cohort are charged with conspiracy in a jurisdiction that follows the common law rule for conspiracy. The most likely result will be:

(A) Both the kidnapper and cohort are guilty of conspiracy because the cohort agreed with the kidnapper to commit the offense.

(B) The cohort is not guilty of conspiracy because he withdrew from the conspiracy by contacting the butler.

(C) The cohort is not guilty of conspiracy because he withdrew from the conspiracy by contacting the butler, and the kidnapper is not guilty of conspiracy with the butler because one cannot be a conspirator by oneself.

(D) The kidnapper is guilty of conspiracy with the butler.

Question 135

A brother and sister decided to hire a professional hit man to kill their parents in order to inherit the family fortune. Shortly after this discussion, however, the sister realized that she could not go through with the plan, and she told her brother that she would not be participating. She then called the hit man and told him that she would call the police if anything happened to her parents. The brother met with the hit man, who accepted a payment but intended to inform the parents of the brother's actions with the hope of collecting a reward. The hit man did so, and the parents had the brother arrested. The brother and sister are charged with attempted murder in a jurisdiction following the modern rules for attempt.

Which of the following statements is most accurate?

(A) The brother can be found guilty, because he paid the hit man.

(B) The brother and the sister can be found guilty, because they conspired to kill their parents.

(C) The brother cannot be found guilty, because the hit man only pretended to agree to the proposal.

(D) Neither the brother nor the sister can be found guilty, because they did not form the mental state necessary for attempt.

Question 93

A felon planned to break into the rental storage unit next to his that contained valuable electronic equipment. He went to a hardware store to purchase a crowbar. The proprietor sold him the crowbar even though he told her that he needed it to break into someone's storage unit. After the purchase, the felon went to the storage facility with his friend. The felon told the friend that he had lost the key to his storage unit and did not have time to contact the facility's manager, so they needed to break into the unit to get his equipment. Because the felon had a bad back, the friend pried open the door with the crowbar and carried the equipment out to the car. A silent alarm was triggered and the pair were apprehended shortly after leaving the facility.

Can the proprietor and the friend be convicted as accomplices to larceny?

(A) Yes as to the proprietor, because she knew that the felon was going to break into someone's storage unit with the crowbar.

(B) Yes as to the friend, because he carried out the theft of the items from the storage unit.

(C) Yes as to both the proprietor and the friend.

(D) No as to both the proprietor and the friend.

Question 119

A factory foreman was suspected of having murdered, for pay, the rival of a local union leader. After the police arrested the foreman at his home and he was taken to the police station, the officers who remained at the house asked the foreman's aunt, who was visiting him for the week, if she knew where any firearms could be found in the house. She went into the bedroom and returned with a pistol. Ballistics experts established that the pistol had been used to murder the victim, and the foreman's fingerprints were all over the pistol. At a subsequent grand jury proceeding, the district attorney introduced the pistol and the related ballistics and fingerprint evidence, and the grand jury indicted the foreman.

If the foreman seeks to quash the indictment, he will:

(A) Not prevail, because the evidence was offered before a grand jury, not a court.

(B) Not prevail, because the pistol was obtained by a private citizen, not the police.

(C) Prevail, because the police did not have probable cause to seize the pistol.

(D) Prevail, because the foreman's aunt was acting as an agent of the police when she obtained the pistol.

Question 1

Federal narcotics officers suspected the defendant of growing marijuana in his greenhouse, which was adjacent to and connected to his house. The narcotics officers learned from an informant that the semi-opaque panes of glass on the greenhouse were being replaced during the night with a newer type of glass that let in more light without an increase in visibility. Without a warrant, the officers flew over the defendant's greenhouse in a

helicopter that night. One of the officers focused on the greenhouse with a pair of "night vision" thermal imaging binoculars supplied by the Department of Defense and not available to the general public. He determined that marijuana was being grown. The officers then went to a magistrate, swore out a warrant, and arrested the defendant.

If the defendant moves to suppress any evidence gathered by virtue of the flyover, the motion most likely will be:

(A) Denied, because the police may conduct flyovers to gather evidence.

(B) Denied, because the defendant did not live in the greenhouse.

(C) Granted, because the "night-vision" binoculars were not available to the general public.

(D) Granted, because the greenhouse was within the curtilage.

Question 143

An undercover agent for a federal drug enforcement agency informed a state law enforcement agency that a large amount of cocaine was being mailed to a resident of that state. The cocaine would be mailed in a large box and wrapped distinctively. The agent further informed the agency that the resident was not the purchaser of the cocaine, but was only acting as an intermediary. The cocaine would be picked up within a few days by the buyer, who was from a neighboring state. The agency immediately placed the resident's house under surveillance. In a few days, a large box wrapped as the undercover agent described was delivered by the post office. The agency did not make an arrest, but kept the house under surveillance. Two days later, a man driving a car with plates from the neighboring state arrived at the house. He entered the house and came back out shortly thereafter carrying what appeared to be the same box. The suspect placed the box in the trunk of his car and drove off. Two blocks later, the car was stopped, the suspect arrested, and officers for the agency searched the entire vehicle, acting without a warrant. The box in the trunk was opened and cocaine was found. The suspect was charged with possession of cocaine. At a preliminary hearing, he moved to suppress the cocaine.

The motion should be:

(A) Denied, because the officers had probable cause to search the trunk.

(B) Denied, because the search was incident to a valid arrest.

(C) Granted, because the officers should have obtained a warrant before opening the package.

(D) Granted, because the officers had no way of knowing that it was the same package that was delivered to the home.

Question 144

A police officer witnessed a car turn the wrong way from a bar's parking lot onto a one-way street. The officer immediately turned on his siren and pursued the car for a couple of miles. During that pursuit, the car repeatedly weaved in and out of its lane of traffic. Eventually, the car pulled over, and the officer placed the driver under arrest. After handcuffing the driver and placing him in the back seat of his squad car, the officer looked under a blanket lying on the floor of the car's passenger compartment. Under the blanket, he found an open bottle of whiskey. Before his trial on charges of drunk driving and driving with an open container of alcohol in the car, the defendant moves to suppress from evidence the open bottle of whiskey.

The motion should be:

(A) Denied, because when the police stopped the car, they had probable cause to search the car.

(B) Denied, because the search was incident to a lawful arrest.

(C) Granted, because the officer did not have probable cause to look under the blanket.

(D) Granted, because, after arresting the driver and placing him in the squad car, the car should have been impounded and a warrant obtained before the search.

Question 127

Based on a tip from a reliable informant that an attorney was illegally selling automatic weapons and ammunition from his storefront office, the police obtained a warrant to search for weapons at the office. When they arrived at the building, they saw a client exiting the attorney's office and placing what appeared to be a weapon inside his jacket. The police stopped the client on the street and an officer patted down his outer clothing but found no weapon. However, the officer felt a bag with several small tube-shaped objects in it, and she immediately placed him under arrest. The contents of the bag were later determined to be marijuana cigarettes.

At a preliminary hearing on the narcotics charge, the client sought to suppress introduction of the marijuana as evidence. The arresting officer testified at the suppression hearing that, based on her long experience as a narcotics officer, she concluded immediately that the bag contained marijuana cigarettes when she first touched it.

If the officer's testimony is believed, the motion to suppress the marijuana evidence should be:

(A)   Denied, because the search was incident to a lawful arrest.

(B)   Denied, because the police had a reasonable suspicion that the client might be armed and dangerous.

(C)   Granted, because the scope of an officer's patdown during an investigatory detention is limited to a search for weapons.

(D)   Granted, because the search warrant did not authorize the police to search the client despite the fact that he was just present at the place to be searched.

Question 128

During the investigation of a large gambling operation, the police obtained a warrant to search a bookie's home based on the affidavit of an informant. The informant was a rival bookie who had never acted as an informant before, and much of the substance of the rival's information came from third-party sources. During the search, the police seized a variety of gambling evidence, including betting slips and a check from the defendant. The bookie and the defendant were arrested for violating the state's gambling laws, and separate trials were ordered. At a preliminary hearing for the bookie, the court held that the search warrant for the bookie's home was not supported by probable cause and suppressed introduction of the evidence seized. The defendant moved to suppress introduction of the betting slips and the check on the same basis.

If the court agrees that the search warrant of the bookie's home was not supported by probable cause, the defendant's motion should be:

(A)   Granted, because the rival bookie was not a reliable informant.

(B)   Granted, because the evidence is the fruit of an unlawful search.

(C)   Denied, because the client's legitimate expectation of privacy was not constitutionally violated.

(D)   Denied, because the police acted reasonably in relying on the issuance of the warrant.

Question 193

The defendant boarded a bus in New York for a trip to Florida to deliver two bricks of cocaine to a drug dealer. En route, in Georgia, an officer for the state motor vehicle department stopped the bus in order to conduct a safety check of the bus. The officer was accompanied by a state trooper. While the motor vehicle officer was conducting the safety inspection, the trooper boarded the bus. The trooper announced that, for homeland security purposes and to combat drug smuggling, he would be asking for identification, for the passengers to identify their luggage, and for permission to search inside the luggage. The trooper stated that the passengers had the right to leave the bus or to decline to show what was inside their luggage. The trooper then walked to the back of the bus to avoid blocking the aisle. The trooper pulled down a bag that another passenger indicated belonged to the defendant. The trooper then asked the defendant if the bag was his and whether he could search the bag, and the defendant responded by nodding his head.

The trooper opened the bag, found the two bricks of cocaine, and immediately placed the defendant under arrest and advised him of his rights under *Miranda*. Approximately one hour later, the motor vehicle officer finished his inspection, issuing the driver a citation for failing to keep his log book up to date. The defendant was charged with possession of cocaine with intent to deliver. Before trial, the defendant moves for suppression of the cocaine.

The most likely outcome is that:

(A)   The cocaine will be suppressed as a violation of the Fourth Amendment.

(B)   The cocaine will be suppressed as a violation of the Fifth Amendment.

(C)   The cocaine will be suppressed as violations of both the Fourth and Fifth Amendments.

(D)   The cocaine will not be suppressed.

Question 54

State statutory law requires that a person who is suspected of committing a crime must be informed of the nature of that crime before questioning may begin. The state supreme court has held that statements obtained in violation of a suspect's statutory interrogation rights may not be admitted into evidence. The defendant, who was arrested on suspicion of committing an arson, was told: "You have the right to remain silent, anything you say can and will be used against you in a court of law, you have the right to the presence of an attorney during questioning, and if you cannot afford an attorney, one will be appointed for you." The defendant immediately gave a statement implicating himself in the arson. He was charged and brought to trial in state court for arson.

At trial, should the statement be excluded from evidence?

(A)   Yes, because the *Miranda* warnings were not proper.

(B) Yes, because the questioning violated state law.

(C) No, because proper *Miranda* warnings were given in compliance with federal constitutional requirements.

(D) No, because the requirement of informing the suspect of the nature of the charges against him is not a state constitutional requirement.

Question 161

While investigating the most recent of a series of murders, a homicide detective was approached by an onlooker who seemed to have detailed knowledge of the murders. The detective recalled the onlooker at some of the other murder scenes, and immediately suspected that he knew something about the crimes. The detective asked the onlooker not to leave until the detective had the opportunity to ask him a few questions. After finishing with the evidence he was gathering, the detective started to question the onlooker at the crime scene without giving him *Miranda* warnings. The onlooker eventually revealed details of the crimes that were never made available to the public. As a result, the onlooker was arrested and charged with several murders. At a preliminary hearing, the onlooker testified that he believed that he could not leave until he had spoken with the detective. The defense counsel moves to suppress the statements made to the homicide detective.

What is the most likely result?

(A) The motion will not be granted because the onlooker was not in custody.

(B) The motion will not be granted because the onlooker initiated the contact with the homicide detective.

(C) The motion will be granted because the onlooker believed that he was not free to leave.

(D) The motion will be granted because the detective was required to give the onlooker *Miranda* warnings once the detective suspected him of having committed the crime.

Question 6

A police officer went to the defendant's house and placed him under arrest for operating an auto theft ring. As the defendant was being arrested, he told his wife, "You had better call our lawyer; I don't want to sign anything unless she's with me." The defendant was given *Miranda* warnings on the way to the police station. Meanwhile, the defendant's lawyer called the station and told the desk sergeant that she was on her way and to have the defendant call her as soon as he arrived. The sergeant assured her that the defendant would be held without questioning for several hours until the district

attorney arrived. When the defendant arrived at the station, the arresting officer and another officer immediately put the defendant in an interrogation room and questioned him about a bank robbery that had taken place two days ago. They did not inform him of the call from his lawyer, but he agreed to talk as long as he did not have to put anything in writing or sign anything without her okay. He made incriminating statements about the robbery, and he was eventually indicted for that crime as well. At a preliminary hearing on the robbery charge, the defendant's lawyer moved to suppress the arresting officer's testimony about the defendant's statements.

The court should:

(A) Deny the motion, because the questioning was about a different crime from the one for which the defendant was in custody.

(B) Deny the motion, because the defendant's statements were made voluntarily after receiving *Miranda* warnings.

(C) Grant the motion, because the defendant was not informed that his lawyer was trying to see him, and his lawyer was misinformed that he would not be questioned right away.

(D) Grant the motion, because the defendant's refusal to write or sign anything indicates that he did not knowingly and intelligently waive his right to the assistance of counsel.

Question 81

Late one night, a young couple in a car was struck by a speeding truck as the couple's car crossed an intersection with the light green in their favor, killing them immediately. Several weeks later, a burglar awaiting trial on burglary charges asked a jail officer to let him speak with a highway patrol officer. When the highway patrol officer came to the cell, the burglar told him that he was the driver of the truck that had struck the car, and had been speeding away from a burglary when the accident occurred.

The burglar was put on trial for felony murder, on the theory that he had not yet reached a place of temporary safety when the accident occurred. The prosecution seeks to introduce the statements made by the burglar to the highway patrol officer regarding the events of the night of the accident. The burglar's attorney objects.

Which of the following is the strongest argument for permitting the statements into evidence?

(A) The burglar had not been charged in connection with the auto accident at the time the statements were made to the highway patrol officer.

(B)   The burglar made the statements spontaneously, without inducement or interrogation by the police.

(C)   The highway patrol officer had no connection with the burglary investigation for which the burglar had been incarcerated.

(D)   The burglar's statements were not the product of coercion by the police officers.

Question 82

At the beginning of the second day of the defendant's trial for arson, a bailiff approached the defendant and got him to admit that he had burned down the house in question. When the trial resumed, the defendant testified that he had nothing to do with the fire in question. In rebuttal, the prosecution seeks to put the bailiff on the stand to testify as to the defendant's statements, but the defendant's attorney objects.

Which of the following is the strongest argument to exclude the bailiff's testimony as to the defendant's statements?

(A)   The bailiff did not give the defendant *Miranda* warnings.

(B)   The bailiff did not tell the defendant's attorney that he was going to question him.

(C)   The statements were made in the absence of the defendant's counsel.

(D)   The statements were made to a law enforcement officer and therefore were not voluntary.

Question 69

A state statute has adopted the common law definition of larceny. Another statute provided as follows:

> It shall be an affirmative defense to a crime if the defendant establishes by clear and convincing evidence that, due to a mental disease or defect, he was unable to appreciate the criminality of his conduct or conform his conduct to the requirements of the law.

A homeowner was leaving town for two weeks and he asked his neighbor to stop by the house each day and water the plants. While at the homeowner's home, the neighbor found the keys to the homeowner's new car. The neighbor took the car and drove it into town to show his friends. The neighbor told all of his friends that he had purchased the car. The homeowner returned home three days early, saw that the car was missing, and called the police. Later that day, the neighbor was arrested and charged with larceny.

At the neighbor's trial, the neighbor testified that he intended to return the car. Additionally, two psychiatrists testified that, due to a mental defect, the neighbor suffered from an extreme inferiority complex and delusions of grandeur. The doctors further testified that his mental condition caused him to take the car and to tell other people that he owned it. At the conclusion of the evidence, the court's instructions to the jury included the following:

1.   If you find by a preponderance of the evidence that the defendant intended to return the car, you should find the defendant not guilty.

2.   If you find by a preponderance of the evidence that, due to a mental disease or defect, the defendant was unable to appreciate the criminality of his conduct or conform his conduct to the requirements of the law, you should find the defendant not guilty.

The neighbor was found guilty and he appealed, claiming that the jury instructions violated his constitutional rights.

The appellate court should rule that:

(A)   Both instructions were constitutional.

(B)   Both instructions were unconstitutional.

(C)   Instruction 1 was unconstitutional; Instruction 2 was constitutional.

(D)   Instruction 1 was constitutional; Instruction 2 was unconstitutional.

Question 118

A masked gunman held up a convenience store. Due to the poor quality of the surveillance recording, it was very difficult to identify the masked gunman. Nonetheless, the defendant was arrested and charged with the robbery. At the preliminary hearing, the magistrate, on seeing the poor quality of the tape, determined that there was not probable cause to prosecute the defendant. After that, the county prosecutor presented the case to a grand jury, but the grand jury refused to indict the defendant. After waiting a couple of months, the prosecutor presented the case to a different grand jury. The grand jury indicted the defendant and the case went to trial. At trial, the jury was unable to reach a verdict. After this trial, the county prosecutor again tried the case before a jury; in this instance, the jury acquitted the defendant of all charges. At a third trial, the county prosecutor was finally successful in having the defendant convicted. The defendant appeals on double jeopardy grounds.

On appeal, the court will find that:

(A) Jeopardy had attached after the magistrate determined that there was insufficient evidence to prosecute.

(B) Jeopardy had attached after the first grand jury refused to indict the defendant.

(C) Jeopardy had attached after the first trial had ended in a hung jury.

(D) Jeopardy had attached after the second trial had ended in an acquittal.

Question 173

The defendant and several of his friends went to a celebration at a club. After consuming numerous alcoholic beverages over a period of two hours, the defendant attempted to drive home. Two blocks away, due to his intoxication, he drove his car across the center line and collided head-on with the victim's car, killing her instantly. However, the defendant was only charged with driving while intoxicated. After a bench trial, he was convicted and sentenced to two years of probation. The resulting public outcry and media attention cost the district attorney the next election. His successor immediately filed a charge of reckless homicide against the defendant for causing the victim's death while driving drunk.

The defendant was tried and convicted of the reckless homicide charge and sentenced to five years in prison. The defendant asserts on appeal that his trial and conviction on the reckless homicide charge violates the Fifth Amendment provision against double jeopardy.

Is he likely to prevail?

(A) No, because the driving while intoxicated charge and the reckless homicide charge each require proof of an additional element that the other crime does not require.

(B) No, because the fact that the charges arose out of the same transaction does not prevent the imposition of separate punishments as long as they are imposed in separate trials.

(C) Yes, because the reckless homicide charge will require proof of the same conduct that constituted the driving while intoxicated charge.

(D) Yes, because the sentence for the reckless homicide conviction was greater than, and not concurrent with, the driving while intoxicated sentence.

Question 75

A farmer was arrested after selling her surplus fruits and vegetables for several days at a vacant lot in the nearby town. A statute provides that it is a misdemeanor, punishable by a fine of up to $500 and/or imprisonment in county jail for up to one year, to sell any product without a business license, except for informal sales held on the property of the seller no more often than once every three months. At the farmer's trial, she requested but was refused appointed counsel.

Assuming that she would otherwise qualify as indigent, if she is convicted of violating the statute, what is the maximum penalty that may be imposed on her?

(A) Imprisonment for six months.

(B) A $500 fine.

(C) Imprisonment for six months and a $500 fine.

(D) No penalty, because her conviction is void as having been obtained in violation of her right to counsel under the Sixth Amendment.

EVIDENCE

Question 40

During the defendant's prosecution for robbery, the prosecutor asks the court to take judicial notice of the fact that at that latitude, the sun is still up at 5:30 p.m. on June 21. The court so finds.

The effect of the court's action is that:

(A) The burden of persuasion is now on the defendant to prove otherwise as to the fact judicially noticed.

(B) The fact judicially noticed is established beyond a reasonable doubt.

(C) The prosecutor's burden of producing evidence on the fact judicially noticed is satisfied.

(D) The fact judicially noticed is conclusively established.

Question 68

In a civil action tried to a jury, the defendant objected to the introduction by the plaintiff of certain evidence without the judge's first making a preliminary ruling on the admissibility of the evidence.

For which evidence is the defendant's objection not appropriate?

(A) Opinion testimony regarding the structural integrity of a building by an engineer called by the plaintiff, without a preliminary determination by the judge that the engineer is an expert.

(B) Hospital records pertaining to the plaintiff offered by the plaintiff, without a preliminary determination by the judge that they were made as a regular activity of the hospital staff.

(C) Contract negotiations between the plaintiff and a third party, without a preliminary determination by the judge that the third party was the defendant's agent.

(D) A paramedic's testimony that the plaintiff's wife, before she died, said that the defendant's car went through a red light before hitting her, without a preliminary determination by the judge that she made the statement under a sense of impending death.

Question 50

At the trial of the plaintiff's breach of contract action against the defendant, the plaintiff called her accountant as a witness to testify about the difference in gross sales, gross income, and net profit caused by the defendant's failure to supply the promised quantity of ice cream to the plaintiff's ice cream shop. When the plaintiff's attorney asked the accountant to state the gross income figures for the year prior to formation of the contract between the plaintiff and the defendant, the accountant replied that he could not remember the exact amounts. The plaintiff's counsel then handed the accountant a copy of the federal tax return submitted by the plaintiff for that year, and asked him to read it. Counsel then asked, "Now that you have read the tax return, can you remember what the gross income of the plaintiff's ice cream shop was for the relevant period?" The defendant's counsel objects.

How should the court rule?

(A) Sustained, because the plaintiff's counsel is seeking to elicit testimony based on inadmissible hearsay.

(B) Sustained, because the accountant's testimony is not the best evidence.

(C) Overruled, because the accountant's hearsay testimony is admissible as a past recollection recorded.

(D) Overruled, because the accountant's testimony is admissible evidence relating to the plaintiff's damages.

Question 179

The defendant is on trial for first degree murder for the shooting of a rival gang member. His defense is that the gun accidentally discharged while he was cleaning it and that he is not in any gang. The prosecution seeks to offer the testimony of an experienced police officer in the gang crimes unit who interrogated the defendant. The officer is prepared to testify that he saw a distinctive tattoo on the defendant's leg and that he recognized the tattoo as one worn by members of a gang that was a rival of the victim's gang, and intends to have the tattoo displayed in court. The defendant's attorney objects to this testimony.

How should the court rule on the admissibility of the testimony?

(A) Inadmissible, because the officer does not have personal knowledge that the defendant is in the gang.

(B) Inadmissible, because the officer has not been qualified by the court as an expert on gangs.

(C) Admissible, as circumstantial evidence that the defendant was a member of the rival gang.

(D) Admissible, because the tattoo will be displayed in court.

Question 60

A state's defamation statutes require as a prerequisite for the filing of a libel suit against a public newspaper that the plaintiff demand in writing that the defendant retract the allegedly defamatory material. In the plaintiff's defamation suit against the defendant, the publisher of a public newspaper, the plaintiff calls as a witness a former employee of the defendant who was the secretary to the editor during the period in which the events underlying the plaintiff's suit occurred. The witness will testify that two days after the allegedly defamatory story was run in the newspaper, she remembers receiving a letter to the editor of the newspaper delivered by the plaintiff. The plaintiff has already testified that he wrote a letter to the editor demanding a retraction, and that the letter was delivered by him the same day that the defamatory story was published.

Should the court admit the witness's testimony over the defendant's objection?

(A) No, because the witness is no longer employed by the defendant.

(B) No, because the letter itself is the best evidence.

(C) Yes, because the witness's testimony is evidence of a matter in issue.

(D) Yes, because the witness's testimony is an admission by a party-opponent.

Question 43

The plaintiff was driving her daughter to school when their car was struck broadside by a car driven by the defendant at an intersection controlled in all directions by stop signs. The plaintiff and her daughter were taken by ambulance to the hospital. In a personal injury action brought by the plaintiff and her daughter against the defendant, pretrial discovery revealed that both cars were in perfect mechanical condition just before the accident, and the defendant was on his way home from work at the time of the accident, but had stopped off at a bar before he reached the intersection at which he struck the plaintiff's car. There is no witness available to testify as to how much the defendant had to drink at the bar that day.

At trial, the plaintiff calls a co-worker of the defendant, who testifies over objection that the defendant has a reputation as a hard drinker who tolerates alcohol well but who always drinks a great deal at any one drinking occasion, as witnessed by the co-worker at numerous company events. Was it error for the trial court to admit his testimony?

(A) Yes, because in a civil matter, evidence of a party's character may not be introduced until he has put his character at issue.

(B) Yes, because the plaintiff may not attempt to prove that the defendant acted in a particular way on one occasion in conformity with his reputation as to that behavior.

(C) No, because the co-worker had personal knowledge of the defendant's drinking habits from having observed him while drinking.

(D) No, because there exists no unbiased eyewitness who can testify as to how much the defendant actually drank at the bar before he had the accident with the plaintiff.

Question 100

A bank hired a security guard after a routine background check of the guard's references. The bank issued the guard a gun that he was allowed to take with him during his off-duty hours. However, bank policy required that all bullets be removed from the gun when the guard was off duty. Each security guard was required to sign a statement that he would abide by the unloaded gun policy. While the guard was driving home one evening, he got into a traffic altercation with another driver. The dispute escalated and the guard jumped out of his car, waving his gun. It was loaded and accidentally went off. The plaintiff suffered a gunshot wound.

The plaintiff brought an action against both the bank and the guard for his injuries. He alleged that the bank was negligent in entrusting the weapon to the guard, and that the guard was negligent in his handling of the weapon. The plaintiff offers the testimony of the guard's former co-worker, who worked with the guard for 10 years at another bank. The former co-worker is prepared to testify that, during the time that he worked with the guard, the guard had a reputation for being a hothead, keeping his weapon loaded during off-duty hours, and threatening people with his gun whenever he got into an argument.

Assuming proper objection, how should the court rule regarding the admissibility of the testimony?

(A) The former co-worker's testimony is character evidence, inadmissible in a civil case.

(B) The former co-worker's testimony is character evidence admissible against the bank if it can be established that the bank knew of the guard's reputation.

(C) The former co-worker's testimony is character evidence admissible against the bank whether or not the bank knew of the guard's reputation.

(D) The former co-worker's testimony is admissible to help establish that the guard may have acted negligently at the time of the accident.

Question 181

The plaintiff brought an action against a major national department store alleging that the electric blanket she bought from them overheated, causing a fire that destroyed her home and all that it contained. The defendant contends that its blanket could not have overheated unless it was left on after the plaintiff left for work on the day of the fire. The plaintiff offers in rebuttal the testimony of her husband, who will state that he has been married to the plaintiff for seven years, that he has slept in the same bed with her for most of that period, and that the first thing she does every morning upon awakening is to turn the control on the electric blanket to "off."

Should this testimony be admitted?

(A)   Yes, because prior conduct may be used to show conformity with habit.

(B)   Yes, because evidence of habit may be used to show that a person acted in conformity with the habit on a particular occasion.

(C)   No, because habit may only be established by opinion or reputation evidence, not specific conduct.

(D)   No, because there is no corroboration of the husband's testimony by a nonparty witness.

Question 140

At the defendant's trial for assault with a deadly weapon, the defendant's counsel calls a witness to the stand and asks him, "What is the defendant's reputation for honesty and veracity in your community?" The prosecutor objects before the witness can answer.

Should the court admit the testimony?

(A)   Yes, because reputation evidence is admissible under these circumstances to establish a character trait.

(B)   Yes, because the prosecution put the defendant's character at issue when they filed charges against him.

(C)   No, because the evidence offered is irrelevant to any material issue in the case.

(D)   No, because the evidence offered is inadmissible hearsay.

Question 83

At the defendant's trial for armed robbery, the prosecutor offers indisputable evidence tending to show that the defendant committed two other armed robberies in the year preceding the present offense, and that he committed all three robberies to obtain money for his heroin habit.

The defendant has no prior convictions and has chosen not to take the stand in his defense.

Should the court admit this evidence over the defendant's objection?

(A)   No, because the defendant was not convicted of the other robberies.

(B)   No, because the defendant has not testified at his trial.

(C)   Yes, unless the court determines that the probative value of the evidence is substantially outweighed by its prejudicial effect.

(D)   Yes, because the prosecution can establish by clear and convincing evidence that the defendant committed the robberies.

Question 91

The defendant is on trial for shoplifting. As part of his defense, the defendant calls to the stand a restaurant cashier, who will testify that the defendant is a regular customer and has corrected an undercharge on her bill several times.

Is the testimony of the cashier admissible?

(A)   Yes, because a defendant may offer evidence of her good character in a criminal case.

(B)   Yes, because the evidence is relevant and its probative value outweighs the danger of unfair prejudice or confusion of the issues.

(C)   No, because the cashier's testimony is hearsay.

(D)   No, because the evidence is not a proper means for proving good character.

Question 44

While driving home after an evening spent drinking at a local bar, the plaintiff passed out at the wheel. His car went through a red light at an intersection and was struck by a car driven by the defendant. The plaintiff, under the influence of alcohol, staggered from his car. The defendant, believing that the plaintiff had been injured in the accident, said "It's my fault. I was not paying attention. I'll take care of all your medical bills." Later that night, the plaintiff was treated for minor injuries at a nearby hospital.

The plaintiff sued the defendant for damages, alleging that the defendant was driving negligently at the time of the accident. The plaintiff offered the testimony of a witness who was prepared to testify that, after the accident, the defendant stated in a clear, calm voice, "I was not paying attention. I'll take care of all your medical bills."

Assuming the proper objection, should the witness's testimony concerning the defendant's statement be admitted?

(A)   No, because the defendant's statement is a settlement offer.

(B)   No, because the plaintiff was negligent per se.

(C)   The defendant's statement "I was not paying attention" should be admitted, but the statement "I'll take care of all your medical bills" should not.

(D)   Yes, as an admission by the defendant.

Question 123

While walking down a city street, the plaintiff was seriously injured when a rotten limb fell off of a tree and hit him on the head. The tree was located on a vacant lot next to the defendant's house. The lot appeared to be a part of the defendant's property. The plaintiff sued the defendant to recover damages for his injuries, alleging that the defendant was negligent with respect to the care of the tree. The defendant's defense was that he did not own the lot or the tree, and that both the lot and the tree were the property of the city. At trial, the plaintiff calls a witness to testify that shortly after the plaintiff was taken to the hospital, he observed the defendant cutting down the rotten limbs on a number of trees on the vacant lot.

The witness's testimony is most likely:

(A)   Admissible, to help prove that the defendant was negligent in not removing the rotten limbs sooner.

(B)   Admissible, to help prove that the defendant owned the lot.

(C)   Inadmissible, because subsequent repairs are encouraged for reasons of public safety.

(D)   Inadmissible, because the evidence does not prove that the defendant owned the lot.

Question 57

The plaintiff is suing the defendant for injuries he suffered when his car was struck by the defendant's truck, allegedly because the defendant had fallen asleep at the wheel after driving all night. At trial, the defendant's girlfriend testified that she had been with the defendant in the truck and had taken over the driving duties for several hours that night while the defendant napped. The plaintiff calls to the stand an acquaintance of the defendant's girlfriend, to testify that the girlfriend told him that she had been unable to get out of bed the weekend the accident occurred because of severe back pain.

The testimony of the acquaintance is:

(A)   Admissible for impeachment purposes only.

(B)   Admissible for impeachment purposes and as substantive evidence as a declaration of physical condition.

(C)   Inadmissible, because this means of impeachment can be done only through cross-examination.

(D)   Inadmissible, because the plaintiff has not first given the girlfriend an opportunity to explain or deny the statement.

Question 200

As a result of an automobile accident at an intersection, the plaintiff sued the defendant, claiming that the defendant's car was traveling at a high rate of speed and went through a red light just before the crash. A witness for the plaintiff testified that he observed the accident and that the plaintiff's car was traveling at a low speed with a green light at the time of the accident.

Which of the following will the court find inadmissible to admit to impeach the credibility of the witness?

(A)   A certified copy of a certificate of conviction for felony assault and battery seven years ago.

(B)   The testimony of the witness's friend that, last month, while having a drink at a bar, the witness told her that the plaintiff's light was red.

(C)   A record of an arrest one week ago for embezzlement.

(D)   On cross-examination of the witness, the question "Isn't it a fact that you lied to your employer last year concerning your meal expenses on a business trip?"

Question 103

The defendant was charged with embezzling $1 million from his employer, a bank, by transferring the funds to a secret offshore account in the bank's name. Only the defendant and the bank's vice president were authorized to draw funds from the account. The defendant testified that he had wired $1 million to the account but had done so at the direction of the bank's vice president. The defendant stated under oath that he had no intent to embezzle bank funds. The government's cross-examination of the defendant concentrated exclusively on his relationship and conversations with the vice president, who has committed suicide.

The defense now seeks to call a second witness, who is prepared to testify that he had worked with the defendant for 10 years and that the defendant had a reputation in both the business and general communities as being a very honest person.

The witness's testimony is:

(A) Admissible, because a defendant has a constitutional right to call witnesses in his own behalf.

(B) Admissible, to help show that the defendant did not embezzle funds.

(C) Inadmissible character evidence.

(D) Inadmissible, because you cannot bolster the credibility of your own witness unless the credibility of the witness has been attacked.

Question 32

The plaintiff sued a local restaurant, claiming that she injured her teeth, gums, and mouth when she bit into a hamburger that contained a large jagged piece of glass. The plaintiff called to the stand a waiter for the restaurant, who testified that, when he heard the plaintiff scream, he looked in her direction and saw her remove a piece of glass from her bleeding mouth. On cross-examination, the defense asked the waiter, "Isn't it a fact that three months ago you were fired by the restaurant for serving drinks to your friends and not charging for them?" The waiter responded, "Yes, but I wasn't trying to steal anything. I just forgot to charge them." The defense then asked, "Isn't it a fact that last month you threw a rock through the plate glass window at the restaurant?" The waiter replied, "That's not true; I was there but I didn't throw the rock." The defense then offered the testimony of a witness who was prepared to testify that she saw the waiter throw the rock through the restaurant's window.

Assuming that there have been no criminal charges filed as a result of the broken window, the witness's testimony is:

(A) Inadmissible, because specific acts of misconduct that did not result in a conviction cannot be used to impeach a witness, either on cross-examination or through extrinsic evidence.

(B) Inadmissible, because specific acts of misconduct that did not result in a conviction cannot be established through extrinsic evidence.

(C) Admissible as evidence of bias.

(D) Admissible to establish that the waiter lied under oath.

Question 187

In a civil lawsuit arising from a car accident, the plaintiff's witness testified that she observed the defendant drive through a red light before striking the plaintiff's car. The defendant then presented evidence impeaching the plaintiff's witness. The plaintiff now wishes to call someone else to testify as to his witness's good reputation for truthfulness.

The court is most likely to permit this testimony if the impeachment was by evidence that:

(A) The plaintiff's witness was convicted of the felony of aggravated battery five years ago.

(B) The plaintiff's witness had a previous dispute with the defendant.

(C) The plaintiff's witness was not wearing her prescription eyeglasses at the time of the accident.

(D) The plaintiff's witness was his mother.

Question 33

In a wrongful death action for the death of his wife in an automobile accident, the plaintiff alleged that the accident was caused by a mudflap assembly that fell off the truck of the defendant. The plaintiff wishes to introduce the testimony of a witness, another truck driver who was on the same highway at the time, who heard someone tell the defendant over CB radio that he had noticed at the truck stop that the defendant's mudflap assembly on his truck was loose. The witness does not know the identity of the person who gave the warning.

If the defendant objects to admission of the testimony, the court should rule that it is:

(A) Admissible to prove that the defendant was notified that the mudflap assembly was loose.

(B) Admissible both to prove that the defendant was notified that the mudflap assembly was loose and as substantive evidence that it was loose.

(C) Inadmissible, because the witness cannot identify who made the statement.

(D) Inadmissible, because it is hearsay not within any recognized exception.

Question 5

A moving company specializing in local moves sent two employees on a typical job: a driver and a helper. The driver's responsibility was to drive the truck and load and unload the cargo. The helper's responsibility was to load and unload the cargo and generally assist the driver. While transporting furniture in a company truck, the driver failed to stop at a stop sign and collided with a car, causing the motorist to be seriously injured in the accident.

In a lawsuit brought by the motorist against the moving company on the theory of negligence by its employee, the motorist offered into evidence a written statement of the helper. The statement said that the driver was adjusting his portable radio and not observing the road when the accident occurred.

The helper's written statement is admissible if:

(A) The helper takes the witness stand and testifies that the driver was adjusting his radio and not observing the road.

(B) The helper is unavailable to testify.

(C) Evidence is introduced to establish that the helper is an employee of the moving company and his written statement is in the scope of his employment.

(D) The helper's statement was given under oath at a trial or other proceeding.

Question 120

The defendant is charged with arson for hire in the burning down of an old office building. The prosecution offers to introduce the testimony of a neighbor of the defendant, who will state that the day after the fire, she went to the defendant's apartment. The defendant had burnt a roast in her oven, and the apartment was full of smoke. The neighbor, coughing and choking, said, "What did you do, burn down that old office building again?" The defendant made no reply. Should this evidence be admitted over the defendant's objection?

(A) No, it is hearsay not within an exception.

(B) No, if the court determines that a reasonable person would not deny such a statement under the circumstances.

(C) Yes, it is an admission by silence.

(D) Yes, it is a declaration against penal interest.

Question 121

The defendant, a competitive athlete, was charged with the murder of another athlete against whom she was scheduled to compete in two weeks. Autopsy results revealed that the victim was poisoned with a lethal mixture containing a variety of substances. During the prosecution's case in chief, evidence was introduced establishing that a bottle of a particular drug, which was among the substances listed in the autopsy report, was discovered in the defendant's medicine cabinet when she was arrested. On direct examination by her own attorney, the defendant states that when she was arrested and the bottle of the drug was found, she told the officers, "My doctor prescribed that for me to cope with the excruciating back pain from which I suffer." If the prosecution moves to strike this testimony, how should the court rule?

(A) For the defendant, because it is a prior consistent statement.

(B) For the defendant, because it tends to explain prosecution evidence.

(C) For the prosecution, because it is hearsay not within an exception.

(D) For the prosecution, because it is a self-serving statement.

Question 106

At the defendant's trial for grand theft auto and other offenses, the prosecution offers to introduce the testimony of a police officer. The officer will testify that he showed a photographic lineup containing the defendant's picture to a witness who had seen the defendant fleeing from the stolen vehicle at the conclusion of a high-speed chase, and the witness selected the defendant's picture. The witness has left the state and refuses to return.

Should the court admit the evidence?

(A) Yes, because the witness is unavailable to testify.

(B) Yes, because it is a prior identification.

(C) No, because it is inadmissible hearsay.

(D) No, because the picture has not been properly authenticated.

Question 96

The plaintiff was injured when the bus in which she was riding braked too abruptly and threw her into a support stanchion, breaking her hip. She has brought an action against the bus company for damages from personal injuries on theories of respondeat superior and negligent hiring.

During the bus company's case in chief, its counsel calls the company's personnel director as a witness and asks him if the driver of the bus had been required to provide proof that he had had no convictions for crimes relating to vehicle use before being hired. The witness answers, "It's been several years since he was hired, but my best recollection is that we did not ask for such proof." Counsel then prepares to question the witness about his statement, made at a deposition taken 18 months before trial, that he had personally requested and received a statement from the driver before he was hired that he (the driver) had no such convictions.

May counsel for the bus company pursue this matter in this fashion?

(A) Yes, but the jury must be instructed that the evidence may be considered only for impeachment of the witness.

(B) Yes, the evidence may be admitted for both impeachment and substantive purposes.

(C) No, because it is hearsay not within any exception.

(D) No, counsel may not impeach its own witness.

Question 113

At the trial of the plaintiff's personal injury action against the defendant, a pedestrian, who was near the accident scene but did not see what happened, testifies that an eyewitness to the accident shouted, "Good Lord! The green car just ran through a red light and hit the red car!" Previous evidence had established that the defendant drove a green car and the plaintiff a red one. The defendant offers to call to the stand the brother of the eyewitness, who will testify that he spoke with the eyewitness the day after the accident, and he said that the light was green when the green car drove through the intersection. The eyewitness had moved to a foreign country prior to trial.

Should this evidence be admitted over the plaintiff's objection?

(A) No, because the eyewitness is not available to explain or deny the contradiction.

(B) No, because it is hearsay not within any exception.

(C) Yes, for the purpose of impeachment and as substantive evidence.

(D) Yes, for the purpose of impeachment only.

Question 189

The victim collapsed at her desk while drinking her morning coffee. Her secretary came rushing to her aid. Gasping for breath, the victim said, "I don't think I have much time left. I want you to remember when they come looking for suspects that I believe my assistant would kill for my job." The victim soon lost consciousness. She regained consciousness briefly after arriving at the hospital, but the doctors would not allow her to speak to anyone, including the police. She again lapsed into a coma, and she remains in this vegetative state. It was determined that she was poisoned. The assistant is arrested and charged with attempted murder.

At the assistant's trial, the prosecution wishes to call the victim's secretary to testify to the victim's statement to him at the office before the ambulance arrived.

The court should find the statement:

(A) Admissible, because it is a dying declaration.

(B) Admissible, because it is a declaration of the victim's state of mind.

(C) Inadmissible, because dying declarations are never admissible unless the declarant is dead.

(D) Inadmissible, because it is hearsay not within any exception.

Question 76

The plaintiff sued the defendant, a computer dealer engaged in buying and selling used computers, alleging that he was not given credit for a DVR drive that he had on the computer that he had sent back for resale. The defendant's bookkeeper testified that it was company practice when a boxed computer was returned to have one clerk open the box and identify the type of computer and its components and have another clerk record the information in the inventory ledger. The defendant seeks to enter into evidence the original ledger entry, which the bookkeeper authenticated, showing that a DVR drive was not checked off on the components list for the plaintiff's computer. The plaintiff objects to the admission of the ledger.

The ledger is:

(A) Admissible, because it is a record of a transaction for which the bookkeeper does not have any present recollection.

(B) Admissible, because it was regular company practice to record receipt of the components in the inventory ledger.

(C) Inadmissible as hearsay within hearsay, because even if a hearsay exception permits introducing the record itself rather than requiring testimony by the employee who made it, that employee was just recording hearsay because he had no personal knowledge of what he was recording.

(D) Inadmissible hearsay, because absence of the notation implies a statement that no DVR return was received, and the evidence is being offered as proof of that assertion.

Question 162

The plaintiff sued the defendant dry cleaner, claiming that it had permanently ruined her $10,000 mink coat by cleaning it with a solvent that left an extremely offensive odor that smelled like "skunk." Further attempts to have the odor removed by other cleaning services were unsuccessful. The odor was so bad that she could no longer wear the coat.

At the trial, the plaintiff testified to the above facts. She then identified a mink coat as her coat that the defendant had ruined. She testified that it still smelled the same as it did after the defendant had cleaned it. The plaintiff's counsel offered to introduce the coat for the purpose of having the jury smell it. Defense counsel objected.

How should the court rule?

(A) The coat is admissible based on the plaintiff's testimony.

(B) The coat is admissible, but the plaintiff must first present extrinsic evidence sufficient to support a finding that the coat is the coat that she had cleaned by the defendant.

(C) The coat is not admissible because the plaintiff's testimony has not been impeached.

(D) The coat is not admissible because its limited probative value in resolving the case would be substantially outweighed by the prejudice that would result from the jury smelling the coat.

Question 141

In litigation over whether an uncle conveyed a parcel of land to his nephew, the nephew wishes to offer into evidence a tape recording of his uncle made by a well-known oral historian at the nearby state university. The voice on the tape is discussing various conveyances of the parcel of land and other property owned by the uncle. The nephew wishes to have the historian testify that the voice on the tape is the uncle's.

If the court allows the historian to testify, it will be because:

(A) The historian is testifying regarding an admission by a party-opponent.

(B) The historian has heard the uncle speak before.

(C) The historian became familiar with the uncle's voice before the dispute over the property arose.

(D) The historian's experience as an oral historian qualifies him as an expert in voice recognition.

Question 137

A balloonist sued the manufacturer of deflation panels for hot air balloons after one of the panels failed while his balloon was descending, causing the balloon to crash and the balloonist to suffer severe injuries. At trial, the balloonist calls as a witness a structural engineer, who testifies that, common to industry practice, her opinion is based on several reports done by an independent laboratory on the burst strength and material composition of the deflation panel closures. The balloonist's attorney then asks the engineer whether, in her opinion, the closures caused the deflation panel to give way. The manufacturer objects. Should the court admit this testimony?

(A) No, because the engineer did not perform the laboratory tests herself.

(B) No, because the laboratory reports are hearsay not within an exception.

(C) Yes, but the balloonist must offer into evidence the reports to which the engineer referred, so that the manufacturer may cross-examine as to them.

(D) Yes, because structural engineers reasonably rely on such reports in the course of their profession.

Question 138

The plaintiff sued the defendant, the owner of an art gallery, alleging that the defendant charged him a price higher than what was originally quoted to him for the purchase of a rare sculpture. During the plaintiff's testimony, he stated that he purchased the sculpture from the gallery on a particular date and then realized two days later that his credit card was charged in an amount over that which he was originally quoted by the defendant. During its defense, the defendant presented the testimony of the art gallery's clerk, who testifies that she remembers the plaintiff coming into the gallery and purchasing the sculpture a week before the date testified to by him, because he signed the purchase order with such an unusual signature. If the plaintiff objects to this testimony, should the trial court admit it?

(A) No, because the content of the purchase order is hearsay not within any exception.

(B) No, because the date of purchase is a collateral matter.

(C) Yes, because the purchase order is a past recollection recorded.

(D) Yes, because the clerk's testimony is relevant evidence as to the date the sculpture was purchased.

Question 58

The defendant is charged with having been one of two men who robbed a tavern and its patrons at gunpoint at 5:30 p.m. on December 16.

The defendant calls a witness to testify that he was at the defendant's house at about 9:30 a.m. on December 16, and that as he was leaving, the defendant said to him, "I'm going to my mother-in-law's house this afternoon for a birthday party."

Is the witness's testimony admissible?

(A) No, it is hearsay not within any exception.

(B) No, it is irrelevant.

(C) Yes, it is not being offered to prove the truth of the matter stated, so it is not hearsay.

(D) Yes, it is hearsay within an exception, and thus admissible.

Question 160

In January of 2007, the defendant proposed to his girlfriend. During the engagement, the defendant confided

in her about various drug deals in which he was participating. The woman swore that she would never reveal any
of his confidences. On January 1, 2008, the couple
married. The defendant continued to share with his wife
information concerning his illegal drug activity. The
wife's only rule was that he could not participate in any
illegal drug transactions in their home. On one occasion
in 2008, the wife came home unexpectedly and saw the
defendant completing a drug transaction in the living
room. The defendant was not aware that his wife had
observed the event. In 2009, the defendant was charged
with 57 counts of illegal drug sales that occurred between
2006 and 2009. The prosecutor wishes to call the defendant's wife as a witness for the state.

Assuming that the defendant's attorney makes appropriate objections, which of the following statements is
correct regarding testimony by the defendant's wife?

(A) She can testify about the defendant's 2008 statements if she desires.

(B) She must testify to the defendant's 2007 statements.

(C) The defendant can keep her from testifying about
his 2007 statements.

(D) She can testify to the drug sale that she observed in
2008 if she desires.

REAL PROPERTY

Question 18

A farmer died, devising his farm "to my wife for life, then to my son and my daughter in fee simple absolute." The wife occupied the farmhouse and operated the farm herself. After expenses of operation, the wife earned about $25,000 per year from the farm. Neither the son nor the daughter did anything to assist the wife with farm chores or expenses. The wife has consistently failed to pay the annual $2,000 county tax assessment and continues to refuse to pay it, despite threats from county tax collection authorities. With the taxes three years in arrears, the county has ordered a tax sale of the farm using proper procedures authorized by state law.

What are the rights and obligations of the parties?

(A)   The wife is personally liable for the taxes, but a tax sale will cut off the rights of the son and the daughter.

(B)   The son and the daughter are personally liable for the taxes if the wife does not pay them.

(C)   The daughter will have to pay one-half of the taxes if the son pays one-half.

(D)   The wife is personally liable for the taxes, and the tax sale will affect only her rights and not the rights of the son and the daughter.

Question 159

Thirty years ago, an owner deeded his land containing a general store to a merchant "for so long as tobacco is not sold on the premises." The deed was promptly and properly recorded. A few years later, the owner died, leaving his son as his only heir but devising "all of my interests in any real property" to his friend by a duly probated will. The next year, the friend conveyed "all of my interest in the general store and its land" to a purchaser by means of a quitclaim deed supported by valid consideration. The purchaser promptly and properly recorded the deed. Two months ago, the merchant began selling tobacco at the general store.

In a jurisdiction in which the common law Rule Against Perpetuities is unmodified by statute, who currently has title to the land and general store?

(A)   The son, because the friend received an executory interest that was void under the Rule Against Perpetuities.

(B)   The friend, because the interest she holds in the land is not transferable inter vivos.

(C)   The purchaser, because tobacco is being sold on the land.

(D)   The merchant, because no party has taken action to terminate her interest in the land.

Question 139

A landowner conveyed her 20-acre tract of land to a developer and his heirs, "provided that no multi-family dwellings may be built on the property for a period of 25 years. If such construction is undertaken, the grantor may terminate the conveyance and retake the land." Two years later the landowner died, leaving her nephew as the sole beneficiary under her will. Shortly thereafter, the nephew discovered that the developer was constructing multi-family dwellings on the land. He promptly brought an ejectment action against the developer. The jurisdiction in which the land is located has a statute providing that all future interests are freely devisable and alienable inter vivos. There are no other applicable statutes.

The court should rule that ownership of the land belongs to:

(A)   The nephew, because the developer began constructing multi-family dwellings on the land.

(B)   The nephew, because the developer began constructing multi-family dwellings on the land and the nephew brought an action for ejectment.

(C)   The developer, because the Rule Against Perpetuities applies.

(D)   The developer, because the restriction in the conveyance is an invalid restraint on alienation.

Question 182

A miner executed his will, bequeathing his property on which a gold mine was located "to my wife for life, remainder to my nephew." When the miner died, the gold mine was producing a net annual value of $100,000 in gold and had proven reserves valued at $2 million. Shortly after the miner's death, the nephew brings an action to enjoin the wife from operating the mine.

The injunction should be:

(A)   Granted, because the nephew has a vested remainder subject to partial divestment.

(B)   Granted, because the nephew has a vested remainder.

(C)   Denied, because the wife has a freehold estate.

(D)   Denied, because of the open mines doctrine.

Question 98

A lumberjack conveyed his forested land by deed "to my sister, her heirs, and assigns; but if my sister should

die without producing issue, then to the American Cancer Society." At the time of the conveyance, the forest produced a net annual value of $25,000 in timber and had proven reserves of $250,000. Shortly after the conveyance, the American Cancer Society brings an action to enjoin the sister from harvesting any more timber.

The court should rule in favor of:

(A) The American Cancer Society, because it has a contingent remainder.

(B) The American Cancer Society, because it has an executory interest.

(C) The sister, because she has a defeasible fee simple.

(D) The sister, because timber was being harvested prior to the lumberjack's conveyance.

Question 150

An owner devised his property by will to a friend "so long as one or more dogs are kept on the property; if dogs are no longer kept on the property, then to the American Society for the Prevention of Cruelty to Animals (ASPCA)." The will also provided that the residuary estate would go to the owner's niece.

In a jurisdiction that has not modified the common law Rule Against Perpetuities, what are the respective interests in the property on the owner's death?

(A) The friend has a fee simple subject to a condition subsequent and the niece has a right of entry.

(B) The friend has a fee simple determinable and the niece has a possibility of reverter.

(C) The friend has a fee simple determinable and the ASPCA has a remainder.

(D) The friend has a fee simple determinable subject to an executory interest and the ASPCA has a shifting executory interest.

Question 175

A landowner devised her land by will "to my husband for life, then to my nieces and nephews for life, then to the children of my nieces and nephews in fee simple." When the landowner died, she had one niece, who had a son. The husband died one year later. The following year, a nephew was born. At that time, the niece and her son were also alive. The jurisdiction's Rule Against Perpetuities is unmodified by statute.

What are the respective interests of the parties in the land at this point in time?

(A) The niece has a life estate, and the niece's son has a remainder.

(B) The niece has a life estate, and the landowner's heirs have a reversion.

(C) The niece and the nephew have a life estate, and the niece's son has a remainder.

(D) The niece and the nephew have a life estate, and the landowner's heirs have a reversion.

Question 25

A husband and a wife owned a parcel of land in joint tenancy. They conveyed a 10% interest in the land to their daughter. Six months later, they conveyed a 10% interest in the land to the daughter's husband, their son-in-law. The jurisdiction in which the land is located does not recognize tenancy by the entirety.

Which of the following best describes the ownership of the land after the conveyances?

(A) The husband and the wife have an 80% interest as joint tenants, the daughter has a 10% interest as a tenant in common, and the son-in-law has a 10% interest as a tenant in common.

(B) The husband and the wife have an 80% interest as tenants in common, the daughter has a 10% interest as a tenant in common, and the son-in-law has a 10% interest as a tenant in common.

(C) The husband and the wife have an 80% interest as tenants in common, and the daughter and the son-in-law have a 20% interest as joint tenants.

(D) The husband and the wife have an 80% interest as joint tenants, and the daughter and the son-in-law have a 20% interest as joint tenants.

Question 169

A parcel of property was devised to a husband and a wife "as joint tenants with right of survivorship" through the will of the husband's mother. After title had passed to them, the husband and the wife experienced marital difficulties and legally separated. Unbeknownst to the husband, the wife quitclaimed her interest in the property to a bona fide purchaser for value. Shortly thereafter, the husband and the wife reconciled. The next month, the wife was killed in an auto accident. The purchaser of the wife's interest filed a suit for partition of the property. The husband filed an appropriate counterclaim for quiet title, asserting that he was owner of the entire parcel by right of survivorship.

How should the court rule?

(A) For the purchaser, because he owns an undivided one-half interest in the property.

(B) For the purchaser, because the husband and the wife are presumed to have taken title from the mother as tenants in common under modern law.

(C) For the purchaser, because the husband and the wife were legally separated when he purchased his interest from the wife.

(D) For the husband, because he succeeded to the entire ownership when the wife died.

Question 114

A landlord entered into a 10-year lease of a building with an auctioneer, who planned to use the building itself for a storage area and the covered porch at the front of the building for auctions. A term in the auctioneer's lease stated, "Lessor agrees to maintain all structures on the property in good repair." Four years into the lease, the landlord sold the property to a buyer. The buyer did not agree to perform any obligations under the lease. As instructed, the auctioneer began paying rent to the buyer. In the fifth year of the lease, the porch roof began to leak. Citing the lease terms, the auctioneer asked the buyer to repair the roof. He continually refused to do so. The auctioneer finally repaired the roof herself at a cost of $2,000. The auctioneer then brought an appropriate lawsuit to recover the money.

Absent any other facts, the auctioneer is likely to recover:

(A) $2,000 from the landlord only, because the sale of the property did not sever his obligation to the auctioneer.

(B) $2,000 from the buyer only, because a covenant to repair runs with the land.

(C) $1,200 from the buyer and $800 from the landlord, because that represents their pro rata shares.

(D) $2,000 from either the buyer or the landlord, because they are both in privity with the auctioneer.

Question 129

A tenant entered into a written five-year lease to rent an office from a landlord for $6,000 per year beginning October 1. The lease required that rent in the amount of $500 be paid on or before the first of each month. Two months before the five-year term was up, the tenant received a new lease identical to the one he had already signed, except that the lease term began on the upcoming October 1 and the stated amount of rent per month was $600. The tenant returned the lease to the landlord unsigned, with a letter stating that he did not intend to renew the lease and would be moving out on September 30. The tenant did not move out on September 30. On October 1, the landlord received a check for $500 from the tenant. The notation on the check indicated that it was for the October rent. The landlord deposited the check in her account. She then sent a letter to the tenant stating that he was $100 in arrears in his rent. The tenant did not move out of the office during October, and the landlord did nothing to remove him.

Most courts would hold that the tenant has:

(A) A month-to-month tenancy at a rent of $500.

(B) A month-to-month tenancy at a rent of $600.

(C) A year-to-year tenancy at $500 per month.

(D) A year-to-year tenancy at $600 per month.

Question 132

A landowner leased a store to a grocer for a term of five years at $10,000 per year, payable in monthly installments. The lease permitted assignments and subleases. After occupying the premises for two years and paying the rent, the grocer transferred the remaining three years of the term to a florist. The agreement between the parties did not have a specific provision regarding payment of rent, instead just referring to the original lease provisions. The florist occupied the premises for two years but paid rent only for the first year. With one year left on the original lease, the florist transferred her leasehold interest to a barber. The barber occupied the premises for one year but did not pay any rent. The landowner brought an appropriate action against the grocer, the florist, and the barber to recover the rent.

Against whom may the landowner recover?

(A) The grocer and the florist jointly and severally for $10,000, and the grocer individually for $10,000.

(B) The grocer and the florist jointly and severally for $10,000, and the grocer and the barber jointly and severally for $10,000.

(C) The grocer and the florist jointly and severally for $10,000, and the grocer, the florist, and the barber jointly and severally for $10,000.

(D) The grocer and the florist jointly and severally for $20,000.

Question 46

An owner of three acres of lakefront property subdivided it and sold two acres to a buyer, retaining the one acre actually fronting on the lake. The deed for the two acres expressly included an easement over the westernmost 30 feet of the one-acre parcel retained by the owner for access to the lake. The buyer recorded his deed in the county recorder's office, which maintained an alphabetical grantor-grantee index only. Fifteen years later, the

owner died, leaving the one-acre parcel to his wife. She sold it to a developer that planned to build condominiums. A month later, the buyer died, and his two acres passed by will to his nephew. Three weeks after taking title to the property, the nephew visited the property and discovered that the developer had erected a chain link fence all along the boundary between the nephew's land and the acre of lakefront land. The nephew brings an action to enjoin the developer from obstructing his easement across the acre of lakefront property.

Which of the following best describes why the nephew should prevail in this litigation?

(A)   Because the developer and the nephew can trace their predecessors in interest to a common grantor whose covenants run with the land, the developer is estopped from interfering with the nephew's use of the easement.

(B)   The nephew's easement is a legal interest that the developer has record notice of, even though there is no tract index.

(C)   Because there is no tract index, the developer was under an obligation to determine the riparian rights of any adjacent landowners before erecting the chain link fence.

(D)   The nephew's easement is a legal interest that attaches not just to a legal estate but to the land itself and, running with the land, it binds successive owners of the servient estate whether or not they have notice of it.

Question 51

A landowner owns 15 acres of undeveloped property. He plans to build a stadium complex on the property to house a football team two years from now, but would like to open the 15 acres to public use for picnicking and similar activities until then.

Which of the following would best accomplish the landowner's goal?

(A)   Dedicate the 15 acres for use as a public park.

(B)   Lease the 15 acres to the city for two years.

(C)   Grant the city an easement for public recreational uses for two years.

(D)   Covenant that the city may use the 15 acres for recreation for two years.

Question 37

A developer owned several acres zoned for mixed use development. The developer prepared a subdivision of his various parcels, filed a subdivision map showing commercial lots, obtained all the necessary approvals, and began selling the lots. Each of the deeds conveying lots sold by the developer contained the following:

> It is hereby covenanted by the seller that the property conveyed shall be used for commercial or residential purposes only, that no industrial, warehouse, or other manufacturing structures shall be erected or maintained thereon, and that this covenant shall bind the buyer, his heirs and assigns, and their successors.

Two years later, after all but two of the lots had been developed as small businesses, the developer sold his remaining two lots to a real estate speculation firm. The deed to the firm did not contain any language restricting the use of the property. The firm then sold the property to a giant supermarket chain, which intended to construct a warehouse and distribution center thereon. A shopkeeper who had purchased a lot from the developer located next to the proposed warehouse brings suit against the supermarket chain seeking to enjoin construction of the warehouse. Her attorney argues that the lots sold by the developer to the firm and then to the supermarket chain are bound by the same restrictions on use that are contained in the deed by which the shopkeeper took her property.

The shopkeeper will likely:

(A)   Win, because the developer established a common development scheme for his entire subdivision and the subdivision appeared to conform to the scheme.

(B)   Lose, because the firm and the supermarket were not aware of the restrictions when they purchased the property.

(C)   Lose, because the restrictions in the shopkeeper's deed bind only the purchaser of the land.

(D)   Lose, because the deed by which the firm took the property from the developer did not contain any restrictions on use.

Question 168

A homeowner owned a parcel of land on which she built a single-family residence. To pay for the construction, she obtained financing from a bank in exchange for a mortgage on the land. The bank promptly and properly recorded its mortgage. When the house was completed, except for the absence of an oven in the kitchen, the homeowner leased the house to a tenant for a three-year term. There was no provision in the lease agreement regarding kitchen appliances. The tenant bought a professional-grade oven from an appliance company and had it installed in the space provided around the built-in cabinets in the kitchen. To make the purchase, the tenant signed a security agreement with the appliance company granting it a security interest in the oven in exchange for financing. The appliance company did not file or record its security interest in the oven.

By the end of the lease term, the homeowner was in serious default on her mortgage payments to the bank and the tenant was in serious default on his loan payments to the appliance company. In preparing foreclosure proceedings against the homeowner, the bank learned that the tenant was planning to remove the oven and take it with him when he moved out within the next few weeks. The bank filed an action against the tenant claiming ownership of the oven, and joined the homeowner and the appliance company as parties.

Which party has a superior claim to the oven?

(A)   The bank, because its mortgage interest attaches to all fixtures on the real estate and it has priority over the appliance company.

(B)   The tenant, because removal of the oven will not cause substantial damage to the real estate.

(C)   The homeowner, because the oven was annexed to the real estate after the mortgage was given.

(D)   The appliance company, because it has a valid security interest in the oven even though it was not recorded.

Question 42

A seller entered into an enforceable written agreement to sell her house to a buyer for $425,000. The agreement provided that closing would take place on September 18, and on that date the seller would provide marketable title, free and clear of all encumbrances. The agreement was silent as to risk of loss if the house was damaged prior to closing and as to any duty to carry insurance. On August 31, the seller cancelled her homeowners' insurance when she moved out of the house. Consequently, when the house was destroyed by wildfires on September 15, it was uninsured. The buyer refused to close on September 18 and the seller immediately brought an action against him for specific performance. The buyer countersued for the cancellation of the contract and return of his earnest money. Both parties stipulate that the value of the property without the house is $225,000.

In this jurisdiction, which has no applicable statute, the seller will most likely:

(A)   Prevail, but the price will be abated to $225,000.

(B)   Prevail for the full contract price.

(C)   Not prevail, because the seller had a duty to carry insurance until the closing date.

(D)   Not prevail, because the seller could not convey marketable title.

Question 145

A seller entered into a written contract to sell her land to a buyer for $200,000. Before the closing date, the buyer received the title search report, which indicated that a rancher conveyed the land to a farmer by quitclaim deed 25 years ago and that a landowner conveyed the land to the seller by warranty deed 13 years ago. The buyer notified the seller that the records did not indicate how the land was conveyed to the landowner (the seller's immediate transferor), and that the buyer was concerned about this. The seller replied that she had no knowledge of the matter but would look into it. At the date and time appointed for closing, the seller informed the buyer that she could not locate the landowner or obtain any information as to the conveyance of the land to him. On hearing this, the buyer refused to tender the purchase money, and told the seller that he was rescinding the contract. The seller sued the buyer for specific performance.

Which party is more likely to prevail?

(A)   The seller, because land is unique and therefore a proper subject for a specific performance action.

(B)   The seller, because she took title from the landowner by warranty deed.

(C)   The buyer, because there is a gap in the title.

(D)   The buyer, because the seller cannot supply marketable title.

Question 13

An owner purchased a parcel of property adjoining a five-foot-wide strip, which was a private right-of-way. Unsure where the exact boundaries of her property were located, the owner planted a garden on the five-foot right-of-way strip and enclosed it with a wire fence two weeks after taking up occupancy. The owner maintained the fence and garden for 20 years, at which time she removed the fence and smoothed out the ground where the garden had been located. Five years later, the owner entered into a written contract to sell the property to a buyer. The description in the contract included the five-foot strip. After research in the county recorder's office, the buyer discovered that the strip was a private right-of-way when the owner purchased the property. After properly notifying the owner of the problem prior to closing, the buyer refused to tender the purchase money to the owner when the closing day arrived. The owner sued the buyer for specific performance of the real estate sales contract. The jurisdiction's statutory adverse possession period is 15 years.

Who will prevail?

(A) The buyer, because the owner failed to provide a marketable title.

(B) The buyer, because the owner surrendered her adverse possession rights when she removed the fence, as her possession was no longer open, notorious, and continuous.

(C) The buyer, because one may not adversely possess a right-of-way.

(D) The owner, because she held the right-of-way for a longer time than the minimum required by the state adverse possession statute.

Question 97

A landowner and his neighbor owned adjoining tracts of land. The boundary line between the two properties was never properly determined or clearly known. Twenty-five years ago, the landowner installed a gas-powered generator on land he thought he owned, but which was in fact owned by the neighbor. The generator was housed in a small shed and surrounded by a fence. Ten years later, the neighbor was found to be mentally incompetent. She died last year, and her executor filed suit to eject the landowner and quiet title. The statute of limitations in ejectment is 20 years.

With respect to the land on which the generator was installed:

(A) The landowner cannot claim title by adverse possession because the statute of limitations was tolled by the neighbor's incompetency.

(B) The landowner cannot claim title by adverse possession because his occupation was not under claim of right.

(C) The landowner has acquired title by adverse possession.

(D) The landowner has acquired a prescriptive easement.

Question 183

A homeowner and her neighbor purchased adjoining parcels of property 20 years ago. During the summer months, the homeowner ran electrical wires from her home to a guest house across land she knew belonged to the neighbor. The neighbor orally consented to the wiring's crossing his land. Two years ago, the neighbor sold his property to a purchaser. The following summer, the homeowner tried to run the wires across the purchaser's land, but the purchaser objected. The statute of limitations in ejectment is 15 years.

With respect to the land over which the electrical wires were laid:

(A) The homeowner has acquired title by adverse possession.

(B) The homeowner has acquired a prescriptive easement.

(C) The homeowner cannot claim any right on title because her use of the land in question was not continuous.

(D) The homeowner cannot claim any right on title because the neighbor consented to her use of the land for the wires.

Question 111

An uncle validly executed a deed conveying his beach house to his nephew, and then validly recorded the deed. When the nephew, who was experiencing financial difficulties, learned of the recordation of the deed, he immediately told his uncle that he did not want the beach house and could not accept such an expensive gift anyway. Later, the nephew filed for bankruptcy and the trustee in bankruptcy asserted an ownership interest in the beach house on behalf of the debtor's estate. The bankruptcy court ruled that the property belonged to the uncle and not to the nephew, and thus was not part of the debtor's estate subject to distribution.

Which of the following is the strongest reason in support of the bankruptcy court's ruling?

(A) There was no presumption of delivery created by recordation of the deed because the nephew did not know of the recordation.

(B) The nephew's statements to the uncle were a constructive reconveyance of the property.

(C) There was never an effective acceptance of delivery of the deed by the nephew.

(D) The recordation of the deed was invalid because it was done without the nephew's permission.

Question 185

A vendor entered into a written contract with a purchaser for the sale of a large tract of land. The contract set forth an accurate metes and bounds description of the land based on a professional survey. At closing, the purchaser discovered that the deed was incorrectly transcribed and did not agree with the description of the land in the contract. The deed described the property to be conveyed as follows:

(i) from the southwest corner of [a specified starting point], proceed South 45 degrees East 200 feet to [a specified point]; (ii) from that point, proceed South 45 degrees West 100 feet to [a specified point]; (iii) from that

point, proceed North 45 degrees West 200 feet to [a specified point]; and (iv) from that point, proceed South 45 degrees East 100 feet to the starting point.

The purchaser refused to proceed with the closing and brought an action to reform the deed to make it conform to the intention of the parties.

Which of the following corrections should be made for the deed to properly describe the land?

(A) Direction (i) should be changed to "South 45 degrees East 100 feet."

(B) Direction (iii) should be changed to "North 45 degrees West 100 feet."

(C) Direction (iii) should be changed to "North 45 degrees East 200 feet."

(D) Direction (iv) should be changed to "North 45 degrees East 100 feet."

Question 78

A buyer entered into a contract with a seller to purchase the seller's farm. The contract of sale referred to the farm as containing 250 acres. The agreed-on price was $1 million. Before the date on which escrow was to close, the buyer learned from a surveyor he had hired that the farm actually contained 248 acres. On the date the sale was to close, the buyer instructed the escrow agent to release all but $8,000 of the purchase money because he was not getting what he bargained for. The seller refused to proceed with the sale. The buyer brings an action for specific performance and also seeks a reduction of the agreed-upon contract price.

What will be the probable outcome of the litigation?

(A) The seller will win, because the buyer refused to tender the contract price when the seller tendered substantially what the contract called for her to perform.

(B) The seller will win, because both parties had seen the farm before the contract was formed.

(C) The buyer will win, because he is not receiving what he bargained for under the contract.

(D) The buyer will win, because the difference of two acres is material and the $8,000 reduction in price is not an excessive variance from the parties' agreement.

Question 149

A father conveyed his property to his son and daughter "as joint tenants with right of survivorship, but if they ever attempt to sell the property during their lifetimes, a right of first refusal based on the sale price is hereby granted to my sister." Unbeknownst to the son or the sister, the daughter quitclaimed her interest in the property to a purchaser. The following month, the daughter was killed in a snowmobile accident. The purchaser of the daughter's interest filed a suit for partition of the property. The son filed an appropriate counterclaim for quiet title, asserting that he was the owner of the entire parcel. The sister also filed a counterclaim, asserting that her right of first refusal was valid and that she was prepared to exercise her option to purchase the property for the contract price.

In a jurisdiction in which the Rule Against Perpetuities is unmodified by statute, how should the court rule?

(A) For the purchaser, because the right of first refusal is invalid as an unreasonable restraint on alienation.

(B) For the son, because he succeeded to the entire ownership when the daughter died.

(C) For the son, because the right of first refusal violates the Rule Against Perpetuities.

(D) For the sister, because she has a valid right of first refusal.

Question 112

An aunt executed and delivered a valid warranty deed conveying her home to her niece as a gift. The niece did not record the deed. Two years later, the aunt was involved in an auto accident. She had allowed her auto insurance to lapse and the other driver's insurance company obtained a judgment against her for $100,000, which it recorded.

A statute in the jurisdiction provides: "Any judgment properly filed shall, for 10 years from filing, be a lien on the real property then owned or subsequently acquired by any person against whom the judgment is rendered."

When the aunt died five years later, her will left all of her property to the niece. The insurance company filed a claim in probate against the estate for $100,000. The niece, as executrix, seeks a determination from the probate court that the home is not part of the aunt's estate, having already been conveyed to the niece.

The court should rule that the home is:

(A) Part of the estate and must be utilized to satisfy the $100,000 claim.

(B) Part of the estate, but is not subject to the $100,000 claim.

(C) Not part of the estate and thus is not subject to the claim.

(D) Not part of the estate, but is nevertheless subject to a $100,000 lien in favor of the insurance company.

Question 26

A homeowner borrowed $50,000 from a bank, secured by a mortgage on his home. Shortly thereafter, the homeowner sold his home to a buyer for $70,000 by a deed containing a recital signed by both parties that title passed "subject to" the bank's mortgage, "which obligation grantee expressly assumes." The buyer paid the homeowner $20,000, took possession of the house, and began making monthly payments of principal and interest to the bank. A few years later, a chemical manufacturing firm built a huge sulfur processing plant just down the road from the home, which caused the house to immediately decline in value to $35,000. Subsequently, the buyer stopped making the monthly payments to the bank. The bank exercised its contractual right of nonjudicial foreclosure and sold the house at a public auction for $34,000. The bank then brought suit against the homeowner and the buyer for $14,000, the difference between the proceeds of the foreclosure sale and the $48,000 principal remaining due on the original loan to the homeowner. The jurisdiction does not bar deficiency judgments.

The bank should be granted a judgment for $14,000 against:

(A) Both the homeowner and the buyer.

(B) Only the homeowner.

(C) Only the buyer.

(D) No one.

Question 4

A landowner sold a parcel of land to an investor for $100,000. The investor did not record the deed, and left the country for an extended trip. The landowner, seeing an opportunity to make a quick profit, partitioned the parcel of land and sold the front half to a friend in exchange for $50,000. The friend, who knew nothing about the investor's interest in the property, promptly recorded his interest. Two months later, the friend sold the front parcel to a buyer in exchange for $55,000. The buyer was aware of the investor's interest in the property but recorded his deed to the front parcel anyway. Meanwhile, the landowner executed a mortgage on the back half of the property to a bank in the amount of $40,000. The bank knew nothing of the landowner's transaction with the investor but neglected to record its mortgage interest. Six months later, the investor returned home and recorded her deed to the parcel of land.

A statute in the jurisdiction provides: "Any conveyance of an estate in land, other than a lease for less than one year, shall not be valid against any subsequent purchaser for value, without notice, unless the conveyance is recorded."

If the investor brings an action to quiet title in the parcel of land, a court will likely determine that her claim to the land is:

(A) Superior to the landowner's rights in the back half and the buyer's rights in the front half, and not subject to the bank's mortgage on the back half.

(B) Superior to the landowner's rights in the back half, inferior to the buyer's rights in the front half, and subject to the bank's mortgage on the back half.

(C) Superior to the landowner's rights in the back half, inferior to the buyer's rights in the front half, and not subject to the bank's mortgage on the back half.

(D) Superior to the landowner's rights in the back half and the buyer's rights in the front half, but subject to the bank's mortgage on the back half.

Question 30

In January, an owner executed and delivered a mortgage on her property to a bank to secure a $50,000 loan. Due to a clerical error, the mortgage was not recorded at that time. On February 15, the owner entered into a contract to sell the property to a buyer for $150,000. On February 16, the owner took out a $30,000 mortgage on the property with a finance company. The finance company promptly and properly recorded its mortgage. Knowing nothing about either of the mortgages, the buyer closed on the property on April 1, tendering $150,000 to the owner. The owner gave the buyer a warranty deed to the property. On April 3, the bank discovered its error and properly recorded its mortgage that same day. The buyer recorded his deed to the property on April 6.

A statute of the jurisdiction in which the property is located provides: "No conveyance or mortgage of real property shall be valid against a subsequent purchaser for value and without notice whose conveyance is first recorded." The bank brings an appropriate action to determine the status of its mortgage on the property.

The court should hold that:

(A) The buyer holds the property subject to both mortgages, and the bank's mortgage is subordinate to the finance company's mortgage.

(B) The buyer holds the property subject to both mortgages, and the bank's mortgage is superior to the finance company's mortgage.

(C) The buyer holds the property subject only to the finance company's mortgage.

(D) The buyer holds the property subject only to the bank's mortgage.

Question 55

A buyer entered into a contract with a seller to buy a parcel of land for $40,000. Although the buyer was expecting to receive a large inheritance in a few weeks, he had very limited funds on hand and was able to personally finance only $10,000. To cover the remaining balance, the buyer obtained a loan from the seller for $30,000, giving the seller a promissory note in that amount secured by a mortgage on the land and orally promising to pay the seller in full when he received his inheritance money. A few weeks later, the seller negotiated the mortgage note to an investor for $25,000 without informing the buyer. The next day, the seller received a check from the buyer in the amount of $30,000. A few days later, the seller left the country with the $65,000 she had made on the sale of the land. The jurisdiction permits deficiency judgments.

If a foreclosure action is instituted by the investor, which of the following correctly states his rights against the buyer?

(A) The investor has no enforceable interest in the land and no rights against the buyer because the seller did not transfer the mortgage to him and the buyer paid the mortgage amount in full.

(B) The investor has an enforceable interest in the land to the extent of $25,000, but cannot recover against the buyer personally for any deficiency.

(C) The investor has an enforceable interest in the land to the extent of $30,000, but cannot recover against the buyer personally for any deficiency.

(D) The investor has an enforceable interest in the land to the extent of $30,000, and can recover against the buyer personally for any deficiency.

Question 56

A driver borrowed $75,000 from a bank to purchase a tract of land on which to operate his trucking company, securing the debt with a mortgage on the land. The bank promptly and properly recorded its mortgage. A few years later, the driver financed the installation of a truck wash on the land with a $50,000 loan from a finance company, secured by a mortgage on the land. The finance company promptly and properly recorded its mortgage. The driver subsequently defaulted on the bank's mortgage, leaving an outstanding balance on the bank's loan of $60,000. However, the driver continued to make payments to the finance company. The bank brought a foreclosure action,

joining the finance company in the proceeding. The jurisdiction provides a statutory right of redemption for lienholders.

Does the finance company have any recourse prior to the foreclosure sale to protect its interest?

(A) Yes, the finance company may pay off the bank's mortgage to preserve its own interest on the land.

(B) Yes, it can exercise its statutory right of redemption.

(C) No, because the driver has not defaulted on the finance company's mortgage.

(D) No, because only the mortgagor holds the right to redeem the property.

Question 176

A buyer purchased a parcel of property from a seller for $100,000, financing the purchase with a loan from the seller secured by a mortgage on the property. The seller promptly and properly recorded his mortgage. Shortly thereafter, the buyer obtained a loan from a credit union for remodeling secured by a mortgage on the property. The credit union promptly and properly recorded its mortgage. One year later, the buyer obtained a home equity loan from a bank secured by a mortgage on the property. The bank promptly and properly recorded its mortgage. A few months later, the buyer stopped making payments on the debt owed to the credit union. With proper notice to all parties, the credit union brought an action to foreclose on its mortgage. At that time, the buyer owed $20,000 on the seller's mortgage, $25,000 on the credit union's mortgage, and $30,000 on the bank's mortgage. At the foreclosure sale, the property was sold for $45,000. The jurisdiction in which the property is located permits deficiency judgments.

After the $25,000 debt owed to the credit union is satisfied from the proceeds, which of the following statements is most correct?

(A) The seller's mortgage and the bank's mortgage are both reduced by $10,000 and remain on the property.

(B) The seller's mortgage is satisfied in full and extinguished, while the bank's mortgage remains on the property.

(C) The seller's mortgage remains on the property, while the bank's mortgage is reduced by $20,000 and extinguished, leaving the buyer personally liable to the bank for the deficiency of $10,000.

(D) The seller's mortgage is satisfied in full and extinguished, and the bank's mortgage is also extinguished, leaving the buyer personally liable to the bank for the deficiency of $30,000.

Question 66

A landowner owned an undeveloped parcel of land, through which a creek ran. The creek also ran through his neighbor's downstream parcel. The neighbor drew off water from the creek to irrigate her crops and to water her livestock. The neighbor's use of her parcel and the creek water has been continuous and uninterrupted for 18 years. Two years ago, the landowner constructed a residence on his parcel and began to draw off the waters of the creek for his domestic use. The following summer, there was adequate water in the creek for all of the landowner's domestic purposes and for all of the neighbor's agricultural purposes. However, the flow of the creek is irregular and the water level dropped dramatically this summer. The amount of water in the creek is sufficient to meet either all of the neighbor's needs and none of the landowner's or all of the landowner's needs and one-half of the neighbor's. Both the landowner and the neighbor file suit, claiming they are entitled to sufficient water from the creek to meet all their respective needs. The jurisdiction in which the parcels are located has a statutory 10-year prescription and adverse possession period, and follows the riparian doctrine of reasonable use.

In the resulting trial of the case, who will prevail?

(A) The neighbor, because she has a prior reasonable use of the water.

(B) The neighbor, because she is entitled to the water by prescription.

(C) The landowner, because his use of the water does not totally deprive the neighbor of water for her needs.

(D) The landowner, because the neighbor's use of the water is not a natural use.

TORTS

Question 45

A logger was confronted by a protester who called him "a moronic treekiller." The logger warned the protester to leave and swung his axe as if to strike her, intending to frighten her away. Unfortunately, the manufacturer of the axe had neglected to insert a metal pin that secured the axe handle to the blade, and the blade had become loosened from previous chopping. Consequently, the blade flew off the handle and struck and injured the protester.

If the protester brings an action for battery against the logger, will she recover?

(A) No, because the logger did not intend to cause harm to the protester.

(B) No, because the defective axe was the cause in fact of the protester's injuries.

(C) Yes, because the logger intended to frighten the protester.

(D) Yes, because the protester provoked the logger.

Question 92

A patient was scheduled to undergo nonemergency surgery for the removal of her appendix by her family doctor. The day of the surgery, the doctor was called out of town because of a family illness. Even though the surgery could be postponed, the doctor asked the surgeon on call, who was an expert in appendectomies, to take his place. The patient was not informed of the switch in doctors.

If the patient sues the surgeon on a battery theory, who will prevail?

(A) The patient, as long as she establishes damages at trial.

(B) The patient, regardless of whether she establishes damages at trial.

(C) The surgeon, because he was at least as qualified as the doctor.

(D) The surgeon, because the doctor requested that the surgeon take his place.

Question 64

A shopper headed out of a store at the same time as a shoplifter, whose stolen items triggered the store's inventory control alarm. A security guard at the exit requested that the shopper stop so that his bags could be checked, but the shopper said he was in a hurry and did not want to wait. The guard then requested that the

shopper immediately step to the side, and pulled out a pair of handcuffs as she reached for his arm. On seeing the handcuffs, the shopper agreed to step over to the side and wait.

If the shopper is not successful in an assault action against the store, it will be because:

(A) The shopper suffered no injury from the guard's actions.

(B) The guard did not intend to injure the shopper when she pulled out the handcuffs and reached for the shopper's arm.

(C) The guard acted reasonably in dealing with a suspected shoplifter.

(D) A reasonable person would have complied with the guard's initial request.

Question 65

A security officer employed by a mall was patrolling the mall parking lot which had suffered numerous thefts from cars when she heard a car alarm go off. She then saw a teenager stand up from behind the car. She immediately stopped the teenager and asked him what he was doing behind the car, and he said he was tying his shoe. Reasonably suspecting that he may have been trying to break into the car, she asked him to wait in the back seat of her car. The teenager complied, and waited in the back of the car while the security officer ate her lunch in the front seat and made a variety of personal calls. The teenager was humiliated because several of his friends and their parents, as well as some neighbors, saw him sitting in the security officer's car. Finally, after about an hour, the officer let the teenager go and advised him not to loiter in the parking lot anymore.

If the teenager brings a false imprisonment action against the mall, will he be able to recover for the humiliation that he felt on sitting in the security officer's car in view of his friends and neighbors?

(A) No, humiliation is not actionable.

(B) No, because the security officer reasonably suspected that he was trying to break into a car.

(C) Yes, if the jury determines that the security officer's conduct was extreme and outrageous.

(D) Yes, because he was falsely imprisoned.

Question 9

A homeowner who regularly borrowed garden tools from his neighbor went to the neighbor's house to borrow

the neighbor's leaf blower. The neighbor was not at home, but the leaf blower was in his unlocked garage with his other garden tools, and so the homeowner took it. Unbeknownst to the homeowner, the neighbor had drained the oil from the leaf blower's motor. The homeowner ran the leaf blower for an hour; the motor was totally destroyed because it had no oil.

The value of the leaf blower at the time that the homeowner took it was $300. An identical, new leaf blower costs $500. The cost of repairing the motor is $150. A new motor will cost $250.

If the neighbor sues the homeowner on a theory of conversion and is successful, he is entitled to:

(A) $300, but the homeowner will keep the leaf blower.

(B) $500, but the homeowner will keep the leaf blower.

(C) $150.

(D) $250.

Question 79

A strawberry farmer held his farm open to the public to pick strawberries for a fee. The farmer knew that many patrons would eat as many strawberries out in the field as they would bring home with them, so he advertised that no chemical pesticides or fertilizers were used on his strawberries. The owner of the land adjacent to the farm began operating a soap factory, a use allowed by the zoning code. Flakes of an unavoidable chemical byproduct of the soap-making process would drift over onto the farm whenever the wind was blowing in that direction and settle onto the strawberry plants. The flakes caused no harm to the plants themselves but detracted from the appearance of the strawberries as well as their taste if eaten right off the plant; consequently, the farmer's business declined. On several occasions, the farmer complained to the factory owner, but the owner did nothing, in part because a visit to the county recorder of deeds office had convinced him that he was the true owner of a large part of the strawberry farm, although in fact it was just a recording error.

Can the farmer recover damages for the harm caused to his business from the factory owner?

(A)   Yes, because the discharge from the owner's factory entered the farmer's land.

(B)   Yes, because the factory owner intended to conduct the activities that caused the particles to fall on the farmer's land.

(C)   No, because the factory owner had no intent to cause harm to the farmer's property.

(D)   No, because the factory owner's belief that he owned the property, although erroneous, was reasonable.

Question 165

A motorist was driving his expensive sports car down a two-lane road at 90 m.p.h. in a heavy rainstorm. Just after cresting a hill, the motorist observed a large tree that had been hit by lightning and was blocking the highway. To avoid hitting the tree, the motorist drove off the road and onto a landowner's property. In so doing, the motorist destroyed the landowner's mailbox and flower bed.

If the landowner sues the motorist for damages to his mailbox and flower bed, he will:

(A)   Prevail, because the jury will likely find that the motorist was not exercising due care.

(B)   Prevail, regardless of whether the motorist was exercising due care.

(C)   Not prevail, because the motorist was acting under necessity when he drove onto the landowner's property.

(D)   Not prevail, because even though the motorist was exceeding the speed limit, the tree in the road was an act of God, and a superseding intervening cause.

Question 188

A woman chastised her roommate when she saw that neither the roommate nor her boyfriend wore a helmet when they rode on the boyfriend's motorcycle. The roommate said that helmets were too restricting. The woman's brother had died in a motorcycle accident because he had not worn a helmet, so she decided to do something to make a lasting impression on her roommate. She called her roommate at work one day and left a message that her boyfriend was in a motorcycle accident and was in the hospital on life support. The roommate was very upset when she got the message and left immediately for the hospital. When she found out later that the message was not true, she became even more upset.

If the roommate brings an action against the woman to recover for her emotional distress, is she likely to prevail?

(A)   Yes, because it was foreseeable that the roommate would suffer severe emotional distress.

(B)   Yes, because the woman knew that there was a high likelihood that the roommate would suffer severe emotional distress.

(C)   No, because it does not appear that the roommate suffered physical injury from her distress.

(D) No, because the roommate and her boyfriend were not related.

Question 153

An American tourist was visiting another country when he was warned by United States health authorities to go immediately to a hospital because he had a serious and extremely contagious disease that required him to be quarantined. He decided to ignore the warning and instead traveled on an airline flight back to the United States. Despite the tourist's belief that he would not be discovered and his best efforts to keep a low profile, the news media were tipped off to what he had done and publicized it. When a passenger who had been sitting next to the tourist on the plane learned about it, she became extremely upset, fearing that she would contract the disease. The passenger brought a negligence action to recover for the distress she suffered.

If the passenger does not prevail, it will be because:

(A) The tourist's conduct was not extreme and outrageous.

(B) The passenger did not suffer physical injury from her distress.

(C) The passenger did not contract the disease from the tourist.

(D) The tourist could not have reasonably foreseen that the other passengers would find out about what he had done.

Question 11

A patient had been taking a prescribed anti-seizure medicine, which had prevented him from having seizures while he had been taking it, but which had caused unpleasant side effects. His physician gradually weaned the patient off the medicine. One year later, the patient was driving when he suddenly suffered a seizure and lost control of his car, which crashed into the car in front of him. The driver of that car suffered serious injuries and sued the patient and the physician.

If the physician is not liable to the driver, it will be because:

(A) It was not reasonably foreseeable that removing the patient from medication could cause harm to third parties.

(B) The physician warned the patient about driving once he was off the medication.

(C) Given the side effects, it was medically reasonable to take the patient off of the medicine.

(D) The patient was judged not liable to the driver.

Question 12

A motorist lapsed into unconsciousness while driving. Her car crossed the center line, which was marked with a double yellow line. A statute made it illegal for any person operating a motor vehicle on the highways of the state to cross a double yellow line. The motorist's car collided with another vehicle, and the driver of that vehicle was seriously injured. The driver sued the motorist for his injuries. At trial, the parties stipulated to the above facts. The motorist testified that she had not previously lapsed into unconsciousness while driving. At the close of the evidence, the driver moved for a directed verdict in his favor.

The court should:

(A) Grant the motion, because the motorist's vehicle crossed into the driver's lane and caused the driver's injuries.

(B) Grant the motion, because the driver has established negligence per se from the violation of an applicable statute that was intended to prevent the type of harm that occurred.

(C) Deny the motion, because the jury could find that the motorist had no reason to believe that she would lapse into unconsciousness.

(D) Deny the motion, because it was impossible for the motorist to comply with the statute.

Question 7

A landowner who had owned and operated a small airport notified the electric company that he was discontinuing operations and that it should shut down the electrical current that had supplied his communications equipment. The equipment was surrounded by a fence with signs warning of high voltage. Because the electric company maintained a transformer next to the landowner's communications equipment that contained many valuable and reusable parts, it decided to leave the power on to prevent theft until it could schedule removal of the transformer. Three days later, a trespasser who knew that the airport had closed went onto the property looking for something to steal. He could find nothing of value except the transformer. He noticed the signs warning of the high voltage but believed that the power had since been turned off. He scaled the fence with the intent to dismantle the transformer. As soon as he touched the transformer, he was seriously injured by the electric current.

If the trespasser asserts a claim against the electric company to recover damages for his injuries, the trespasser will:

(A) Prevail, because the electric company was not the owner of the land on which the trespasser trespassed.

(B) Prevail, because the electric company used unreasonable force to protect its property.

(C) Not prevail, because the trespasser was a trespasser on the landowner's land.

(D) Not prevail, because the trespasser intended to steal the electric company's transformer.

Question 166

A state statute prohibits leaving a child under the age of five years unattended in an automobile. A mother parked her car at a supermarket parking lot. She left her four-year-old son in the car with his seatbelt fastened while she did her grocery shopping. While the mother was shopping, the son undid his seatbelt, left the car, and started riding on the grocery carts that customers had left in the parking lot. The son crashed one of the carts into another shopper's car, causing damage. The shopper brought a negligence action against the mother to recover for the damage caused by the son. At trial, the shopper presented evidence of the statute and the facts stated above. At the conclusion of the shopper's case, the mother moved for a directed verdict in her favor.

Should the court grant the mother's motion?

(A) No, because the shopper has established negligence per se based on the mother's violation of the statute.

(B) No, because the jury could find that it was foreseeable that the son would cause damage to cars in the parking lot if the mother left him unattended.

(C) Yes, because the shopper has not presented evidence that the statute was designed to prevent children from causing damage to the cars of other customers.

(D) Yes, because a parent is not vicariously liable for the negligence of her child.

Question 84

A backpacker came upon another hiker who had been bitten by a rattlesnake. The backpacker carried the bitten hiker back to his vehicle and drove him toward the nearest hospital. On the way there, while exceeding the posted speed limit, the backpacker lost control of his vehicle and crashed into a tree by the side of the road. He was uninjured, but the snakebitten hiker's leg was broken. An ambulance soon arrived and took the hiker to the hospital. The emergency room physician committed malpractice that resulted in the loss of the hiker's leg. The hiker is now suing the backpacker.

Which of the following is the most likely reason why the backpacker will be held liable for the hiker's injuries?

(A) Having undertaken to rescue the hiker, the backpacker is strictly liable for injuries resulting from the rescue.

(B) The emergency room physician's malpractice is a foreseeable intervening cause that does not relieve the backpacker of liability.

(C) The backpacker did not conduct himself as a reasonably prudent person in carrying out the rescue of the hiker.

(D) The backpacker committed negligence per se when he exceeded the posted speed limit.

Question 95

An off-duty mall security guard was at a bar with his girlfriend when he got into an argument with another patron. The argument escalated and the guard drew out the pistol he had been given at work and shot the patron in the chest, killing him. The survivors of the dead patron brought a wrongful death action against the security agency that hired the guard. At trial, they established that the guard had been required to fill out an application listing references and indicating whether he had any prior convictions for offenses involving violence or use of a weapon, which would disqualify him by law from a position as a security officer. The guard had listed as references some aunts and uncles who had not seen him in some time, and he stated that he had no prior convictions. In fact, the guard had several times been convicted of violent assaults using firearms, and records of these convictions were available in a public database. The agency, however, had not investigated the statements on his application.

The survivors will likely:

(A) Prevail, because a reasonable employer would have discovered the guard's prior convictions.

(B) Prevail, because the agency employed the guard and gave him the pistol he used to kill the patron.

(C) Not prevail, because the agency owed no duty to the patron which was violated.

(D) Not prevail, because the guard's actions occurred while he was acting outside the scope of his employment.

Question 104

A patient went to a dermatologist for treatment of a skin condition on his face that had resisted standard treatment. The dermatologist prescribed a new topical antibiotic cream that was recommended by her associate. She gave the patient instructions on how and when to

apply the cream but did not discuss potential side effects. The patient purchased the cream at his local pharmacy and applied it as instructed. Shortly thereafter his skin turned a distinct shade of green and he felt a strong burning sensation when he tried to wash it off. The color took almost a week to fade away, during which time he avoided going out in public and took time off from work.

The cream was packaged with a lengthy printed insert that listed a number of possible side effects of varying degrees of probability. A "green pallor" and "irritation" were listed as uncommon side effects. The patient sued the dermatologist for prescribing the medicine and established the above facts. He also testified that he would not have taken the medicine had he been informed of all of the potential side effects.

If the patient does not prevail, it will be because:

(A) A reasonable person in the patient's position would have used the cream even when told of the potential side effects.

(B) The printed insert that came with the cream listed possible side effects similar to the reaction the patient experienced.

(C) The severity of the reaction the patient experienced was unforeseeable.

(D) The jurisdiction does not apply a "national" standard of care to specialists.

Question 133

A 12-year-old boy took his radio-controlled model airplane to the park to show his friends the stunts he could do with it. The weather that day was rainy, and the instruction manual for the plane warned against flying it in the rain, but the boy was able to get the plane off of the ground. However, because of the rain, he had trouble controlling it with the transmitter. He tried to have the plane make a loop but it veered off course and crashed through the fabric roof of a convertible, which was parked nearby on the street.

If the car owner sues the boy for damages to his car and prevails, it will be because:

(A) A child of the boy's age, education, intelligence, and experience would not have flown the airplane that day.

(B) A reasonable person would not have flown the airplane that day.

(C) The airplane instruction manual warned against flying in the rain.

(D) The boy committed a trespass to chattel with his airplane.

Question 115

A resort maintained an outside bar adjacent to its pool. When the bar was closed, it was secured by a metal gate that reached up towards the roof of the bar, but which left about a three-foot gap between the top of the gate and the roof. The resort had installed motion detectors inside the bar linked to an alarm system because of several previous thefts of liquor by persons climbing over the gate. Late one night, an intoxicated guest of the resort who wanted to keep partying after hours began to climb over the gate to get into the bar through the gap at the top, intending to take some bottles of wine. The brackets attaching the gate to the walls, which had been gradually deteriorating and pulling away from the walls for some time, suddenly gave way as he reached the top. The gate collapsed, causing him to fall back onto the concrete patio. He sustained a severe concussion and other serious injuries.

If the guest sues the resort for his injuries, is he likely to prevail?

(A) No, because the guest did not have invitee status when he was climbing over the gate.

(B) No, because the guest intended to steal alcohol belonging to the resort.

(C) Yes, because the resort operators were aware that persons had climbed over the gate in the past.

(D) Yes, because the brackets attaching the gate to the walls were in a weakened condition that could have been detected by a routine inspection.

Question 86

A passenger on a commuter train left his seat to go to the lavatory at the front of the car. While he was in the aisle, the car moved across intersecting tracks, causing the car to rock. He stumbled and bumped his knee against the lavatory door, aggravating a preexisting circulation problem in his leg that had been controlled by medication. As a result, he had to have several surgeries to correct the circulation problem.

The passenger brought suit to recover damages against the agency that operated the train system. At the jury trial, the following evidence was presented: The passenger testified as to how he was injured and introduced evidence of his medical expenses. His physician testified that the bump aggravated the circulation problem. The engineer of the train testified that the train had not been exceeding the speed limit for that stretch of track, and the agency introduced a report indicating that a subsequent inspection disclosed no problems with the track. The agency also presented uncontroverted evidence that a person in normal health would not have been injured by

the bump. At the close of the evidence, the agency moved for a directed verdict.

The court should:

(A) Grant the motion, because there is no evidence that the agency or its employees operated the train negligently.

(B) Grant the motion, because the agency established that a person in normal health would not have been injured by the bump.

(C) Deny the motion, because the jury could find that the agency, as a common carrier, breached its high duty of care to its passenger.

(D) Deny the motion, because the fact that the severity of the passenger's injuries was not foreseeable does not cut off the agency's liability.

Question 101

A petroleum company operated refineries in several states and was also engaged in the manufacture of a variety of petrochemical products. The company hired an industrial cleaning service to thoroughly clean one of its refineries. While one of the cleaning service's employees was engaged in routine cleaning activities at the refinery, one of the support legs on a crane suddenly gave way, causing part of the crane to fall onto a pipe carrying hot oil, cracking it open. The employee had his back to the pipe at the time and hot oil squirted over his back and legs, causing severe burns. The employee filed suit against the petroleum company for his injuries.

The parties stipulated for trial that the crane had been designed and constructed by a crane construction specialist and was serviced at regular intervals by a reputable crane maintenance company selected by the crane construction company. The employee testified at the trial that he was injured when the pipe cracked open and submitted his medical bills and other evidence of damages. The employee introduced no further evidence. At the conclusion of the employee's case, the petroleum company moved for a directed verdict in its favor.

Should the directed verdict be granted?

(A) Yes, because the employee has done nothing to connect the petroleum company to any negligent activity that might have caused the accident.

(B) Yes, because the petroleum company did not owe a duty to an employee of an independent contractor.

(C) No, because the petroleum company is strictly liable to the employee for his injuries.

(D) No, because a jury could reasonably conclude, based on the evidence presented by the employee, that the petroleum company was negligent.

Question 17

The driver of a Zamboni machine at an ice rink began to clean the ice without making sure that all of the doors to the rink were closed, contrary to established procedures. A young child who had just completed a skating lesson went back onto the ice through an open door to retrieve a water bottle from the bench. A bystander saw what was happening and worried that the Zamboni driver would not see the child, and the machine's engine was too loud to yell to the driver or child. Intending to get the child off of the ice, the bystander darted through another door to the rink just in front of the approaching Zamboni machine, but she slipped and fell in front of it. She suffered serious injuries when she was struck by the machine.

The bystander sued the ice rink to recover damages for her injuries in a jurisdiction that has adopted a modified ("partial") form of comparative negligence. The trier of fact determined that the bystander was 45% at fault and the Zamboni driver was 55% at fault. The Zamboni driver was employed by a reputable rink maintenance company that contracted with the ice rink for its services.

The bystander will:

(A) Recover 45% of her damages from the ice rink because she was less at fault than the Zamboni driver.

(B) Recover 55% of her damages from the ice rink because she was less at fault than the Zamboni driver.

(C) Not recover damages from the ice rink because she assumed the risk of falling by going onto the ice.

(D) Not recover damages from the ice rink because the Zamboni driver was employed by a rink maintenance company rather than by the rink itself.

Question 192

A pedestrian brought a negligence action against a motorist who struck him with her car in a shopping mall parking lot. The trier of fact determined that the pedestrian suffered $100,000 in damages and that he was 25% at fault for crossing in front of the motorist's car. The shopping mall was determined to be 30% at fault for allowing bushes to obscure the view of drivers, and the motorist was found to be 45% at fault for striking the pedestrian.

The jurisdiction involved has adopted pure comparative negligence and uses a comparative contribution system.

How much can the pedestrian recover from the motorist?

(A) $45,000, because the jurisdiction uses a comparative contribution system.

(B) $75,000, because the pedestrian's fault was less than the fault of the motorist.

(C) $75,000, but the motorist can recover $30,000 contribution from the shopping mall.

(D) $75,000, and the motorist cannot recover contribution from the shopping mall because the motorist's fault was greater.

Question 156

A plaintiff was injured when the steering mechanism of a snowmobile failed. He brought a negligence action against the snowmobile manufacturer. The steering mechanism was designed and manufactured by a component manufacturer; the snowmobile manufacturer merely assembled the snowmobile, branded it, and distributed it directly to retailers.

To prevail against the snowmobile manufacturer, the plaintiff will need to prove that:

(A)   The steering mechanism was in a defective condition unreasonably dangerous to users.

(B)   The steering mechanism was in a defective condition unreasonably dangerous to users, and the plaintiff was the purchaser of the snowmobile, a member of the purchaser's family, or a guest of the purchaser.

(C)   The steering mechanism was in a defective condition unreasonably dangerous to users, and the defect could have been discovered and corrected if the component manufacturer had exercised reasonable care in its quality control process.

(D)   The steering mechanism was in a defective condition unreasonably dangerous to users, and the snowmobile manufacturer failed to inspect the mechanism before assembly of the snowmobile.

Question 157

A testing lab purchased a wind tunnel as a complete unit from a machinery company. The machinery company used an electronics company for the design and installation of the unit's electronic control systems, which regulated air speed and triggered the emergency shut-off devices.

A technician was installing a scale model of a prototype aircraft that was to be tested in the wind tunnel when the electronic control system of the tunnel malfunctioned, causing the huge fans that created the air flow to start up. The powerful air flow pinned the technician against the grating covering the intake ducts, asphyxiating him before he was discovered and the fans could be shut off.

In an action by the technician's survivors against the electronics company, proof that the machinery company failed to inspect the wind tunnel has which of the following legal effects?

(A)   If the electronics company is held liable to the plaintiffs, it may bring an action for indemnity against the machinery company based on the failure to inspect.

(B)   The failure of the machinery company to inspect the tunnel is a superseding cause that relieves the electronics company of liability to the plaintiffs.

(C)   The failure of the machinery company to inspect the tunnel is attributable to the electronics company under the doctrine of respondeat superior.

(D)   The failure of the machinery company to inspect the tunnel has no legal effect on the electronics company's liability.

Question 71

A motorist purchased a new sport utility vehicle from his local dealer. Standard equipment on the vehicle included a set of top-of-the-line tires from a premium tire company. However, the motorist was able to save $400 on the purchase price by allowing the dealer to substitute a lower priced tire manufactured by a discount tire manufacturer. Unbeknownst to the motorist and the dealer, the tire manufacturer had negligently designed the tires, with the result that a tire would occasionally blow out when the car was traveling at a high rate of speed in hot weather. On an exceptionally hot day, the motorist was traveling 80 m.p.h. in a 55 m.p.h. zone. A tire exploded, resulting in damage to the vehicle and injury to the motorist.

If the motorist sues the dealer on a theory of strict liability, is he likely to prevail?

(A)   Yes, because the tire was in a dangerously defective condition when the motorist purchased the car.

(B)   Yes, because the dealer is responsible for the negligence of the tire manufacturer, because the dealer used its tires.

(C)   No, because the motorist assumed the risk when he substituted the discount tires in exchange for $400.

(D)   No, because the motorist was misusing the tire when he was traveling at 80 m.p.h.

Question 190

A father took his six-year-old son to a shopping mall. While the father was looking at the mall directory, the son went over to a small electric trolley that traveled around a small oval track. Four children, whose parents had paid admission to the ride operator, were already seated in the

four seats in the trolley, and the operator started the ride. The son climbed over the low fence surrounding the ride and ran to the rear of the trolley. He grabbed onto the upper edge of the trolley and stood on a narrow ledge at the bottom as the ride advanced. He lost his grip as the trolley was moving and fell backward onto the track, injuring his head.

The son brought an action, through his guardian ad litem, against the manufacturer of the trolley ride on a theory of strict liability. The jurisdiction follows traditional contributory negligence rules.

Which of the following would provide the best defense for the manufacturer in this litigation?

(A) There is not privity of contract between the son and the manufacturer.

(B) The son was contributorily negligent in riding on the rear of the trolley.

(C) The trolley was not being used by the son in a reasonably foreseeable manner.

(D) The father was negligent in his supervision of the son.

Question 99

A company manufactured parachutes that it sold exclusively to the United States Army. To meet the standards required by the Army, each parachute was subjected to a 15-point inspection by the company before it could be approved for sale. When a parachute did not pass inspection, it was stored in another section of the company's plant. At a later time, a further inspection of the defective parachute would be made to determine whether the defects could be corrected or whether the parachute should be destroyed.

One night, the plant was burglarized through no fault of the company and a large number of parachutes, including the defective ones, were stolen. The defective parachutes eventually were sold on the black market to a member of a skydiving club who made purchases for the club. One week later, the member was using one of the parachutes when it failed to open, causing his death.

If the member's estate brings a wrongful death action against the company on a theory of strict liability in a jurisdiction retaining traditional contributory negligence rules, the company's best defense would be that:

(A) The company acted reasonably in storing the defective parachutes.

(B) The company did not sell or place into the stream of commerce the defective parachute.

(C) The member did not purchase the parachute from the company.

(D) The member was negligent when he purchased the parachute on the black market.

Question 152

The owner of a self-propelled mower started the engine in preparation to mow when the clutch of the mower suddenly engaged, and it jerked forward rapidly. The owner was unable to grab the handle in time before the mower was out of reach and heading for the street. As he caught up with the mower and attempted to restrain it in the street, a motorist driving down the street swerved to avoid the mower and struck a tree. The motorist was injured and her car damaged. The motorist brought an action against the owner of the mower and was awarded damages. The owner then sought indemnification from the manufacturer of the mower in a jurisdiction following traditional indemnity rules.

If the owner prevails, it will be because:

(A) The owner was found to have taken reasonable care in maintaining the mower.

(B) The mower clutch engaged because of some defect in manufacture.

(C) The clutch assembly was manufactured and assembled by the manufacturer.

(D) The jurisdiction apportions damages based on relative fault in contribution cases.

Question 72

A farmer kept a pet bear at his farm. The bear was very old and had no teeth, no claws, and very little energy, but people liked to see the bear when they visited the farmer because no one else in the region had a pet bear. When the farmer first obtained the bear many years ago, he had a large steel cage constructed to house the animal. The cage had an electronic lock that only opened with a security code. Even though the bear was now old and harmless, it was always kept locked in the cage. One night during a severe storm while the farmer was out of town, a bolt of lightning hit the cage and the door opened. The bear left the cage and wandered off. The next morning, a 10-year-old girl was waiting on a rural road for her school bus. The bear emerged from a wooded area about 100 feet from where the girl was standing and headed towards her. She screamed and turned to run, tripping on the road and breaking her arm when she fell.

If the girl sues the farmer on a theory of strict liability for her bodily harm, will she prevail?

(A) No, because the bear was in fact a nondangerous animal.

(B) No, because the damage she suffered was not the type of damage that a bear would normally cause.

(C)   Yes, because the bear is a wild animal.

(D)   Yes, because pet bears were not commonly kept in the community.

Question 177

A chemical company located in a small city stored the components of a deadly nerve gas in its underground vaults. The two chemical agents that combined to create the nerve gas were harmless when kept separate, and the canisters for the delivery system had been manufactured under detailed specifications to stay intact for decades without deterioration. The chemical company's vaults were adjacent to an old underground storage chamber of the city's cable car system. Unbeknownst to the chemical company or the city, children living nearby had gotten access to the city's underground chamber and played in there from time to time. After a period of time, several of the canisters in the delivery systems began to leak, permitting the mixture of the two harmless agents into the deadly nerve gas. The chemical reaction caused by the mixture released a great deal of heat, which melted through the walls of the storage vault where it adjoined the city's underground storage chamber. The children playing in the chamber at the time were able to scramble out through a ventilation shaft, but one child fell and cut his leg while escaping. Fortunately, the authorities were able to flood the chamber with a neutralizing agent that rendered the nerve gas inert, and no one was harmed by its effects. Through his parents, the injured child brings an action against the chemical company.

Will he prevail?

(A)   Yes, because the chemical company was engaged in an abnormally dangerous activity.

(B)   Yes, because the chemical company was negligent.

(C)   No, because the child's injuries were not foreseeable.

(D)   No, because the underground chamber in which the child was injured was owned by the city, not by the chemical company.

Question 178

A consumer bit into a hamburger at a restaurant and cut her gum on a piece of bone in the meat. The bone was over an inch long. The consumer sued the meat processor in strict liability and negligence. At trial, she presented evidence that the processor supplied the ground beef that the restaurant used to make its hamburgers and that she was injured from the piece of bone in the meat. The meat processor presented evidence that restaurant employees prepared the hamburger patties by hand from the ground beef supplied by the processor, and asserted that one of the employees would have found the piece of bone had they made a reasonable inspection of the meat while preparing it. At the close of the evidence, the meat processor moved for a directed verdict on the consumer's negligence claim.

Based on the facts above, the court should:

(A)   Grant the motion, because the consumer has failed to show negligent conduct by the meat processor.

(B)   Grant the motion, because the restaurant employees' failure to inspect the meat and discover the bone cuts off the processor's negligence liability.

(C)   Deny the motion, because the jury could find that the bone was in the ground beef as a result of negligence by the processor.

(D)   Deny the motion, because the jury could find that the processor was more at fault than the restaurant.

Question 52

After leaving ceremonies at which the chief justice of a state supreme court had been named distinguished jurist of the year, an associate justice was interviewed by the press. The associate justice told a reporter that the chief justice "is a senile imbecile who lets his clerks write all his opinions. He hasn't had a lucid thought in decades, and he became a judge by being on the payroll of the mob." Enraged, the chief justice brought an action for defamation against the associate justice.

Which of the following, if established by the chief justice in his defamation action, would permit recovery against the associate justice?

(A)   The associate justice negligently made the statements, which were false, and caused the chief justice actual injury.

(B)   The associate justice made the statements knowing they were false.

(C)   The associate justice made the statements because he hated the chief justice and wished to destroy his reputation in the legal community.

(D)   The associate justice made the statements in order to ensure that the chief justice's political career was nipped in the bud.

Question 27

A patient sought psychiatric treatment from a psychiatrist. During the treatment, which consisted of hour-long analysis sessions twice a week, the psychiatrist, unbeknownst to the patient, videotaped her. No sound recording was made of the sessions, but the psychiatrist was

conducting a study on "body language" and planned to use the videotapes in those experiments. The patient learned that the psychiatrist had been videotaping their analysis sessions and brought an action against him on a theory of invasion of privacy.

Which of the following arguments best supports the patient's claims in this action?

(A) The psychiatrist has placed the patient in a false light.

(B) The psychiatrist has publicly displayed private facts of the patient's life.

(C) The psychiatrist has misappropriated the patient's likeness.

(D) The psychiatrist has intruded upon the patient's physical seclusion.

Question 80

At a popular barbecue restaurant, the barbecue was prepared in a large, outdoor pit in the back of the restaurant. Cooking meat outdoors in a commercial establishment violated a city health code regulation, designed to assure that the food was not exposed to flies and other insects. On windy days, smoke from the barbecue pit sometimes blew into a neighbor's backyard. Although most people would not be bothered by the smoke, the neighbor had extremely sensitive eyes. They watered and stung every time that he was exposed to any form of smoke. When the barbecue smoke drifted onto his property, the neighbor could not use his backyard.

If the neighbor sues the restaurant because he often cannot use his backyard, the neighbor will likely:

(A) Prevail, because the restaurant's action interfered with the neighbor's use and enjoyment of his yard.

(B) Prevail, because the restaurant was violating a health code regulation.

(C) Not prevail, because the smoke would not disturb a person of ordinary sensibilities in the community.

(D) Not prevail, because the health code regulation was not designed to protect against the type of harm suffered by the neighbor.